THE
PRAGMATIC
SUPERPOWER

THE PRAGMATIC SUPERPOWER

WINNING THE COLD WAR IN THE MIDDLE EAST

RAY TAKEYH

and

STEVEN SIMON

W. W. NORTON & COMPANY

Independent Publishers Since 1923

New York • London

For information about permission to reproduce selections from this book,
write to Permissions, W. W. Norton & Company, Inc.,
500 Fifth Avenue, New York, NY 10110

For information about special discounts for bulk purchases, please contact
W. W. Norton Special Sales at specialsales@wwnorton.com or 800-233-4830

Manufacturing by Berryville Graphics
Book design by Dana Sloan
Production manager: Anna Oler

ISBN 978-0-393-08151-0

W. W. Norton & Company, Inc.
500 Fifth Avenue, New York, N.Y. 10110
www.wwnorton.com

W. W. Norton & Company Ltd.
Castle House, 75/76 Wells Street, London W1T 3QT

1 2 3 4 5 6 7 8 9 0

To Alex and Nick

For Virginia

CONTENTS

AMERICAN APOGEE

The Cold War was one of the most momentous and unpredictable con-flicts in the annals of modern history. The conflict spanned nearly five decades and reached every corner of the world. Two nuclear-armed ideological rivals sought global hegemony by enlisting allies worldwide and denying each other vital resources. The underreported story of the Cold War is that the United States succeeded in achieving many of its objectives in the Middle East. To sustain the walls of containment in Europe, the United States had to deploy a massive number of troops and nuclear weapons, while in the Middle East a small naval contingent seemed sufficient. Unlike as it had in East Asia, the United States did not fight prolonged and inconclusive wars in the Middle East. While Latin America was beset by leftist revolutions, the conservative order in the Arab world largely held its own. America became the indispens-able power, as both Israel and the Arab states came to value its ability to steady the region.

The Cold War came to the Middle East early. In 1946, the Soviet Union laid claim to the Iranian province of Azerbaijan, precipitating the first of many confrontations with America. As it entered the region, the United States' principal objective was to ensure stability. The European empires that had held sway in the Arab world were fading from the scene but leaving behind a region aligned with the West and an elite that saw its fortunes to be bound up with the West. For the next forty years, successive U.S. administrations struggled to preserve this status quo. The final tally shows that despite setbacks Washington met its objective with reasonable success.

It is the argument of this book that although America's objectives in the region may have been uncomplicated, they were hardly modest. Washington sought to prevent Soviet infiltration of the region, preserve its considerable petroleum wealth for the West, and resolve the conflict between a Jewish homeland and the Arab states. In this context, stability had its virtues and a reliable ruling class had its share of benefits. A stable order in the Middle East could resist Soviet pressure and maintain a free flow of oil. And politicians tied to the West were best positioned and more likely to make peace with Israel.

The question then is how did Washington view threats to stability? The most obvious peril was direct Soviet military intervention in the Middle East. This would prove a rarity, as during much of the Cold War, the superpowers relied on proxies and allies to subvert each other's interests. A more recurring problem was the rise of radical leaders who were unreliable custodians of America's Cold War concerns. Iran's Prime Minister Muhammad Mossadeq, Egypt's Colonel Gamal Abdel Nasser, and the assorted Arab officers who took command of Iraq and Syria would fit that description. It is not true, as some have argued, that U.S. presidents could not distinguish between communism and nationalism, but they were wary of the neutralist tendencies of such rulers. America may have plotted against these actors but it was always open to a constructive relationship with them.

Wars plagued the Middle East during the Cold War and threatened to unhinge its order. A series of Arab-Israeli wars and conflicts in the Persian Gulf between Iraq and its neighbors would challenge the stability that Washington sought to ensure. American diplomacy had to resolve the conflict between Israel and its neighbors and find ways to mitigate the impact of the Arab-Israeli wars. Iraq and its impetuous leader Saddam Hussein offered America a similar set of problems. Wars by their nature are destabilizing, yet the record demonstrates that the United States handled these conflicts with a measure of skill, preventing them from unraveling the regional order.

A search of the U.S. archives reveals that promoting democratic regimes was not Washington's goal during the Cold War. To the extent that policy makers focused on domestic affairs in the countries of the Middle East, they hoped that strong leaders and durable institutions would suffice to maintain internal control and resist Soviet encroachment. In Washington, notions of reform were usually limited to the economic sphere: distributing wealth more equitably, creating self-sustaining agricultural and industrial sectors, and reducing rampant corruption. On occasion, the issue of human rights abuses would surface, but usually in a manner that did not disrupt the fundamentals of bilateral relations. The notion of implanting democratic polities and refashioning the political culture of the Middle East along liberal lines was very much a post–Cold War innovation. The overwhelming threat of the Soviet Union propelled successive administrations to see virtue in authoritarian allies that shared their strategic concerns. It is difficult to retrospectively censure this impulse on utilitarian grounds, given the overall success the United States experienced in preserving its essential interests during the Cold War.

To make its case, this book focuses on ten of the most consequential crises in the Middle East during the Cold War. We selected episodes that had the potential to provoke a wider regional conflict, threatened key U.S. allies, or could have entangled the superpowers in an actual war. To be fair, the Middle East featured many more crises than the ones we assess. There were certainly tensions in Yemen, Lebanon threatened to implode in the 1970s and 1980s, and Algeria waged its own war of colonial liberation and later a vicious civil war. These conflicts were not unimportant but they did not reach a point where they could have destabilized the entire Middle East or brought about superpower confrontation. Thus, we limit ourselves to surveying the rise and fall of radical actors and militant ideologies in key states, the Arab-Israeli wars, and the region's most significant interstate conflicts. We believe that our selections best illustrate the dilemmas and opportunities that the United States confronted in the Middle East during the Cold War era.

In studying the Cold War in the Middle East the absence of Soviet military intervention is a striking fact. Still, in 1946, Russia did try to carve out Iran's Azerbaijan province as a Soviet possession. As part of an allied wartime agreement, the Soviet armed forces occupied northern Iran while the British claimed the south. It was stipulated by the allies that six months after the end of the war all foreign troops would leave Iran. Britain complied only to see Stalin attempt to impose a sphere of influence in northern Iran. The Persian court at that time still produced statesmen such as the cagey prime minister Ahmad Qavam, who could outmaneuver even Stalin by virtue of his talent for manipulation. However, without the firm backing of the Truman administration, it is hard to see how the Iranians could have succeeded. Faced with American resistance, United Nations censure, and Iranian protest, Stalin decided to leave—the only time during his rule that the Soviet strongman relinquished his territorial gains.

Iran would be the linchpin of another crisis in 1953 when Prime Minister Muhammad Mossadeq nationalized the country's oil industry and provoked a crisis with Britain. Despite sincere American mediation efforts, the stubborn prime minister refused all compromise offers. As Iran drifted into chaos, there were fears in Washington that communist forces inside the country could take advantage of the situation and come to power. In the fateful month of August 1953, a joint Anglo-American coup was staged only to fail. At that time, the United States and Britain gave up the idea of toppling Mossadeq and even considered mending fences with him. Despite all the later recriminations about the role of the CIA in Mossadeq's overthrow, the second (and successful) coup was very much an Iranian initiative. The same political establishment that had outwitted the Soviet dictator deposed the troublesome premier. If this was a U.S. success, it was purely an accidental one that owed more to the determination of the Iranian royalists than to the genius of American planners.

Iran would also be the locus of America's most spectacular setback in the Middle East, the revolution of 1979. The capable political class that had navigated Iran through so many crises had been largely destroyed by Muhammad Reza Shah Pahlavi in the years after the 1953 coup. What remained were a monarch who faded from the scene during times of tension and a new elite composed of second-tier politicians and unimaginative military officers. In Washington, a new president, Jimmy Carter, seemed more offended by the shah's right-wing dictatorship than by the Islamist revolutionaries Carter mistook as moderates. A cascade of misjudgments by the White House and the royal court ensured the triumph of an improbable revolution. Unlike 1953, by the late 1970s neither Iran nor America had strong, prudent leaders. The shah's indecisiveness and Carter's confusion led to a rise of a militant theocracy that continues to imperil America's interests in the Middle East.

The rise of radical actors was not limited to Iran. The decline of European influence in the aftermath of World War II led to a transformation of Middle East politics. Arab nationalism and its call for self-determination and opposition to the fading remnants of European empires captured the popular imagination. In the aftermath of the Suez War in 1956, Egypt emerged as the vanguard of the Arab campaign for independence and self-reliance. Nasser soon launched his challenge to the conservative monarchies, enshrined socialism as the basis of economic planning, and upheld nonalignment as the region's preferred international orientation. An Arab Cold War engulfed the Middle East, with the radical republics confronting conservative monarchies.

The United States did not stand aloof from this enveloping Cold War-within-a-Cold War. In the hinge year of 1958, the Middle East could have gone in either of two dramatically different directions, with radicals sweeping the region or the conservatives holding their own. U.S. president Dwight D. Eisenhower stepped into this arena, resuscitated the conservative order, and pushed back the frontiers of Pan-Arabism. While Nasser and his radical disciples bickered among themselves, the monarchs regained their confidence. Nasserism would soon be endangered by the militant forces it helped to unleash, causing Cairo to look for tactical accommodation with the West. America was not instinctively hostile to post-colonial nationalism and was willing to make common cause with it, so long as it served U.S. interest in stability.

The Arab-Israeli conflict would produce four wars that discredited successive ruling elites. The 1948 war ended the reign of landlords and urban notables, an overlapping group that saw its interests as largely aligned with those of their imperial patrons. The 1956 Suez War demonstrated the folly of the European powers and the miscalculation of Israeli leaders. The invasion spurred publics to lionize Nasser and strained the Western alliance. Still, these tensions were not lasting and the alliance overcame its divisions. The short 1967 war discredited the very Arab nationalist leaders who had risen to power by castigating the complacent ways of their predecessors. And the 1973 war and its limited gains for the invading Arab armies proved to be both the crescendo and finale of Arab-Israeli wars.

Although many argue that U.S. support for Israel thwarted Washington's strategic aims in the Arab world, this book claims that—by strange irony—the outcome was in fact the reverse. For many conservative rulers, the United States was the only outside power with the capacity to restrain a disproportionately potent Israel. America was the only nation with the ability to get Israel to relinquish territory and address Palestinian grievances. Thus, in some ways, the conservative rulers became more dependent on the United States. The radical regional states chose a different path, relying on Soviet arms and diplomacy to secure their cause. It was in the aftermath of the 1973 war that Egypt recognized the futility of depending on Moscow and switched sides in order to regain lost territory in the Sinai Peninsula.

Wars in the Middle East were not limited to Israel and the Arab states, as the Persian Gulf also saw its share of rivalry and violent conflict. Much of the world's oil still flows through the gulf, giving the waterway and surrounding territory an outsized impact on the global economy. The longest interstate war in the annals of modern Middle East history took place in the gulf and was triggered by Iraq's catastrophic invasion of Iran in 1980. The intriguing aspect of the Iran-Iraq war was how the United States managed to hold its alliance together, ensure global access to gulf oil, and eventually help facilitate the end of the conflict.

The first Gulf War would constitute the apex of American power in the Middle East. In August 1990, Saddam Hussein would once again test the durability of the regional state system by annexing Kuwait. By then, however, the Soviet Union was led by men more interested in reviving their fortunes through cooperation with the West than in embracing a chronically errant client. Moscow would try to mediate the conflict and persuade Saddam to withdraw from Kuwait. But by the end, the Kremlin proved unwilling to risk humiliation by trying to block an ineluctable American invasion. As the administration of President George H. W. Bush lined up allies, won U.N. endorsement, and marshaled a huge military force, a dying Soviet state uneasily acquiesced in a Western war against Iraq. This was a pivotal moment. The Cold War was no longer sufficiently present to require the huge deployment of U.S. armed forces in Germany, so the troops required to dislodge a sometime Soviet client were available. There would be no risk that the Soviet Union would exploit the redeployment of much of America's armor from Europe and even less risk that the Kremlin would protest Saddam's ejection from Kuwait. In many ways, the Gulf War reflected the transition from the bipolarity of the Cold War to a more unpredictable dispensation, wherein America's preeminence would be challenged not by a fellow superpower, but by emerging states and unconventional threats.

During the Cold War, the United States faced an array of challenges in the region even as its involvement there deepened. Washington had to corral Arab regimes that detested each other and get what the United States needed from them, while maintaining its strong relationship with Israel. Successive administrations had to deal with recalcitrant leaders, revisionist states, and Soviet mischief. The United States did not always succeed, and at times its successes resulted from luck rather than foresight. However, by the time the Cold War ended, the United States did achieve its core objectives—the exclusion of a rival superpower, establishment of a robust system of air and naval bases, preservation of a steady supply of oil, and emergence of a secure Israel—without significant cost in blood or treasure. This feat was managed by leaders who by and large had a sound strategic vision that they followed throughout the fraught epoch. Amid the anarchic conditions of the twenty-first century, characterized by a new normal of military intervention, regime change and vast social engineering projects, there is an urgent need to look back at a period when the United States got it right, recognizing that the domestic and international order in which Washington succeeded is inexorably receding.

THE

PRAGMATIC
SUPERPOWER

CHAPTER 1

THE IRAN CRISIS OF 1946 AND THE COLD WAR'S FIRST CONFLICT

It is nearly impossible to convey how precarious the global scene appeared in the aftermath of the Second World War. President Franklin D. Roosevelt's lofty dreams of great power cooperation vanished as the Soviet Union busily extended its reach across Eastern Europe. Meanwhile, in Western Europe, the Soviets and proliferating homegrown communist parties exploited rampant starvation to gain political influence.[1] The specter of nationalist clamor in Asia and a civil war in China compounded Europe's problems. And the British edifice in the Middle East was eroding by the minute. As senior State Department official Dean Acheson acknowledged, "Destruction is more complete, hunger more acute, exhaustion more widespread than anyone realized."[2] The United States would be preoccupied with preserving the balance of power at a time of political unrest and economic turmoil.

The year 1946 would mark the United States' shift from perceiving the Soviet Union an ally—albeit a difficult one—to considering it an adversary whose ambitions had to be thwarted. Containment would become the touchstone of American foreign policy. The Grand Alliance—forged by the necessity of defeating Nazi Germany—would collapse as Stalin's brutal tactics disillusioned all but the most ardent

1

leftists. America, armed with its new doctrine, searched abroad for an occasion to validate its strategy. Iran may have been distant from the core of the conflict, but it offered a venue for the superpowers' test of wills. As it has throughout history, Iran would play a role in international politics hardly commensurate with its actual importance.

1946: TRUMAN'S TURN TO CONTAINMENT

In one of the paradoxes of history, a series of speeches and a memorandum would define the evolving international order of the Cold War. On February 9, Joseph Stalin delivered to great fanfare a speech in the Bolshoi Theater. Although the speech was ostensibly intended to congratulate the army and the nation for their heroic sacrifices during the war, Stalin also used the occasion to call for a significant increase in industrial production. The new economic buildup was necessary preparation for the coming conflict with the West. He noted the incompatibility between communism and capitalism and how previous wars had been the consequence of uneven distribution of wealth within the capitalist bloc. The Soviet dictator implied the possibility of war so long as capitalism persisted as a system of economic organization. Although such crass denunciations of capitalism were common features of Marxist rhetoric, in the context of 1946 they appeared particularly ominous. Russia did not want war, Stalin insisted, but it had to prepare for one.

Stalin's speech set off alarm bells in Washington. Supreme Court Justice William O. Douglas warned Secretary of the Navy James Forrestal that the speech was "the declaration of World War III."[3] The head of the Eastern European Division in the State Department, H. Freeman Matthews, perceived the speech as "the most important and authoritative guide to postwar Soviet society."[4] In America's corridors of power, the relationship between communism and Russian foreign policy now became one of the most crucial debates.

George F. Kennan had been leery of communist fanaticism since he first witnessed Stalin's murderous show trials and the convulsions of the agricultural collectivization process that killed millions of peasants. From his perch in Moscow, the American diplomat had "bombarded the lower levels of Washington bureaucracy with analyses of communist evil."[5] All were ignored; the 1930s intelligentsia had been mesmerized by the Soviet Union as a laboratory of social reform. The eventual Grand Alliance would cement these feelings, turning the Soviet Union in the eyes of many into a gallant and important ally against Nazi tyranny. Warm feelings lingered after the war. Thus, Kennan was surprised in 1946 to receive an urgent request from Washington for an assessment of Russia's behavior. "They asked for it—now they're going to get it," exclaimed Kennan.[6]

In a five-thousand-word telegram, Kennan described a Soviet cosmology that divided the world between two blocs without the possibility of coexistence or pragmatic adjustment. "We have here a political force committed fanatically to the belief that with U.S. there can be no permanent modus vivendi," stressed Kennan.[7] Russia's traditional anxieties married to Marxist pathologies meant that Soviet leaders required an external enemy to justify their hold on power. Marxism was a "fig leaf of their moral and intellectual respectability. Without it they would stand before history, at best, as only the last of that long succession of cruel and wasteful Russian rulers."[8] In more subtle passages, Kennan described how the Soviet appetite for global dominance was cleverly fed by a strategy of gradual, yet relentless, expansion of its influence. Unlike Nazi Germany, the Soviet Union would not resort to an explicit use of force but would exploit all vulnerabilities to subvert the Western democracies.[9] The implication of Kennan's analysis was ominous. It suggested that gestures of goodwill and acknowledgment of Russia's legitimate concerns were foolhardy. Soviet hostility toward the West was intrinsic, ideologically animated, and undeterred by gestures of accommodation.

Unlike most policy advisors, Kennan did not simply outline the problem in his "long telegram"; he offered an acceptable alternative to the existing U.S. approach. The Soviet Union that Kennan described was not impervious to the logic of power. Confronted with determination and resolve, it would retreat. Kennan stressed that Russia would seek to avoid war but may lapse into one if it "underestimated American strength and patience."[10] However, in the deformed political order that Stalin had created it was impossible to determine how information was being conveyed and how it was being received. A judicious Soviet functionary would likely offer assessments that affirmed his superiors' misjudgments as opposed to challenging them. Unable to rely on traditional diplomatic messaging, redlines had to be drawn and American decisions directly transmitted to Soviet authorities. Once convinced of such resolution, Stalin would concede, back down, and even adjust his objectives.

The success of Kennan's telegram stemmed from the fact that it affirmed sentiments already percolating within the Washington bureaucracy. American officials presented a picture of an unaccountable, dogmatic communist party invigorated by historic Russian expansionism. High-ranking officials, including Dean Acheson and various envoys to Russia, were already exasperated by the Kremlin's obstinacy. As early as the summer of 1944 Acheson had compared negotiating with the Soviet Union to "dealing with an old-fashion penny slot machine. . . . One could sometimes expedite the process by shaking the machine, but it was useless to talk to it."[11] Ambassador Laurence Steinhardt, who had succeeded the disreputable Joseph Davies as America's ambassador to Russia, noted, "My experience has been that they respond only to force and if force cannot be applied, to straight oriental bartering."[12] The State Department's assessment echoed Kennan, noting the precarious nature of the international system and a balance of power that had swung entirely in the Soviet favor. The shift had benefited a state whose aim was "the complete subversion or forcible destruction of the machinery of government and structure of society in the countries of the non-Soviet world and their replacement by an apparatus and structure subservient to and controlled from the Kremlin."[13] The Soviet Union would take advantage of all opportunities because "it possesses and is possessed by a world-wide revolutionary movement, because it is the inheritor of Russian imperialism, because it is a totalitarian dictatorship."[14]

As Washington contemplated its response, a call for confrontation was issued from a world leader of considerable esteem. Winston Churchill had been unexpectedly ousted as prime minister by his constituents in the aftermath of the war. However, he maintained the considerable prestige gained by his solitary and courageous opposition to the Nazi scourge in Europe. On a trip to the United States, the aging orator was determined to arouse the American public to the new threats shadowing Europe. At President Harry S. Truman's invitation, he accepted an offer to give a speech on March 5, 1946, at Westminster College in Fulton, Missouri. Although it would become known as the "Iron Curtain" speech, its original title was "The Sinews of Peace." The speech proved as alarming as it was prophetic. Churchill began cautiously, "Nobody knows what Soviet Russia and its Communist international organizations intend to do in the future or what limits, if any, there are to their expansive and proselytizing tendencies."[15] However, he soon moved to the essence of his argument:

> From Stettin in the Baltic to Trieste in the Adriatic, an iron curtain has descended across the Continent. Behind that line lie all the capitals of the ancient states of central and eastern Europe . . . what I must call the Soviet sphere, and all are subject in one form or another, not only to Soviet influence but to a very high and, in some cases, increasing measure of control from Moscow.

Churchill quickly pointed to the next arena of conflict, noting that "Persia and Turkey are both profoundly alarmed and disturbed by claims made upon them." In this sense Churchill was reinforcing

Kennan's telegram, which had similarly pointed to the eastern Mediterranean as the next target of Russian intrigue. Although the ostensible purpose of the speech was a call for an Anglo-American alliance resisting Soviet aggression, Churchill echoed Kennan in claiming that power alone, not lofty sentiments, would forestall the Soviets.[16]

When Truman assumed office in 1945, persistent Soviet transgressions did not jolt him away from sustaining Roosevelt's legacy of great-power cooperation. Uncertain of himself and surrounded by men with a superior knowledge of foreign affairs, Truman was prone to follow the existing path. Whether in deliberations over Poland or dealing with Soviet aid requests, Truman sought to reconcile his call for self-determination in Eastern Europe with his desire to sustain security cooperation with the Soviet Union. To be sure, Truman grew uneasy about his circumstances and was somewhat confused about his options, but the gravitational pull was toward the Yalta Accords and its spirit of accommodation.[17]

The key challenge for an administration facing conflicting priorities is when to admit a policy has failed. To declare Roosevelt's prized Soviet-American partnership doomed was a difficult decision. The consensus among historians is that by 1946, Truman was ready to take this step. The sheer scale of Stalin's aggression and his disregard for the interests and sensibilities of his allies transformed Truman's perspective. As an upright person who believed that politicians should keep their word, Truman was predisposed to arguments that Moscow be held accountable for its treaty violations. Along the way, Kennan's famed telegram and Churchill's powerful oratory provided the intellectual justification to a president equally uneasy about his current path and searching for a different strategy.

The essence of the containment doctrine held that the Soviet Union was not bent on war with the militarily and economically superior West. A ruthless but clever strategist, Stalin wanted to consolidate his sphere of influence with limited cost. Thus, Moscow was always open to diplomacy and dialogue as a means of lulling the West into a belief that accommodation was possible. The Kremlin sought the improbable: to sustain the Grand Alliance while advancing the frontiers of the Russian empire. The policy was not without its successes, as Stalin had managed to impose his totalitarian grip on Eastern Europe while pledging great-power harmony at diplomatic conclaves. It was also bound to be short-lived. Inevitably, a crisis would call into question Soviet pledges of goodwill.

Given the global aspirations of the containment doctrine, the question of means became crucial. To block the systematic advance of the new enemy, the United States required a patient, long-term strategy. Defense budgets that were slashed after the war had to rise, but the great task of containment demanded allies in Europe and in the Third World. The American military buildup combined with strong defense networks in key theaters would gradually isolate the Soviet Union and accentuate its weaknesses. Accordingly, the Kremlin would have to either accept the rules of the international system as defined by the United States or confront a slow, but inevitable, demise.[18]

The containment imperatives were bound to resonate in the Middle East. The region's petroleum assets were critical for the recovery of Western Europe, while its vast borders with the Soviet Union made it a tantalizing strategic prize. Truman captured this sentiment in his Army Day Address on April 6, 1946, declaring that the region "contains vast natural resources. It lies across the most convenient routes of land, air, and water communications."[19] The American defense line had to encompass the Middle East as a means of denying its lands and resources to the Soviet bloc. Iran soon found itself thrust into this emerging superpower rivalry.

THE ORIGINS OF THE IRAN CRISIS

Even prior to the outbreak of the Cold War, Iran's strategic location and its warm-water ports had enticed successive generations of Russian rulers. As early as 1921, the hard-pressed Qajar dynasty agreed to a treaty granting Russia the right to intervene in Iran should it encounter threats on its southern periphery. This accord paved the way during World War II for an allied intervention in Iran that in August 1941 deposed the country's leader Reza Shah Pahlavi because of his pro-Nazi sentiments. The terms of the Tripartite Agreement, signed by the United States, Britain, and the Soviet Union in January 1942, stipulated that allied forces would be withdrawn six months after the conclusion of the war. The Soviets would occupy the northern portion of Iran while the British maintained their traditional southern sphere of influence. Although the United States was a party to the agreement, it dispatched few troops and limited itself to an advisory role.

During the latter stages of World War II, Soviet ambitions for the Middle East began to crystallize. As with other parts of the world, Moscow was unwilling to concede the region to the West and was determined to become an active player in Middle Eastern politics. In order to gain traction, the Soviets recognized that they had to undermine the British Empire, the principal bulwark of Western presence in the Middle East. Given Britain's vulnerabilities in terms of limited financial resources and America's preoccupation with sustaining the Grand Alliance, Stalin sensed that tantalizing opportunities awaited him south of his border. Iran would prove his first foray into the Middle East, pursued with the dictator's usual determination and force.[20]

As Soviet troops marched into Azerbaijan in 1942, as part of the Tripartite Agreement, they encountered a collapsing government, fleeing officials, and economic misery. Throughout the country, allied forces had commandeered Iran's transportation network and much of its food supply. The effect was widespread dislocation, if not outright famine. Such a dire situation made the task of consolidating the Soviet sphere of influence in the country much easier. The Russian occupation authorities, backed by sixty thousand Red Army troops, quickly installed sympathetic functionaries and purged the rest. As the British consulate reported, "One by one, the government officials in Azerbaijan are being removed from the scene."[21] Under the banner of reform and autonomy, the Soviets and their clients were busy taking over all administrative functions.

The primary instrument of Soviet domination was the Red Army. Soviet forces obstructed the movement of Iranian troops, shielded Kurdish and Azeri separatists who were attacking Iranian garrisons, and even prevented allied diplomatic representatives from performing their legitimate duties. Behind the façade of the Red Army, the Tudeh Party—an Iranian communist party—was allowed to carve out a zone of influence for itself. The Tudeh members now openly agitated against the central government, organized labor and youth groups, and stimulated ethnic separatism among the Kurds and Azeris. Protests from Tehran were curtly dismissed by Moscow. In the midst of great-power amity and the need to deal with weightier issues of war, neither London nor Washington was inclined to confront Stalin over developments in northern Iran. Whatever the terms of the Tripartite Agreement, Russia was busy carving out the northern portion of Iran for itself.

Oil even more than territory appeared to have motivated Stalin's moves in Iran. The German assault on the Soviet Union, particularly its surge toward oil refineries in Baku and Grozny in 1942, convinced Stalin of the need to increase his country's oil reserves. The Soviet dictator feared that in a future conflict Russia's adversaries would emulate Hitler and try to paralyze the Soviet industrial sector by destroying its oil facilities. Russia's historical quest for influence on its southern periphery now merged with Stalin's well-established fear of resource wars.[22]

On the surface, Soviet oil demands were neither new nor unprecedented. As early as 1925, Moscow and Tehran had established the Kavir Khurian Company that exploited various depositories. The company soon floundered under mismanagement and lack of capital investment. As the Soviet Union became mired in its own political crisis and later its war with Nazi Germany, the Kremlin did not seek to revive the agreement. For their part, the Iranians decreed the 1925 project null and void.

By 1944, the Soviet eye had again fallen on Iranian oil. Sergie Kavtarzade, then vice chairman of foreign affairs, arrived in Iran ostensibly to discuss the defunct oil company. However, in his talks with Iranian officials, he sidestepped the previous concession and signaled Russia's desire for general exploration rights in the vast area stretching from the northern province of Azerbaijan all the way to the eastern region of Khorasan.[23] In the meantime, the Soviets were increasing their troop presence in an area from which they had agreed to withdraw at war's end. It appeared that Moscow had more expansive ambitions for Iran than a wartime contingency.

Iran's domestic political scene may have appeared chaotic and unruly. Reza Shah had abdicated and his young son, Muhammad Reza, seemed uncertain and indecisive. However, Iran was hardly a passive actor in the drama unfolding all around it. Given its long history with foreign interventions, Iran had produced a coterie of agile politicians capable of maneuvering their way to independence. Through much of the early decades of the twentieth century, reformist nationalists such as Muhammad Mossadeq and clever aristocrats such as Ahmad Qavam had wrestled with imperial powers that coveted Iran's land and resources. Whether dealing with Britain's imperial concerns or tsarist Russia's interventions, the Iranian political class had demonstrated an uncanny ability to play the great powers against each other.

Traditional Iranian suspicions of Britain have obscured the fact that Tehran usually perceived Russia as a greater threat. The proximity of Soviet power and Russia's historic drive southward had led successive Iranian regimes to seek an alliance with a countervailing external power. From the Iranian vantage point, Britain was hardly reliable ballast to Russian influence. During the interwar years, Iran had worked to entice the United States to be more involved in its affairs, and offered it oil contracts and a foothold in the Middle East. In Iran at the time, as indeed throughout the Middle East, the United States was perceived as a more benign and enlightened nation, devoid of the crass material preoccupations of the European states. Yet, happy in its splendid isolation and later preoccupied with the economic woes of the Great Depression, the United States showed scant interest in Iranian entreaties. It was then that in an act of desperation and miscalculation, the elder shah had reached out to Nazi Germany. Such a disastrous act not only cost Reza Shah his throne but also precipitated the allied invasion of his country.[24]

As World War II was drawing to an end, Iran once more settled on the United States as an ally to fend off Soviet encroachment. To tempt the budding superpower, Iran dangled oil concessions to firms including the Standard Oil, Vacuum Oil, and Sinclair Oil companies. The fields of Baluchistan in the east were initially offered but Tehran was open to other types of U.S. investment. Although some preliminary discussions did take place, in the end, the American firms remained on the sidelines. Hardly deterred, in 1945 Iran asked the United States to pressure Russia into allowing Iranian troops to enter Azerbaijan and quell the ethnic insurrection there.[25] Still in pursuit of its Grand Alliance, Washington had little motivation to antagonize its Soviet partner over such a tangential issue. For Washington, the Tripartite Agreement, which stipulated withdrawal of all allied forces after the cessation of hostilities, had settled the issue of respecting Iranian sovereignty.

During the war neither Washington nor London necessarily had objected to Soviet oil concessions in Iran. While both powers were disturbed at the conduct of Russian troops and insisted that Moscow adhere to the terms of the Tripartite Agreement, neither country discouraged Russia's commercial pursuits. Secretary of State Edward Stettinius had already stipulated that Washington had no objection to a Soviet oil grant.[26] Given his devotion to the Grand Alliance, Roosevelt seemingly hoped that Moscow could advance its claims in a manner consistent with its international obligation.

Britain's position was even more complicated and less altruistic than that of the United States. The Anglo-Iranian Oil Company (AIOC) that dominated Iran's southern oil fields was Britain's largest overseas asset and an important contributor to its treasury. The British oil concessions had long been a source of contention. For many Iranians, the AIOC was a symbol of imperial abuse, a company that usurped their natural wealth without improving their welfare. Given its own situation, London could hardly complain about Soviet oil demands. Foreign Secretary Anthony Eden assured his Soviet counterpart, Vyacheslav Molotov, that it was "not part of British policy to prevent the Soviet Union from obtaining oil in Northern Iran."[27] Devoid of real leverage, Iran had to figure out a way to preserve its independence and safeguard its resources at the same time.

The overriding issue for Tehran was the withdrawal of Soviet forces from its territory. Iran well understood that Soviet machinations best succeeded when shielded by the Red Army. Iranian diplomats sought to cleverly untangle their many knots and tie the issue of oil concessions to the evacuation of foreign forces. In a move that surprised and angered the Russians, Tehran announced that so long as its territory was occupied it would be politically difficult for its parliament—the Majlis—to consider commercial ventures. If Russia wanted the country's oil, then it had to withdraw its troops. Two issues that had appeared unrelated to the allied powers were now joined together by Iran's claim that the occupation of its territory meant no new oil contracts. Although uneager to compound tensions in U.S.-Soviet relations, Washington did endorse Iran's position, informing Moscow that "American policy in this case is based on the American government's recognition of the sovereign rights of an independent nation such as Iran, acting in a nondiscriminatory manner, to grant or withhold commercial concession within its territory."[28] In a single move, Iran had reset the diplomatic framework and ensured that all of its concerns would be taken into account by the great powers.

In 1945 there were many dark clouds on the horizon. Iran had managed to defer the issue of oil concessions, but a sizeable portion of its territory was still occupied by the Russian forces. The Tripartite Agreement had ostensibly ensured the country's sovereignty, but the Soviet approach in Eastern Europe was not reassuring. Would the Kremlin abide by its treaty obligations? The Americans were still hoping to preserve their Grand Alliance and the British were more than willing to reach an accommodation with Russia at Iran's expense. It would be up to Iranians to salvage their sovereignty. And the ensuing Cold War offered them ample opportunity to manipulate their way to independence.

THE COLD WAR'S FIRST CRISIS

With the war over, Soviet moves became more brazen and their objectives more transparent. Both Turkey and Iran became the targets of Russian expansionism southward. Both countries had important strategic locations, ample resources, and access to key waterways. Stalin's preferred method of territorial acquisition was to stimulate aggrieved nationalism—in Iran's case Azeri separatism. In 1946, the Politburo decided to "create inside the Iranian state a national autonomous Azerbaijan region with broad jurisdiction."[29] Behind the protective façade of Russian power, the Azerbaijan Democratic Party (ADP) headed by the pliable Ja'afar Pishevari came into existence and pressed for independence from Tehran. In a worrisome move, the Tudeh Party in Azerbaijan dissolved itself, with its cadre joining ADP. In a gesture of defiance, the party introduced a new flag and postage stamps. The educational system was revamped with emphasis on Azeri historical and cultural themes. The monuments and tributes dedicated to the shah were systematically dismantled. The new authorities even accepted Moscow standard time, which ran thirty minutes behind Tehran. They launched an ambitious public works program designed to bolster their popularity. For all practical purposes a new state was emerging in northern Iran.

To justify its moves, Moscow offered a series of increasingly absurd arguments. During a meeting with U.S. envoy Averell Harriman, Stalin insisted that given Iran's hostility to the Soviet Union and the need to protect the Baku oil fields, a Russian presence in Azerbaijan was required.[30] Stalin was essentially claiming that the Soviet Union was being threatened by Iran. True to form, the Soviet dictator kept pushing beyond the limits of his allies' forbearance. It is clear that for Stalin, Eastern Europe mattered far more than Iran. Yet his use of the same tactics in both places allowed Americans to sense a pattern of global aggression. This miscalculation in an area peripheral to Stalin's core concerns endangered his more essential interests. Had the Soviet dictator behaved with more circumspection, he may have forestalled the arrival of the Cold War.

Instead of attempting to ease tensions, the Kremlin began signaling wider objectives in Iran. Radio Moscow now stressed, "Is it only the Azerbaijanis who demand the same standard of living and reasonable political freedom as enjoyed by all nations of Europe. No! The people of Gilan and Mazandaran as well as vast masses of Tehran are voicing the same demands." [31] Suddenly, Moscow seemed to reach beyond Azerbaijan and target other Iranian provinces. In one of his trips through Iran, Harriman was pointedly informed by Russia's envoy, Mikhail Maximov, that "since the Iranian government did not truly represent the Iranian people and since the Soviets knew what the Iranian people wanted, it was proper for the Soviet government that this opinion find political expression."[32] The provocative nature of Russia's conduct and its crude propaganda campaigns enmeshed the noncontroversial oil issue in the larger Cold War context.

As Washington deliberated over Moscow's latest provocation, it was besieged by alarmist cables from its diplomatic missions in both Russia and Iran. For Kennan, the Soviet moves in Iran appeared eerily similar to its behavior in Eastern Europe. The Russians were once more stimulating ethnic grievances as a way of putting in place parties and politicians devoted to their cause.[33] From Tabriz, the American consulate official reported, "I cannot overstate the seriousness and magnitude of current Soviet troop movements here. This is not ordinary reshuffling of troops but a full-scale combat deployment."[34] If nothing else, Russia had succeeded in solidifying the opinion of local American representatives against its ambitions.

Although Iran was ostensibly an absolutist monarchy, the new shah was largely a bystander in his country's most traumatic foreign confrontation.[35] In decades to come the shah would evolve into a dictator with limited tolerance for dissent. However, at the beginning of his reign, the untested monarch turned to his more seasoned advisors. Preoccupied with his palace intrigues, he was more than happy to defer to elder statesmen. No one exemplified the diplomatic acumen of Iran's aristocratic class more than Prime Minister Ahmad Qavam. At this point in Iran, prime ministers and parliaments still exercised much authority with the shah not just soliciting but yielding to their advice.

Qavam had been involved in national affairs since 1905 and had held nearly every important office in Iran. Among the country's scheming aristocratic class, he had earned a reputation as a particularly slippery and skilled manipulator. Nonetheless, the prime minister's accomplishments were remarkable. He would eventually manage to preserve his country's sovereignty at a time when all the great powers were ready to compromise the principle of Iran's independence. Under the banner of "positive neutralism," Qavam sought a balance between the competing interests of the United States and the Soviet Union. His objectives remained unaltered—ensuring his country's territorial integrity—however, his tactics would prove supple and his promises always tentative.

Qavam soon embarked on a diplomatic mission that sought to conciliate the Soviet Union while engineering its expulsion. Already, the Kremlin had identified Qavam as a politician it could deal with. In Iran's aristocratic circles, Qavam was known to be independent of Britain and had avoided the strident anticommunist rhetoric common among some of his contemporaries. Qavam indicated that he was prepared for direct talks with the Soviet Union and often spoke of Russian rights that were "long overdue."[36] After coming to power in 1946, Qavam journeyed to Moscow in an attempt to assuage Stalin's concerns. This was to be conciliation without compromise. Qavam insisted that Soviet troops must withdraw and that Azerbaijan was part of Iran's territory. As far as the oil concessions were concerned, Qavam was quick to invoke his parliament's prohibition against any deals while Iranian territory remained occupied. However, the prime minister pledged to Stalin that should the Soviets evacuate their troops, he would hold new parliamentary elections and resubmit the Soviet oil request. The implication was that a Soviet military departure would alter the national political scene and produce a parliament prone to concede to Russia's demands. Qavam never actually promised any oil concessions, but he was happy to leave the Kremlin with the impression that, in a different political environment, they might be granted.

Qavam's promises and pledges seemed to have had a limited impact on Stalin. After returning to Tehran, the prime minister received a letter from Molotov urging him to recognize the Azerbaijan republic's autonomy. The foreign minister similarly insisted on creation of a joint Soviet-Iranian oil firm with wide exploratory authority. Even more ominously, Molotov suggested that according to the 1921 treaty with the Qajar dynasty, the Soviet Union had a right to maintain troops in Iran until order and stability were restored. Moscow had begun to predicate its presence on the 1921 treaty, not on the Tripartite Agreement that had called for Soviet troop withdrawals six months after the war ended. Molotov ended his letter by complaining about Tehran's "discriminatory and hostile attitude."[37]

As a politician practiced in the art of power politics, Qavam understood that Iran needed the American stick. Qavam proved a more
judicious reader of international politics than Stalin and recognized
that Russia's persistent violations of its wartime agreements in Eastern
Europe were straining the Grand Alliance. He also understood that
the Tripartite Agreement continued to provide the Soviet Union with a
veneer of legality. He resolved to drag out the negotiations with Russia
past March 1946, when the Soviet troop presence in Iran could be seen
as yet another treaty violation. If Stalin wanted to mobilize Azeri separatism as leverage on Iran, then Qavam was happy to inflame great-
power tensions as a means of taming the dictator.

The initiative for placing Iran's case before the newly constituted
United Nations actually came from Tehran. From Iran's perspective,
the United Nations' emphasis on national sovereignty made it a suitable venue for addressing Soviet transgressions. Qavam sensed that
Moscow would not want to be the first state censured by the nascent
international organization. In January 1946, Iran's ambassador to the
United States, Hussein Ala, began floating to the State Department
the idea of submitting Iran's case for violation of its sovereignty before
the United Nations.[38] While previous Iranian requests to put the Azerbaijan issue on various wartime conferences' agenda had been given
polite but largely perfunctory hearings by the United States, Tehran's
latest entreaty found a more receptive audience in Washington.

By 1946, the headlines in America's leading newspapers were breath-
lessly reporting Moscow's latest provocations. The situation in Eastern
Europe continued to fray, as Soviet satraps imposed a rigid Stalinist system on the ancient capitals of the continent. In Asia, the intractable Chinese civil war had entered a new stage, with Mao's communist troops
advancing steadily on nationalist strongholds. The European colonial
possessions were being assailed from Africa to South Asia by the newly
aroused nationalist forces. Churchill and Kennan had already made an
impression on those uneasy about continued accommodation of Soviet

power. Stalin's moves were no longer seen as the defensive spasms of an insecure Russia, but as expansionist surges of an ideological adversary.

As if Truman needed further motivation for a more aggressive policy, he also obtained a highly explosive report from his trusted aide Clark Clifford. The report began with the familiar refrain that "the language of military power is the only language which the disciples of power politics understand."[39] The best means of preserving American security would be to deter the Soviet Union from absorbing areas vital to U.S. interests. The increasing overlap between Iran and the new U.S. "get tough" policy was clearly expressed in the report, as "our continued access to the oil of the Middle East is especially threatened by the Soviet penetration of Iran."[40] The strategy of containment now had an Iranian venue to play host to its precepts.

Harry Truman was fortunate to inherit from his predecessor sober minds such as Dean Acheson and Averell Harriman, who fed him a steady stream of criticisms of Stalin's rule and the impracticality of uncritical engagement. After a period of dithering and confusion, Truman finally embraced the more confrontational policy.[41] The newly invigorated president informed his latest envoy to Moscow, General Walter Bedell Smith, to advise Stalin "that it would be misinterpreting the character of the United States to assume that because we are basically peaceful and deeply interested in world security we are either divided, weakened, or unwilling to face our responsibilities."[42] The president quickly came to see Iran as a critical pillar of his containment policy, stressing that "if the Russians were to control Iran's oil, either directly or indirectly, the raw material balance of the world would undergo a serious loss for the economy of the Western world."[43] An Iran that had been peripheral to America's global outlook now assumed center stage.

Despite Churchill's anti-Soviet oratory, British policy was conditioned more by commercial considerations than anticommunist sentiment. Given the AIOC's centrality in London's calculations, the British initially proved reluctant to challenge Russia's oil claims. Foreign Secretary

Ernest Bevin was lukewarm about dispatching the Iran issue to the United Nations, and the Foreign Office was concerned about exposing Britain's own oil interests to similar international arbitration. In Iran, Britain glimpsed a problem that it would encounter elsewhere in the Middle East as the Cold War unfolded. While British officialdom recognized the need for American support in checking Soviet ambitions, their policy was often pulled in contradictory and self-defeating directions.

British perspective changed when the Foreign Office began to fear that a spheres-of -influence arrangement with the Soviet Union could not be sustained. The Tudeh Party's agitation among laborers in the southern oil field had already provoked its share of strikes and protests. London became alarmed that a Soviet presence in the north of Iran was bound to endanger its financial interests in the south. Britain's envoy to Iran, Reader Bullard, warned that "appeasement of Moscow in the last analysis threatens our vital oil supplies in the south."[44] In an about face, the Foreign Office also stipulated, "Britain has to face the unpleasant possibility that a government entirely subservient to the Soviet government might soon be operating in Tehran and that government might either cancel the AIOC concession or by stirring up labor riots make the operation of that concession ultimately impossible."[45] Given its fear that Russia's power could not be insulated in the north, Britain focused on dismantling the entire Soviet enterprise in Iran by joining the United States in plotting against Moscow at the United Nations. The convergence of Anglo-American perspectives on the Iranian issue resulted less from shared anticommunist convictions than from Britain's desire to sustain its mercantile empire.[46]

The initial Iranian appeal to the United Nations filed on January 30, 1946, focused on its twin concerns: Soviet involvement in Iran's internal affairs and its troop presence in Azerbaijan. Iran stressed that the "interference of the Soviet Union through the medium of its official and armed forces" constituted the basis of its petition.[47] Since the

Tripartite Agreement gave Moscow the right to maintain forces in Iran until March, Tehran refrained from formally charging the Soviet Union on that point. All along, Qavam's strategy was to establish a legal basis for Iran's case at the United Nations and then drag out the negotiations until Russia was formally in breach of its treaty obligations. As such, Qavam not only called for continued bilateral discussions but also agreed to a suspension of U.N. deliberations until those talks concluded. The making of the Soviet case fell to the Deputy Foreign Minister, Andrey Vyshinsky, who quickly fell into Qavam's trap. Vyshinsky initially engaged in the type of bullying and deception that he had perfected as Stalin's henchman at the show trials, and called for the complete removal of the case from the United Nations' docket. Having failed to intimidate the Security Council, he had few options but to accept the proposed bilateral discussions.

Despite his petition at the United Nations, Qavam launched a charm offensive to placate the Russians and make it easy for them to escape their predicament. The prime minister relaxed controls on the Tudeh Party and even incorporated some of its members in his government. Qavam assured the Soviets that he would consider approaching the separatist government of Azerbaijan for talks, a position anathema to a Tehran that had considered the breakaway republic illegitimate. Despite these overtures, Moscow remained dogmatic, augmenting its troop levels and further buttressing the power of the Azerbaijani regime. In the meantime, the Soviet chargé d'affaires warned Qavam that persisting with the Security Council protest "would be regarded as an unfriendly and hostile act and would have unfortunate results for Iran."[48] The Soviet threats coupled with increased troop deployments in the north might have softened Qavam if not for American backing.

To steady the prime minister, U.S. policy makers offered both public and private assurances of support. In public, the United States insisted on Iran's sovereign rights and refused to remove the issue from the United Nations. As the recently appointed secretary of state James

Byrnes conceded, this was a means of putting "an escalator under the feet of Persia."[49] In private messages to Tehran, American and British representatives pledged their support once the issue returned to the Security Council. Having been fortified by the Western powers, Qavam refused to acquiesce to Soviet mandates and again played the parliamentary card, stressing that the Majlis would impeach him should he accept Russia's terms. Qavam advised the Soviet delegation that to settle the oil issue Stalin had to withdraw his troops. In the meantime, Iran filed another complaint at the United Nations.

In a remarkable turnabout, a new Soviet ambassador was dispatched to Tehran with a different offer. Ambassador Ivan Sadchikov stipulated that Russia would withdraw its forces if Iran signed a letter assuring it of an oil concession. The final text of the accord was somewhat different. It agreed that the Red Army would begin its departure on March 24, after which an agreement on a joint Iranian-Soviet company would be presented to the Majlis. Azerbaijan was still viewed as an internal Iranian matter, although Qavam had already hinted that he would look upon its quest for independence with favor. Shortly after the withdrawal of Soviet forces, the Majlis rejected the oil agreement by a vote of 102 to 2 while Iranian troops forcibly dismantled the breakaway republic, executing some of its leaders. Pishevari managed to escape to the Soviet Union, where his complaints so irritated Stalin that he conveniently died in a car accident.

During the Iran crisis the behavior of Stalin, a tyrant sensitive to subtle power shifts, was a curious mixture of defiance and conciliation. The Soviet dictator had been effective in consolidating his European realm and making significant inroads into Asia. However, this was aggression with impunity. The lingering legacy of the Grand Alliance and seeming American indifference had propelled Stalin to stand firm behind his demands on Iran. The sudden Western resolve surprised and perplexed the Soviet dictator. That both the United States and Britain were willing to go to the Security Council reflected a type of commitment that Stalin had not seen before. Moreover, the U.N. deliberations revealed how isolated the Soviet Union had become. As Molotov confessed, "We began to probe on Iran but nobody supported us."[50]

The Soviet dictator's core miscalculation was his failure to see how his adventurism would precipitate a new containment doctrine and how his acquiescence would affirm the logic of that doctrine. Stalin perceived that he could test the limits of his allies' patience without provoking a fundamental change in the structure of international relations. A perplexed Stalin confided to Molotov, "What does the Cold War mean? We were simply on the offensive. They became angry at us; of course we had to consolidate what we conquered."[51] Given the peripheral nature of the northern tier of the Middle East to his global ambitions, Stalin must have concluded that the costs far outweighed the advantages of belligerency.

Of all the actors in the Cold War's first melodrama, Qavam emerges as the most intriguing figure. The Soviets came away with a belief that Qavam had double-crossed them. Given how the issue resolved itself there is little in the Russian account that one can dispute. However, American representatives also did not fully trust Qavam. His flirtations with the Soviet Union, his inclination to countenance the Tudeh Party, and his seeming willingness to concede to a semiautonomous Azerbaijan Republic had alarmed his American supporters. Perhaps the British came away with the most accurate characterization of Qavam as a "sly old bird." In the end, Qavam entered the conflict with the weakest hand and somehow emerged in the strongest position. And this was no small achievement given the leaders arrayed against him.

WHY WAS THE CRISIS RESOLVED?

The Truman administration was the first to define the Middle East as critical to America's global containment struggle. Stability in the Middle East was crucial given its strategic location and immense oil reserves.

The threat that Truman faced in 1946 would prove an unusual one: a direct Soviet military intervention. It was the misfortune of Stalin that his military foray came at a time when America defined the Soviet moves as part of a larger Russian assault on the remaining outposts of the free world. While Soviet gains in Eastern Europe may have been irreversible, Washington was determined to limit Soviet expansionism. Truman and his advisors crafted an imaginative alternative to both war and appeasement. They mobilized the international community and used the nascent United Nations to good effect. But perhaps most telling was that the United States got very lucky in terms of the priority of its adversary and the resolution of its allies.

While Iran assumed a central role in America's calculations, it was never critical to Stalin. The Soviet dictator was an opportunist who continuously probed the West for weaknesses to see how much he could gain. In many ways, Stalin was a nineteenth-century strategist who remained fixated on Europe and did not always see the opportunities that awaited him in the vast colonial region. It would fall to Stalin's successors to take full advantage of the ongoing nationalist uproar in Africa and the Middle East. Long accustomed to Roosevelt's benevolence and perennially misreading American politics, Stalin seemed surprised by Truman's determination. Ultimately, given Iran's peripheral nature, Stalin was not about to crash with Truman over Azerbaijan's autonomy.

The other key to America's success was a reliable if not an ingenuous Iranian ally. The fact that Qavam was determined to preserve Iran's sovereignty made the task of American diplomacy much easier. Qavam understood that he could not prevail without U.S. support and was hopeful that Stalin's excesses in Europe would redound to his advantage. The prime minister withstood Soviet threats, provocative troop deployments, and attempts to carve out portions of his country. The crisis may have worked out differently had Tehran been intimidated into accepting the Soviet mandates. Instead Qavam challenged one of history's most ruthless tyrants at the zenith of his power.

Great Britain also fortuitously reinforced U.S. policy. Often denigrated as a declining power, Britain's global military network remained crucial to the success of America's containment policy. The British had long been active in Iranian politics, recruiting and bribing numerous politicians and parliamentarians. As we have seen, given the contentious nature of London's own oil interests, the Foreign Office was initially reluctant to press the Soviet case at the United Nations. The critical switch in Britain's policy came when it perceived that Soviet influence may not remain restricted to the north. The Tudeh Party's agitation against British firms did much to disabuse London of the possibility of working out a suitable arrangement with Moscow. Britain and America soon cooperated to evict Soviet forces.

An unexpected convergence of events ensured the success of America's policy. The Truman administration was quick to draw redlines and communicate them to Moscow. For Stalin, Iran was not Poland and he saw limited utility in provoking another confrontation with America. The unique confluence of all these factors would prove difficult to replicate as America confronted the hazards of a turbulent Palestine.

CHAPTER 2

THE PALESTINE QUESTION

The second flashpoint of the Cold War in the Middle East—the question of Palestine's future—would crystallize the superpowers' thus far inchoate regional policies. Both the United States and the Soviet Union would be forced to evaluate their interests in the region and determine their relationships with its major players.

The British Mandate for Palestine, in place since the end of World War I, was seen by both Arab and Jewish Palestinians as the precursor to an arrangement that each believed would satisfy their national aspirations for independence. Indeed, London had fueled such expectations by deals struck with both Zionists and Hashemites during Britain's struggle for strategic advantage during World War I. The Hashemites were one of two families and their tribal allies who vied for control of the Arabian Peninsula. The Hashemites held sway over the western region of the peninsula, the Hejaz, while the al-Saud controlled in varying degrees the east and much of the center. As the current name of the country indicates, the al-Saud ultimately won. The Mandate in Palestine was punctuated by violence between Arabs and Jews and between these communities and British authority. The near destruction of European Jewry in World War II altered the situation by focusing international humanitarian concern on the Jews victimized by Nazi genocide. In the wake of the war as many as two hundred fifty thousand Jews were living in displaced persons camps in European zones occupied by the Allies and in a host of other ad hoc facilities. Palestine emerged as a destination for these refugees in part because many wished to go there, but also because other potential receiving countries preferred that this population not be a burden on themselves. Jewish immigration to Palestine had long been an issue both for Arabs and Jews living in Palestine and therefore for Great Britain, the mandatory power responsible for Palestine. A British "White Paper" in 1939 aimed to win Arab support for the Allied cause by sharply limiting the entry of Jews into Palestine. Arab anxieties were stoked by the economic competition of incoming Jews, but more fundamentally by the fact that the larger the Jewish population, the firmer its claim to self-rule. Jewish sovereignty was seen as incompatible with the corresponding nationalist impulse that had begun to infuse Palestinian Arab politics. Jewish immigration therefore became a pivotal issue in an intensifying brawl over Palestine's future.

Expanding awareness in the United States of the horrors of the Holocaust also affected the political posture of American Jews. The American Jewish community had been relatively well organized for decades and, like other ethnic groups, sought to advance its interests in the realm of politics. But self-assertion was counterbalanced by the fear of persecution that might follow. There had been a particularly strong aversion to interfering in diplomatic matters. The war altered these instincts. It led to a vast increase in membership in Jewish civil society groups. Enrollment in these organizations swelled from sixty-five thousand in 1933 to one million within two years of the war's end. This vast increase was mobilized in large part by an interest in the fate of European Jews, which, in turn, was intertwined with the immigration issue and ultimately the establishment of a Jewish state in Palestine.[1]

Britain was saddled with the task of resolving the incompatible demands of Arabs and Jews in this exceedingly complicated environment. Historian Peter Hahn succinctly captures the British government's dilemma: "Two rounds of Anglo-Arab-Jewish talks between September 1946 and February 1947 produced an irreconcilable deadlock: the Jews demanded a state, but the Arabs refused to approve one. Foreign Minister Ernest Bevin realized that to endorse partition would infuriate the Arabs, to oppose it would provoke the Jews, and to impose a settlement on both parties would require financial and military resources that his government lacked."[2] Unable to resolve this dilemma, Bevin announced on February 19, 1947, that the government intended to refer the question of its Palestine Mandate to the United Nations, conceding that Britain could no longer mediate effectively or foster a compromise between the leaders of the contending populations. Bevin's advisor on Near Eastern affairs, Harold Beeley, seemed to think that the foreign minister's gambit would, in the end, perpetuate the status quo. He told David Horowitz, the representative of the Jewish Agency—the Zionists' proto-government—that the United Nations would not be able to devise a successor arrangement because success would require a two-thirds majority vote at the United Nations, which presupposed an inconceivable suspension of Cold War rivalry. "That," said Beeley, "has never happened, it cannot happen, and it will never happen."[3]

Such an outcome might well have pleased Bevin, despite his dour assessment of Britain's ability to sustain a mandatory arrangement or trusteeship in the face of determined Jewish resistance and the Arabs' inability to unify under a leadership that enjoyed a degree of popular legitimacy. Bevin had long endorsed British primacy in the Middle East. He envisioned a federated, unitary state in Palestine, ruled by an Arab majority and linked to the British Commonwealth. This was essentially a Churchillian vision of a postwar British empire. In Bevin's view, the Commonwealth "family," as he liked to describe it, would preserve Britain's long-term strategic needs, while accommodating to the burgeoning nationalism within the region. A U.N. imprimatur would thus facilitate the British interest.[4]

The process Bevin kicked off in February 1947 resulted in the creation of the United Nations Special Committee on Palestine (UNSCOP) in April; the committee was instructed to report to the U.N. General Assembly when it convened in September. The committee consulted widely with stakeholders in Europe, the United States, and the Middle East. The message they received was clear. Compromise between Arabs and Jews was unachievable. The gap was simply too wide. There being no other alternative, the committee concluded that partition was the course to take and that the British mandate was unsustainable. Jerusalem would be covered by a trusteeship. Bevin's hopes for a continued British role gave way to bitter exclusion. The last commander of British forces in Palestine would urinate on the ground before departing.[5]

The subsequent vote on the UNSCOP recommendations would draw the United States and Soviet Union into the debate over the future of Palestine, forcing each to take a public stand on an issue that carried major geopolitical implications for their emerging Cold War rivalry.

THE PARTITION RESOLUTION

The United States, unlike the British, had no imperial scheme defining its interest in Palestine. American interest had historically been religious in inspiration. As a policy matter, issues devolved to the protection of missionary institutions established by Americans in the region. During World War II, the United States was focused on defeating Germany and Japan and therefore had little reason to tread where Britain was already in control. The Cold War necessarily enlarged this conception of interest, but without endowing policy makers with new and better approaches to the intercommunal violence that had blighted the British mandate. The fact that Moscow had not declared for one side or the other liberated Washington from having to make any fateful choices.

On the other hand, there were domestic political considerations that could not be ignored. In the waning days of the 1944 presidential campaign, Franklin Roosevelt attempted to mollify his Jewish constituency by joining his opponent, Governor Thomas E. Dewey of New York, in endorsing unlimited Jewish immigration to Palestine and statehood. But strategic concerns still lurked in the background and would come to the fore when necessary, as they did shortly after the election when Roosevelt opposed a pro-Zionist congressional resolution signed by 399 members. The president assured his counterparts in the Arab world that "no decision altering the basic situation of Palestine should be reached without full consultation with both Arabs and Jews."[6]

Roosevelt's laissez-faire approach did not bequeath to his successor, Harry Truman, a carefully considered policy. Nevertheless, Truman did not long enjoy the luxury of cost-free vacillation on the Palestine question. The awful circumstances of Jewish displaced persons in Europe forced the issue. Roosevelt had appointed Earl G. Harrison, a former administration official, as the U.S. representative to the Intergovernmental Committee on Refugees in March 1945; in June he ordered Harrison to tour the displaced persons camps administered by the U.S. Army. In August 1945, Harrison presented his report. He wrote, "Many Jewish displaced persons . . . are living under guard behind barbed-wire fences . . . including some of the most notorious concentration camps . . . [have] no clothing other than their concentration camp garb. . . . Most of them have been separated three, four or five years and they cannot understand why the liberators should not have undertaken immediately the organized effort to re-unite family groups. . . . Many of the buildings . . . are clearly unfit for winter. . . . We appear to be treating the Jews as the Nazis treated them except that we do not exterminate them. They are in concentration camps in large numbers under our military guard instead of S.S. troops. One is led to wonder whether the German people, seeing this, are not supposing that we are following or at least condoning Nazi policy." He concluded the United States should support "the quick evacuation of all non-repatriable Jews in Germany and Austria, who wish it, to Palestine."[7]

The bleak irony of Harrison's recommendation spurred Truman to get British prime minister Clement Attlee to propose an Anglo-American Committee of Inquiry into the Palestine question. The committee's April 1946 report advocated the immigration of one hundred thousand Jewish refugees and a U.N. trusteeship that would lead to a binational state. The possibility that renewed, large-scale Jewish immigration might prejudge the political dispensation by strengthening the Zionists' hand and biasing the outcome toward partition was clearly on the minds of both the British and the Arabs. Samuel I. Rosenman, one of Truman's advisors who sympathized with the Zionist cause, took pains to assuage Truman's own qualms. He maintained that one hundred thousand immigrants would not significantly change the demographic balance in Palestine and, in response to the argument that Roosevelt had implicitly pledged to Arab leaders that the United States would not jeopardize the situation of Palestinian Arabs, Rosenman noted that Roosevelt's pledge had been to consult rather than obtain prior consent.[8] Truman's insistence that the United Nations adjudicate the post-mandate future of Palestine suggests that he remained somewhat uneasy about approving the one hundred thousand new entrants.

These doubts might have been offset to a degree by a contemporary Gallup poll showing that 78 to 80 percent "of Americans who had followed the issue favored Jewish immigration to Palestine."[9] The political salience of Palestine for Jewish voters was clearly growing. Prudence required that it be taken into account, especially around elections. Thus, as the holiest night of the Jewish liturgical year corresponding to 1946 was ushered in by Jews throughout the country just weeks prior to mid-term elections, Truman endorsed a "viable Jewish state . . . in an adequate area of Palestine instead of in the whole of Palestine."[10] Truman was immediately accused of pandering to a key voting bloc, a charge he brushed aside with claims of humanitarian concern for Jewish refugees. According to Dean Acheson, a senior State Department official at the time, Truman's statement was necessitated by the certainty that Thomas Dewey was going to back the creation of a Jewish state in Palestine and Truman could therefore do no less.[11] Truman, however, could not outbid Dewey, who called for unlimited immigration. The president's statement failed to impress voters and, for a number of reasons, Congress went Republican that November.[12]

Truman was also thinking about the strategic aspects of the Palestine problem. Several things were clear. The United States faced a perilous situation in Europe, and a commitment to Palestine would be a dangerous distraction. It would be an intractable one, too, if the British experience was any guide. On the other hand, the United States had an interest in denying Palestine to the Soviets, even if the British were incapable of controlling it and the United States did not want to. And as a corollary to these factors, the United States would want to avoid any arrangement that might necessitate the allocation of troops to managing a crisis in Palestine.[13]

The last point was an especially sensitive one. The War Department had studied prospects for deployment to Palestine even as the smoke was clearing over Europe in 1945. Its analysis was released in a September 1945 memorandum. As defense officials have done since time immemorial, they sought to kill the concept in the crib by concluding that any deployment would have to be very large and would likely spawn the need for further deployments. The estimate could not be dismissed, however, in view of the fact that Britain's armed forces and police in Palestine had hovered at the seventy thousand mark.[14] This judgment was carried over to a June 1946 assessment disseminated by the Joint Chiefs of Staff, which concluded that no U.S. troops be involved in implementing the Anglo-American Committee's recommendations.[15] The truth was that the U.S. military was shrinking rapidly. As of August 15, 1945, when Japan surrendered, there were more than twelve million Americans in uniform. By the summer of 1947, there were a bit more than 1.5 million. Yet as this remarkable demobilization was taking place, the specter of war with the Soviet Union was appearing just over the horizon. It was therefore to be expected that Truman would concur in the Pentagon's reluctance to send increasingly scarce man-power to the region. Middle East military commitments would limit Washington's flexibility to respond to challenges in other areas seen to have higher strategic value, especially Europe, just as tensions there were rising. Truman's later instruction to the U.S. delegation to the United Nations that "we are not going to pick up . . . responsibility for the maintenance of law and order in Palestine" reflected these worries.

Truman also had to consider the conduct of international politics in a postwar world. The UNSCOP report recommendations put the credibility of the United Nations as an impartial arbitrator in the Cold War at risk.[16] As a matter of policy, the United States was committed to supporting the United Nations, which had been established to pro-vide collective security and resolve disputes that might lead to major war. Truman might have been reluctant to contemplate partition in Palestine, but to oppose the UNSCOP recommendations would have amounted to rejecting the consensus of the new international organiza-tion just as it was getting off the ground. His attitude regarding parti-tion was thus intertwined with his intent to reinforce the integrity of the United Nations at a crucial moment in its history.

The national security departments and agencies—the Department of State, the Department of Defense, and the intelligence agencies—came to a different conclusion. Partition, they judged, could not be carried out without the participation of American troops. Secretary of State George Marshall prophesied that partition could necessitate U.S. troops in Palestine.[17] His service as Army chief of staff during World War II endowed this judgment with substantial credibility. At the Pen-tagon, the Joint Chiefs of Staff contended that partition would embroil U.S. troops in Palestine and in the region more broadly, potentially triggering unwelcome clashes with the Soviet Union.[18] The dangers of a troop commitment had actually become an argument against both trusteeship and partition.

Apart from higher U.S. priorities in Europe, the support for partition with the implicit acceptance of a Jewish state in Palestine was thought to carry serious regional risks. The State Department lamented that perceptions of U.S. backing for a Jewish state would wreck U.S.-Arab relations. Loy W. Henderson, the head of the Near East and African Affairs Division (NEA) of the State Department, was a forceful exponent of this reasoning. "We are not," he said, "only forfeiting the friendship of the Arab world, but we are incurring long-term Arab hostility towards us."[19] He predicted that the Arab states would flock to the Soviet Union.[20] He had high confidence in the Soviets' ability to exploit the disturbances that the creation of a Jewish state would trigger throughout the region.[21] Henderson and his NEA colleagues consequently rejected the recommendations of the UNSCOP report. Not for the first time, the State Department misread Arab political tendencies and the region's evolving alignments.

Marshall naturally concurred with his functionaries. Later that autumn, he averred that "adoption of the majority report . . . would mean very violent Arab reaction," and that U.S. support for partition could shift the Arab world toward "rapprochement with the Soviet Union."[22] The State Department's view was buttressed by an apocalyptic CIA assessment that partition "is capable of changing the development of the Arab World from one of evolution in cooperation with the West, to one of revolution with the support of the U.S.S.R."[23]

There were dissenting voices within the bureaucracy. In strategic terms, the U.S. stake in the Middle East was access to oil, especially to assure a steady supply for vulnerable allies in Europe. Ibn Saud, the founder of the modern Saudi state and its first king, had stoked these fears, saying that "he may be compelled, in certain circumstances, to apply sanctions against the American oil concessions [due to the American recognition of Israel] . . . not because of his desire to do so but because the pressure upon him of Arab public opinion was so great that he could no longer resist it." State Department analysts, however, concluded that the Arab Middle East supplied only 6 percent of global oil consumption, which, if lost, would not cause "substantial hardship to any group of consumers."[24]

Whether the Saudi monarch would ever have taken this step was open to doubt in view of his reliance on the immense wealth flowing into his coffers via the Arabian American Oil Company (Aramco) and his perceived need for U.S. protection from supposed British machinations to replace the al-Saud with his Hashemite rivals. The need to protect his kingdom from Soviet aggression no doubt reinforced Ibn Saud's reliance on the United States.[25]

Curiously, the contention that U.S. support for partition would push the Arab world into the arms of the Soviets was advanced in the apparent absence of any insight into Moscow's rather flexible position on the UNSCOP recommendations. Whether this was a matter of poor intelligence or the diplomats' resistance to information at odds with their preconceptions is not obvious at this remove. Whichever the case, two days after Truman overruled his chief diplomat and instructed the U.S. delegation to support the UNSCOP's recommendation on October 11, 1947, the Soviet Union also voted in favor.

Like the United States, Moscow had avoided expressing a clear policy toward Palestine prior to 1947. Ambiguity on Palestine would preserve room for maneuver once the matter went to the United Nations. Moreover, given the Soviet Union's modest assessment of its ability to influence regional developments, an ambiguous posture would obscure Soviet weakness by postponing policy decisions until the context was clearer. Moscow "felt certain that Britain would eventually be compelled to refer the Palestine issue to the international community. When that occurred, the U.S.S.R. would have ample opportunity to commit itself to one or another solution in such a way as to make its influence felt."[26]

The Soviets addressed the question of Palestine's future at the United Nations on May 14, 1947. In the hope of maximizing his government's limited influence on the parties, Andrey Gromyko, until recently the

Soviet ambassador to the U.S. but now Moscow's U.N. representative in New York, declared that "the legitimate interests of both the Jewish and Arab populations of Palestine can be duly safeguarded only through the establishment of an independent, dual, democratic, homogeneous Arab-Jewish state . . . If this plan proved impossible to implement, in view of the deterioration in the relations between the Jews and the Arabs—and it will be very important to know the special committee's opinion on this question—then it would be necessary to consider the second plan . . . which provides for the partition of Palestine into two independent autonomous states, one Jewish and one Arab. I repeat that such a solution of the Palestine problem would be justifiable only if relations between the Jewish and Arab populations of Palestine indeed proved to be so bad that it would be impossible to reconcile them."[27]

As might have been expected, the Zionists were more than content with a Soviet speech that held the door open to partition. A diplomatic report of a meeting with Moshe Sharett, the de facto foreign minister of the pre-state Zionist administration in Palestine, summarizes the Zionist reaction: "Mr. Sharett referred to the recent Special Session of the General Assembly of the United Nations and said that the Jewish Agency in general was somewhat encouraged at what transpired . . . In particular, the Jewish Agency was pleasantly surprised at the attitude displayed in the fine speech of Mr. Gromyko . . . It would appear from that speech that the Soviet Union, which heretofore had been considered as favorable to the Arab side of the case, had finally decided to support partition . . . the pronouncement was extremely helpful to the Zionists, particularly since it should assist in removing concern lest the Soviet Union would back the Arabs in case the United States and Great Britain should decide in favor of partition."[28]

Gromyko's tantalizing reference to partition notwithstanding, the official Soviet position still favored a federated, binational state.[29] Private communications by Soviet and East European officials tacitly acknowledged the ambiguity of Moscow's line by cautioning the Zion-

ists not to leap to convenient conclusions. Yugoslav deputy foreign minister Vladimir Velebit, for example, warned the Zionists in Palestine
not to overinterpret Gromyko's statement as advocating the creation of
a Jewish state.[30]

These early, if uncertain, signs that the Soviet Union might back
partition did not appear to affect the State Department perceptions of
Soviet intentions. U.S. diplomats understood the Soviet position at the
First Special Session as "non-committal" but expected the Soviets' next
step would be "to come out forthrightly on the side of the Arabs."[31] Over
the long run, this understanding would prove valid, but it misread the
Soviet near-term objectives. A State Department position paper circu-
lated at the end of September, which aimed to gauge the likely Soviet
approach to a partition vote, concluded: "The Soviet Union has thus
far avoided taking a position, but the Embassy in Moscow and other
observers are convinced that, in the final showdown, the Soviet Union
will support the Arab states."[32]

Zionist diplomacy watchers had a more nuanced understanding of the
evolving Soviet position. Eliyahu Epstein, the Jewish Agency representative in Washington, proffered a less pessimistic appraisal of the Soviet
position to former State Department official and one-time Roosevelt confidant Summer Welles. Israeli historian Yaakov Ro'i summarized it this
way: "The traditional Anglo-American fear that sympathy for Jewish
aspirations might drive the Arabs into an alliance with the U.S.S.R. no
longer seemed valid. Moreover, just as there was no cause to fear Soviet-
Arab cooperation for other reasons—specifically that the ruling Arab
circles feared the implications for the domestic political, social economic
spheres—so too there were no grounds to apprehend that the fundamentally democratic *Yishuv* [the term denoting the Jewish community in
Palestine prior to the establishment of the State of Israel] would become
affiliated with Soviet Communism and totalitarianism."[33]

On October 13, 1947, the Soviet Union voted in favor of partition, explaining its decision in terms of the logic of the situation on

the ground: "Relations between Arabs and Jews had reached such a state of tension that it had become impossible to reconcile their points of view on the solution of the problem; the minority plan therefore appeared impracticable. In the circumstances therefore, the partition plan proposed by the majority offered more hope of realization."[34]

Cold War interests explain the Soviet decision. Moscow needed a policy that would promise a degree of influence in an area of the eastern Mediterranean that it increasingly saw as strategically important. The Soviets grasped Palestine's geopolitical role as an oil junction crucial to efficient transporting of the Persian Gulf's petroleum to Europe. A contemporary analysis featured in the Soviet newspaper *Pravda* explained to readers that Palestine "lies at the center of the world trade routes passing through the Mediterranean" and had been "converted into a principal British strategic [*sic*] base in the Arab East."[35] Soviet strategy therefore required the end of the British mandate as a first step toward weakening Britain's still formidable position in the Middle East.[36] Combined Arab and Jewish rejection of British mandatory authority that relied, in turn, on despised Western client regimes in Egypt, Jordan, Lebanon, and Syria would have made Palestine seem like low-hanging fruit.

Abetting the creation of a Jewish state in the Middle East was, ironically, the most efficient way to puncture the carapace of British and French control that had solidified in the aftermath of World War I. The most plausible alternative to partition, some variation of the 1946 Morrison-Grady Plan—which envisaged a federalized arrangement under British trusteeship—would only have legitimized the British role in Palestine. Even worse, according to *Pravda*, was that under the plan's provisions, "the sanctity of Jerusalem, like the sanctity of the oil fields . . . [would] remain a British preserve." Unsurprisingly, the Zionists were hearing the same thing from "reliable sources" in Palestine, namely, that "the general trend in Soviet political quarters is opposed to the conversion of Palestine into a purely Arab state." From a Soviet perspective, this would consolidate "British mastery of the Middle East."[37]

Given this strategic priority, a tactical alignment on partition with the United States at the United Nations was a small price to pay for hamstringing Britain in the Middle East.[38] That this was such a surprise to the State Department could be explained by the stew of hardline anticommunist thinking—Loy Henderson portrayed himself as such a hardliner—and subtle anti-Semitism simmering in the Near East Department. Yet, Stalin had sounded a collaborative note about Palestine to Roosevelt at Yalta in 1945 and struck Roosevelt as amenable to cooperation.[39] Similarly, a State Department Memorandum of Conversation with Nahum Goldmann, a leading Zionist, characterized Czechoslovakia's foreign minister Jan Masaryk as "in line with what the Zionists had been told by President Roosevelt on his return from Yalta, when he had remarked that, to his surprise Stalin had not appeared opposed to Zionism."[40]

Cooperation with the United States had the additional benefit of driving a wedge between Washington and London. The Soviet press crowed, "the Palestine question is the focus of one of the sharpest clashes between British and American interests in the Middle East."[41] Moscow clearly intended to take advantage of Anglo-American friction to reduce or at least deflect attention from Soviet-American tensions, while hastening the end of Britain's presence in Palestine.[42]

Despite the critical diplomatic and subsequent military support the Soviets offered to the Zionists, they did not see in the unfolding Jewish state an enduring ally. Moscow correctly anticipated that the new Jewish state would ultimately side with the West as the Cold War played out. The Soviets did understand that Britain and the Zionists were parting ways, but concluded that this was not an unalloyed blessing, since the United States was simply replacing Britain in Zionist affections. Domestic U.S. political support for Zionism was scarcely secret and Moscow drew the obvious conclusion about the impact this would have on U.S. policy. A flavor of Soviet thinking about the future orientation of a Jewish state was captured by the Soviet consul in Beirut, M. N. Agronov, who described his colleagues as unpersuaded of the "independence" of the Zionists from the West, despite the "progressive" spirit of the movement as a whole. In his view, it was unclear whether pro-Western or "progressive" factions would ultimately determine the direction of Zionist foreign policy. Others were less agnostic. One Soviet diplomatic cable alleged that the speeches of David Ben-Gurion, the chairman of the Jewish Agency executive and the leader of the Yishuv, had a fascist ring to them and that "Jewish Agency materials might lead a reader to suppose that Arabs do not exist in Palestine at all."[43]

Eliyahu Epstein discounted these Soviet suspicions regarding socio-political proclivities of the Yishuv. In his report to the Jewish Agency executive of a dinner conversation at the residence of Mikhail Vavilov, a Soviet embassy officer in Washington, Epstein quotes his host saying that the Soviets "are well aware that the social and economic struc-ture of the Yishuv is a capitalistic one and that our social experiments in collectivism have nothing to do with the Marxist interpretation of collectivism. They believe, however, that we are building a peaceful, democratic and progressive community in Palestine which can block anti-Soviet intrigues. . . ." Epstein noted that Vavilov ". . . ridiculed the 'vicious propaganda' of some anti-Soviet circles in the U.S., including Jewish circles, that Mr. Gromyko's statement did not intend to help the Jews but was the springboard for an attack on the British, intended to cause further trouble for the British and American governments with the Arabs rather than help the Jews." Vavilov continued, "If this were indeed the case, Mr. Gromyko would not have had to come out in sup-port of Jewish statehood and to commit the Soviet government to a definite policy in this respect."[44]

As skeptical as the Soviets were of the Yishuv, their disregard for rul-ing Arab regimes as British pawns and political reactionaries was even more pronounced. Any arrangement that left all of Palestine under Arab rule was tantamount to leaving it under Britain's control. The official Soviet assessment was that "the basic Arab feudal-bourgeois organizations—the Arab Higher Committee and the Arab Office—backed by the British, have spoken out against the partition of Palestine . . . Traitors and quislings from all over the world have begun to flood into Palestine and are taking part in the struggle on the Arab side."[45]

Regional considerations were not the only ones to shape Soviet thinking in this period. The Soviets also saw Palestine as an opportunity to influence American Jewry, which they defined as both progressive outsiders and controlling insiders.[46] Moscow's overestimation of Jewish influence, fueled by persistent anti-Semitic tropes relating to obscure Jewish influence over world powers, resembled the spurious assumptions underlying Britain's endorsement of Zionism thirty years before in order to bolster its efforts to bring the United States into the war.

Yaacov Ro'i summed up Soviet diplomacy during the fluid events that preceded the outbreak of war this way: "Moscow's short-term policy calculations directed at precipitating the end of the Mandate seemed, then, to require the consideration of Jewish national claims and aspirations without any thought of a long-term commitment. . . . Despite current opposition to the Arab League [a group of seven key Arab states that had formed a pact in 1945 to 'safeguard their independence and sovereignty'], Moscow would one day win over the Arabs. Palestine's remoteness from the Soviet Union meant that direct national interests did not determine the Soviet stand. It was therefore plausible that just as currently the U.S.S.R. seemed to be coming closer to the Jews, so, when the international political arena changed, as it was constantly doing, Moscow would be compelled to abandon them."[47]

FROM PARTITION TO WAR

Following the adoption of the partition resolution at the United Nations, Palestine exploded into civil war and forced Washington to reexamine the situation. The British mandate was set to expire on May

15, 1948. The Cold War context dictated that a workable solution had to be in place to prevent a vacuum that the Soviets might fill. There were clear constraints, however, on the U.S. role in whatever solution might be devised. At a press conference on January 15, 1948, Truman clearly reaffirmed his desire not to send American forces to Palestine.[48] This was not just a public posture. Truman explained privately to his trusted aide Clark Clifford that although he had gone to great lengths in support of partition, "he was not about to mobilize troops."[49]

The State Department continued to stress that support for partition just as Arab-Jewish violence was escalating would put the United States on a slippery slope to a military entanglement. They feared that as the violence worsened and the Yishuv suffered military losses, domestic pressures to intervene would grow to prevent another Holocaust, this time in Palestine. The United States, warned the State Department, must not find itself holding "major military and economic responsibility for the indefinite maintenance by armed force of a status quo in Palestine fiercely resented by the bulk of the Arab world."[50] Yet this exact outcome, in their assessment, was where current policy would lead. A subsequent National Security Council report indicated that it would take a minimum of 160,000 troops to enforce partition.[51]

Moreover, opponents in the bureaucracy were still bitter over Truman's decision the previous fall. They attributed Truman's support for partition largely to domestic politics and lack of concern for the U.S. stake in the friendship of the Arab world.[52] Hence the determination with which the State Department argued that support for partition would hand the region to the Soviets on a silver platter.

On January 19, the first of two substantial memoranda on the subject, signed off by George Kennan, then the director of the State Department's Policy Planning Staff, forecast that partition would rupture relations with Saudi Arabia; shutter the American University in Beirut; isolate Greece, Turkey, and Iran, all important U.S. allies; cut off Western access to Middle East oil and expose Aramco to retaliation; and create a Zionist state hungry for additional territory and likely to corrupt the integrity of U.S. political and policy processes through unscrupulous lobbying.[53]

The surprise Soviet endorsement of partition at the United Nations, however, prodded the State Department and others to reassess the Kremlin's intentions. Why had Moscow so confounded U.S. expectations?[54] The answer was that Russia had foreseen the probable need to police a partition arrangement, which would offer a legitimate pretext for deployment of Soviet troops. Not everyone believed this. Walter Bedell Smith, a former Army general and future Director of Central Intelligence then serving as U.S. ambassador in Moscow, did not foresee Soviet military intervention. He characterized Soviet strategy rather more shrewdly:

(3) [Soviet] support of the UNSCOP majority recommendation would place Soviet Delegation in optimum position to secure "appropriate" implementing measures and ensure adoption of the partition plan. This solution, though second-choice, would serve Soviet interest in softening up area by:

a) Securing withdrawal of British and ensuring against their replacement by other great-power influence;

b) Launching unsettling and disruptive Jewish-Arab conflict which could be kept going indefinitely by covert Soviet aid and incitement to both sides through local Communist parties who will be heavily reinforced by Communist indoctrinated emigrants from Eastern Europe; thus threatening and damaging major U.S. and British interests in an area where U.S.S.R. has nothing to lose.

c) Soviet offense in Arab eyes would be minimized by the prior endorsement partition by the UNSCOP majority and USA and by the Soviet record in support of Syria, Lebanon, and Egypt. Moreover, given shortness of man's memory and flexibility of Soviet tactics, Kremlin could quickly recapture Arab good will by sudden reversal of its position if and when its interests should so dictate.[55]

Smith's cold calculation of the interests of the ruling Arab regimes led him to conclude that capturing this goodwill would be easier said than done: "Both Europe and Asiatic colonial areas are at present more critical and considerably 'softer' for Soviet exploitation than 'harder' Arab East, unshaken either politically or economically by war and enemy occupation, shielded by firm U.S. stand in Greece, Turkey and Iran, bolstered by strong U.S. and British interests and commitments and controlled by feudal anti-Communist ruling class, susceptible to limited political 'deals' but unlikely to open doors to Soviet penetration."[56]

Back in Washington, George Kennan had come to a different conclusion, unleashing a second acid critique of Truman's Palestine policy.

In the Mediterranean and the Middle East, we have a situation where a vigorous and collective national effort, utilizing both our political and military resources, could probably prevent the area from falling under Soviet influence and preserve it as a highly important factor in our world strategic position. But we are deeply involved, in that same area, in a situation which has no direct relation to our national security, and where the motives of our involvement lie solely in past commitment of dubious wisdom and in our attachment to the U.N. itself. If we do not effect a fairly radical reversal of the trend of our policy to date, we will end up either in the position of being ourselves militarily responsible for the protection of the Jewish population in Palestine against the declared hostility of the Arab world, or of sharing that responsibility with the Russians and thus assisting at their installation as one of the military powers of the area. In either case, the clarity and efficiency of a sound national policy for that area will be shattered.[57]

Clark Clifford remarked drily: "If anything has been omitted that could help kill partition, I do not know what it would be."[58] Yet the drumbeat of these analyses was felt; it resonated, after all, with the president's own sense of Soviet intentions. Kennan's depiction of a daisy chain that would begin with deployment of U.S. forces to Palestine and end with the deployment of Soviet troops, and resulting in the collapse of "the whole structure of strategic and political planning which we have been building on," leveraged preexisting concerns about the ineluctable requirement for U.S. troops to effectuate a partition of Palestine. The CIA's own analysis predicted the same devolution.[59] U.S. analysts also foresaw partition as an irritant in the transatlantic relations. "Unrest within the Arab world might topple conservative Arab governments, creating opportunities for the small Communist movements. At the very least, Arabs would demand that the United Kingdom provide them munitions to match those the Israelis were securing from Soviet satellites. British compliance would create enormous Anglo-American tension; their not complying would further undermine the Western position in the Arab world."[60] The bottom line was that partition would suck in the armies of the United States, the Soviet Union, or both and that this would raise the specter of superpower confrontation.

Events on the ground initially appeared to confirm these warnings. From March 1948 onward, successive UNSCOP reports made it clear that the partition plan could not be implemented by peaceful means.[61] This timeframe coincided with the crisis in U.S.-Soviet relations that followed a Soviet coup in Czechoslovakia. Policy makers could not help but see Soviet maneuvering in regard to Palestine as a precursor to expansionism in the Middle East. Indeed, many Americans expected war between the United States and the Soviet Union to break out soon.[62] In this atmosphere of crisis, Kennan's recommendation seems to represent the most prudent way forward.[63] Truman therefore told Marshall to approve U.N. trusteeship "in principle" while insisting that "nothing should be presented to the Security Council that could be interpreted as a recession on our part" from partition.[64]

The inherent ambiguity of Truman's guidance afforded State Department opponents of partition an opportunity to seize control of a policy that career diplomats believed had gone off the rails. There is evidence of deliberate deception on the part of the State Department, in the form of a memorandum in which State Department officials in Washington wring their hands over the possibility that U.S. Ambassador to the United Nations Warren Austin might communicate with Truman before the vote and receive clear, incontrovertible instruction to endorse partition: "At one point yesterday there seemed to have been considerable danger lest Ambassador Austin find himself in outright disagreement with his instructions and that he had been tempted at least to discuss this disagreement with the President."[65] This contingency was evidently averted. Both Marshall and Robert A. Lovett, the undersecretary of state, had departed Washington at this juncture, probably so as to be unavailable in the event that Austin sought their clarification of the president's murky instruction.

When the Security Council met on March 19, the three permanent members of the council, the United States, Britain, and France, quickly agreed that partition was going to be too difficult to implement. This consensus enabled Austin to propose a temporary trusteeship as a substitute for partition.[66]

Truman was outraged when he read the U.S. statement at the Security Council in the newspapers the following day and told Clifford to investigate.[67] Whether the president was upset more by the embarrassing public appearance of policy confusion, or by the apparent abandonment of partition as the preferred U.S. policy option, is difficult to determine. There is no question that Truman had been swayed by his administration's forecast of disaster if partition were attempted, but there is also evidence that he saw no real alternative to partition. His awkward instruction to Marshall seems to have reflected an attempt to reconcile these contradictory views. Marshall's ex post facto explanation to Chip Bohlen of Truman's anger tends to support this interpretation; he portrays the president as "so much exercised in the matter . . . [because] . . . Austin made his statement without the President having been advised that he was going to make it at that particular time. He had agreed to the statement but said that if he had known when it was going to be made he could have taken certain measures to have avoided the political blast of the press."[68] Yet it remains unclear whether Marshall's readout to Bohlen was inaccurate or perhaps even tendentious. Truman's reaffirmation the very next day of his support for partition, in a meeting with Chaim Weizmann, the distinguished Zionist leader, suggests that Marshall might have mischaracterized Truman's response to Austin's debacle in New York.

Regardless, the administration still had to stitch together a policy statement that would allay the confusion over the U.S. stance on partition. The result was a March 25 statement proposing "temporary trusteeship" [not as a] "substitute for [a] partition plan but as [an] effort to fill [the] vacuum soon to be created by termination of [the] mandate on May 15."[69] This expedient only succeeded in enraging both sides in the spiraling struggle over the U.S. position on partition. American Jews were disconcerted by an unexpected and potentially indeterminate delay in their quest for a Jewish state. Marshall, Lovett, and Defense Secretary James Forrestal all expressed serious consternation over White House persistence regarding partition. In the meantime, the tempo of violence in Palestine was increasing. By the end of the following week, the scale of the fighting spurred Truman to urge Britain to keep its troops in Palestine, and to signal his readiness to insert a U.S. contingent.[70]

Intervention, however, was still anathema to the military leaders who would have to carry it out. Dean Rusk, then a senior State Department official, presented the case for deployment to the Joint Chiefs of Staff on April 4. His first point was that inaction would pave the way for Soviet control of the eastern Mediterranean: "If we did nothing," he said, "the Russians could and would take definite steps toward gaining control in Palestine." His second argument was that intervention would enable the United States to gain vital base access. It would, he continued, "give us the opportunity to construct bomber fields in the

Middle East." The Joint Staff was uninspired by these arguments. For them, such benefits would be offset by the need for a large occupation force, which would entail reversing a vast demobilization that had only just been completed, as well as more funding.[71]

Nevertheless, events on the ground soon rendered this debate irrelevant. Israeli forces had adopted a more aggressive strategy when they realized that the United States might walk away from partition because it looked as though Jewish forces might be defeated. The new strategy was largely successful. Israeli forces were soon to break the Arab blockade of Jerusalem and gained control of Haifa and Jaffa.[72] At this stage the declaration of statehood upon the expiration of the mandate was a foregone conclusion. Whether the United States would recognize the fledgling country was still unsettled.

The question was debated by Clifford and Marshall at the White House on May 12. Clifford emphasized the inevitability of Jewish statehood, showcasing a *New York Times* article reporting that the Arab armies were "incapable of preventing the establishment of a Jewish state in Palestine."[73] He also played the Cold War card, pointing to another article suggesting that "the Soviets plan to give further impetus to de facto partition by recognizing the Jews."[74] This press piece aligned with diplomatic reporting from the U.S. mission to the United Nations suggesting that the Soviets intended to wrong-foot Washington by recognizing the Jewish state.[75] The gist of Clifford's argument was that statehood was a fait accompli, which would not be changed by withholding recognition; but that withholding recognition would hand the initiative to Moscow. Dismissing the thrust of Clifford's logic, Marshall and Lovett insisted that the White House was motivated by nothing more than pursuit of the Jewish vote, rather than strategic advantage vis à vis the Soviet Union, which was the real issue. And, they argued, since there was no way to know which side in the Cold War the Jewish state would actually choose, it would be better to decide on the basis of U.S. interests in the Arab world. The general and his diplomatic

sidekick also argued that recognition would run counter to ongoing
U.S. efforts at the United Nations to win a truce between the combatants in Palestine.[76] The last argument would appear in retrospect to be
particularly weak given that a truce would have been unacceptable to
the Arabs, while the Zionists were certain to declare statehood. It must
have sounded flimsy even then. And trusteeship, which was linked to
the concept of an unattainable truce, was by then a dead letter. Further-
more, enforcement of a truce would require peacekeepers, which most
Washington officials had said could lead to the deployment of Soviet
troops to Palestine under U.N. authorization.

Nor would this be the only unintended consequence. According to
Evan Wilson, then head of the Palestine Desk at the State Department,
"had the Americans pressed on with trusteeship, they likely would
have found themselves in the impossible situation of having to use force
against the Jews, in contravention of a U.N. Resolution.[77]

These points were academic, however, since it was implicitly understood by all the players on the U.S. side that the violence was going to
spike upon Israel's declaration of statehood no matter what the United
Nations decided.[78] Truman, unpersuaded by Marshall, opted for recognition. In the final analysis, recognition elicited political benefit from
an unavoidable event, while the risk of an Arab backlash that might
benefit the Soviet Union had been obviated by Moscow's readiness to
recognize Israel.

The Soviets did so on a de jure basis on May 17. They went beyond
mere recognition by authorizing their Eastern European clients to
transfer an array of weapons to the new Israel Defense Forces. Ivan
Bakulin, who was head of the Middle East department at the Soviet
foreign ministry, advised his superior, Deputy Foreign Minister Vale-
rian Zorin, ". . . to let the Czechs and Yugoslavs know confidentially
via our ambassadors in Prague and Belgrade about the desirability of
extending aid to the representatives of the State of Israel in the pur-

chase and dispatch to Palestine of artillery and airplanes in view of the fact that, despite the Security Council Resolution forbidding the import of arms to Arab countries, the latter have every opportunity to receive the requisite quantity of arms from British depots." It was important to the Soviets that this assistance be deniable, the better to protect whatever equities the Soviet Union might have or attempt to acquire in the Arab world. Thus, Bakulin further advised Zorin "not to permit representatives of the government of Israel to travel to the U.S.S.R. from Czechoslovakia in order to conduct negotiations on purchasing airplanes in Russia."[79]

Speaking in support of Israel's accession to the United Nations, Iakov Malik, the Soviet delegate to the United Nations, recalled that since Israel's birth, it had "declared that it wished to live in peace and entertain peaceful relations with all its neighbors and with all the nations of the world. It is not to blame for the fact that this appeal did not meet with any response either from its neighbors or from some of the most distant states."[80] Such expressions of Soviet empathy became increasingly scarce over the following decades, just as they became a staple of American discourse. For a brief moment, however, this sentiment was shared by the two Cold War rivals.

THE RIGHT CALL

In overruling the famed General George Marshall and the diplomatic corps and recognizing Israel, Truman made not just an independent decision, but the right one. In 1949, the United States settled on a strategy of support for both conservative Arab monarchies and Israel. This approach evolved from the challenge posed by a number of interlocking developments: the Holocaust, Britain's inability to sustain its mandate in Palestine, the success of the Zionist movement, the importance of regional energy resources for the consolidation of democracy in Western Europe in the wake of World War II, and the emergence of a politically engaged American-Jewish community. The Truman administration was initially divided against itself, but a rough consensus that the United States would cast its lot with Israel, Jordan, and the Arab Gulf monarchies had come together by 1949, thus setting the foundation of U.S. Middle Eastern policy that has endured for decades.

For the Soviets, after an initial tactical dalliance with Israel prompted by the desire to pry Britain from the Middle East, the future lay clearly with the Arab side. Arab bitterness over their defeat by Israel provided fertile ground for the revolutionary nationalist coups of the 1950s. The Soviets were in a position to capitalize on these regime changes because they had less at stake and fewer domestic political considerations than did the United States. This fixed the trajectory of Soviet policy in the Middle East until the collapse of the Soviet Union.

Ultimately, the Palestine crisis of 1947–48 set the pattern that regulated superpower involvement in the Cold War. On the U.S. side, the division within the government about how best to balance American commitments to Israel and the Arabs and, relatedly, the political salience of the U.S.-Israel relationship persists to this day as does the indispensable role of the White House in setting policy toward Israel. Turning to Israel, the early Cold War was the period during which Israelis made the strategic decision to join the U.S. camp, rejecting Soviet patronage despite links to the Soviet Union. The Soviets' divide-and-conquer approach to the region came into view in this period as they manipulated the crisis over Israeli independence to lever Britain from Palestine and drive a wedge between the United States and Britain. The struggle over partition also shaped the pattern of interaction between the conservative Arab monarchies and the United States. In this diplomatic dance, the Arabs opposed U.S. ties with Israel, but valued them nevertheless owing to a perception that Israel's dependence on the United States would enable Washington to extract concessions from Jerusalem that would otherwise be unavailable. The U.S. relationship with its allies on the Arab side of the Persian Gulf would inevitably turn on Arab threat perceptions. The Arab conservatives' displeasure with the United States was subordinated to their pressing need for American security guarantees. At the same time, their reliance on the United States placed insurmountable barriers to Soviet encroachment.

CHAPTER 3

AMERICA, IRAN, AND THE COUP

In 1901 the gold speculator and oil entrepreneur William D'Arcy pur-chased the right to exploit Iran's oil fields. In return for the contract, he offered Iran's rulers twenty thousand British pounds in cash and 16 percent of his annual revenues. Soon, a British government eager to convert its navy from coal to oil purchased 52.5 percent of the compa-ny's shares. A 1933 agreement adjusted the terms of the original conces-sion, granting Iran additional revenues in exchange for adding another sixty years to the deal. Thus was born the Anglo-Iranian Oil Company (AIOC). In the postwar years, the AIOC would play a pivotal role in Britain's strategy for maintaining imperial predominance.

The company's profits and privileges made it a tantalizing target for Persian nationalists. An agreement conceived in the early twentieth century appeared anachronistic in an era of postcolonial awakenings. By the 1940s both Mexico and Venezuela had negotiated fifty-fifty profit-sharing arrangements with American oil firms, making the British concession seem unjust. At a time when Iran was in dire finan-cial straits resulting from postwar devastation, Whitehall was receiv-ing more money from the AIOC in taxes than Iran was in the form of revenues.[1] Tehran's grievances were not limited to profit sharing, as the British company refused to open its books to inspection or pay its majority Iranian workforce decent wages. The AIOC and the Foreign Office routinely interfered in Iran's politics by installing governors, tribal leaders, police officials, and politicians favorable to their cause. From bribing parliamentarians and press barons to manipulating Iran's ethnic minorities, British conduct was bound to be controversial in the age of nationalism.

The crisis enveloping Iran came at an inauspicious time for Britain. The immediate postwar years were difficult for a British government burdened by a depleted treasury and public demands for expansion of the welfare state. As such, London had to extract as much in taxes from the AIOC as it could. Given its financial predicament, even a progressive Labour government was in no mood to seriously consider Iran's demands for greater profit sharing. From the British perspective, Iran should have been grateful to the Western allies for ensuring its territorial integrity from a prying Soviet Union in 1946. London's fiscal difficulties and the AIOC's avarice ensured an intransigent British response to Iran's quest for national autonomy.

All this is not to suggest that the British officials did not recognize the nationalist surge sweeping their domain and the sheer impracticality of resisting such a force. However, as any global power would, Britain considered Iran within the context of its worldwide commercial interests and sought to craft an agreement that did not unduly jeopardize its remaining overseas assets.[2] As Defense Minister Emanuel Shinwell acknowledged, "If Persia is allowed to get away with it, Egypt and other Middle Eastern countries would be encouraged to think they could try things on."[3] Although they often diverged on details, the Foreign Office diplomats and AIOC officials agreed on the legitimacy of their various offers and were quick to dismiss Iran's nationalistic claims as the ploy of a political class eager to divert attention from its misrule by pointing to British exploitation. In the end, the gap between Iran's aspirations and British expectations proved largely unbridgeable.

In midst of these tensions stood the United States. From Washington's perspective the global scene in the early 1950s was unsettled. The Iran crisis unfolded in the midst of the Korean War, a conflict the Truman administration saw as an indication of a renewed Soviet offensive. Washington was concerned that Korea presaged total war. The intelligence community reinforced this perception by claiming that the Soviet Union had "resolved to pursue aggressively their worldwide attack on the power positions of the United States and its allies regardless of the possibility that global war may result."[4] China's military intervention in the Korean peninsula further inflamed official opinion, as the Soviets were seen as relying on dogmatic proxies. British power and Middle Eastern oil were both critical for an American administration focused on prosecuting this new and dangerous phase of the Cold War.

The United States did appreciate the rise of regional nationalism and the inevitability that these forces would target Western commercial interests. For successive American administrations, the Iranian nationalists were not a unique case, but representatives of a movement whose aspirations had to be accommodated. At the same time, the Korean War accentuated the importance of Britain in the global struggle against communism. As British forces were dispatched to Asia in large numbers, it became difficult for Washington to disregard all of London's claims. America's attempt to balance recognition of new forces of nationalism with the interests of an intimate ally taxed its diplomatic ingenuity.

In the end, the Americans were often reduced to lecturing both the British and the Iranians to see the crisis through the prism of geopolitics. The United States warned Iranian premiers that rash conduct was destabilizing their country and creating an opening for Soviet mischief. They should put aside their nationalistic imperatives and come to terms with London. The Americans stressed to the British that the dispute could not be seen as a commercial disagreement, but had to be cast instead within the context of Soviet containment. Thus, Britain had to concede and accept half a loaf, because the greater task of restraining Soviet ambitions required such generosity. The problem for Washington was that the British were not willing to be more munificent and the Iranians less patriotic to facilitate America's anticommunist objectives. At some point, America was bound to set aside mediation diplomacy and choose sides. When it did, it opted for Britain and the conservative political establishment in Iran rather than forces of radical nationalism.

A MISSED OPPORTUNITY? 1949–1951

In May 1949, sensing the changing mood in Iran, the AIOC reconsidered its existing contract in an effort to assuage Iranian nationalism. Britain offered Iran a revised Supplemental Oil Agreement that ensured royalties would not fall below four million British pounds a year. In light of the Majlis's rejection of the oil agreement with the Soviet Union in 1946, the latest British offer was bound to stoke controversy. The attendant diplomatic intrigues and complex commercial negotiations provided the backdrop to an aroused Iranian nationalism that sought not to renegotiate the terms of British imperial preference, but to reclaim Iran's resources once and for all.

At the outset of the crisis, the royal court and many of Iran's conservative politicians favored coming to terms with Britain. As members of a political class concerned about Soviet designs, they were prepared to barter for better terms but not sever links with an important Western state. To ensure parliamentary passage of the Supplemental Agreement, Muhammad Reza Shah Pahlavi turned to General Ali Razmara in 1950, an officer the monarch had once called a "viper that must be crushed."[5] The shah was always wary of military men and their penchant for coups. After all, this was how his father had come to power and inaugurated the Pahlavi dynasty. But the appointment to premier of a seemingly strong-willed military officer who had pledged to improve relations with the Western powers and was dubious of nationalization caused much consternation in liberal circles. Many feared that Razmara was determined to impose an agreement on the Majlis and had sufficient royal and external support to make it so.

However, in many ways, Razmara was not an ideal candidate for such a contentious task. His reputation as a decisive military leader was belied by his opportunism and propensity to dither. Distrusted by the shah, uneasy with parliamentary procedures, and risk averse, he allowed the Supplemental Agreement to languish. The more months that passed, the more the opposition to the agreement grew. The forces of outright nationalization gained strength, making a compromise accord difficult to achieve for a diffident monarch and his politically hesitant premier.

The leadership of the nationalization movement soon passed to an Iranian politician of an illustrious pedigree, Muhammad Mossadeq. Born in 1882 into an aristocratic family and educated in Switzerland, Mossadeq belonged to a narrow class of Iranian elite that considered high government office its patrimony. Respectful of the monarchy and the traditions of its class, this cohort manned the cabinets, parliaments, and civil service that ruled Iran. An ardent nationalist, Mossadeq was dubious of foreign control and came to articulate the concept of "negative equilibrium" under which Iran would preserve its autonomy by exempting itself from the great-power struggles. Prone to histrionics of Persian politics, he would weep while making speeches, feign illness, and play the part of a fragile old man. Mossadeq appeared eccentric, even bizarre, but he was also a genuine patriot seeking to emancipate his country from the clutches of the British Empire. Mossadeq was very much a royalist, however, one who believed that the monarchy should conform to the constitution.[6]

Mossadeq's political party, the National Front, was born out of a dispute about vote rigging, a practice that was all too common in Iran's politics. In 1949, to highlight electoral abuse, Mossadeq and his closest aides marched to the palace and agreed to curtail their demonstration

only after the shah promised clean elections. The National Front came
into existence soon after. The Front was essentially composed of liberal
reformers, the intelligentsia, and middle-class professionals. Although
the nationalization of oil would become its central cause, the party's
agenda called for improved public education, the establishment of a
health care system, freedom of the press, judicial reforms, and a more
democratic government.[7] From its inception, one of the key shortcomings of the party was that it did not recruit members, but asked like-
minded organizations to join it. As such, the party never developed a
disciplined cadre that would not break as political pressure mounted.[8]

The clerical estate also would play a controversial role in the unfolding nationalization crisis. By mid-twentieth century, the clerical community was focused on strengthening the institutions of faith. The
shrine city of Qum had been financially devastated by World War II
and stressed by the anticlerical policies of the elder shah. Under the
leadership of Ayatollah Muhammad Hussein Bourjerdi, the clerical
leaders concentrated on refurbishing the seminary and developing a
patronage system that could accommodate a large number of students
and instructors. At ease with the younger shah and his deference to the
clergy, the mullahs were happy to abjure public affairs. In February
1946, an important gathering of more than two thousand clergymen
had passed a resolution prohibiting the clergy from joining political
parties. However, such a prohibition did not stop the more ambitious
mullahs from participating in national affairs. The priestly class certainly agitated against female suffrage and pressed for the persecution
of the minority Baha'i faith. When discussions of the nationalization
of oil began in earnest, it was too important an issue and too popular a
cause for the clergymen to remain on the sidelines.[9]

The cleric at the epicenter of the nationalist struggle was Ayatollah Abdel-Qassem Kashani. Kashani was a mullah known more for
political activism than theological erudition. Arrested and exiled many
times by the British authorities, he had emerged as an implacable foe of

Her Majesty's government. He would soon become the speaker of the Majlis, embracing the cause of nationalization and Mossadeq's political party. Kashani was no stranger to violence and seemed to have had connections to the Islamist group Feda'iyan-e Islam and its clandestine terrorist network. However, as the British embassy reported, Kashani was so corrupt that for the right sum he could be persuaded to switch sides.[10] Still, at the early stages of nationalization, the clerics subtly sided with Mossadeq.

Although fears of the communist Tudeh Party would eventually lead Western nations to conspire against Mossadeq, it is important to note that at the beginning the Tudeh opposed the nationalization of Iran's oil. Steeped in Marxist cant, the Tudeh considered nationalization an American ruse to supplant Britain and turn Iran into a reliable Cold War ally. As we have seen in the Azerbaijan Crisis of 1946, Britain and the Soviet Union implicitly acknowledged each other's spheres of influence and were ready to peacefully divide Iran's spoils. Such imperial manipulations were at odds with America's straightforward anticommunism. The Tudeh Party would switch sides again, pending the preferences of its Russian patron, thus discrediting its cause and evaporating whatever appeal it may have had to working-class Iranians.

From the outset, London was determined to hold a hard line. Both the embassy and AIOC representatives discounted the nationalist surge and claimed that the Iranians were incapable of mastering the intricacies of the oil industry. To be fair, the British were ready to offer Iran a more generous profit-sharing arrangement and to accept some cosmetic changes in the formalities of their operations. However, all this did not distract London from its core objective of sustained control over Iran's oil.

The United States' position suffered from its own set of contradictions. A Cold War–focused Washington urged both Britain and Iran to be more forthcoming. The National Security Council (NSC) resolved that "the primary objective of our policy toward Iran is to prevent the domination of that country by the USSR and to strengthen Iran's association with the free world." Along these lines, the NSC stipulated that "the United States should use its utmost influence to persuade the British to offer, and the Iranians to accept, an equitable concession agreement."[11] Simultaneously, Washington was concerned about the potential impact of Iranian nationalization on its own global investments. The Americans thus advocated that Iranian rights be acknowledged, but in a manner that preserved the sanctity of Western property. For the United States an ideal agreement would concede greater control of the oil industry to Iran while preserving a role for the AIOC. The only problem with this approach was that both Britain and Iran found it unacceptable.[12]

For his part, Razmara agreed with the British that Iran did not have the technical capacity to manage the oil industry. The prime minister admonished the parliamentarians pushing for nationalization, stressing, "Gentlemen, you cannot even manage a cement factory with your own personnel."[13] Razmara's preferred approach was to quietly bargain with the AIOC in hope of securing a better deal.

The Supplemental Agreement was dealt a devastating blow in December 1950 when the Arabian-American Oil Company (Aramco) negotiated a fifty-fifty profit-sharing arrangement with Saudi Arabia.[14] Although both Mexico and Venezuela had already negotiated such an accord, this was the first time a Middle Eastern country had achieved such a split. The British were taken aback by what they called the "McGhee bombshell," attributing the Saudi deal to U.S. Assistant Secretary of State George McGhee, a former oilman and Rhodes Scholar that they had come to distrust. The Foreign Office was determined to "persuade the Americans to delay the announcement."[15] When that gambit failed, the AIOC and the Iranian government confronted an altered national environment. Calls for nationalization grew even louder in both the parliament and the street.

Razmara found himself in an impossible position. His initial instinct was to calm the national temper by dissolving the parliament, which only the shah could do. The prime minister seemed confident that he could engineer the election of a more pliable Majlis and oust cantankerous troublemakers such as Mossadeq. However, obsessed with threats to his throne, the shah worried that such a move would strengthen his prime minister. The monarch demurred and eventually rejected Razmara's plea. In the meantime, Razmara had more success with the British. Initially, the Foreign Office had blamed the prime minister for the disturbances and claimed that had he been more resolute he could have explained to his countrymen the benefits of the Supplemental Agreement. This position soon gave way to more sober analysis, as the AIOC finally offered Iran a fifty-fifty profit-sharing scheme. As it would often happen in Iranian politics, the compromise came too late.

On March 7, 1951, a member of Feda'iyan-e Islam assassinated Razmara in Tehran's central mosque. To any politician who wanted to compromise with the British, this was a clear signal of dangers that lay ahead. Ever the opportunist, Kashani left no mystery about his feelings, as he praised the assassination as a "brilliant stroke of great courage and virtue" and stressed that other "traitors would be similarly struck down."[16] The nationalist faction in the Majlis voted in Mossadeq as the new premier. In a clever move, Mossadeq insisted that he would not assume the responsibilities of the office unless the parliamentary oil commission's recommendation for nationalization was endorsed. By unanimous vote, the parliament followed suit and nationalized Iran's oil industry. The easily intimidated shah, recently the target of an assassination attempt, capitulated to the parliament's demands. Iran now entered a new and more dangerous crisis.

From the perspective of either the United States or Britain, Razmara had not been an ideal prime minster. He often procrastinated and did not always have the courage of his convictions. In many ways, Razmara may also have misread the public mood. Mossadeq and the National Front had done so much to popularize nationalization that a revamped

Supplemental Agreement was hardly acceptable to the aroused masses. Beset by an inflamed public opinion, an obstinate parliament, and a recalcitrant Britain, Razmara still managed to navigate the pathways of Iran's politics and secure an agreement similar to those offered to other oil producers. In the aftermath of his assassination, it was hard to see how any Iranian politician would take command of the oil issue and press for compromise.

The events of March 1951 also brought the Truman administration back into Iranian politics in a more decisive manner. From Washington's perspective, the inability of the British and Iranians to settle their dispute threatened to destabilize the region and possibly even paved the way for Soviet intervention. The administration now resolved, "We believe that we should be prepared to help both the Iranians and the British to work out a new arrangement which would satisfy Iranian political requirements and at the same time assure the flow of petroleum to Britain."[17] The Americans would soon realize the challenge of reconciling the two antagonists in one of the great oil disputes of the twentieth century.

THE DANCE OF DIPLOMACY

To the Americans, Iran's new prime minister seemed erratic, odd, and even absurd. U.S. officials could not always understand a politician who conducted negotiations in his pajamas, often fainted, and cried when the occasion moved him.[18] Even when acknowledging Mossadeq, the American press seemed incredulous of his antics. In its selection of him as the man of the year in 1951, *Time* still managed to call him an "appalling caricature of a statesman."[19] The *New York Times* pointedly asked, "Mossadeq: Prophet or Buffoon?"[20] As we have seen, Mossadeq has to be understood in the context of Iran's politics in the mid-twentieth century. Bursts of hysteria, pretensions of illness, and shrewd negotiations went together as Iranians bargained, cajoled, and often deceived each other. Mossadeq made mistakes, but as a proud nationalist he was focused on advancing his country's interests.

In many ways, Mossadeq belonged to a new generation of Third World leaders that rejected Cold War alignments in favor of carving out an autonomous space for their country in a contested international system. Along with Jawaharlal Nehru of India and Josip Broz Tito of Yugoslavia, Mossadeq came to view the Cold War power blocs as a manifestation of superpower domination. Instead of seeking to preserve Iran's independence by playing the great powers against each other, as Persian politicians had historically tried to do, Mossadeq articulated a new concept of international relations. The best means of ensuring Iran's autonomy was not to manipulate the superpowers but to exempt Iran from their struggles. This proved impractical for a country of such immense geopolitical gravity. Mossadeq's idyllic notions of foreign policy eventually came to be rejected by American Cold Warriors and his own countrymen alike.

The forces of nationalism altered Iran's political landscape in a manner that made a negotiated settlement nearly impossible. The prime minister and his allies dismissed compromise measures that would preserve any aspect of British power. As Mossadeq informed a startled American envoy, Henry Grady, "I assure you, Excellency, that we value independence more than economics."[21] The new premier castigated the AIOC for its plunder of Iran, its manipulation of domestic politics, corruption of its elites, and deforming of its society. In essence, Mossadeq saw the nationalization as an act of liberation. Once diplomacy is infused with such evangelical spirit, technical agreements and profit-sharing arrangements are overwhelmed by a desire for emancipation.

Britain entered the dispute with its own set of prejudices and misapprehensions. The British politicians' hysterical denunciations of the nationalization act concealed the fact that they knew the AIOC's concession had to be adjusted. After all, a Labour government led by Clement Attlee that was nationalizing industries at home appreciated that hanging on to an anachronistic contract was untenable in the age of colonial awakenings. However, this did not mean that Britain was inclined to forfeit its access to Persian oil. In practice, Labour leaders were prepared to accept Iran's formal nationalization without conceding to its legitimacy. Both Whitehall and the AIOC were confident that they could craft an arrangement whereby Iran's nationalization did not impinge on the fundamentals of their power.

As the Labour government wrestled with the Iran conundrum, its diplomatic maneuverability was constrained by Britain's inflamed domestic politics. The Conservative opposition led by the venerable Winston Churchill hammered the Labour Party for its lack of resolution. The aging premier, long enchanted by Britain's imperial grandeur, castigated Attlee as "unequal to the enormous and complicated" Iran situation.[22] For many English leaders, the AIOC was the symbol of Britain's prestige and global standing. Any attempt by the Labourites to acquiesce to Iranian mandates was bound to be opposed by that large segment of the British public still unable to accept the empire's decline. The year 1951, being an election year, further exposed Attlee to charges of appeasement and pusillanimity.

London's opening salvo lodged a complaint with the International Court of Justice at The Hague. The British petition accepted that Iran had the sovereign right to nationalize its resources but claimed that in this case, Iran had breached a legal contract. In an act of brazenness, Britain accused Iran of discrimination as only Britain's property among all the other foreign-owned assets was actually being nationalized. Finally, Britain demanded extravagant compensation, calling for payment for the contract's remaining forty-three years. Iran's counterargument rejected a role for the British government in a dispute between a sovereign nation and a private company. The court would go through its own endless cycle of deliberations and arcane legal arguments before rendering a judgment that was bound to have only symbolic importance as it lacked an ability to enforce its verdicts.

Britain did not limit itself to legal arbitration, as it successfully obstructed the export of Iran's oil. British technicians in Iran left their posts, while skilled workers from other countries tempted to replace them were warned off by the Foreign Office. London also began informing European companies doing business in Iran that they would be sanctioned unless they limited their dealings at once. In the meantime, the British navy interdicted tankers carrying Iranian oil on the grounds that they were transporting stolen cargo. The embargo quietly gained adherents as key consumers of Iran's oil such as Germany and Japan stopped issuing licenses for its purchase. Given the fact that the Western oil giants owned nearly all of the fifteen hundred tankers then in existence, it is hard to see how Iran's petroleum could reach any destination. By 1952, Iran's oil exports fell from six hundred sixty thousand to a mere twenty thousand barrels per day.[23] The once-vibrant Abadan refinery began to grind down its operations.[24]

This economic warfare was not meant to compel Iran to settle the oil issue, but to displace the Mossadeq government. In today's parlance, the British policy was regime change. Urged on by an embassy relishing intrigue more than analysis, the Foreign Office grew confident that it could replace Mossadeq with a more pliable figure. The sheer availability of scheming Iranian politicians buoyed hopes in London for an easy solution. Foreign Secretary Herbert Morrison now calmly mused that the oil issue could be expeditiously resolved if the "Shah dismissed Mossadeq and dissolved the Majlis."[25] In this sense, the foreign secretary underestimated the popularity of nationalization and the difficulty of actually compelling the shah to take decisive action.

Behind the scenes, Britain also indulged in saber rattling to buttress its diplomatic moves. Contingency plans labeled "Operation Buccaneer" envisioned an invasion force of seventy thousand troops backed by a significant naval deployment. While the Royal Navy would bomb southern Iranian fortifications, a militia would occupy the refinery and the adjacent areas. It is hard to see how the British military chiefs could have devised a plan that was bound to destroy the installations they were hoping to preserve. Moreover, at a time when Britain was appealing to international institutions regarding Iran's illegal seizure of its property, it would find it difficult to sanction a war of aggression.

Britain's military planning did have one effect: it provoked the White House into a frenzy of diplomatic activity. The NSC warned the president that "the entry of British forces in opposition to the military forces of Iran might split the free world, produce chaos in Iran, and might cause the Iranian government to turn to the Soviet Union for help."[26] Truman impassionedly warned Attlee, "I am sure you can understand my deep concern that no action should be taken in connection with the dispute which would result in disagreement between Iran and the free world."[27] Washington established impossible conditions for military intervention, suggesting that force could only be used at the invitation of the Iranian government or in the case of Soviet invasion or a communist coup.[28] Reclaiming the oil fields by force thus was rejected by the United States and ultimately shelved by Britain.

The U.S. dismissal of military intervention was not its only point of contention with Britain. By 1952, the United States was providing 23.4 million dollars of aid to Iran per year. It was an American Cold War axiom that financial assistance bolstered the local regime's resistance to communist subversion. After all, similar impulses had guided the Marshall Plan, which offered massive amounts of aid to postwar Europe. Yet, the British government that once had been the beneficiary of American largess claimed that in Iran's case such aid was reinforcing Mossadeq's intransigence and mitigating the impact of economic sanctions. Such calls fell on deaf ears at the State Department as the United States continued to provide aid to Iran, much to Britain's annoyance.

In Iran, a peculiar pattern emerged with Mossadeq seemingly interested in an agreement but restrained by the nationalist agitation that he had stimulated. After much prodding by the United States, a British delegation led by the cabinet member Richard Stokes arrived in Iran in hope of mediating the dispute. On the surface, Stokes's offer fell considerably short of Iran's expectations. His eight-point proposal recognized the nationalization act but reserved the right of marketing and production of Iran's oil to a committee that was responsible to Tehran in name only. Still, Mossadeq had established an easy rapport with Stokes and seemed interested in exploring his proposals. As the talks proceeded, Ayatollah Kashani voiced warnings while the nationalist parliamentarians inveighed against Stokes. The vociferous complaints did affect Mossadeq, as Stokes suddenly found him as "obstinate as a mule."[29] Mossadeq may have had no intention of accepting Stokes's offer, but whatever the reason an uneasy political atmosphere hovered over the talks, making the task of diplomacy even more difficult.

The stalemate in the Anglo-Iranian discussions led Truman to appoint the seasoned diplomat Averell Harriman as his mediator. A shrewd politician, Harriman appreciated the dilemmas and opportunities that nationalization had created for Mossadeq.[30] Harriman arrived in Tehran in July 1951 and quickly dismissed the British notion that the Mossadeq government was unpopular and ripe for overthrow. However, he also sensed that the popularity of nationalization constrained the prime minister's options and created a real obstacle to an agreement. Harriman noted that Mossadeq "appears obsessed with the idea of eliminating completely the British oil company's operations and influence in Iran."[31] In a sense, Harriman's mission validated Stokes's observations on the difficulty of securing an agreement with a country mired in the frenzy of nationalism.

Harriman sought to break the impasse by explaining to Mossadeq the complexities of the oil industry and the technical challenges of operating such a vast infrastructure. The presidential emissary hoped that his subtle elucidations would induce Mossadeq to concede to a continued British role. In such a framework, the AIOC would be involved in the production of Iran's oil, however, the scope of that involvement would be tweaked to assuage Iranian nationalism. This was in line with

American thinking that nationalization had to be somehow reconciled with a continued British presence. Harriman was quickly disabused of such accommodating notions, as Mossadeq remained steadfast.

As Harriman lingered in Tehran, he realized that for Mossadeq the central issue was the impact of an agreement on Iran's political rivalries and factions. Mossadeq was perennially concerned about how compromising with the British would affect his reputation and national standing. Given Razmara's fate it was not unreasonable for Mossadeq to fear that an accord would put his life in jeopardy. However, beyond his physical safety, Mossadeq was reluctant to engage in a compromise that would betray his nationalism. An exasperated Harriman concluded that "there is a chance his emotions can be tempered with realism. It is more unlikely, however, that he can be convinced that the political aspects of the problem would permit him to seek an amicable settlement with the British." [32] It soon became apparent to Harriman that factors beyond distribution of profits would guide Iran's approach to the negotiations. Tehran's position remained consistent: it was prepared to offer reasonable compensation to the AIOC for the property that it seized, but it envisioned no role for Britain in Iran's oil industry.

From his very first encounter with American emissaries, Mossadeq played the communist card. The premier warned Harriman that the failure to address the oil issue largely on his terms could lead to a communist coup. Such threats were being made at a time when the Soviet Union's new envoy to Tehran was the same ambassador who had engineered a communist takeover of the Czechoslovakian government in 1948. While the Tudeh was not yet seen by the United States as strong enough to assume power, it appeared that Russia had not given up its ambitions south of its border. The fear of communist takeover had always defined America's approach to Iran and in due course would cause it to tilt against Mossadeq. Ironically, the Soviet moves were affirmed by Mossadeq, who persistently warned that his rule was threatened from the left.

Mossadeq's playing of the communist card was not completely ineffective. The fear of Iran's collapse, after all, had compelled the Truman administration to offer Iran aid and press the British for a quick settlement. However, Mossadeq's fearmongering could not compel Washington to provide him with sufficient aid to offset the loss of oil revenue. Nor could he compel the United States to jettison its British ally and embrace his cause. Given the centrality of Britain in the wider containment effort and its growing role in the Korean War, there were limits to how far the United States was prepared to antagonize the United Kingdom over Iran. In the end, anticommunism would naturally lead the United States to side with Britain and against Iran's obdurate prime minister. Mossadeq may not have been wrong in invoking the communist threat, but he was misguided in not seeing the limits of the ploy.

As the negotiations ebbed and flowed, both sides attempted to press their perceived advantages. In October 1951, Mossadeq took the alarming step of ordering AIOC employees to leave Iran. The British government responded with more saber rattling and referred the issue to the U.N. Security Council. The Foreign Office hoped that a U.N. censure would get Iran to back down. After all, the Azerbaijan Crisis of 1946 had been resolved when the allies employed the United Nations to get Stalin to withdraw his forces from northern Iran. Perhaps a similar injunction would have the same effect on Mossadeq. As the venue for diplomatic maneuvering switched to the United States, the crisis had its best chance of resolution.

Mossadeq arrived in New York to personally present Iran's case to the United Nations. The prime minister's arguments echoed those made by Iran at The Hague months earlier, namely that the United Nations did not have jurisdiction over a dispute between a sovereign state and a private company. In his speech at the United Nations, the premier repeated his litany of grievances about the company's discriminatory and abusive practices. At the same time, Mossadeq emphasized Iran's readiness to pay fair compensation and honor its existing contracts. The British representative Sir Gladwyn Jebb offered a series of legalist arguments that failed to sway the majority of opinion. Mossadeq's masterful performance carried the day at the United Nations, as many developing countries such as India that were taking their place at the international gathering had also been victims of British imperialism. The Security Council refused to take any action on the British petition until The Hague had issued its judgment. In Iran, this was widely seen as a triumph for Mossadeq. If the British had hoped that the U.N. deliberations would weaken Mossadeq at home, they were gravely disappointed.

While in the United States, Mossadeq held meetings with Truman and Acheson; however, his most important negotiations were with McGhee. The American diplomat, who had been pivotal in devising the Saudi oil deal, devised a clever scheme whereby the Royal Dutch Shell company would operate the oilfields on behalf of Iran. A special oil purchase agreement would be negotiated with AIOC, offering it generous compensation for its lost property. All this seemed reasonable to Mossadeq, but he insisted on one additional condition, namely that no British technician could participate in the operation of the oil industry. While Mossadeq and McGhee were involved in their delicate talks, the British public returned the Conservatives to power, putting Churchill once more at the helm of what remained of the British Empire.

The Conservatives who had excoriated the Labour Party for its appeasement of Iran were in no mood to consider McGhee's shrewd formulations. Foreign Secretary Anthony Eden, appalled by the provision barring British technicians from the oilfields, flatly rejected McGhee's proposal, stressing that it was better to have "no agreement than a bad one."[33] The British government continued to hope that intensifying economic pressures would induce the shah or the parliament to remove Mossadeq from power. As Eden acknowledged in his memoirs, "The situation in Iran was gloomy, but I thought one should be better occupied looking to alternatives to Mossadeq rather than trying to buy him off."[34] For Churchill, agreements that salvaged Mossadeq's premiership and validated his precepts of nationalism were too dangerous to contemplate.[35] Instead of considering various negotiating proposals, the British focused their efforts on bringing the United States in line with a policy of regime change.

If Mossadeq desired an agreement, it was not entirely obvious. To American official Vernon A. Walters, who served as a translator throughout the negotiations, Mossadeq confessed that he would be in tough political shape if he had to sell an accord "to his fanatics."[36] Even if all his requirements were met, Mossadeq informed McGee he would forward the agreement to "the parliament without publicly endorsing it."[37] Mossadeq had to confront the real possibility of Iran's economic collapse, but he perceived that the communist card could solicit aid from the United States. The premier returned home triumphant from his U.N. trip, and without an agreement.

The ever-enterprising Truman administration devised still another proposal before its time in office expired. In the new scheme, the International Bank for Reconstruction and Development would get a neutral entity to distribute Iran's oil and manage its facilities. The profits would be apportioned equally among Iran, the managing organization, and an escrow account that would compensate the AIOC. This temporary measure would be in place until a permanent resolution was negotiated. Bank officials and American functionaries now journeyed to Tehran and London in the hope of persuading both parties to accept the arrangement. Once more, it appears that the Americans were more interested in resolving the issue than were either the British or the Iranians.

Mossadeq was the first to raise objections that effectively derailed the bank's proposal. Among the bank's recommendations was that British technicians with experience in Iran's oil infrastructure not be barred from participation. This proved unacceptable to Mossadeq. And then there was the question of on whose behalf the bank would be operating. For Mossadeq, Britain's refusal to formally accept Iran's nationalization meant that it had forfeited any role in Iran's oil market, and thus, the bank had to operate on his authority. Not only were Mossadeq's proposals unacceptable to the British, they were also viewed as impractical by the bank. The bank could not acknowledge Iran's possession of the oilfields so long as the issue was being adjudicated at various international institutions. Moreover, the bank officials did not think there were sufficient non-British technicians to run the oil facilities. Given the passions that Mossadeq had unleashed, he found it impossible to concede to an agreement that did not explicitly recognize Iran's nationalization.

By 1952, Iran's economic free-fall remained unabated. Deprived of its oil wealth and facing a mounting budget deficit, the Mossadeq government was increasingly incapable of meeting its payroll. Various seven-year development plans were either incomplete or shelved altogether. The government's attempt to find ways to sell its oil could not overcome Britain's embargo. In the meantime, the attempts to operate an oil-less economy proved illusory; the government relied on petroleum sales for much of its budget outlays. Mossadeq's response to such dire economic conditions was to blame foreign conspiracies and seek to centralize power.

In one sense, Mossadeq was right to suspect that the British and their subsidized politicians were intriguing against him. However, his responses to such plots were unconstitutional and illegal. Mossadeq attempted to tame Iran's national institutions by bringing them under his control. He sought to take charge of the armed forces and the Ministry of War—which had long been monarchical prerogatives. Along this path, he demanded special powers to deal with the unfolding national crisis. An aristocrat who had historically appreciated the rule of law, he was now transformed into a rabble-rouser leading the masses against the traditions of the state. Mossadeq's failure to obtain more authority from the shah led to his resignation on July 6, 1952, and to yet another crisis in Iranian politics.[38]

The news of Mossadeq's resignation led to massive protests throughout Iran engineered by the National Front, the Tudeh, and Kashani. The communists and the mullahs looked at the political crisis not so much as a means of empowering Mossadeq but to enhance their own standing. The Tudeh, which had initially been lukewarm about nationalization, called for opposition to all forms of oil settlement and the eviction of all American personnel from Iran. In the meantime, Kashani issued a fatwa calling on the armed forces not to resist the protesters. Fearful of losing control, the shah backed down and reappointed Mossadeq prime minister six days later. As with Razmara, every time the shah recoiled from confrontation he had to cede more ground to the opposition. The monarch's failure to compel his ministers to settle the oil issue or to forcibly put down his opponents only eroded his authority.[39]

Upon reclaiming the premiership, Mossadeq moved fast to complete his power grab. The prime minister assumed control over the armed forces by taking over the Ministry of War and prohibiting the shah from direct contact with the officer corps. The court's political involvement also had to be circumscribed. Mossadeq was essentially transforming the shah into a constitutional monarch with limited and largely symbolic powers. Along this path, Mossadeq also purged the armed forces and the judiciary of unreliable elements that were not loyal to him. The military's budget was further reduced. His next target was the parliament, where he forced legislation through the chamber giving him the ability to carry out financial, economic, and legal reforms without its approval for six months. So long as the oil negotiations were proceeding, the opposition to Mossadeq was willing to remain quiet. However, if Mossadeq could not reach an agreement and end Iran's economic distress, then his assumption of autocratic powers was bound to be challenged.

Mossadeq's return to office via street riots established a depressing precedent that would soon subvert his rule. At his core, Mossadeq was a principled politician with deep reverence for Iran's institutions and constitutional arrangements. He had spent his entire public life defending the rule of law and limitations of power. But the pressure of governing at a time of deepening crisis accentuated the troubling aspects of his character. Suddenly the champion of democratic reform and account- ability seemed to indulge in the same arbitrary behavior that he had spent much of his political career condemning. Even more ominously for Mossadeq, the popular passions that brought him back to power could as easily be used against him.

Having rebuffed previous Anglo-American offers, Mossadeq needed to divert attention from his misrule and shore up his base. On October 22, 1952, in a vitriolic speech, he announced the severance of diplomatic relations with Britain. His accusations of British interfer- ence in Iranian politics and of the corrupting influence of the AIOC are indisputable. Brandishing British conspiracies certainly helped his public standing, as Iranians had long harbored suspicions of Britain and its manipulation of their national affairs. Still, such a move made a negotiated settlement even more difficult at a time when shortages and rations were becoming the order of the day in Iran.

As the Truman presidency came to the end, the United States had failed to broker a compromise between Iran and Britain. The adminis- tration was ingenious in formulating various proposals and it went far in tempering both British expectations of support and Iranian demands of assistance. Washington's mediation role meant it could not side deci- sively with either party. However, the administration failed to grasp the sheer difficulty of trying to devise an accord that would assuage Iranian nationalism while preserving Britain's imperial preferences. As the crisis deepened, both sides became more entrenched in their ani- mosities and more invested in their narratives. "Once again one reflects on Oxenstierne's [sic] question: 'Dost thou not know, my son, with how little wisdom the world is governed,'" Acheson mourned in his mem- oirs.[40] The administration may have been an honest broker but it simply could not bring the two antagonists together. The task of managing the

Iran imbroglio now transferred to the victor of World War II, Dwight D. Eisenhower.

EISENHOWER AND A VERY IRANIAN COUP

In the election of 1952, the American people gave an overwhelming victory to Dwight Eisenhower. Although portrayed by the press at the time as an indifferent president more comfortable on the golf course than in the Oval Office, Eisenhower today is regarded as a master politician firmly in control of his administration's policies. By avoiding the limelight and allowing his cabinet secretaries center stage, the president cleverly avoided responsibility for any failed initiatives. Thus, at all times, his popularity and power remained intact.[41] No other presidency has undergone more interpretive revisions than that of Eisenhower, whose stature has steadily risen over time among both historians and the public alike.[42]

In the management of foreign affairs, Eisenhower preferred to delegate power to loyal, able subordinates. Secretary of State John Foster Dulles fit perfectly Eisenhower's idea of a useful deputy.[43] Dulles, a respected international lawyer, followed his chief's advice assiduously. Although Dulles was granted latitude in initiating policy toward the Middle East, the president always made the final decision. The relationship that eventually evolved between the president and his secretary of state was one of mutual respect, with Eisenhower serving as the senior partner while Dulles concentrated on everyday management of affairs.

The other bureaucracy that gained prominence during this period was the Central Intelligence Agency. Given the impossibility of war between the superpowers in the atomic age, covert operations became a prime instrument of the Cold War. This was particularly true in the Third World, as both blocs attempted to influence political developments in these countries. The new director of the CIA, Allen Dulles, resoundingly endorsed this strategy. The institutional power of the

CIA was enhanced further by the fact that the new director was the secretary of state's brother, granting him ample access to the administration's inner circle. Although covert operations were always a feature of U.S. Cold War policy, they became a significant instrument of national security strategy during the Eisenhower era.[44]

The Eisenhower administration soon encountered the same obstacles as its predecessor. The principal antagonists in the Persian Gulf melodrama seemed far from reaching an agreement. The gap between British imperial mandates and Iran's nationalistic claims remained largely unabridged. In a letter to Churchill, Eisenhower pointedly noted that "it was disturbing to gain the impression that your government now considers the situation absolutely hopeless and believes that it would be preferable to face the probability of the whole area falling under Russian domination than to look for a new approach."[45] In a similar vein, Washington sought to prod Mossadeq to compromise. As with Truman, Eisenhower could not press either party to fundamentally adjust its perspective.

It was inevitable that the newly inaugurated Eisenhower administration would prove susceptible to the British preference for regime change. Although such impulses are at times attributed to the administration's attraction to covert operations or its senseless anticommunism, the context does matter. By 1953, Washington feared that Mossadeq was unwittingly paving the way for Tudeh's assumption of power. Had Truman remained in office, he might have arrived at the same conclusion. Eisenhower appreciated the arrival of nationalism and he was sophisticated enough to recognize the difference between neutralism and communism. The new president's concern was that Mossadeq's unfolding dictatorship of the left could easily slide into communist rule. By this time Mossadeq had rejected a string of settlement proposals and was not even superficially interested in negotiations. In the meantime, Iran's domestic stability continued to deteriorate, empowering radical forces on both the left and the right.

As his rule crumbled, Mossadeq seemed immured in a cycle of his own making. On the one hand, he dealt with domestic dissent by expanding his powers through constitutionally dubious means. Yet, such enhanced authority was not used to resolve the oil dispute and end Iran's economic crisis. As we have seen, the National Front was always a diverse coalition whose unifying principle was opposition to British imperialism. Mossadeq's arbitrary concentration of power inevitably alienated his partners. The prime minister increasingly ruled by relying on a few trusted aides and largely excluded senior politicians from his inner circle.

Even before the Western intelligence services devised plots against Mossadeq, the National Front had started to crumble. Middle-class elements of coalition, concerned about their declining economic fortunes, gradually looked for an alternative to the prime minister. Even the reliably pro–National Front intelligentsia and the professional syndicates were chafing under Mossadeq's authoritarian tendencies. A number of smaller political parties that had been associated with Mossadeq's movement were also contemplating an exit. Even more ominous, the armed forces, which had stayed quiet despite Mossadeq's periodic purges of the senior officer corps, grew vocal and began to participate in political intrigues.

Among Mossadeq's coalition partners, the clergy would play the most curious role. As with most historical events, the Islamic Republic has neglected the role that the clerical estate played in Mossadeq's demise. As we have seen, the Grand Ayatollah Bourjerdi had initially supported the nationalization act and had encouraged the shah to oppose Britain's imperial designs. However, the liberal policies advocated by the National Front and the growing influence of the Tudeh Party disturbed the clerics. Although Mossadeq and Bourjerdi had been respectful toward each other, the mayhem sweeping Iran in 1953 and fears that the monarchy might be displaced by a republican, if not a communist, regime caused the clerical community to shift its allegiance. Kashani would lead the charge, but behind him stood a clerical cohort skeptical of Mossadeq and alarmed at his continuation in power.

In the meantime, Mossadeq's attempt to hollow out the monarchy finally provoked protest from the shah. In February, the royal court suddenly announced that the shah intended to leave the country for medical reasons. The news of the monarch's departure caused the most serious confrontation between Mossadeq and his growing list of detractors. Kashani joined forces with disgruntled military officers and purged politicians to implore the shah to stay.[46] Tehran and many provincial cities were engulfed in protests against the shah's departure, as crowds even attempted to sack Mossadeq's residence. Sensing the mood of the public, the shah informed the jubilant protesters that "my going out of country for health reasons does not meet with your approval."[47] This episode is particularly important because no one has suggested that these demonstrations were engineered by the CIA. The coalition in opposition to Mossadeq was in full view, its strength amply demonstrated in the streets. This same coalition, with greater reinforcement from the armed forces, would spearhead Mossadeq's ultimate downfall six months later.

Mossadeq responded to the erosion of his base by simultaneously alarming the Americans and further estranging Iran's political class. The parliament had now become the seat of anti-Mossadeq agitation and an obstacle to his political aggrandizement. The prime minister responded to these critics by seeking to dissolve the parliament. Because he did not have the constitutional authority to simply do away with the Majlis, Mossadeq contrived a legally dubious means of discharging this task. The National Front deputies resigned their posts, depriving the chamber of the necessary quorum to function. Then a referendum was scheduled to decide the fate of the paralyzed parliament. The plebiscite that took place on August 3 was marred by boycotts, voting irregularities, and mob violence. The results surprised no one: the referendum was approved by 99 percent of the vote. Mossadeq won his rigged election and lost what remained of his constituency.

To an American administration alarmed about the prospect of communist takeover, Mossadeq did all he could to affirm its fears. The key figure that resurfaced in the Iran drama was once again Loy Henderson, who, having failed to obstruct Truman's recognition of Israel, would now, as U.S. ambassador to Iran, have to untangle the situation in Tehran. Mossadeq warned Henderson that unless the United States purchased Iranian oil "there would be a revolution in Iran in thirty days."[48] In another meeting with Henderson, Mossadeq once more invoked the specter of communist rule by claiming that "if the National Front government should pass out of existence only confusion or Tudeh would take over."[49] Along these lines, Mossadeq threatened to sell oil to Eastern bloc countries and reach out to the Soviet Union for assistance. In the past, such tactics had succeeded in spurring the Truman administration to pressure the British for an early settlement, but they fell on deaf ears in Dulles's State Department.

The failure of this gambit led Mossadeq to approach Eisenhower in June. In a breathless tone, Mossadeq asked in a letter for direct U.S. economic assistance, warning that "if prompt and effective aid is not given to this country, any steps that might be taken tomorrow to compensate for the neglect of today might well be too late."[50] Eisenhower took nearly a month to respond and when he did suggested that the path out of Iran's predicament was to settle the oil dispute with Britain.[51] Mossadeq's latest missive had sealed his fate in Washington.

The idea of a coup was promoted by a coterie of Iranian politicians who stressed that given Mossadeq's new supplementary powers, there was no legislative way to end his rule. Figures such as General Fazlullah Zahedi, a one-time member of Mossadeq's cabinet turned oppositionist, readily offered themselves to the U.S. embassy. Zahedi, with his links to the armed forces and ties to the clerical establishment, assured the embassy that a robust anti-Mossadeq network already existed and could discharge its functions with minimal U.S. support.[52] The chorus of scheming Iranians offered Washington a simple path out of its dilemma.

The British government not only endorsed these views but also provided the United States with its own extensive network of plotters. The rupture of diplomatic relations between Iran and the United Kingdom meant that London had to rely on the U.S. diplomatic mission to advance its plans for regime change. Given its history of interference in Iranian politics, the British government and its spy agency MI6 had an impressive array of actors that they had subsidized and cultivated. Within the merchant class, London could count on Asadollah Rashidian, who controlled various bazaar guilds such as the butcher and baker unions, as well as assorted toughs that he could mobilize for street action. Senior clerics such as Seyyed Ziaeddin Tabatabai and Muhammad Reza Behbahani were known to have contacts with the British. To this list, one must add a variety of parliamentarians, politicians, and journalists. This infrastructure was made available to the Americans as they contemplated their next move. It should be stressed that the CIA took a rather dim view of British agents, believing that the "assets had been far overstated and oversold."[53]

The U.S. embassy now became a vocal champion of overthrowing Mossadeq. In a stream of cables, written in summer 1953, Henderson warned that chaos in Iran was bound to benefit the Soviet Union and its Iranian proxy, the Tudeh. For Henderson, Mossadeq was an obdurate politician emotionally incapable of resolving the stalemate with Britain. The ambassador assured Washington that "most Iranian politicians friendly to the West would welcome secret American intervention which would assist them in attaining their individual or group political ambitions." To make his point clear, Henderson warned "only those sympathetic to the Soviet Union and International Communism have reason to be pleased at what is taking place in Iran."[54]

By May, the joint CIA-MI6 task force finally completed its plan of action, codenamed TPAJAX. The key to the plot was to gain the shah's cooperation, given that he retained the legal authority to dismiss his premier.[55] A series of emissaries would be dispatched to obtain the support of the diffident monarch. General Zahedi emerged as the linchpin of the plan as he was seen as the only figure with sufficient "vigor and courage to make him worthy of support."[56] A propaganda campaign would augment the orchestrated demonstrations and protest marches by Britain's clients.[57] The Westerners and their Iranian accomplices were well placed to execute their conspiracy.

On July 11, Eisenhower approved the final plan. By that point the erosion of Mossadeq's support was obvious. Kashani had defected to the opposition, a large segment of the National Front had abandoned Mossadeq, and the military's top brass was agitating for action. The prime minister's arbitrary manner had alienated many legislators while key clerical figures were already in touch with the royal court regarding their apprehensions. All the signals coming out of Tehran were that the shah still had popular appeal: should the shah intervene decisively, Mossadeq would have to yield. As with most well-laid plans, the actual course of events did not conform to expectations.

The first phase of the CIA's operation was to inflame the existing disorder in Iran. Conservative politicians were encouraged to continue their agitation against the prime minister while newspapers published articles critical of Mossadeq. Many of the defamatory press reports were distributed in the mosques by mullahs who used their sermons to inveigh against the National Front. Various street toughs and tribal leaders were encouraged to provoke acts of violence. The CIA propaganda machine churned out stories fed to the Iranian press about how Mossadeq was corrupt, power-hungry, and even of Jewish descent.[58] Forged documents were produced suggesting that the National Front was secretly collaborating with the Tudeh in establishing a "people's democracy" that would expunge religion from public life. It is hard to see how such obviously crude claims could be effective or persuasive.

The recruitment of the shah proved a more difficult task. The monarch seemed to welcome Mossadeq's demise but would not sign an official order dismissing him. As always, seeking to evade formal responsibility, he instead offered to verbally encourage the rebelling army officers. To stiffen his spine, the CIA arranged for a series of emissaries including the shah's twin sister, Princess Ashraf, and General Norman Schwarzkopf Sr., who had trained the Iranian police force in the 1940s, to visit the palace. Another furtive guest of the court was the operational leader of the coup, Kermit "Kim" Roosevelt, the head of the CIA's Near East and Africa division. Still, the shah remained noncommittal and seemed reluctant to directly engage the plot. Roosevelt subsequently warned the shah that he "should realize that failure to act could lead only to a Communist Iran or a second Korea . . . [the U.S.] government was not prepared to accept these possibilities and that some other plan might be carried through."[59] Roosevelt directly warned the monarch that his failure to act would cause "General Zahedi to be informed that the United States would be ready to go ahead without the Shah's active cooperation."[60] Faced with such concerted pressure, the shah finally relented, issuing two orders—one dismissing Mossadeq and the other appointing Zahedi as his prime minister.

On the night of August 15, Colonel Nematollah Nasiri, the commander of the Imperial Guards, attempted to deliver the orders to the prime minister's residence. The coup failed. Colonel Nasiri and his troops were overwhelmed and quickly arrested by forces loyal to Mossadeq. General Zahedi went into hiding. As was his wont, the shah fled Iran, going first to Iraq and then to Italy. It appears that Mossadeq had been tipped off by the Tudeh, who had penetrated the armed forces.[61] All the discussion of the coup should not obscure the fact that the shah did have the constitutional authority to dismiss his prime minister. For Mossadeq to remain in office after the monarch's orders was itself an illegal act according to Iranian law.

After the apparent failure of the coup, a mood of resignation descended over Western capitals. The State Department acknowledged that the "operation has been tried and failed."[62] The British position was equally glum: "We cannot consider going on fighting."[63] Eisenhower's close aide and confidant, General Walter Bedell Smith, informed the president that "we now have to take a whole new look at the Iranian situation and probably have to snuggle up to Mossadeq if we are going to save anything there."[64] As Washington despaired, the initiative passed on to the Iranians.

In a chaotic and confused Tehran, political fortunes swayed back and forth. A number of radical politicians took to the airwaves denouncing the monarchy and castigating the shah as a bloodthirsty tyrant. In a paradoxical manner, the Tudeh did much to arrest the capital's revolutionary surge. During those hectic August days, the Tudeh perceived a unique opportunity to flex muscles and finally depose the shah. Tudeh cadres toppled statues of the two Pahlavi kings and called for the establishment of a democratic republic. A prominent member of the Tudeh, Babak Amir-Khosravi, subsequently acknowledged that such conduct led to much "quarrelling with shopkeepers, ordinary folks and clerics, affronting, even alienating them from the government of Dr. Mossadeq."[65] Paradoxically, this perception was validated by the chief representative of Western capitalism in Iran, as Henderson cabled to Washington that the masses were outraged by Tudeh's "gang of hooligans bearing red flags and chanting Commie songs."[66]

The radicalizing mood of the street did not sit well with Mossadeq. Throughout his memoirs, he retains his respect for the monarchy. Despite his usurpations of power, Mossadeq did not seek the demise of the monarchy or the overthrow of the shah. Although some members of the National Front did join Tudeh's call for a republic, these views did not conform to Mossadeq's dispositions. Mossadeq desired a monarchy that reigned, not ruled, and a shah that adhered to constitutional limits. The prime minister's reverence for the institution of the monarchy reflected the penchant of an aristocrat at ease with Iran's political traditions.

Whatever the mood in Western chancelleries may have been, Zahedi and his coconspirators continued the resistance. The determination of the Iranian plotters was largely independent of Kermit Roosevelt and the CIA. Zahedi now took two distinct initiatives. First, he sought to broadcast widely the shah's dismissal of Mossadeq and appointment of himself—Zahedi—as prime minister. The CIA seemed to have had a hand in distributing this message through both domestic and foreign media. In a more important move Zahedi alerted the armed units in the capital and provinces that still remained loyal to the shah. Through his son Ardeshir he made contact with district and provisional commanders, asking them to mobilize their forces.

By August 19, a momentum had swept the street that surprised all the participants. Military units began clashing with Tudeh activists while pro-shah protesters took to the streets. Given that he was a partisan of the coup, Ardeshir Zahedi's memoirs have to be discounted, but in them he does suggest that the popular outpouring in favor of the shah surprised even his father.[67] Some of these demonstrators were paid by the CIA, it later came to light, but marches by toughs and thugs only would have been too small and too erratic to determine the fate of Iran. As Henderson cabled from Tehran, the marches were "not of hoodlum type customarily predominant in recent demonstrations in Tehran. They seem to come from all classes of people, including workers, clerks, shopkeepers, students, et cetera."[68] The best that can be said about the CIA is that its paid demonstrators sparked a pro-shah cascade.

In many ways, Mossadeq expedited his own demise. Determined to restore order, the premier commanded the military to put an end to the disturbances—but the military's loyalty was increasingly in question. Mossadeq rejected the Tudeh's offer of assistance to help him battle the insurgent soldiers, demurred at calls for disbanding the monarchy, and essentially revealed himself to be an establishmentarian uncomfortable with the mayhem sweeping the country. Mossadeq proved too humane to countenance violence and too liberal to rely completely on Iran's communist party.

The street that Mossadeq had relied on was now in full rebellion.

Tehran was engulfed with vast crowds with no apparent connection to the Western intelligence services. In due course, armed units took over key installations and ministries, forcing the prime minister to flee his home. Mossadeq was too much a man of the system to remain on the run, and he quickly turned himself in at General Zahedi's headquarters, where he was treated with courtesy and respect. Mossadeq received a three-year prison term and spent the remainder of his life confined to his native village. He would write his memoirs, which observed a respectful tone toward the monarchy while offering a spirited defense of his record. Many of Mossadeq's core supporters were given light sentences and soon resumed their previous lives.

A coup that would be subject to much historical contention was not merely an Anglo-American conspiracy against a popular government but in fact the reassertion of Iran's traditional institutions alarmed at the radicalization of national politics. Many chronicles of TPAJAX seemed to overlook that the shah was still a popular figure. To be sure, this was not the shah that would come to rule by 1979, an imperious autocrat with limited tolerance for dissent, but a hesitant monarch inclined to yield to elder statesmen. The army officers, landowners, mullahs, and even average citizens had confidence in the monarchy and were fearful that its absence would open the way for the communists.

In the aftermath of Mossadeq's demise, it took another year of contentious negotiations to conclude the oil dispute. Eventually a consortium of American and European oil companies was put together that in conjunction with a revamped AIOC revived Iran's petroleum sector. Iran received a fifty-fifty profit-sharing arrangement and the AIOC obtained a modest compensation package. Iran reentered the international oil market and would eventually emerge as one of its most independent-minded actors.

As a postscript to the coup, it is important to stress its complex origins. In his memoirs, Mossadeq spends significant time bemoaning foreign intrigues against his rule. However, in a curious passage, he identifies the shah's departure as a turning point of the event. "What happened after 16 August, was a reaction to His Majesty's unannounced departure from the country [that day] which has been seen by the society as running away, and which prompted every party and clique to try and turn the situation to their own favor," noted the premier.[69] In one of his last meetings with Henderson, Mossadeq judiciously identified the coalition arrayed against him and acknowledged its diversity and power. The premier castigated the "fanatical religious groups led by irresponsible mullahs, disgruntled politicians and reactionary elements in the army and bureaucracy" that challenged him.[70] Mossadeq was not unaware of the Anglo-American plotting, but more so than his contemporary defenders, he appreciated how his power base had diminished over the years.

In the coming decades, CIA alumni including Kermit Roosevelt would embellish their role, but the United States government's own after-action report was more modest.[71] The CIA noted that the event that turned the tide was the shah's departure. "The flight of the Shah brought home to the populace in a dramatic way how far Mossadeq had gone, and galvanized the people into an irate pro-Shah force," stressed the agency.[72] The British assessment did not diverge from that of the CIA. Less than a week after the coup, the Foreign Office reported to the Cabinet that "a spontaneous demonstration in favor of the Shah started in the bazaar and spread throughout Tehran . . . The rank and file of the army apparently largely went over to the demonstrators, and by the evening [Zahedi] had emerged from hiding and taken over all the centers of government."[73] In the end, the coup of 1953 was very much an Iranian affair.

THE SHAH VERSUS MOSSADEQ

The events of 1953 have often been seen as a nefarious U.S. plot to overthrow a nationalist politician with considerable public support.

This is certainly the narrative cultivated by the Islamic Republic and readily accepted by the Western intellectual class. The reality is more complex, as the nationalization crisis came to pit two politicians representing two different coalitions against each other. The shah and the Pahlavi dynasty represented the traditional classes: landowning aristocracy, the clergy, and the military. Mossadeq came to lead the intelligentsia and the growing urban middle class. The power struggle between these two actors should not obscure that they were nationalists who wanted to preserve Iran's interests. Both the shah and Mossadeq perceived the United States as a useful ally to be deployed against Britain. At some point, the shah seemed more amendable to a compromise on the oil issue, while Mossadeq was too invested in the conflict to be able to resolve it. Ultimately, the shah's coalition managed to overthrow an isolated and beleaguered premier whose allies had abandoned him. In this scenario, the CIA's machinations are important but hardly consequential.

In the traditional narrative of the Iran saga, the British have often been exempt from responsibility. The fact remains that the Labour government sought an agreement that nodded to the nationalization act while preserving Britain's control over Iran's resources. Whatever the shortcomings of the Labourites' approach to Iran may have been, their Conservative successors did not even feign interest in an accord. The British government desired a change of regime in Tehran and was not unhappy about a stalemate that was producing fissures and fractures in the Iranian body politic. At every juncture, diplomacy was bedeviled not only by Iranian intransigence but also by British obduracy.

By August 1953, Muhammad Mossadeq was bound to fall. Operation TPAJAX did not create the opposition to the prime minister though it did provide some of its key leaders with guidance. Those who stress the centrality of the CIA maneuvers conveniently ignore the shah's popular appeal and public disillusionment with Mossadeq. Moreover, it is important to stress that the shah had the constitutional authority to dismiss his prime minister. The key to the plotters' success seemed to have been their widespread distribution of the shah's orders to the news media. The Iranian people faced a choice between an increasingly despotic Mossadeq and a hesitant monarch who wanted to give Iran a second chance. They opted for the shah and his path of compromise and conciliation.

For the United States, Mossadeq was the first of a long line of radical leaders in the Middle East that would challenge the parameters of its Cold War policy. He was not a communist nor was he inclined to submit to Soviet dictates. Washington's concern was that his chaotic rule would lead to ascendance of the Tudeh Party and eventual absorption of Iran into the Eastern bloc. Iran's oil and location were too important to be left to a leader who seemed incapable of stemming the tide of the crisis. Stability in the Middle East hinged on restoring order in Iran.

Can the U.S. policy toward Iran during this period be considered a success? On the surface, the principal objective of American policy was realized and Iran did not collapse into the Soviet orbit and its oil continued to flow to the West. A troublesome prime minister was deposed in favor of a reliable monarch who shared America's anticommunist zeal. Yet a closer look reveals that both Truman and Eisenhower failed in important respects. The Truman administration invested considerable time and energy in mediating the oil dispute. Yet by the time it left office, the disagreements between Britain and Iran were hardly resolved. Truman's diplomacy was sincere and imaginative but ultimately did not persuade either party to abandon its maximalist claims. For his part, Eisenhower launched a coup that failed to overthrow Mossadeq. On the eve of its botched coup attempt, a befuddled White House was at a loss about how to move forward in Iran.

The 1953 episode reveals an important aspect of America's Cold War successes in the Middle East, namely that too often the United States prevailed because it had the support of credible local allies. In the end, Iran's military and traditional classes had more to lose and more at stake. At a critical juncture they claimed the initiative and deposed a prime minister who was threatening their country with his ruinous policies. Washington was the beneficiary of its allies' ingenuity and determination, but did little to conceive such friends.

In yet another bid of mythologizing, it is at times suggested that events of 1953 made the revolution of 1979 and the rise of theocracy inevitable. History rarely moves in such a predetermined manner. Upon reclaiming his throne, the shah had many opportunities to create an inclusive government that could have withstood the revolutionary tremors of the 1970s. The shah who returned from his brief exile had the support of his public, the endorsement of Iran's important social classes, and the validation of a superpower benefactor. He had ample means at his disposal with which to create a resilient political state that would have continued his modernization drive. Instead, he opted for autocracy and corruption that proved his undoing. Neither the Truman nor Eisenhower administrations should be blamed for not foreseeing, much less preventing, the shah's subsequent misfortunes.

CHAPTER 4

THE SUEZ WAR

The 1950s would prove a tumultuous decade for the Arab world. The rise of nationalist forces led by Egypt's charismatic Gamal Abdel Nasser challenged the remnants of the British Empire, the conservative monarchies, and the state of Israel. The defining event of the decade was a war fought over the Suez Canal by America's closest allies that served only to further discredit their cause. When the war was finished, the United States had displaced Britain as the external power with primary influence over the region.

Eisenhower's troubles in the Middle East started with a misreading of Arab politics. While judicious in accepting postcolonial nationalism and Nasser's ability to mold Arab public opinion, United States policy was motivated by the imperatives of the Cold War. Neutralism would guide Egypt's rulers as they rejected being pawns in the great-power conflict. A clash between a global power preoccupied with the Soviet Union and a regional actor focused on more immediate foes was inevitable.

The decade closed with the announcement of the Eisenhower Doctrine, a momentous policy that has often been overshadowed by the conflagration of the Suez War. After initially hoping to play a minor role in the Middle East, America entered fully into the region's conflicts and rivalries. The United States was now to be a participant in the Arab Cold War. Successive U.S. administrations would be suspicious of revolutionary change and maintain a close alliance with the conservative monarchies such as those of Saudi Arabia and Jordan. This aversion to change is the enduring legacy of the Eisenhower Doctrine. Gone were the heady days of optimism about Arab nationalists as American policy aligned with regimes that resisted not just Soviet communism but also any hints of neutralism.

A NEW LOOK AT OLD PROBLEMS

Eisenhower's understanding of the Soviet Union did not differ much from that of his predecessor.[1] The president and his chief aides accepted the notion that the Soviet Union sought global domination. The Russians employed propaganda, subversion, covert action, and proxy war to achieve this sinister aim. Moreover, as the Korean War seemingly revealed, Moscow's focus extended beyond Europe, to countries whose turbulent political environments provided unique opportunities to project Russian power. The Soviets were clever and patient and would exploit all vulnerabilities to achieve their objective of undermining the Western democracies.[2] Unaccountable to public opinion or a prying press, the Politburo could adopt a long-term policy. In the nuclear age, superpower war might not be imminent, but superpower conflict and certainly competition would be a fundamental aspect of international life.

The one point of divergence between Eisenhower and Truman was the new president's greater concern for the financial cost of the simmering conflict.[3] This budgetary concern had an important impact on the administration's containment policy. For the authors of National Security Council Paper 68 (NSC-68)—the guiding document of the Truman administration's Cold War policies, published in April 1950— economic considerations came second to the overall strategic necessity of subduing the Soviets. Eisenhower's fiscal conservatism caused him to reject this aspect of Truman's policy. The president reminded his aides that "we are engaged in defense of a way of life, and the greater danger is that in defending this way of life, we find ourselves resorting to methods that endanger our existence."[4] This was Eisenhower's most significant contribution to the Cold War, as he recognized the existence of certain interests, such as economic health, as distinct from other threats, namely Soviet communism. The strategy for containing the Soviet menace had to recognize economic factors.

This complex set of considerations formed the basis of the New Look, as the Eisenhower administration's strategy came to be called. The policy was not without contradiction, as Eisenhower accepted the containment doctrine's definition of global threats while rejecting the economic measures it prescribed. The apparent conundrum would be resolved by relying on nuclear weapons (that were less costly than conventional forces) and a series of alliances. The new administration perceived that Truman had been slow to utilize the free world's resources and spread the cost of defense obligations.[5] Multilateral and bilateral defense pacts would encircle and contain the Russians. This alliance strategy made Europe and the Middle East critical in the administration's planning, as both lay on the periphery of the Soviet Union.

In its survey of the Middle East, Washington recognized the passing of an older age and the implausibility of relying on landlords and tribal chiefs to sustain the Western presence. The rising urban middle class, as represented in professional syndicates such as lawyers' and doctors' guilds and the officer corps, would be the focus of American policy. The Eisenhower administration's initial assessment identified Arab nationalism as a potent force that could not be ignored.[6] In the absence of a constructive U.S. policy, the nationalists were inclined to embrace neutralism at best—at worst, communism. Global competition reinforced the urgency of the issue, as the United States sensed Russia's intent of "using Arab nationalism as an instrument for substituting Soviet influence for that of the West."[7] It was absolutely imperative for

the United States to co-opt the nationalists and reorient their governments toward the task of Soviet containment.

The Eisenhower administration's initial assessment soon moved
beyond nationalism as an amorphous force and settled on Egypt as
its designated agent. By mid-twentieth century, Egypt's population
was greater than that of the entire Arab East, and its geographic size
dwarfed that of other Arab nations. Egypt's encounter with modernization was the longest, its industrial and educational structures were
the most extensive, and its cultural and intellectual output was the most
prolific.[8] It was hard to conceive of greater Arab political integration
without Egypt's consent and active leadership. Moreover, in Egypt,
dynamic military officers had come to power seeking a path of modernization. As the State Department noted, if Egypt "exerted her influence in the right direction she can swing the rest of the Arab world and
may be the key to [the] Israeli question also."[9]

Besides Egypt, the Eisenhower administration also had to contend
with Britain's role in the Middle East. The Cold War challenges of the
early 1950s required close Anglo-American collaboration. In the Arab
world, where the British establishment was assailed by the nationalists, the United States still perceived that a "rapid abandonment of the
British position would leave a military vacuum that the United States
would have difficulty in filling and which would accentuate insecurity
and create further opportunities for Soviet or local Communist exploitation."[10] Yet Washington could not ignore the dark legacy of imperialism and the difficulty of reconciling a continued British presence with
Arab nationalism. Britain would have to make certain compromises
and expunge some of the unpalatable characteristics of its presence. A
reformed Britain remained a cornerstone of America's policy in the
Middle East.

Finally, the administration had to address the issue of Israel. The creation of an independent Jewish state in 1948 had led to an Arab-Israeli
war whose reverberations continued to destabilize the region. The Arab-

Israeli conflict deflected regional attention from the Soviet threat, thus complicated the implementation of the containment doctrine. Accordingly, the Eisenhower administration decided to resolve the conflict through a comprehensive settlement package. Israel would be asked to moderate its demands and concede vital territory to the Arab states. In exchange, the Arab regimes, led by Egypt, would recognize Israel and begin trade and diplomatic relations with the Jewish state.

At first, it seemed all the actors were inclined to follow Eisenhower's script. On July 23, 1952, a group of young soldiers calling themselves the Free Officers had overthrown the monarchy of King Farouk and promised a new dawn in Egyptian and Arab history. The new military junta led by Colonel Gamal Abdel Nasser had already cultivated close ties with the American embassy and longtime CIA hands Miles Copeland and the indefatigable Kermit Roosevelt. The embassy and the CIA station abandoned analytical objectivity and became powerful advocates of the Free Officers. A litany of cables and reports from the embassy and the station suggested that the new team was prepared to pragmatically negotiate with Britain and even come to terms with Israel. A Washington desperate for credible local allies was thrilled at the prospect of transforming Cairo into the linchpin of its regional containment strategy.

The reality was more complex. The Free Officers had arrived in power to assert Egyptian leadership in the Arab world, not to implement America's containment doctrine. In his political manifesto, aptly titled *The Philosophy of the Revolution*, Nasser sensed that "an important drama is to be played which awaits a hero. I know not why, but it seems to me that this role is wandering through this vast region around us. We have responded to that appeal."[11] The new Arab hero was greatly influenced by Prime Minister Nehru of India and his ideas of neutrality and its insistence that emerging powers should exempt themselves from the Cold War struggle. Even before his journey to Bandung, India, for a summit of nonaligned powers in 1955, Nasser had long talks with

Nehru and was beginning to perceive Arab nationalism as a facet of the
Third World struggle against the great powers. Clearly influenced by
the Indian leader, Nasser stressed to his aides that "the only wise policy
for us would be one of positive neutralism and non-alignment."[12] The
1950s would epitomize Nasser's Arabism, as he supported revolutionary movements throughout the Middle East, broke the Western arms
monopoly and obtained hardware from the Soviet Union, nationalized
the Suez Canal, and even unified Egypt with Syria.

The question then becomes how to reconcile Nasser's ambitions with
his subtle promises to the U.S. representatives in Cairo. When the Free
Officers assumed power, Egypt was still a virtual colony of the United
Kingdom and there were eighty thousand British troops occupying the
Suez Canal base. The ruling junta needed economic aid and arms to
refurbish its military after the 1948 war. Israel had to be held at bay
while the Free Officers consolidated their power. The best means of
achieving these objectives was to dangle pledges of cooperation before
the Americans. Should the U.S. administration be convinced of Egypt's
reliability as a Cold War ally, then it might press Britain to evacuate its
forces, convince a parsimonious Congress to offer assistance, and restrain
Israel from undertaking any attacks on Nasser's regime. In due course,
Nasser's measured mendacity would alienate his American patrons, but
at the outset his ploy was clever, and not without achievements.

The initial American assumptions regarding Cairo were acknowledged in Britain. The British approach to the region was greatly influenced by the varying sentiments within the ruling Conservative Party.
Winston Churchill, back at the national helm with a slim parliamentary majority, was hardly a leader prone to abandoning imperial missions.[13] The prime minister's stubborn instincts were buttressed by
approximately forty Conservative backbenchers, led by Julian Amery
and Charles Waterhouse, who were extremely hostile to a further contraction of Britain's presence in the Middle East. For a generation of
Tory leaders, the Suez installations were the basis of Britain's power

and a symbol of its imperial prestige.[14] Although economic realities in Britain made retrenchment a necessity, for an influential portion of the British body politic, acquiescing to postcolonial realities was a wrenching prospect.

Against the backbenchers, Foreign Secretary Anthony Eden led another faction of the Conservative Party. Although Eden would be remembered as the British leader who waged an ill-fated war over Suez, at this point he was a leading advocate of compromise with Egypt. Had Eden retired from public life in 1955, he would likely be commemorated as one of the great diplomats of his time. Since the 1930s, when he emerged as a dogged opponent of appeasing Hitler, he had displayed calm judgment and cogent analysis of international trends. During this period, Eden was a discerning observer of the Arab world and attempted to reach some kind of an accommodation with the Egyptian regime.

Eden did not favor abandoning Britain's position in the Arab world. He fully shared the idea that Britain's world power status was contingent on its continued presence in the Middle East. However, the foreign secretary believed that a settlement of the question of what to do with the Suez base might open a chance to favorably approach Arab nationalism. Eden advised the cabinet that "in the second half of the twentieth century we cannot hope to maintain our position in the Middle East by the methods of the last century."[15] Moreover, the Foreign Office was already eyeing the Hashemite monarchies of Jordan and Iraq as more suitable platforms for British power than cantankerous Egypt. As an aged and ailing Churchill faded in and out of his premiership, Eden took command of Britain's foreign policy and beat back the forces of reaction.

The year 1954 would be the high point of the Eisenhower administration's Middle East policy. This was the year when an Anglo-Egyptian Treaty was finally hammered out under U.S. auspices. As part of the accord, Britain would withdraw all of its troops from Egypt in eighteen months, leaving behind four thousand technicians to keep the base in working condition. Egypt agreed that allied forces had a right to reoccupy the base in a regional crisis. This was a model agreement from Washington's perspective. Egypt's sovereignty was upheld, the Cold War requirements were noted, and Britain's presence was refashioned in a manner acceptable to local opinion. The contradictions inherent in U.S. policy would become more fully obvious in the shoals of the Arab-Israeli conflict.

WORKING WITH NASSER

The aftermath of the Anglo-Egyptian Treaty saw the launch of two mutually undermining initiatives. The first was a Cold War defense perimeter along the northern tier of the Middle East, composed of the northern borders of Turkey, Iraq, Iran, and Pakistan. The second was a plan to settle the Arab-Israeli conflict. While Washington's Soviet containment line was bound to empower Egypt's conservative rivals in the Arab world, its peace plan relied on Cairo to sell the reconciliation to the Arab people. Washington's plans were bedeviled by the region's poisonous politics and the conflicting ambitions of its allies.

From the outset, the administration appreciated that it had to tread gently in erecting its containment barriers. An NSC analysis had warned that "until progress can be made in settling the dispute between Arabs and Israelis, there is little possibility of including both Arab states and the West in a formal defense organization."[16] As long as the Arab masses were fixated on the plight of the Palestinians, Soviet machinations were unlikely to disturb them. By limiting its defense line to Turkey, Iraq, Iran, and Pakistan, Washington hoped that it could achieve some of its containment aims without antagonizing Egypt. Once more, the administration misread Nasser's ambitions and the politics of the Arab world.

The consensus within the historical literature is that 1954 was the year when Egypt made Arab unity the foremost aim of its foreign policy and gave content to Arab nationalism.[17] Soon after the final resolution of the Suez base dispute, Nasser made his choice clear in a speech:

> Every Arab speaking country is our country, and our country absolutely must be liberated. The role in question is political action throughout the Arab countries, to liberate them, that is deliver them from the yoke of imperialism and ensure their full independence under the shield of the greater Arab brother country, Egypt.[18]

The Arab world offered many tempting opportunities to the Free Officers. The Hashemite states of Iraq and Jordan brimmed with social tensions, while in Syria the Ba'ath Party was ascending with the declared goal of seeking closer ties to Egypt. Nasser recognized that borders could not obstruct the appeal of his message, confessing, "the frontiers end where my propaganda arouses no echo. Beyond this point something else begins, a foreign world that doesn't interest me."[19] Over time, individual states would complain about Egypt's interference in their internal affairs and would even plot against the Free Officers. However, so powerful was the message of reform and anti-imperialism that the masses sided with Nasser against conservative regimes whose credibility had been dealt a severe blow in 1948.

Given Nasser's regional pretensions, Cairo was bound to be suspicious of an American alliance network that would exacerbate Arab divisions and perpetuate Western influence. The Free Officers' reluctance to join the pact meant that its establishment would result in dispatch of Western arms to their Iraqi rival. Egyptian-Iraqi competition predated the rise of Nasser, as the rulers of the Nile and of Mesopotamia had long vied for influence in the land between the two rivers. Cairo realized that the pact had to be defeated, for it contributed to the deflation of pan-Arabism by buttressing conservative monarchical regimes. Moreover, Nasser, better than some U.S. policy makers, real-ized that the northern tier arrangement would give Britain another opportunity to resurrect its influence.

Cairo would also reject U.S. plans to resolve the Arab-Israeli con-flict. Until 1954, the Free Officers' attitude toward Israel had ranged from public neglect to private assurances to the Americans of future reconciliation once British forces withdrew from the canal. However, the 1948 Arab-Israeli War and the emotional issue of Palestine had undermined the old order. The Free Officers recognized that compro-mise with Israel would delegitimize their rule and subvert the tenets of Arab nationalism. The Arab ethos stressed that any prospective leader had to assert himself against Israel, the very existence of which severed links between Egypt and the Arab world. The pursuit of pan-Arabism was not compatible with peace with Israel.

Nonetheless, for Nasser ideology and pragmatism were always inter-twined. Thus, U.S. cooperation was as vital in 1955 as it had been dur-ing the negotiations over the Suez base rights. The new U.S. peace plan could be an effective way to thwart British and Iraqi designs on the Fertile Crescent, as well as replenish the stocks of the Egyptian army. Thus, Cairo persisted with its diplomacy of promising potential coop-eration with Israel if the United States restrained the growth of the pact. Despite this tactical ploy it is obvious that by this point the United States and Egypt viewed the Middle East from very different perspectives.

Eisenhower's problems were not limited to Egypt, as his allies also displayed an independent streak. Since the armistice ending the 1948 war, Palestinian paramilitary forces had often attacked Israeli settle-ments, leading to massive retaliation by Jerusalem. The patriarch of Israeli politics, Prime Minister David Ben-Gurion, was determined to severely punish such cross-border raids. On August 22, 1955, in response to yet another guerrilla attack, Israeli forces occupied key points in Gaza. In response, Egypt permitted further raids by Palestin-ian guerrillas. Retaliatory Israeli strikes in Khan Yunis claimed thirty-six Egyptian lives. The issue of military aid now preoccupied Nasser, as his rule was partly contingent on the approbation of the armed forces.

Nasser's appeal to the United States for arms was complicated by bureaucratic hurdles and the politics of peacemaking. The Free Officers' refusal to accept the Mutual Security Assistance Program that required U.S. military advisors to accompany American hardware meant that Egypt's arms request would encounter resistance in the U.S. Congress. Having recently evicted the British troops from Suez, Nasser was not about to invite another set of Western military officers to Egypt. Moreover, the White House was conscious of Israeli objections and feared that any dispatch of arms to an Arab state bordering Israel would diminish Jerusalem's willingness to consider a peace plan. Washington was simply not in a position to dispatch arms to Nasser.

The Soviets eagerly seized on U.S. reticence. Having abandoned Stalinist rigidity with its focus on Europe, Moscow's main intention in the Third World was to foil U.S. containment designs. Arab nationalism and its inherent neutralism was welcomed by the Soviets, as it opposed a revived Western presence in the region. For their part, the Free Officers were not averse to dealing with the Russians; Cold War blocs meant little to them. Nasser was determined to show that nonalignment could be an effective means of security, and that the bipolarization of the international arena did not mean that the smaller states had to choose sides.

As early as the Bandung conference of nonaligned nations, Nasser had confessed to Zhou Enlai, the Chinese foreign minister, that Egypt required a steady source of arms. Zhou sympathized but, given China's own dependence on the Soviet Union, there was not much Beijing could offer. Still, the foreign minister promised to pass on Nasser's request to the Russians. Moscow now dispatched Dmitri Shepilov, the editor of Tass, the main Russian news agency, with an offer to trade one hundred MiG fighter jets, two hundred tanks, and a few Ilyushin jet bombers for Egyptian cotton. In addition, Shepilov hinted that a similar barter arrangement could be worked out to finance the jewel of the Free Officers' domestic development program, construction of the Aswan Dam. On September 27, 1955, Nasser shocked and surprised many by announcing a package deal with Czechoslovakia. To placate American concerns, Cairo chose to procure the arms from the Czechs, but the real source was well known. After countless White House deliberations about containing the Soviet Union, the Kremlin had simply leaped over U.S. defense lines and established a presence in the heart of the Arab world.

Eisenhower's nascent northern tier perimeter, now christened the Baghdad Pact, was not only breached by Russia but also hijacked by Britain, which was not yet a member of the pact. Behind the scenes, the administration had worked assiduously to bring Iraq, Iran, Turkey, and Pakistan into the same defense grouping. However, Washington feared that a premature expansion of the pact beyond these four states would plunge the enterprise into inter-Arab political squabbles. The State Department warned that Britain's aims "seemed to go beyond the limits explicitly sanctioned by the United States."[20] Eisenhower soon discovered that Britain was prepared to stretch the pact to fit its parochial interests.

Given its eviction from Egypt, Britain's strategy in the Middle East was increasingly tied to the fortunes of the monarchies in Iraq and Jordan. For a Conservative government that was being assailed by its own backbenchers over the scuttle in Egypt, the Baghdad Pact offered many advantages. Among them was access to Iraqi military facilities. The Foreign Office emphasized that to remain passive after Britain's recent departure from the Suez installations "would endanger the Turco-Iraqi agreement and consequently our best interests in the Middle East."[21] Iraq welcomed Britain's attempt to expand the pact to Jordan, as an alliance with Iranians and Turks was bound to isolate Iraq from the Arab world. On April 5, 1955, Britain took the first important step in enlarging the pact by formally joining the organization. The American call for the pact to remain an indigenous group focused on the northern tier was being defied by its closest allies.

Jordan now became the focal point of the region's intrigues and tensions. As he finally assumed the premiership in April 1955, Eden, sensing American qualms, seemed reluctant to press King Hussein of Jordan to join the pact. But pressure on the prime minister soon began to mount. From Amman, General John Glubb, the commander of the Arab Legion, as the Jordanian army was still called, warned of the growing Egyptian influence and Nasser's determination to "dominate the Middle East"; and to this purpose, he continued, "it is essential for them to get rid of the British and American influence."[22] Charles Duke, the British ambassador to Jordan, reemphasized this point, stating that "I am convinced that we must act very soon. . . . even a few days might make a difference."[23] The crucial voice seemed to belong to Foreign Secretary Harold Macmillan, who stressed the need for "a fresh attempt to draw the Arabs away from the growing ambition of Nasser and the increasing temptations dangled before them by the Soviet Union."[24] Eden now relented and agreed that it was necessary for Britain to "tie to the treaty all the Arab states we now can."[25]

To obstruct Britain's moves, Nasser took his case to the Arab street. Cairo announced that it would counter the Baghdad Pact by establishing an "Arab bloc, free from imperialist influence to protect the interests of Islamic, Asiatic and African peoples."[26] The new Arab pact drew interest from Syria and even Saudi Arabia, a long time U.S. ally that was alarmed by Britain's support for its historic Hashemite rivals. As always, Nasser's pronouncements on Radio Cairo electrified the region. The Arab world was now inflamed as forces of nationalism were pitted against the old order.

In the midst of this regional tumult, Whitehall dispatched General Gerald Templer of the British Imperial General Staff to facilitate Jordanian inclusion in the Baghdad Pact. By all accounts, the Templer mission was a disaster. Initially King Hussein seemed to disregard the nationalistic surge in his own divided kingdom and considered joining the pact, tempted by aid and arms. The Jordanian cabinet's approval of pact membership, however, was blocked by the resignation of the body's four Palestinian ministers. Meanwhile massive demonstrations engulfed Amman. The situation only calmed down when the new prime minister, Samir Rifai, pledged that his government would not participate in the pact. Despite his reliance on British subsidies, King Hussein recognized that his tenuous grasp on power could not withstand membership in the Baghdad Pact.

The Templer disaster confirmed the American assessment of the British policy. Confiding to his diary, Eisenhower bemoaned the British move: "We tried to make Britain see the danger of including or pressuring Jordan to join the Northern Tier. They went blindly ahead and only recently have been suffering one of the most sever diplomatic defeats Britain had taken in many years."[27]

By 1956, U.S. policy in the Middle East was in shambles. The Eisenhower administration seemed able to neither restrain its allies nor compel its adversaries to adjust their views. A defense alignment that was supposed to protect the northern tier of the Middle East was entangled in inter-Arab politics. The region was more polarized and divided against itself than at any point in its recent past. As usual, Washington confronted its dilemmas by contemplating a massive aid package.

The great prize offered by the Western powers for Egyptian cooperation was the financing of the Aswan Dam. Secretary of State Dulles conceded that the "U.S. could not fight the Soviet Union on the political front with the existing resources programmed for the Middle East."[28] The dam had been the recurring dream of Egyptian politicians: their people's survival had long depended on the Nile, and the project would create a lake reservoir that regulated the flow of the great river. The United States agreed to provide 80 percent of the funding needed to build the dam while the British would match the two-hundred-million-dollar contribution of the World Bank. After much American arm-twisting, Britain agreed to play its part by providing its share of funds in the massive construction project.

The Aswan Dam came with many political strings. Dulles believed that the United States' aid program for Israel was providing it with influence in Jerusalem and he was searching for a similar position in Cairo. The dam would provide leverage for the United States to redirect Egyptian policy in the proper direction. The secretary confessed to the cabinet that "implicit in this proposed program of assistance would be the fact that the Egyptians were going to reach some genuine understanding with Israel."[29] Preoccupation with the domestic economy coupled with gratitude to the United States was supposed to defuse Cairo's attachment to its long-standing objectives of extending its influence in the Middle East.

Despite the problems lingering in the background, Washington and London forged ahead with their much-vaunted peace plan. A joint Anglo-American team headed by Francis Russell, the former chargé d'affaires at the United States embassy in Israel, and Evelyn Shuckburgh, the assistant undersecretary for the Middle East at the Foreign Office, devised a secret plan code-named Alpha. The plan called for the end of belligerence between Israel and Egypt. The Jewish state would be asked to repatriate seventy-five thousand Palestinian refugees, while financial compensation for the rest would come through international effort. Above all, Israel would make territorial concessions, particularly in the Negev desert. The sensitive issue of Jerusalem was to be resolved by placing the holy sites under international auspices. In return for such concessions, the Western powers would guarantee Israeli borders and seek to persuade the Arab countries to end their trade embargo on the Jewish state. Egypt was to take the lead in convincing Arab states to make peace with Israel. As part of his strategy of manipulating Washington, Nasser appeared receptive to Western mediation.

The peace plan arrived at the right time for Nasser. The Egyptian leader was embroiled in both a border conflict with Israel and tensions over the Baghdad Pact with Britain. So long as negotiations proceeded, the United States could be counted on to restrain Israel and curb British appetite for expansion of the pact. For Cairo, a protracted diplomatic process was far more conducive to its goals than actually accepting a controversial peace plan.

For his part, Ben-Gurion was always ready to discuss peace; he was simply not willing to concede large amounts of territory. Far from ceding land to Egypt, the patriarch hoped to settle thousands of new Jewish immigrants in Negev. The desert, properly irrigated, would provide a new haven for Jewish immigration as well as enable Israel's economic development. In accepting American mediation, the Israelis insisted on some fundamental points. First, they stressed their suspicion that Cairo was going along only to gain time for the absorption of the Czech weapons. Second, although the Israelis were willing to meet with Western officials, they would not accept an agreement that involved substantial territorial concessions or mass refugee repatriation.[30]

The fate of American policy was now in the hands of Robert B. Anderson, a former deputy secretary of defense appointed by the White House as its official mediator. The American emissary was a confidant of the president and was to receive maximum logistical support. In Cairo, he would be accompanied by the CIA's Kermit Roosevelt and in Jerusalem he was assisted by the agency's rising star James Angleton. Eisenhower's confidence in Anderson was so great that he confessed, "I feel nothing could give me greater satisfaction than to believe that next January 20, I could turn over this office to his hands."[31] In 1987, Anderson would go to prison for tax evasion and operating an illegal offshore bank.

Robert Anderson's first meeting with Nasser in January 1956 should have been instructive. The Egyptian leader spent most of his time bemoaning how the Baghdad Pact was fracturing Arab unity. Nasser stressed that the only way to solve the Palestinian refugee problem was to give the refugees the option of returning home. On the issue of territory, Nasser held out for all of Negev, as "Israel forms a wedge between the two halves of the Arab world."[32] The colonel employed all the dilatory tactics at his disposal to avoid committing to a settlement. He insisted that first the inflamed regional tensions must be tempered. Only then could Arab opinion be readied for coexistence with Israel. After such steps, which could take years, he would be willing to sign a favorable accord.

Anderson's reception did not get warmer once he landed in Israel. Ben-Gurion stressed that no real negotiations could take place unless he met directly with Nasser. The very skeptical Israeli premier insisted that such an encounter was necessary to test Nasser's sincerity. To Anderson, Ben-Gurion emphasized, "If only we could meet, I know there would be peace in ten days."[33] Such a meeting was unacceptable to Nasser. If revealed, it would undermine his political standing and even endanger his life. It is difficult to determine whether Ben-Gurion was placing impossible barriers in front of an accord or if he really did believe that a meeting could facilitate an agreement. Certainly if the Egyptian colonel was unwilling to meet secretly, it is hard to see how he would publicly champion a peace compact to the Arab world.

Given the looming U.S. presidential election, in his next round of talks, Anderson pressed for an agreement within six months. Further delay would entangle the issue in America's domestic politics and potentially spur the Israelis to take matters into their own hands with a preemptive assault before Egypt absorbed the Czech arms. Anderson claimed that "while we appreciate [Nasser's] concerns in molding Arab public opinion and the decisive factor he attributed to the Baghdad Pact, it was necessary that some definite action be taken by Egypt that would establish its alignment with Western powers."[34] Anderson further emphasized that "we cannot afford the time of weeks and months which he apparently envisions for a settlement."[35] Nasser curtly informed the American envoy that his projected timeline was hope-lessly insufficient and that months were required to iron out his disagreements with Israel.

The final breakdown of the talks came when Nasser stressed that even after a favorable accord was reached "Egypt [would] not put the proposal forward as its own, but we will have to discuss the appropriate outside source to make the proposal that will be submitted to Egypt and other Arab states."[36] This was a direct contravention of the U.S. policy that since 1953 had sought to exploit Egypt's prestige for the execution of the American vision. Nasser further anguished the White House by claiming that even a final agreement with him might still be subject to modification by other Arab leaders. The idea of rehashing the terms of the accord with individual Arab rulers was anathema to the administration. This was hardly the type of leadership that the United States had in mind for Nasser, nor was it the kind of assistance that he had been subtly promising. Disillusioned, Anderson concluded that Nasser "obviously does not look forward to any early resolution of the problem."[37]

The failure of Anderson's mission led Eisenhower to contemplate a change of policy. To Secretary Dulles the president confessed, "It looks as if Egypt under Nasser is going to make no moves whatsoever to meet the Israelis in an attempt to settle outstanding differences."[38] The once-promising Gamal Abdel Nasser was now seen as duplicitous and cynical. Eisenhower stressed that "if Egypt finds herself isolated from the rest of the Arab world, and with no allies in sight except Soviet Russia, she would very quickly get sick of that prospect."[39] Nasser's shifting promises finally caught up with him, resulting in the antagonism of a superpower that had invested much in his pledges.

The American switch to a coercive policy would be welcomed in Britain. Since the tumult in Jordan, Eden had been fulminating against Nasser and seeing Russia lurking behind the colonel's objectionable practices. From Whitehall's perspective, its inability to cement the Baghdad Pact had much to do with Nasser's incendiary rhetoric and his clever manipulations of Arab opinion. The task at hand was no longer to placate the colonel but to remove him from power.

WORKING AGAINST NASSER

By April 1956, the Eisenhower administration's strategy, code-named Omega, had begun to coalesce. The plan envisioned weakening Egypt's economy while eroding its regional standing. The purpose of the new policy "would be to lead Colonel Nasser to realize that he cannot cooperate as he is doing with the Soviet Union and at the same time enjoy most-favored national treatment from the United States."[40] Throughout the Omega documents, the notion of bringing Nasser back to the fold is often stressed. And yet given Washington's suspicions of Nasser it is hard to see how the colonel could be redeemed.

In devising its plan, the United States recognized the importance of cooperating with Britain. However, the British and American perspectives differed on key issues. Far from hoping to reorient Nasser, Whitehall was already contemplating his ouster. An apoplectic Eden made his feelings known to aide Anthony Nutting, exclaiming, "What's all this nonsense about isolating Nasser as you call it? I want him destroyed. Can you understand that?"[41] In more tempered language, Britain's ambassador to the United States, Roger Makins, informed John Foster Dulles that "with respect to Egypt, the British take a somewhat dimmer view of the possibility of bringing Nasser around."[42] Omega's gradualist approach would prove inconsistent with the prime minister's preference for fast, dramatic action.

A critical part of Omega involved undermining Egypt's regional position by buttressing alternative power centers. The administration stipulated that a "major effort will be made to build up the Baghdad Pact."[43] Far more important, however, was the idea of bolstering the position of Saudi Arabia. Eisenhower was fond of stressing that "Arabia is a country that contains the holy places of the Muslim world and the

Saudi Arabians are considered the most deeply religious of all peoples. Consequently, the King could be built up, possibly as a spiritual leader. Once this was accomplished we might begin to urge his right to political leadership."[44] Although the House of Saud's feuds with the Hashemite monarchies had drawn it toward Nasser's Arab Pact, it was at best an incongruous alliance. The Arab world was gradually fracturing along radical and conservative lines, pitting the Saudi monarchy against the secular republics. The United States that once had seen Arab nationalism as a vehicle for extension of its influence was increasingly looking to traditional monarchies as the foundation of its regional power.

Omega's attempt to isolate Egypt would take a special note of Syria. From the American perspective, the political situation in Damascus was deteriorating, as previous parliamentary elections had already cemented a pro-Egyptian sentiment. This problem was compounded by the election of Shukry Quwatly to the presidency, since the pro-Western right-wing parties could not coalesce around a single leader. The new president had long enjoyed close ties to Cairo and was committed to the Egyptian-led Arab Pact. Once the effort to counter Egypt's influence was under way, a more specific program against Syria, code-named Operation Straggle, was initiated by the CIA and MI6. Straggle involved Turkey provoking incidents along its border with Syria and British agents stirring up tribal unrest, while the American operatives organized reliable politicians. All this was designed to create instability and trigger an internal coup that would displace the leftist regime in Syria.[45]

Beyond isolating Nasser politically in the region, Omega also focused on Egypt's domestic affairs. Economic pressure once more formed the basis of American strategy, as the funding for the Aswan Dam would be permanently shelved and all other forms of financial assistance gradually suspended. Even under the cumbersome secrecy rules, there is sufficient evidence to suggest that an effort to overthrow Nasser was afoot. Washington was to "establish contact and discreetly encourage political opposition groups in Egypt."[46] The administration justified its covert operation by claiming that after all the purpose of Omega was to "limit Egypt's influence and actions in the Near East and Africa and undermine the Nasser regime at home."[47] Evidently, the United States hoped that by isolating Egypt and undermining its economy it could generate internal opposition to Nasser.

Not long after Eisenhower's approval of Omega, an entire range of economic assistance programs such as CARE and dispatch of surplus agricultural goods to Egypt were delayed. Along the established line, a variety of high-ranking American delegations began to take active part in various Baghdad Pact committees, particularly those that were involved in counter-subversion and military activities. Existing arms deliveries to Saudi Arabia were also increased and included sophisticated tanks and aircraft. In the meantime, American officials made a concerted effort to convince King Saud of the dangers that Egypt posed to his rule. The Syrian angle was not neglected, as covert operations there were accelerated to decouple Damascus from Cairo.

The American machinations did provoke a response from the Free Officers but hardly the one that the administration had anticipated. Nasser took to the airways to mobilize the Arab masses, denouncing the "great plan to wipe out our Arab nationalism." Nasser went on to proclaim, "They have no good intentions toward us. They will not leave us alone as an independent country, but we are independent and strong."[48] Instead of complying with the American mandates, Egypt officially recognized the People's Republic of China. Nasser had at this point purchased arms from the Eastern bloc and was now officially recognizing a revolutionary communist regime that the United States sought to isolate.

The Aswan Dam became the touchstone of Egypt's relations with the Western powers. Despite his flirtations with the Soviet bloc, Nasser was reluctant to become entirely dependent on the communist powers. Sensing the shifting mood in the United States, the colonel dispatched his envoy Ahmad Hussein to Washington to accept all conditions on the Aswan Dam funding. However, Nasser failed to understand that the withdrawal of the dam funding was part of the Omega plan. The issue at hand was not hashing out financial arrangements, but economic coercion as a means of discipline.

On July 19, 1956, Dulles finally met Hussein in the State Department. The secretary began by couching the American withdrawal of the offer in terms of the weakness of Egypt's economy. Dulles stressed that "the Aswan Dam was a huge project representing a heavy burden on the Egyptian economy."[49] Just so that the Egyptian envoy did not miss the point, Cairo's conduct came under indictment. Dulles was quick to assert that "developments during the past six or seven months had not been such as to generate goodwill toward Egypt on the part of the American people."[50] Hussein responded by brandishing the Soviet card, particularly in light of a forthcoming Nasser visit to Russia. The crude attempt to play the two superpowers against each other failed to dissuade Dulles, who had settled on a policy of pressuring, and if necessary undermining, Nasser's regime. The secretary officially rescinded the American offer.

Nasser was outraged at the revocation of the agreement. He declared to his foreign minister, Mahmoud Fawzi, that "this is not a withdrawal. It is an attack on the regime and an invitation to bring us down."[51] Cairo needed a bold move to sustain its ascendancy in the Arab world and maintain its nationalistic credibility. The Egyptian reaction once more exceeded Western expectations.

On July 26, 1956, Nasser shocked everyone when in a speech in Alexandria he declared Egypt's intention to nationalize the Suez Canal Company as a means of funding the construction of the Aswan Dam. The colonel demonstrated his penchant to uphold Egyptian independence by foregoing the Soviet offer of funding Aswan. The nationalization of the canal had far-reaching consequences for U.S. policy and the Anglo-American approach to the Middle East. The latent disagreements between Washington and London now surfaced to complicate relations between the two allies.

GOING TO WAR WITH NASSER

Upon hearing the news, the White House indulged in its share of histrionics. Dulles pointed to the colonel's slim volume, *The Philosophy of the Revolution*, and claimed that it clearly reflected how Nasser was "dreaming of a great buildup of Arab power, and a corresponding diminution in the power of the West." The canal seizure, Dulles added, "was one of a series of steps to this end, and had accordingly raised basic questions involving the balance of power and the future of Western Europe."[52] Charles E. Wilson, the secretary of defense, not only endorsed his colleague's views but claimed that "the collapse of colonialism had been too rapid and was having as much effect on the world as the rise of communism."[53] In a sense, Wilson was correct in noting the difficulty of influencing postcolonial nationalism. The nationalization of the canal and Nasser's flirtations with the Eastern bloc reflected the tensions between a global power preoccupied with the threat of communism and a prickly nationalist regime focused on parochial ambitions.

In contemplating its response, the administration was quick to rule out the use of force. Eisenhower never wavered from his belief that a precipitous resort to arms would only embolden Arab nationalism and validate its claims that the West had merely remodeled, not removed, its colonial presence. The president warned that the use of military force "might well array the world from Dakar to the Philippine islands against us."[54] An armed intervention, led by the Western powers, would lionize Nasser and marginalize his Arab detractors. Eisenhower preferred to stay with the more subtle Omega plan and gradually subvert Nasser's power.

The American stance was quickly challenged by Britain. Given

Eden's belief that Nasser was the source of all Western difficulties in the Middle East, the latest Egyptian move was seen as another step in a concerted attempt to undermine the British presence. The undersecretary of state for foreign affairs, Ivone Kirkpatrick, warned of a dark future if Egypt emerged triumphant, envisioning "in two years' time Nasser will have deprived us of our oil, the sterling area falling apart, no European defense possible, unemployment and unrest in the UK and our standard of living reduced to that of Yugoslavs or Egyptians."[55] Eden not only endorsed such outlandish claims but emphasized that the health of the Western economies was imperiled by Nasser's move. In its deliberations, the British cabinet viewed nationalization of the canal as an extraordinary act of defiance that required a firm response.

The situation became even more complicated with the intrusion of yet another Western power in the Suez melodrama. The French reaction to Nasser's act was nearly as apoplectic as the British. Long accustomed to blaming the Algerian insurrection against their rule on Radio Cairo's invectives and Egypt's modest material assistance to the rebels, Paris saw Nasser's seizure of the canal as the perfect opportunity to eliminate a perceived source of difficulty. Foreign Minister Christian Pineau exclaimed to the U.S. ambassador to France, Douglas Dillon, that "the French government takes a most serious view of the affair and links it to the seizure of the Rhineland by Hitler."[56] The French now joined their British counterparts in seeing Hitler's dark shadow over Middle Eastern developments.

The inflammatory nature of the debate in European capitals led Eisenhower to dispatch Undersecretary of State Robert D. Murphy to London for a careful assessment of continental views. Upon arriving in Europe, Murphy met the full force of Anglo-French resolution. Harold Macmillan, who had recently left the Foreign Office and assumed the post of chancellor of the exchequer, set the tone early on when he greeted the American diplomat by stressing that "if Britain did not accept Egypt's challenge it would become another Netherlands."[57] This impression was reinforced by the recently installed foreign secretary, Selwyn Lloyd, who informed Murphy that irresolution would mean that "NATO, Western Europe and other parts of the world will be at the mercy of a man who has shown himself irresponsible."[58] Reflecting the French preoccupation with Algeria, Pineau bluntly declared that "one successful battle in Egypt is worth ten in North Africa."[59] The American diplomat assured his hosts that although the United States viewed the use of force as ill-considered, it was prepared to employ other means to temper Nasser's ambitions. Still, the British and the French seemed committed to military intervention.

As Eisenhower contemplated Murphy's urgent cables, he grew apprehensive about his allies' intentions. The president considered Eden's thinking "unwise" and "out of date." Dulles advised that "we could make Nasser disgorge what he has seized and agree to internationalize the canal—by means other than force."[60] It was incomprehensible to the White House that its allies were rejecting a policy designed to defuse Egypt's influence in favor of a war that was bound to make a hero out of Nasser.

The task of American diplomacy was to gain time and make Eden realize his folly. A series of international conclaves was held in fall of 1956 and numerous emissaries were dispatched to various capitals. Nasser received his share of intermediaries and diplomatic démarches. The interesting aspect of all these conferences and high-wire diplomatic maneuvers was that no one had much confidence in their success. Nasser was entrenched, the British and the French were determined to salvage their prestige through the force of arms, and the Americans hoped to prolong the talks while Omega unfolded. In the meantime, the Israelis were eyeing Nasser's army and its absorption of the Czech weapons. In the end, the dance of diplomacy failed to head off the coming calamity.

In October 1956, the noisy Anglo-French military preparations and the evacuation of their civilians from the canal zone had caused much consternation in the White House. Eisenhower tried to head off Eden by assuring the prime minister that "I do not, repeat do not, differ from your estimate of [Nasser's] intentions and purpose. The place where we disagree is on the probable effect in the Arab world."[61] The problem of canal seizure and Arab nationalism had to be separated. Eisenhower was convinced that even though Nasser's ambitions had disturbed the conservative monarchies, they would have no choice but to react vehemently against European reversion to gunboat diplomacy. The best solution was to defuse the crisis and then proceed with Omega. Increasingly, the president's calls for patience were falling on deaf ears in both Europe and Israel.

At this point Eden was finally offered a pretext for action against Nasser. Two French representatives, General Maurice Challe and Labor Minister Albert Gazier, arrived at the British prime minister's country residence at Chequers and presented their collusion scheme. The French plan called for Israel to attack Egypt, and then on the pretext of separating the combatants and securing the safety of the canal, the French and British forces would intervene. The threat to the Hashemite Kingdom of Jordan was emphasized by the French, who argued that given the persistent border clashes between Israel and its neighbors, Jerusalem was bound to attack an Arab country. It would serve everyone's purpose if Israel attacked Egypt rather than Jordan. Clearly, the prime minister was searching for a justification for a war that had thus far eluded him. The coming winter pushed Eden farther toward collusion, as military operations were likely to be postponed for yet another season. The conspiracy fulfilled the prime minister's determination to deflate Nasser's influence and make use of assembled British troops.

The French plot would not have worked without the participation of Israel. To properly examine Israel's position we must grapple with the ideology of its most influential politician of the 1950s, Prime Minister David Ben-Gurion. In pursuit of Israel's security, the premier was determined to establish its deterrent power. His approach to any Arab attack or contemplated attack was massive retaliation to emphasize the strength of Israeli armed forces. In Ben-Gurion's telling, once the Arab states were disabused of destroying Israel, then they would finally make peace with it. Thus, in his view, all forms of military confrontation, ranging from massive reprisals to preventive war, were a useful means of promoting an overall settlement.

In 1956, the Israelis held a very dim view of the developments that had taken place in the Middle East since Eisenhower's inauguration. They bemoaned the 1954 Anglo-Egyptian Treaty, for it had led to the withdrawal of British forces from Egypt that could have acted as a restraint on Nasser. They were concerned about the Baghdad Pact, for it supplied U.S. arms to an Iraqi state that remained hostile to Israel. And naturally, they were fearful about the pace of Egypt's absorption of the Czech arms. The tensions on Israel's borders and the persistent infiltration of Palestinian guerrillas from both Egypt and Jordan further inflamed Ben-Gurion's anxieties. The Israelis had pleaded with the Eisenhower administration for security guarantees that were not forthcoming. Everywhere the Israelis looked they saw armed Arabs threatening their state.

It was natural for Israel to be responsive to French pleas for taking on Nasser. During the 1950s, France had emerged as Israel's leading supplier of military hardware and an important backer of its nascent nuclear program. At a time when the United States demurred formal security guarantees to Israel, Ben-Gurion was searching for a Western benefactor. When presented with the French plan to attack Egypt, the patriarch noted that "this is the birth of the first serious alliance between us and a Western power. We cannot not accept."[62] The plan offered Ben-Gurion a way of cementing Israel's alliance with France while striking a blow against his principal Arab foe.

At this point, Foreign Secretary Lloyd returned to the Paris suburb of Sèvres to seal the deal for the invasion of Egypt. Initially, Lloyd attempted to induce the Israelis to assume greater responsibility by outlining a plan where they would endanger the canal, followed by a joint Anglo-French ultimatum against both sides to cease military operations. Then after a suitable interval, the British and the French would militarily intervene. Ben-Gurion refused the deal and insisted that British air attacks occur simultaneously with Israel's land invasion. Such a move would effectively dispel the idea that the Anglo-French intervention was the result of the Israeli assault. In essence, Britain agreed to participate directly in a tripartite conspiracy against Nasser with the most superficial of covers.

The Americans were completely in the dark when the deal was being consummated. Days prior to the Israeli invasion, Dulles protested to the U.S. ambassador to the United Kingdom, Winthrop Aldrich, "we are quite disturbed here over the fact that there is apparently an elaborate British plan of keeping us completely in the dark as to their intentions with reference to the Middle East matters generally and Egypt in particular."[63] The allied relations were strained to the point where long-standing practices such as information sharing had been halted.

The British and French intelligence blackout functioned effectively, as the United States came to see Jordan as the likely target of any forthcoming military campaign in the area. The chaotic internal conditions of Jordan made it vulnerable to predatory neighbors. Dulles reported that "it seems to be taken internationally as a forgone conclusion that Jordan is breaking up, and of course, all the surrounding countries are anxious to get their share of the wreckage."[64] Israel engaged in its share of deception by issuing a statement acknowledging its nationwide mobilization and claiming that "units are being moved to the Jordan border in view of the recent threats that foreign troops may enter that country."[65] In conversation with Aldrich, Lloyd emphasized that he was "inclined to believe that an Israeli attack more likely [would] be directed against Jordan than Egypt."[66] As part of their collusion, the British and Israelis were busy deceiving Eisenhower in the hope that once their military operations commenced he would acquiesce to the fait accompli.

On October 29, 1956, Israeli forces attacked Egypt, directly imperiling the operation of the canal. This was followed by the Anglo-French ultimatum, warning both sides to fall back ten miles on each side of the canal, meaning that Israeli would remain on Egyptian soil.[67] Nasser's rejection of the ultimatum led to direct European intervention. The military aspect of the conspiracy worked efficiently, as Nasser's army was soon in ruins. Neither the colonel's words, transmitted so often through Radio Cairo, nor his army could salvage his fortunes. That task would be up to America's foremost military leader turned politician.

To the U.S. administration, the Anglo-French action had come at a particularly inauspicious time. The simultaneous Soviet attempt to forcefully put down a Hungarian uprising was a glaring indication of the failure of socialist solidarity. But the allied conduct in Suez obscured Soviet brutality by highlighting a degree of moral equivalency between the two blocs. Dulles bemoaned that "the intended action in Egypt may well obliterate the success that we have long awaited in Eastern Europe."[68] The Anglo-French invasion eliminated any propaganda advantage that the United States may have gained from the Hungarian situation to further fracture the Eastern bloc.

The outbreak of the hostilities in the Middle East clearly perplexed and confused officials in Washington. An angry Eisenhower stressed to his aides, "I must say that it is hard for me to see any good final result emerging from a scheme that seems to antagonize the entire Muslim world."[69] The military solution ran contrary to the administration's ambition to undermine the Egyptian regime through subtle measures. Eisenhower complained to the British chargé d'affaires "that we had a great chance to split the Arab world. Various other countries were becoming uneasy at Egyptian developments."[70] All this was gone as the president immediately recognized that the Arab world would coalesce behind Nasser and his radical nationalist allies.

Far from acquiescing to the course of events, Eisenhower was determined to end the war. The United States went to the United Nations and sponsored a resolution calling for an immediate cessation of hostilities and withdrawal of all invading forces. Eisenhower was not beyond using economic pressure to get his way. The Egyptian blockade of the Suez Canal meant that oil had to be transported around the Cape of Good Hope, thus increasing its price. In the meantime, British gold and financial reserves were quickly depleting. The prospect of American aid seemed unlikely as Eisenhower had privately decided that the "purpose of peace and stability would be served not by being too quick in attempting to render extraordinary assistance."[71] With its solvency threatened, Britain confronted a Washington that blocked its loan petition to the International Monetary Fund. This placed unbearable pressure on the much-anguished prime minister. On November 6, in the midst of financial distress, international condemnation, and domestic discontent, Eden finally consented to a cease-fire. France and Israel were not far behind. They could not continue the conflict without their senior partner.

Since the Suez War, there has been occasional lament in Britain and even the United States about whether Eisenhower should have backed the invasion. After all, Nasser was a thorn in the side of the West and had opened the way for Soviet penetration of the Middle East. Such views are shortsighted when one considers the temper of Arab politics in the 1950s and the sheer incompetence of Eden's folly. It was never clear who Whitehall thought would replace Nasser and how his successor would differ from him. Moreover, the aroused forces of Arab nationalism that were conditioning the politics of the Middle East could hardly have been assuaged with such a transparent imperial intervention. At a time when Washington was trying to reach out to credible local actors, it could not be associated with a colonial enterprise that was widely unpopular in the region. Moreover, Eisenhower did have plans for disciplining and potentially even displacing Nasser, but he sought to do so in a subtle way using economic pressure and cultivating officers and politicians opposed to the colonel. It is unclear whether such covert machinations would have succeeded, but after an invasion that lionized Nasser such schemes were simply impractical.

The end of the Suez Crisis did nothing to diminish the United States' problems in the Middle East. Egypt's defiance of the Anglo-French military adventure elevated Nasser's prestige in the Arab world and reinforced his quest for regional preeminence. For the Arab masses, already inspired by Nasser's rhetoric, the war confirmed fears and suspicions that they had harbored all along about Western imperialism. The pro-Nasser forces were further energized in their opposition to the conservative regimes allied with America. It was feared in Washington that the Suez Crisis had realigned the power relations in the Middle East to the distinct benefit of the Soviet Union. The United States was now compelled to take dramatic steps to reverse these ominous trends.

PICKING UP THE PIECES

As the crisis wound down, Eisenhower received more grim news from his advisors. In November, the Operations Coordinating Board (OCB), whose task was to pull together the federal bureaucracy's wisdom, informed the president that "the opportunistic and nationalistic Nasser government of Egypt has gained influence throughout the area and other Arab heads of state are less able to resist the formation of governments which cater to this surge of nationalism."[72] Throughout the region power vacuums were being created that the Soviet Union was bound to fill.

Washington appreciated that a direct injection of its power was necessary to stabilize the situation. The British were still too toxic to influence events and the conservative monarchies were too frightened to play the role the United States had in mind for them. Dulles stressed that "if we do not act, the Soviets are likely to take over the area, and they could thereby control Europe through oil on which Europe depends."[73] The question then was how to assert U.S. power. The administration initially contemplated joining the Baghdad Pact, but given that organization's close identification with Britain, overt American involvement was ruled out. To persist with Omega and its covert schemes also seemed at odds with the regional temper. America needed a bold stroke.

After carefully examining the issue, the State Department gave concrete expression to Eisenhower's preferences. In a White House meeting, Undersecretary Herbert Hoover Jr. elaborated on how best to construct an anti-Nasser coalition. Once more, Saudi Arabia was the starting point. The mystique of overseeing Islam's holiest shrines gave the king a unique standing among the Arabs. However, the sparsely populated kingdom needed to partake of the resources of the better-endowed Arab states. The task here was to "draw Saudi Arabia and Iraq closer together."[74] Similar measures were contemplated for the besieged Jordanian monarchy. The significant Palestinian population of Jordan had always been susceptible to Nasser's pan-Arabist appeal and his pledge to confront Israel. The Palestinian agitation made the Jordanian king's hold on power at best tenuous. The administration resolved to "assist Jordan financially, and perhaps militarily in the context of a closer federation with Iraq."[75]

Nor was Eisenhower prepared to completely give up on Britain, particularly one led by his wartime friend and new prime minister, Harold Macmillan. Having been one of the anti-Nasser hawks, Macmillan opportunistically abandoned Eden as the invasion turned disastrous and managed to secure a promotion for himself. At any rate, whatever the differences in British and American perspectives may have been, Cold War requirements and regional exigencies demanded renewal of ties. A U.S. administration that had come to see Cairo's policies as prime obstacles to the implementation of the containment doctrine in the Middle East was inclined to seek assistance from all corners. Britain would have to be rehabilitated and its remaining assets in the region mobilized for the deflation of the Egyptian regime.

As part of their new initiative, Eisenhower and Dulles began lobbying Congress for a program of economic assistance and the authorization for the use of force if necessary. This was the first expression of what would be known as the Eisenhower Doctrine. The precedent of the Truman Doctrine guided Eisenhower's decision to seek legislative authority for providing aid and possibly using military force. As had Truman, Eisenhower overcame legislators' objections by brandishing the communist card and by claiming that the Suez Crisis had "given Russia an opportunity to improve its position in an area having vital resources and strategic location."[76] The president went on to stress that the "existing vacuum in the Middle East must be filled by the United States before it is filled by Russia."[77] Accustomed to acquiescing to executive claims of communist danger, congressional leaders accepted the administration's approach.

On January 5, 1957, the president officially unveiled the Eisenhower Doctrine to a joint session of Congress. The doctrine called for measures including the use of U.S. armed forces to "secure and protect territorial integrity and political independence of such nations, requesting such aid, against covert armed aggression from any nations controlled by International Communism."[78] In his subsequent Senate testimony, Dulles also invoked the Soviet threat, claiming, "It would be abhorrent and dangerous if this area were ruled by International Communism. Yet that is the present danger."[79] It is hard to properly identify what exactly international communism was and in what manner it was threatening the Middle East. However, the basic purpose of the Eisenhower Doctrine was to assure America's allies of its commitment to the region and signal to its adversaries that the United States was prepared to take urgent action to redeem its interests.

A PROBLEM WITH NO END

Eisenhower's foray in the Middle East during his first term was a failure. He had hoped to limit America's involvement in the Arab world and somehow implement the containment doctrine there on the cheap. The new forces of nationalism as embodied by Egypt's Gamal Abdel Nasser appeared to be ideal allies as they were legitimate and seemingly pragmatic. Nasser and his cohort were to make peace with Israel, come to terms with their reformed imperial tormentors, and hold aloft the banner of anticommunism. To be sure, such impressions were carefully cultivated by Nasser, who sought to manipulate the American leverage against his many foes. Still, Eisenhower and his aides should have paid closer attention to what Nasser was doing in the Arab world and what he was saying to his domestic audiences. Should they have done so, they would have realized that Nasser's pan-Arabism was indifferent to U.S. Cold War imperatives. It was Israel and the Arab monarchs that Nasser sought to undermine, not Nikita Khrushchev or Mao Zedong. The administration's entire Middle East policy was predicated on a series of wrong assumptions and optimistic misapprehensions.

Along the way, America's path was twisted by the machinations of its allies. At a time when the United States was preoccupied with multiple global crises, it had hoped that Britain would take the lead in the Middle East. This was not to be. Anthony Eden somehow convinced himself that his provocative military invasion would not inflame Arab politics and further imperil the conservative rulers that America was seeking to buttress. Three middle powers, conspiring behind their superpower benefactor, launched an attack that not only lionized Nasser but polarized the Middle East. This would be Britain's last gasp in the heart of the Arab world. London would spend another decade policing the Persian Gulf principalities before giving up on that modest task. Eden's final legacy was a diminished Britain, an enraged America, and a divided Arab world.

In the end, Eisenhower had to come to terms with the contradictions of his policies. The only way that the region's pro-Western title could be maintained was for the United States to become more involved in the Middle East. Still, Eisenhower's doctrine was a hesitant one, making his administration careful with its adversaries and wary of its allies. Whatever his dispositions may have been, there is no denying that Eisenhower's doctrine was contrary to his desire for a light footprint in the Middle East. Washington would gradually take sides, empower its allies, and plot against its detractors. Once America settled down to a new policy it proved surprisingly adroit in navigating Arab politics.

CHAPTER 5

1958: THE YEAR OF THE REVOLUTIONS

Dwight Eisenhower's second term coincided with the high-water mark of pan-Arabism and its ideological companion, anticolonialism. The merger of Egypt and Syria and the overthrow of the conservative Iraqi monarchy seemingly heralded a new age. As with most storms, the latest epoch passed, leaving in its wake the same acrimony and division that had long plagued the Arab world. Still, in the aftermath of the Suez Crisis, Nasserism appeared menacing and empowered. At a time of superpower conflict, many Americans saw the Kremlin's shadows behind Nasser's façade. Eisenhower's critics accused his administration of passivity and lack of imagination in dealing with the region's problems.

As with most of the criticism levied against Eisenhower, his handling of Middle Eastern affairs was more competent and thoughtful than his detractors suggest.[1] In many ways, Eisenhower offers a model of how to deal with adversaries. While initially Eisenhower had hoped for Nasser's cooperation, he soon came to appreciate that the colonel was an autonomous actor who would alternate between Cold War power blocs without committing to either one. Arab nationalism's neutralist tendencies had to be thwarted, but the United States was open to tactical cooperation with the nationalists when mutual interests were at stake. Despite the occasional inflamed rhetoric that laces official documents, Eisenhower did not view Nasser in categorical terms. He accepted that each side could disagree in a manner that did not jeopardize future cooperation.

In the aftermath of the Suez War, Nasser searched for a way out of his predicament. Cairo may have been at the height of its power, but the regime appreciated the need for measured steps. To begin with Nasser understood that it was the United States and not the Soviet Union that had tipped the scales in his favor during the Suez conflict. He was wary of being too dependent on Moscow and understood that the United States remained the predominant power in the region. Nasser's message to Washington was that he had no plans to infringe on its core interests, such as obstructing access to the region's oil supplies. Nasser portrayed nonalignment as his guarantee that Egypt would not concede to Soviet mandates or facilitate Moscow's inroads into the Middle East. As the Arab world entered a period of unpredictable transitions, Eisenhower at times would rely on Nasser to check the forces of radicalism.

Dwight Eisenhower succeeded in the Middle East in his second term because he adjusted his assumptions and reconsidered his failures. He was also aided by factors not of his own making, namely he had good allies and flexible adversaries. The conservative order held its own against the revolutionary reverberations of the 1950s. The radical republics such as Egypt and Iraq abjured communism while exploiting the Soviet Union as a source of arms and assistance. Soviet communism did not penetrate the Middle East because no one wanted it. Nikita Khrushchev may have sought to extend Russian influence to the postcolonial realm, but in the Middle East he found an inhospitable terrain for his message of communist empowerment. A combination of foresight and luck allowed Eisenhower to stabilize the region and secure U.S. concerns without undertaking unwise interventions.

FROM SYRIA TO UNITED ARAB REPUBLIC

No Arab country lent itself more to foreign intervention than Syria. The Syrian military caste routinely meddled in politics, at times encouraged by civilians seeking to displace their rivals. All Syrian actors looked abroad for redemption and leverage. Syria's tribulations became internationalized, partly because Syrians wanted it that way. An intellectual class attuned to pan-Arabism, an officer corps seeking power, and bickering politicians plotting against each other made Syria a place that invited intrigue and intervention.

The Suez War had severely damaged the position of those in Syria who were predisposed to the West. The popular revulsion against Europe's gunboat diplomacy was compounded by the disclosure of Operation Straggle's intent to restore a friendly regime in Damascus. The United States relied on a conservative coalition of landed gentry, religious leaders, and businessmen who seemed dispirited and disorganized. The conservative forces were reeling under pressure from Ba'athists and communists while the moderate president, Shukry Quwatly, was busy purging them from his government. The left seemed cohesive and ascendant, not to mention energized by the region's tumult.[2]

The radicalization of Syria's domestic politics colored its international relations.[3] The Syrians severed ties with the Europeans while condemning the Eisenhower Doctrine and America's priorities in the Middle East. Soon, a barter agreement with Moscow was announced exchanging Syrian agricultural products for Russian arms. Along with Soviet weapons came technical advisors and intelligence operatives. The unsettled politics of Syria seemed to lean toward the Soviet Union and its domestic accomplices.

The oil issue also surfaced as Washington contemplated its policy options. During the Suez Crisis, the Americans grew alarmed by the war's potentially crippling effect on oil shipments to Europe. The closure of the Suez waterway and the sabotage of the Iraqi oil pipeline that traversed Syria had diminished oil exports to a stressed European economy. The United States was concerned that if radical regimes came to power in Syria and Egypt, forces unfriendly to the West would have sudden, enormous influence over the petroleum market. Given Nasser's firm position in Egypt, regime change in Syria became a tantalizing goal of the newly established Eisenhower Doctrine.

As we have seen, Eisenhower placed a premium on covert operations. In Iran, Egypt, and Syria itself, Washington had embarked on attempts to undermine the established authorities through black operations. Even after the failure of Operation Straggle, the United States still perceived that it could manipulate the situation in Syria through clandestine measures. A careful reading of the Eisenhower administration's covert action record reveals that the president's confidence in such programs was exaggerated if not altogether misplaced.

Although evidence on such matters is ordinarily circumspect, by May 1957 the Eisenhower administration seemed to have embarked on a conspiracy. Secretary Dulles confided to his brother Allan, the head of the CIA, "We need a good fellow in government [in Syria] to run it." The younger Dulles assured his brother that "we are working on it."[4] Shortly after that conversation, Dulles cabled the U.S. embassy in Damascus insisting that it "encourage elements opposed to the present Syrian policies."[5] The CIA, working with conservative elements in the country, plotted its schemes. The inevitable discovery of the plot by Syria's intelligence services essentially eliminated coups as a policy option. As John Foster Dulles conceded to Senator Mike Mansfield, "The difficulty is that we do not have any valuable subversive assets within Syria itself."[6] If Washington was going to reverse the situation, it had to consider more drastic steps.

In the aftermath of the failed coup, the Eisenhower administration contemplated fantastic measures for stemming the communist tide in Syria. Given the long shadow of the Suez War and the fact that a case could not be made that Syria was controlled by international communism, Eisenhower could not sanction an American military intervention. Despite his excited claims, Eisenhower was loath to intervene militarily in a conflict without an obvious exit path. Syria had the trappings of a quagmire: disorderly politics, a complicated ethnic composition, and unreliable politicians. The president—and former general—may have ruled out direct American involvement, but he was not beyond instigating a regional war. As a gesture of burden sharing, Eisenhower hoped to induce Syria's neighbors to depose the country's troublesome regime.

As White House deliberations continued, the leaders of Turkey, Jordan, and Iraq—Adnan Menderes, King Hussein, and King Faisal II, respectively—met in Ankara. Eisenhower decided to take advantage of the gathering and cabled the assembled leaders that "if Syria's Muslim neighbors felt necessary to take action against aggression by the Syrian government, the United States would expedite arms sales."[7] To provoke such Syrian aggression, Washington advised riling up the tribes and staging border incidents. The president assured his allies that the Soviet Union would not intervene, but still as a confidence-building measure dispatched additional naval forces to the Mediterranean. The veteran diplomat Loy Henderson was sent to the region in 1957 to elicit opinion and mobilize support.

As Henderson embarked on his tour of Middle Eastern capitals, he found that Turkey was the most ardent supporter of intervention—the country was quietly amassing troops on its border. This proved a lonely struggle, as the conservative Arab rulers who were so dogmatic in private were reticent in public. Damascus quickly filed a complaint against Turkey in the United Nations regarding violations of its territorial integrity with ample support from the Arab states, including some of the conservative ones that had inveighed against Damascus in private. The Soviet Union began well-publicized military exercises on Turkey's periphery. Beyond the fear of a superpower confrontation, Eisenhower appreciated that Turkey, without an Arab cover, could not attack Syria. The president conceded that "while a Muslim country, her domination of the region before World War I was too unfavorably remembered by the Arabs for them to accept her leadership."[8] As Washington ran out of options to arrest the communist surge in Syria, Nasser paradoxically came to its rescue.

Syria's political uncertainties and the prospect of Western intervention demanded a response from the champion of Arab self-determination. Never one to pass up a public relations opportunity, Nasser responded to the turbulence of the Levant by deploying a small contingent of Egyptian troops in Syria's northwest frontier. The colonel was once more acclaimed in the Arab street as his resolution was credited with aborting another Western conspiracy against a Middle Eastern state. However, Nasser did not foresee how he was being drawn into Damascus' web of intrigue. Syria's poisonous factionalism was about to ensnare Cairo. In Syria, Nasser would pay a steep price for his radical infatuations.

Despite his apparent triumph, behind the scenes Nasser was concerned about developments in Syria. The colonel was left in the dark as Damascus and Moscow negotiated their trade agreement and he feared that a power vacuum in Syria would only benefit the communist party. As Soviet advisors and intelligence operatives arrived, they would inevitably rely on and empower the local communists. Suddenly it was possible that Syria could escape Nasser's clutches and join the Soviet bloc. Ironically, on the eve of his latest anti-Western victory, Nasser and Eisenhower shared the same anxieties.

As often happened in the region's history, the weakest actor took the most consequential initiative. Syria's domestic turmoil led some of its factions to seek a political merger with Egypt.[9] The Ba'ath party perceived that, with Soviet backing, Syrian communists could win the power struggle within the left. The political calendar further aggravated these anxieties, as the Ba'athists feared that the communists might do well in the forthcoming parliamentary elections, setting them up to contest the presidency. Indeed, given the behavior of the communist parties in Eastern Europe, some thought the Syrian communists might even forego such electoral formalities and stage a coup.

The Ba'ath party's agitation for union with Egypt transcended political expediency and was deeply rooted in its ideological self-image. The Ba'athists had always pressed for Arab unity, and a merger with Egypt was seen as a critical first step toward their pan-Arabist aspirations. For the Ba'athists, Nasser's charisma and prestige proved alluring. By anchoring their fortunes on Nasser's authority, they could nurture their Arabist dreams and rescue their endangered party. A union with Egypt would advance their ideals as well as enhance their power.

For parochial and institutional reasons, the military backed the notion of unity. In most Arab countries, the military exhibited a sense of discipline not found among the civilian politicians, but this was not the case in Syria. The disunity of the political class was mirrored in the armed forces, and the officer corps had fragmented among competing factions of Ba'athists, communists, and conservatives. Ironically, senior military leadership sensed that through a union with Egypt, the institution could temper cantankerous civilians while restoring its own cohesion.

On January 12, 1958, without informing their own government, a delegation of Syrian officers traveled to Cairo and petitioned for an immediate and complete unity between the two states. Nasser attempted to stall and claimed that he could not discuss such national matters without the consent of responsible constitutional authorities. At that time, the officers summoned Syrian foreign minister Salah ad-Din al-Bitar, who also pleaded with Nasser that only unity could save their country. It appeared that Cairo's allies were finally seeking to redeem its pan-Arab exhortations.

The unity scheme presented Nasser with a difficult choice. The colonel viewed pan-Arabism as a means of influencing the foreign policy of individual states without necessarily burdening their domestic problems. Yet as a proclaimed champion of Arab unity he could not easily reject Syria's proposal without loss of prestige. As we have seen, Nasser was also concerned about the growth of the communist party's influence in Syria and the disarray that was sweeping that country. Egypt itself had previously called for unity with Syria once there was a sufficient degree of military and economic integration. Nasser slyly had assured his confidant Muhammad Heikal that such unity could not happen for at least five years. Now the colonel had to make a decision on a much more compressed timeline. Nasser demurred but in the end he had no choice but to go along. In February 1958, the United Arab Republic (UAR) was born, bringing together two of the Middle East's most important nations.

Still, if unity had to take place, it had to be on Nasser's terms. The Syrians had to dissolve their political parties, the army had to abandon politics, and power would rest in Cairo, not Damascus. The Ba'athists, who perceived that their privileged position as Nasser's ally would ensure their influence, agreed to dismantle their party. As with most intellectuals they assumed that ideas have greater sway in the real world than they actually do. The Ba'athists convinced themselves that Nasser would heed their advice and yield to their judgments. By contrast, the suddenly beleaguered communists—and the military that had instigated the unity talks—had no choice but to concede.

The advent of the UAR meant that pan-Arabism had transcended slogans and found practical territorial expression.[10] The charismatic Nasser had finally given substance to his rhetoric and laid the foundation for greater regional unity. The colonel was in control of two states and the master of the Suez Canal. The hesitations that plagued Nasser were concealed from an adoring public busy commemorating the historic Arab moment. It remained unclear whether Nasser could exert influence over Syria's unruly political class. But all this was in the future, as the jubilation of the crowds was matched only by the consternation of conservative Arab rulers.

As Washington considered its options, its allies went ahead with their own policies. King Hussein of Jordan quickly initiated unity talks with his Hashemite cousin in Iraq, Faisal II. Hussein's dilemma mirrored that of Syrian Ba'athists as Faisal II stood in better light. The Arab Union was to be a loose federal arrangement that called for coordination of foreign and defense policies. The two parties would maintain separate domestic institutions while presenting a united front in the region. The conservatives wanted to demonstrate that they could also compete on a pan-Arabist terrain and were not about to cede this ground to Nasser. The enveloping unity schemes left the region badly divided against itself. The two blocs now engaged in vicious propaganda attacks, with King Hussein the victim of various coup attempts.[11]

The polarization of the Arab world caused a gradual Saudi shift away from Nasser. During his state visit to Washington in 1957, King Saud had applauded Eisenhower's commitment to the region and his determination to fill the vacuum left by the European powers. Saud was a virulently anticommunist conservative in command of a state that oversaw Islam's holiest shrines. He was concerned about the impact of Nasser's pan-Arabism on the region and even among his own countrymen. All this may have reinforced Eisenhower's instinct to use the Saudi kingdom as a counterweight to Nasser. However, Saud's reckless conduct soon undermined such conceptions.

In March 1958, Syria's intelligence chief, Abdel Hamid al-Sarraj, revealed that he had been approached by the Saudis to lead a coup in Syria. The Saudi emissary allegedly offered him 1.9 million pounds and an additional 2 million pounds should he engineer the assassination of Nasser. In his press conference revealing the plot, Sarraj showed the checks that had been issued by the Arab National Bank of Riyadh. This may not have been news to Washington—in February, the Saudis had cryptically informed the administration to anticipate a change of government in Syria. Given their own failed coup attempts, the Americans had demurred and warned the Saudis to be aware of potential problems. As Allen Dulles confessed, "Saud has engaged in a lot of intrigue against the leaders of these countries which have now been unmasked by Sarraj and Nasser. We had tried to warn Saud that he was falling into a trap."[12]

The failure of such a maladroit coup attempt embarrassed the Saudi kingdom and proved the undoing of Saud. The king would remain the titular head of state, but Crown Prince Faisal assumed effective control of the monarchy and proved a judicious custodian of the state. Disciplined and self-assured, he quickly instituted austerity measures that helped stabilize Saudi finances that had been neglected by the profligate Saud.[13] He sought to maintain a balance both at home and in the region. On the one hand, he placated the monarchy's domestic critics and seemed sensitive to Nasser's appeal among younger Saudis. Yet, he also restored diplomatic ties with Britain and France that had been severed during the Suez War and was supportive of the Hashemite monarchies. On occasion when politics demanded, he would be critical of the United States, yet he rejected Arab nationalists' calls for terminating U.S. base rights. Faisal's Saudi Arabia appreciated the need for American protection and remained an important pillar of U.S. containment policy in the Middle East.[14]

As U.S. allies were sorting themselves out, Nasser tried to mend ties with Washington. The colonel insisted to his American interlocutors that he had no intention of subordinating himself to the Soviet Union. Raymond Hare, America's capable ambassador to Egypt, affirmed Nasser's claims and reported to the White House that Cairo was looking for a way out of its predicament. The National Security Council endorsed Hare's judgment, stressing that Nasser was conveying signals that "he would like to be friendlier with our nation provided he could bring this about without humiliation to himself."[15]

For his part, Eisenhower appreciated that in the aftermath of the Suez Crisis, Nasser's domestic position had become unassailable. Although Washington continued to depict Cairo's policies as "inimical to the interests of the West," it also acknowledged that "the U.S. cannot become involved in attempts to unseat Nasser's regime."[16] The Eisenhower administration sensed that Nasser was more pragmatic than it had perceived and potentially the colonel was searching for some kind of an accommodation with the United States. Once Eisenhower recognized that Nasser's demise was not likely and that his moderation could be harnessed, he was open to tactical cooperation between the two states.

On the surface, Syria seemed to offer the United States a platform for a new pragmatic approach to Egypt. Nasser was busy persecuting communists, even causing the head of the Syrian communist party, Khalid Bakdash, to flee the country. The intelligence community noted Nasser's anticommunist vigor and reported that the union between Syria and Egypt was not a Kremlin design. The National Intelligence Estimate even noted the anti-Soviet features of the merger by stressing that "Nasser probably agreed to go forward with the union this time because he was convinced that it was necessary to forestall a communist takeover in Syria."[17] Eisenhower did not ignore such reports and even relaxed economic sanctions that the United States had imposed on Egypt.

Still, there were limits to how far the United States could reach out to Nasser. Washington had to be mindful of its friends and maintain its alliance system. In the end, its options limited, the United States did acquiesce to the formation of the UAR. Given the frenzied Arab reaction to the news of the union, the Eisenhower administration did not want to be seen as defying public opinion. But Eisenhower still kept Nasser at arm's length. The fact that Washington quietly conceded to Nasser's creation testifies to the complexities of the region's political alignments.

In retrospect, the conservative Arab states' fear of the United Arab Republic seems exaggerated if not unwise. The UAR was an experiment that was bound to fail. The Arab masses that were so inspired by Nasser's rhetoric did not have to live in Egypt and experience its stagnant economy and police-state atmosphere. The Syrians that were brought into this union soon grew disenchanted with the reality of Nasserist governance. Nasser's proconsul in Damascus, General Abdel Hakim 'Amr, disregarded collaboration and abolished local authorities in favor of central control. The Syrian politicians, army officers, and merchants that had once agitated for the union were soon chafing under Cairo's heavy hand. Given the nature of Syrian politics, the culmination of this discontent was naturally a coup. In 1961, a group of army officers staged a coup and declared Syria's independence from the UAR. Nasser initially contemplated military intervention but, given his lack of allies, he thought better of it.

The UAR was beset by contradictions that haunted Nasser. The colonel and his Free Officers could always fall back on pragmatism, as they viewed pan-Arabism as a means of enhancing Egypt's influence and prestige. They were military men who relished power more than ideas and saw tactical adjustments as a necessity of political life. The Ba'athists by comparison were doctrinaire ideologues led by university-bred intellectuals who saw limited virtue in practical solutions. When they spoke of assaulting the old order and the Zionist state, they meant it. Nasser could not always afford their belligerence and in 1967 would fall victim to their militancy. This may not have been obvious in 1958, but the merger with Syria planted the seeds of destruction of Nasserism itself.

Through the regional tumult, the United States had persisted with its two-track policy of bolstering the conservative states while taking a more measured view of Nasser. These two tracks were seemingly in contradiction to one another. The more the United States aided the conservative monarchies, the more displeased Nasser became. And the Eisenhower administration's willingness to cooperate with Nasser was thoroughly despised by its conservative allies. Yet, Washington managed this policy with some success. In the end, the communist surge in Syria was arrested and Nasser found the burdens of pan-Arabism more daunting than he had anticipated. Despite accusations that Eisenhower and Dulles were incapable of calibrated policies, the official record reveals a thoughtful administration searching for solutions to the region's quandaries.

Eisenhower's triumph was not merely the product of his genius, but the fact that he had flexible adversaries and a superpower rival that could not take advantage of the inflamed situation in Syria. No matter how much aid Russia was prepared to offer, it could not alter the political alignments in Damascus. At some point, Eisenhower, Nasser, and even Syria's radicals shared the same goal of arresting the communist surge. Nasser reached out to the United States and sought its forbearance while he stabilized the situation. The White House came to appreciate that Nasser had conflicting motives and his desire to enhance his power meant that he would diminish the influence of the communist party. As such, Washington was prepared to live with the UAR, knowing full well that it would redound to the disadvantage of the Soviet Union and its allies. As the Syrian crisis ebbed, both sides' pragmatism would be severely tested in the turbulent waters of Lebanon.

LEBANON AND ITS TRIBULATIONS

Lebanon in the 1950s was a feudal country ruled by a religiously diverse elite. Lebanese politicians competed for power yet adhered to the sectarian parameters of their unusual state. This small country of 1.5 million inhabitants had somehow managed to hold its confessional tensions in check. Lebanon was destined to play a large role in the Cold War's early struggles. Its history, geography, and ethnic diversity conspired to fracture a nation that had based its politics on reconciliation and tolerance.

One of the most notable inventions of Lebanon's elite was the 1943 National Pact that had neatly distributed power among its religious groups. The National Pact granted the presidency to the Christians, the premiership to the Sunni Muslims, and the office of parliamentary speaker to the Shia Muslims. To preserve its political equilibrium, Lebanon tried to shield itself from the vagaries of Arab politics. Beirut looked neither to the conservative monarchs nor to the radical republics for salvation. In principle, Lebanon aimed for friendly relations with its neighbors without conceding to their disparate alignments. It is hard to see how this compact could have survived in ordinary times, much less in the turbulent year of 1958.

The custodian of Lebanon's order was a politician uniquely ill-suited for such a task. Camille Chamoun had been elected to the office of the presidency in 1952 with the promise to uphold Lebanon's constitutional limits. Initially, he adhered to the spirit of the National Pact, as he refused to join the Baghdad Pact or yield to Egypt's pan-Arabist imperatives. Chamoun's foreign minister, Charles Malik, was known as an advocate of nonalignment and along with other champions of neutralism had attended the Bandung conference. Yet in the post-Suez period, Chamoun would seek to prolong his tenure in office even if that meant provoking an international crisis.

As a prelude to his power grab, the president began to upset Lebanon's international relations by embracing the West. Chamoun refused to sever relations with the European states after their invasion of Egypt. At a time when even the conservative monarchies placated their publics by breaking ties with Britain and France, Chamoun sustained his diplomatic ties. The Lebanese leader further bucked the Arab consensus when he endorsed the Eisenhower Doctrine and in private urged the Americans to depose the leftist Syrian regime. As Chamoun placed Lebanon in the region's crosshairs, he faced the full Nasserist assault with its usual share of propaganda and subversion.

The spark that ignited the flame was Chamoun's decision to defy the constitution and seek another term as president. The parliamentary election held in June 1957 was marred by violence and vote rigging.

Prominent and independent politicians were gerrymandered, allowing the sitting government to secure fifty-three out of sixty-six seats. Given that the chamber would select the next president, Chamoun paid particular attention to manipulating the vote. Although the CIA was involved in the plot, Washington still hoped that constitutional prohibitions would be observed. For Chamoun, however, the vote rigging presaged his quest for an additional term in office.

In March 1958, Chamoun announced his intention to run for the presidency. Opposition to Chamoun transcended the sectarian divide, as influential Christians such as the Maronite patriarch Boulos Meouchi were also concerned about his ambitions. Many of Lebanon's factions were invested in preserving the fragile balance between Lebanon's Arab and Western orientations as enshrined by the National Compact. Chamoun's aspirations threatened the stability of his country and the durability of its accord.

Lebanon's politics seemed to spiral to a new level of violence as both sides hurled accusations against each other. The opposition to Chamoun encompassed important parties such as the United National Front, the Third Force, and the Progressive Socialist Party. The president's opponents accused him of diverting attention from his mischief by invoking foreign threats. Chamoun in turn castigated his critics as agents of the UAR. It seemed unusual for Chamoun to complain about foreign intervention when he was desperate for U.S. involvement in Lebanon's affairs.

Lebanon's susceptibility to Nasser's appeal was not fiction, and the attraction grew after the merger of Syria and Egypt. Sunni politicians as well as many other segments of society were enthusiastic about the union and journeyed to Damascus in large numbers to express their solidarity. The fact that the newly constituted UAR was intriguing against Chamoun is beyond doubt. Still, it was Chamoun's opportunism and indifference to regional temper that caused much of his difficulties.

As Chamoun and his detractors squared off, both sides welcomed, even solicited, foreign intervention. This was not so much foreign meddling, as meddling by invitation. Chamoun sensed that by tying himself to the United States he could secure his position at home. But he overestimated the importance of Lebanon and Eisenhower's willingness to sustain a president who was exceeding his constitutional authority. The United States desired a stable Lebanon that was not an Egyptian client, but perceived that the best way to achieve that aim was to preserve its delicate confessional balance.

By May 1958, Lebanon's crisis had yielded to full-scale violence. Chamoun was quick to blame the mayhem on Nasser, a claim that may have been exaggerated but was not without evidence. Armed bands had been infiltrating from Syria and the Egyptian embassy was funneling guns and money to opposition forces. Such measures were all too familiar features of Arab politics, as Nasser often relied on subversion and propaganda to advance his cause. To offset the UAR's intrigues, Chamoun appealed to America for military intervention. The Lebanese president insisted that the Soviet Union was behind Nasser's mischief and that he was being punished for his outspoken support for the United States. Chamoun, who had presented himself as Eisenhower's most dependable ally in the region, was hoping to leverage that stance for American support.

Washington was caught in the dilemma as the needs of its ally conflicted with its sense of prudence. Chamoun was one of the few Arab leaders to publicly embrace the Eisenhower Doctrine and openly proclaim the virtues of pro-Western alignment. To abjure calls for assistance from a steady ally could dishearten other actors seeking better relations with the United States. John Foster Dulles warned, in his typically inflated language, "Our failure to respond would destroy the confidence in the U.S. of all countries in the Soviet periphery and throughout the Middle East and Far East."[18] Yet, Eisenhower still did not want to intervene in the morass of Lebanese politics. The costs were potentially high and the rewards not obvious. So soon after the Suez War, Washington was concerned that a Western military intervention would validate Nasser's rhetoric and further inflame the region. Eisenhower's penchant toward caution and the traditional American imperative of constantly demonstrating credibility now collided, as the president searched for an exit from this latest Middle Eastern trouble.

As Lebanon lurched from crisis to crisis, Eisenhower and Nasser began a back-channel conversation. The pragmatism of both sides was on full display, as the colonel approached the embassy with an offer to help stabilize Lebanon. Eisenhower was thinking along the same lines and had empowered Hare to consult Nasser. Given the sensitivity of America's conservative allies, Hare was to present this as a private initiative whose premature disclosure could have been denied by the White House. The colonel's price for cooperation was that Chamoun leave power after his term expired and be replaced by General Fouad Chehab, a moderate Christian officer. The United States also perceived that the best means of restoring order was for Chamoun to honor the constitution and forgo an additional term in office. The State Department passed the offer on to Chamoun, who summarily rejected it. As often in the past, Washington was bedeviled not just by its adversaries but also by the intransigence of its allies.

When American presidents find themselves in a tough spot and need to buy time, they usually defer the issue to the United Nations. Washington made it clear to Beirut that it required the fig leaf of the United Nations for any potential intervention. The United Nations played its part and soon disappointed Chamoun by dispatching an observatory group to Lebanon. Given that portions of Lebanon's border with Syria were controlled by rebels, the United Nations did not have access to the most contentious areas. Despite these limitations, the U.N. team issued a report denying large-scale intervention by the UAR. Chamoun justifiably complained that given the observers' circumscribed purview, their conclusions were wrong if not misleading. Whatever Chamoun's criticisms may have been, for Eisenhower, the U.N. report gave him an excuse for standing idle.

By June 1958, the need for an American military intervention had receded. Chamoun finally pledged not to seek a second term. The Lebanese president had assumed that by invoking the Soviet threat, he could trigger an American involvement on his behalf. When that appeared not to be the case, he retreated.

The Eisenhower administration had all along sensed that 1958 would be a test of its resolve. Its adversaries were looking for signs of equivocation and its allies were searching for indications of commitment. The need to impress allies and deter enemies did not prevent Eisenhower from searching for ways to defuse crises. He had adopted a tempered approach to the emergence of the UAR and avoided intervention in Lebanon. On both occasions, Eisenhower was open to cooperation with Egypt and explored opportunities for coming to terms with Nasser. For his part, the colonel also tried to limit his conflicts with the United States and looked for ways to put distance between himself and Moscow. But when revolution engulfed Iraq, both sides would find it difficult to sustain their pragmatism.

IRAQ ERUPTS

On July 14, a group of army officers rushed into Baghdad and overthrew a Hashemite monarchy that had ruled since 1921. In one of the more gruesome displays of Arab politics, King Faisal, Crown Prince Abdullah and Prime Minister Nuri al-Said were all assassinated, their bodies subsequently dragged through the streets. On the surface, the events were an eerie reminder of Cairo six years earlier. A group of military men calling themselves the Free Officers had followed the path of their Egyptian counterparts and established cells in the Iraqi military. Humiliated by the defeat of 1948, they turned against a political class they blamed for the creation of Israel. Then came Iraq's isolation from the main currents of Arabism, and its role in fortifying America's containment lines in the Middle East. The usual charges of corruption and economic mismanagement followed, as the monarchy had rewarded its allies to the detriment of Iraq's growing middle class.[19]

Given the self-identification of the plotters as Free Officers, it was not unusual for the Western powers to assume that Nasser had engineered the events. Undoubtedly, the Iraqi officers had attempted to contact Nasser. They were inspired by his model of political activism. In his monumental study of Iraq, Hanna Batatu suggests that these connections were made by the Iraqi politician Saddiq Shanshal, who visited Cairo in 1958.[20] According to Heikal, however, Nasser did not take such entreaties seriously and dismissed the Iraqis until they actually succeeded.[21] Irrespective of such casual contacts, the coup was an Iraqi initiative and a product of the armed forces' frustrations with a complacent monarchy. Iraq and Egypt were destined to remain rivals, whether Baghdad was ruled by monarchs or by military men.

The fate of Iraq was now in the hands of two officers who had engineered the coup, Brigadier General Abdel Karim Qasim and Colonel Abdel Salam Arif. Qasim's principal ideology was Iraqi nationalism and he would prove a reluctant pan-Arabist when such regional unity schemes infringed on Iraq's sovereignty. For his part, Arif was a more committed Nasserist who saw Arab unity as the future. Arif also hoped that by bringing Iraq firmly into the Nasserist fold, he could best secure his domestic position. The rivalry between these two men, and their contending ideological orientations, would define the future of Iraq.[22]

Arif was undone as much by his pan-Arabist proclivities as by his recklessness. Days after the coup, he journeyed to Egypt and promised Iraq's deliverance to the Nasserist camp. When asked by Nasser how Qasim would react to such a step, Arif assured him that the general was a mere figurehead. When pressed further by Nasser, who seemed to know better, Arif stressed that this was not a dispute that a single bullet could not resolve. For his part, Qasim continued to warn that Iraq's national institutions had to mature before he could contemplate any unity schemes. As Arif traveled around Iraq, talking up his pan-

Arabist cause, Qasim patiently consolidated his position. Before long, the champion of Arabism was dispatched to Germany as Iraq's envoy. Once Arif made known his displeasure with diplomatic duty, he was quickly recalled, tried, and sent to prison. This would not be the end of Arif, but it did remove him from the stage at a critical moment.

As master of Iraq, Qasim had no intention of subordinating himself to Nasser and his professions of Arab unity. Iraqis would not behave like Syrians, as their regional pretensions and domestic complications militated against conceding to Nasser's leadership. Iraq's Shias and Kurds, who constituted the majority of the population, saw pan-Arabism as a means of subsuming them in a political structure dominated by Sunnis. In the meantime, Iraq's well-organized communist party also opposed Nasser's unity scheme given his persecution of their brethren in Syria and Egypt. Iraq's new leaders wanted their country to play a prominent role in the Middle East, but that role had to be defined by Iraq's interests and not by Nasser's ambitions.

The complexities of Iraq were largely lost on Western chancelleries, who were shocked by the coup and its aftermath. The revolt had taken place in a bastion of British presence and a reliable American Cold War ally. The pivotal state of Iraq, with its powerful military and ample oil reserves, had seemingly joined the Arab radical caucus. Although Eisenhower was taken by the idea of promoting Saudi Arabia as a counterweight to Nasser's Egypt, Iraq was still the seat of the Baghdad Pact and the linchpin of containment in the Middle East. Coming on the heels of the merger between Syria and Egypt and the disturbances in Lebanon, the rise of the Free Officers in Iraq appeared to herald an age in which the Middle East would be free of relics of the past with its conservative monarchies and their imperial lineage.

As Eisenhower huddled with his advisors, he unwisely and incorrectly attributed events in Iraq to Nasser and the Soviet Union. The president grimly acknowledged that "We must act or get out of the Middle East entirely."[23] For Eisenhower this would be "far worse than the loss in China, because of the strategic position and resources of the Middle East."[24] The internal motivations for the coup and the rivalries that had always divided Baghdad and Cairo were casually set aside.

If the reaction in Washington was one of concern, the mood among its allies was borderline apoplectic.[25] Chamoun quickly summoned the U.S. ambassador to Lebanon Robert McClintock and stressed that the coup was part of a larger Nasserist assault on the existing order. The embassy reported that Chamoun had asked for "U.S. military action in Lebanon within 48 hours."[26] Chamoun's cynicism was on full display, as despite his pledge to honor the constitutional limits on presidential succession, he looked at the latest crisis as a means of enhancing his powers. The Lebanese reaction may have been discounted if it had not been joined by a chorus of conservative anxiety.

In his capacity as the titular head of state, Saud chimed in with his own warnings. The monarch stressed that if the United States and Britain reacted passively, "they are finished as powers in the Middle East."[27] The Saudis demanded an immediate dispatch of troops to fortify the beleaguered front-line conservative states of Jordan and Lebanon, as well as the reversal of the coup in Iraq itself. Barring such drastic action, Saudi Arabia warned that it may have to consider placating Nasser and his allies.[28] In the coming years, such claims would be repeated often. Whenever the Saudis grew disenchanted with Washington, they would threaten to cozy up to America's nemeses.

The region's crisis also unsettled a British officialdom nursing its own objections to Nasser. After its eviction from the Arab East, Britain had preserved its imperial trappings by maintaining a presence in the Persian Gulf region. The decapitation of Hashemite rulers that London had placed on the throne of Iraq caused considerable consternation in Whitehall. Prime Minister Harold Macmillan once more rekindled the British animus toward Nasser with comparisons to Hitler and Europe of the 1930s. Macmillan advised that the Iraq issue be dispatched to an emergency session of the U.N. Security Council, where the inevitable

Russian veto would free the United States and Britain to intervene. As the allies contemplated their moves, the next country on the verge of implosion was the Hashemite Kingdom of Jordan.[29]

Given its daunting internal challenges, Jordan's position seemed perennially combustible. The sizeable Palestinian population that had settled there after the 1948 war brought with it its own set of grievances. In the view of the Palestinians, the Hashemites had always collaborated with imperial powers to expand their kingdom at the Palestinians' expense. The tale of King Hussein's grandfather, King Abdullah, conspiring with the fledgling Zionist entity to divide up Palestine had led to his assassination in 1951 and had forever tarnished the reputation of his descendants. This aggrieved Palestinian population would be difficult to absorb in the best of times; 1958 was hardly an ideal year, as the temper of the region was bound to excite Palestinian protest.

Simmering tensions came to a head with the discovery of a military coup against King Hussein planned a few days after the overthrow of his cousin Faisal. The murder of Iraq's royal family and the break of its union with Jordan had already enraged Hussein, who had even contemplated military intervention. Once disabused of such notions, he had to confront a plot within an armed forces that was supposed to be the source of his authority. The chief culprit this time was Lieutenant Colonel Mahmoud Pusan, who had previously served in Washington. Pusan was alleged to have received support from Syria, thus directly implicating Nasser. News of the coup led Hussein to go public and officially ask for assistance. Although the king was not beyond fulminating against communists as a means of getting more American aid, this time the threats against his rule and life seemed genuine.[30]

The regional turmoil caused the Eisenhower administration to move into high gear. The surprising aspect of Iraq's revolt was how it blindsided both Washington and London. Baghdad had been seething with rumors, conspiracies, and intrigues of all sorts. It is hard to see how the United States did not anticipate a coup. Still, after the uprising,

Eisenhower mourned to Dulles that "it looks as if we have a solid Arab world against us."[31] The secretary of state agreed, responding, "We must regard Arab nationalism as a flood which is running strongly, we cannot successfully oppose it but we can put up sand bags around positions we must protect."[32] The CIA and the State Department affirmed these forebodings by stressing that the Middle East was at a crossroads, with the radical forces in ascendance.

Despite these anxieties, there was no clear consensus within the administration about how to proceed. Dulles and Vice President Richard Nixon seemed most eager for armed intervention in Iraq. However, such schemes were unacceptable to a military leadership that had witnessed the undoing of the Anglo-French invasion of Egypt two years earlier. Eisenhower, always parsimonious about forceful interventions, also did not relish overturning Iraq's revolution by war. As an astute student of history, Eisenhower appreciated that assaulting revolutionary states seldom redounds to the advantage of the conqueror. Still, the Arab conservatives were panicking. The United States had to reassure them.

The Eisenhower administration now resolved to make Lebanon the example of its commitment to the region.[33] Jordan seemed a less desirable candidate, as American officialdom had convinced itself that King Hussein's improbable country could not survive in the long run.[34] The notion of international communism threatening Lebanon may have been absurd, but it proved convenient. Whatever Chamoun's limitations, the Lebanese government was the most pro-Western regime in the region and it was being challenged by forces that were bound to be less friendly to the United States and its Cold War mandates.

Having made the decision to intervene, Eisenhower turned to his skeptical legislators. Falling dominoes and loss of credibility once more proved powerful instruments of persuasion. Dulles unleashed the usual case, stressing, "Turkey, Iran and Pakistan would feel—if we do not act—that our inaction is because we are afraid of the Soviet Union."[35] Senators Mike Mansfield and William Fulbright pushed back, challenging the notion that U.S. standing was at stake in a distant civil war. Nonetheless, Eisenhower's stature and fears of Soviet communism carried the day.

On July 15, 1958, Operation Blue Bat was launched, deploying fourteen thousand U.S. personnel to Lebanon. The U.S. deployment in Lebanon was accompanied by the dispatch of diplomatic trouble-shooter Robert Murphy. Murphy's mission was to forge a political compromise and make sure that Chamoun adhered to his commitment to vacate the presidency. Murphy proved a diligent diplomat as he operated effectively in Lebanon's bewildering political environment. General Chehab was elected as the new president, and for the time being Lebanon's fragile National Pact was preserved. The American role may have been symbolic, but symbolism has its uses. The fact that U.S. intervention was greeted with Soviet passivity helped undermine the notion popular in leftist circles that Moscow was capable and willing to stand up to the United States in the Middle East. After the landing of U.S. troops, conservatives across the region were less nervous and the radicals more anxious.

Although it is popular in recent historiography to denigrate the intervention in Lebanon as Marines landing on beaches populated by tourists and vacationers, the operation was not logistically simple. The landing of such a large number of troops required careful coordination between the U.S. embassy and the Lebanese army. The American forces took up positions throughout Beirut and yet still managed to avoid an altercation with Lebanon's many armed groups. It is a credit to Eisenhower that the landing remains the largest military deployment of his presidency. The fact that he managed the incursion carefully and avoided other military entanglements presented to him is a testimony to his caution and common sense.

As we have seen, Washington wanted to demonstrate resolve in the region but seemed indifferent to the fate of the Jordanian monarchy. The Americans were willing to steady Lebanon, but were reluctant to prop up Hussein. Having come to view Jordan as an unlikely country, Washington sensed that sooner or later it would succumb to its predatory neighbors. Moreover, Eisenhower had assured domestic lawmakers that he would not pursue military action beyond Lebanon. Here British prodding proved a useful antidote to American pessimism, as Whitehall was not prepared to concede another Hashemite monarchy to Arab nationalism.

Britain's pressure finally compelled a degree of American support. Eisenhower endorsed the deployment of British paratroopers to Jordan while rejecting Macmillan's calls for a joint operation.[36] The United States sustained its modest aid program and persuaded Israel to allow passage of British aircraft over its territory. Robert Murphy was dispatched to Cairo to warn Nasser to stay out of Jordan. The tireless American emissary cautioned the colonel that violence against the kingdom "could not be confined to Jordan itself. . . . .It is in the interest of everybody concerned that steps be taken to prevent creation of a situation that might result in such hostilities."[37]

In a sense, Murphy did not have to concern himself with Nasser's mischief. The reaction of the Arab republics was symbolic and muted. Nasser released a perfunctory statement denouncing the twin interventions as endangering the region. Radio Cairo did not thunder with its typical bombastic denunciations. The Syrian military went on alert but stayed within its borders. The Suez Canal remained open and the Iraqi oil pipelines traversing Syria went unmolested. Once Nasser was rebuffed by Khrushchev for more active gestures of support, he recognized that caution was his best approach. The Eisenhower administration had succeeded in preventing Iraq's crisis from enveloping the conservative states of Lebanon and Jordan, and in the process, the administration had obtained Britain's help and Nasser's grudging acquiescence.

By August, the situation in Lebanon and Jordan seemed to improve as both sides regained confidence. Nasser eased up on Jordan and toned down his broadsides against Hussein. In Lebanon, the political settlement allowed curfews to ease and militants to disarm. The United Nations stepped up its activities in both countries, enlarging its presence and enhancing its monitoring systems. The new U.N. infrastructure allowed the Western powers to begin withdrawing their troops. As the Anglo-American forces departed, all eyes once more turned to Baghdad, where Iraq would set the surprising stage for yet another rapprochement between Cairo and Washington.

REAPPRAISALS

The Iraqi communist party under the leadership of Hussein al-Radi had emerged as an effective political organization with a presence throughout the country. Active among the peasantry as well as the urban working class, the party was capable of organizing vast demonstrations. Beyond street politics, the party created a popular resistance militia that gave it paramilitary muscle. As with its Eastern European counterparts, the Iraqi communist party began taking over professional associations and civil society groups. While held in check during the monarchy, the communists took full advantage of the postrevolutionary chaos to solidify their gains.

For Qasim, the party's tight structure and cohesive networks made it an ideal instrument of his power. Locked in conflict with Nasserists and Arab nationalists, Qasim needed allies and granted the party freedom to conduct its activities. Qasim's lenient attitude toward the communists paved the way for better relations with a Soviet Union already disenchanted with Nasser's independence and looking for a new base in the Middle East. In due course, Qasim would crack down on the communists, driven as he was by authoritarian nationalism rather than Marxist affinities. Still, Qasim's infatuation with the communists set off alarm bells in Washington and Cairo.[38]

As Eisenhower was sorting out Lebanon, a stream of alarmist reports about the impending communist takeover of Iraq confronted him. The National Intelligence Estimate predicted that Qasim "lacked the ability to stem the movement toward a communist takeover."[39] The U.S. ambassador to Iraq, John Jernegan, similarly stressed that the "basic question remains whether Qasim and the government of Iraq are too far along the road to Communism to turn back."[40] Allen Dulles summed up the collective judgment of the bureaucracy by claiming that "events seem to be moving in the direction of ultimate Communist control."[41] The U.S. intelligence and diplomatic services that had failed to foresee the Iraqi coup were now confidently predicting a communist takeover.

The simmering in Baghdad also distressed Colonel Nasser, who recognized that far from being subservient to Egypt, Iraq, with Soviet support, was reviving its claim to regional leadership. It was easy for Nasser to decry the Iraqi monarchy as a lackey of the West, but now he was being challenged by revolutionaries with impeccable anti-imperialist credentials. In a typical move, Nasser began attacking Qasim for dividing the progressive wing of Arab politics and being submissive to a foreign power. The Egyptian president was even less subtle when he denounced Qasim as the "Red butcher." Qasim responded by denigrating Egypt and belittling Nasser's achievements.[42] The conflict between the two states was not limited to a war of words, as Nasser soon activated his covert network of spies and saboteurs.

In March 1959, a military coup led by nationalist officer Abdel al-Wahab Shawaf implicated the UAR. The plot apparently began when Syrian officials made contact with tribal leaders and anticommunist officers. The plan envisioned tribal chiefs starting an insurrection that the military would be compelled to suppress. Once armed units were deployed, they would move against the central government. The entire affair fell apart in a matter of hours and Colonel Shawaf was summarily executed.[43]

Nasser's participation in such a clumsy plot reflected the unique challenge that Qasim posed to his aspirations and power. The colonel seemed baffled that his usual techniques of propaganda and subversion had not generated real opposition to Qasim. Given his nationalist credentials and his power base, Qasim could withstand Radio Cairo's invectives and Nasser's machinations better than the region's monarchs could. Moreover, Iraq challenged the principal tenet of Nasserism, namely that if an Arab state emancipated itself from reactionary rule it had to join the pan-Arabist crusade led by Egypt. Suddenly, a revolutionary leader had come to power and instead of joining Cairo's regional enterprise, was busy assaulting Nasser from the left. The rise of Qasim proved worse for Nasser than the conservative monarchies and their Western benefactors had.

The Iraq imbroglio also complicated Nasser's relations with the Soviet Union. At a time when Baghdad was complaining about Egyptian intrigue, Moscow took Iraq's side. Khrushchev was never at ease with Nasser's notion that all Arabs belonged to a single community free of external influence. Such sentiments could awaken Central Asian Muslims that were themselves struggling under a different form of Western domination. Moreover, unlike Nasser, the Kremlin welcomed the rise of the communist party in Iraq and even sought to shift its support from Cairo to Baghdad.[44]

In the aftermath of Iraq's revolution, Nasser was once more a leader in search of a role. He had to defang Qasim and isolate his revolutionary state. That meant mending fences with Jordanian and Saudi monarchies that Radio Cairo had been eviscerating as reactionary relics. Nasser also offered soothing words to the United States. In an interview with *Life* he boasted about jailing communists because of "their opposition to Arab nationalism and the UAR."[45] In a sly note, he even chided Israel for not banning its communist party the way Egypt had done. Perhaps, Nasser realized that the pendulum had swung too far to the left and that he needed an American leverage.

The Eisenhower administration was also reexamining its assumptions and dispatched Assistant Secretary of State William Rountree for a tour of the region. Rountree reported that "Nasser is showing real concerns over Communist penetration of the Middle East" and recommended better ties with Cairo.[46] The thrust of the new policy was codified in NSC 5820/1, which called for a fresh approach to Arab nationalism. The NSC study claimed that the United States had a range of interests in the Middle East, and that the most important was thwarting Soviet advances in the region. Nasser and his nationalist allies had done much to diminish the power of the communists in Egypt and Syria. As such, there was a basis for greater accommodation between the two parties. At the same time, Washington would continue to buttress the conservative monarchies.[47]

Eisenhower's nuanced approach to regional politics and his essential pragmatism once again came to the surface. The president stressed that the overriding purpose of the U.S. containment policy was to deny the region to the Soviet Union. If Nasser was willing to cooperate with that objective for his own reasons, that was fine with Eisenhower. The collapse of Iraq to communism was too dire to contemplate and Nasser's help in preventing that outcome could be rewarded. In the end, Eisenhower concluded that "we could support Nasser when this is not contrary to our interests."[48] After all, the president mused to his advisors that Nasser could probably resist communism in the Arab world better than the occidental powers could.

The culmination of these reassessments was Eisenhower's meeting with Nasser at the edge of the U.N. General Assembly in September 1960. In their first and only meeting, Eisenhower found Nasser to be an impressive and decisive leader. For his part, Nasser was effusive in his praise of U.S. conduct during the Suez War. The Egyptian colonel assured the American general that there was no tension between Arab nationalism and legitimate American interests in the Middle East. Nasser regurgitated the usual Arab complaints about U.S. support for

Israel and its excessive Cold War preoccupation, but such gestures were the hallmark of the times and hardly obscured the fact that the relationship between the two sides rested on a firmer setting.

As Cairo and Washington edged closer to a common outlook on Iraq, Qasim once more surprised his critics and allies alike. Having survived various challenges to his rule, Qasim grew suspicious of his erstwhile communist allies. The Iraqi communist party was growing more vocal, staging rallies and demanding a greater presence in government. Qasim turned the table on them by proclaiming, "Groupings, parties and party politics [are] not at the moment beneficial to the country."[49] Thus began the purging of the communists from state institutions, trade unions, and the armed forces. This was probably Qasim's design all along—he had cynically used the communists to vanquish his other enemies.

By the close of the 1950s, the Iraqi regime appeared less menacing than its blood-soaked rise to power would suggest. Baghdad began assuring Washington that it had no interest in joining with Nasser and merging with the UAR. The Iraqi government also honored its existing oil agreements and refrained from nationalization measures. This was partly an economic imperative, as the petroleum market was awash in oil and the producing states did not have the leverage that they would one day wield. Iraq had to lure customers and not repel them. The lesson of Muhammad Mossadeq in Iran was that no country was indispensable to the world oil market. From Washington's perspective, it suddenly garnered another win over the Soviet Union that had invested in yet another opportunistic Arab officer.

POSTSCRIPT

The UAR that was to launch a political avalanche in the region ultimately failed to displace the old order. Jordan teetered on the brink but refused to yield. In Lebanon, the American intervention may not have extinguished international communism but it did permit an orderly transition from Chamoun's government. In Iraq, whose politics have been perennially misdiagnosed, discontent among its social classes may have decapitated a monarchy but hardly created loyal Nasserists. The radicals soon bickered among themselves, discrediting the notion that Arab solidarity transcended national boundaries. The Western interventions of 1958 provided a psychological boost to rulers who feared the tide of history. Assured by Western pledges and buttressed by Anglo-American troops, the conservatives not only rebounded but reclaimed the region. By 1967 an altogether different wind would blow though the Arab world, sweeping away the edifice of pan-Arabism once and for all.

The superpower that perennially misread the region's politics was not the United States but the Soviet Union. The advent of the Egyptian revolution initially raised hopes in Moscow that it could anchor its presence on a nationalist foundation. Nasser proved feckless, independent, and difficult to manage. Then he went about persecuting communists throughout the region while receiving Soviet aid. The rise of Qasim and his close collaboration with Iraq's communist party excited the Russians into believing that they had finally found a durable foothold in the Arab world. The Soviet propaganda praised Qasim's revolutionary model and admonished Nasser for his truculence. Moscow failed to appreciate the ephemeral nature of Arab officers' ideological attachments. As with Nasser, Qasim was a nationalist who used the communist party to advance his goals and then quickly discarded it.

It is often lamented by scholars that anticommunism blinded the United States to regional complexities. Granted, the containment of the Soviet Union was the overarching American objective. But the Eisenhower Doctrine's rhetoric about international communism should not obscure its clever and nuanced implementation. The administration benefited from having cagy allies. The American intervention helped the Lebanese preserve their National Pact and discipline Chamoun.

In Jordan, the British took the lead while King Hussein took command of his situation. And Saudi Arabia's opaque palace politics still managed to empower a crown prince whose judicious stewardship may have saved the kingdom.

Yet another cause of Eisenhower's success was his ability to reexamine his assumptions and reconsider his adversaries. During his second term, Eisenhower decoupled his policy from the notion that Nasser would serve as a surrogate of American power in the Middle East. The resolution of the Arab-Israeli conflict also took a backseat, paradoxically allowing Washington to improve relations with both Cairo and Jerusalem.[50] Eisenhower came to understand that Egypt would neither embrace the U.S. Cold War mandates nor become a Soviet satellite. The best that Washington could hope for was tactical cooperation between the two sides when their interests coincided. And that was fine with Eisenhower.

The challenge of alliances also taxed Eisenhower's considerable diplomatic skill. Eisenhower was mindful of his allies' sensitivities and his outreach to Nasser was always conditioned by those concerns. Yet, his overall record indicates that he shrewdly discharged his competing obligations to sustain the alliance system and respond to Nasser's entreaties. The two-track policy may have had its share of contradictions but those inconsistencies were usually managed.

At the end of his tenure, Eisenhower could step back and take a measure of Arab politics. The Suez War was the nadir of Western fortunes in the Middle East. Britain stood discredited and crestfallen while the Arab conservatives were on the brink of despair. Four years later, the conservative order displayed a resilience that surprised even its American benefactors. Britain found a useful place in the region as a junior partner to the United States. More importantly, Nasser was cut to size with the UAR imploding and the Syrians going their own way. The colonel seemed at odds with Iraqi Free Officers, whose radicalism and opportunism offended even him. Eisenhower appreciated the different shades of Arabism and Nasser's inability to shape the contours of that powerful force.

The rivalries of the Arab world always benefited America, as it was well positioned to take advantage of the region's fissures. The United States was the only actor capable of restraining Israel, rehabilitating Britain, safeguarding the monarchies, and rescuing the radicals from predicaments of their own making. Eisenhower was never uncritical of his allies or unforgiving of his adversaries. Everyone had to deal with Washington because America had something to offer all the parties. And that is something that neither Nasser's Egypt nor Khrushchev's Russia could claim.

CHAPTER 6

THE SIX-DAY WAR

The Six-Day War of June 1967 was an inflection point in the history of the modern Middle East. The Israeli defeat of combined Arab forces marked the beginning of the end of Soviet regional influence. Conversely, the war solidified the position of the United States as the most influential outside power in the Middle East.

The war was also a classic Cold War proxy struggle, and was seen in this light by the United States and the Soviet Union. Soviet Middle East strategy aimed to enhance its regional influence by drawing "progressive" Arab nationalists to its side through arms transfers and diplomatic support. The United States sought to counter Soviet maneuvering by triangulating between its nascent security relationship with Israel and its support for Jordan and the oil monarchies on the Arab side of the Persian Gulf. Still, neither superpower saw the Middle East as the primary locus of Cold War confrontation. During the 1960s, both sides had spent incomparably more bureaucratic, military, and financial resources on Central Europe and, in the case of the United States, on Southeast Asia than on the Middle East. Born of distraction, superpower policy in the Middle East was largely neglected for other theaters where the stakes were thought to be greater.

The consequent policy drift had cleared the space for regional pow-ers to maximize their local political interests. On the Arab side, a micro-cosmic cold war between the Arab nationalist "confrontation states" aligned with Egypt's Gamal Abdel Nasser and the conservative Saudi and Jordanian monarchies drove regional politics.[1] This cold war had little to do with the global Cold War; it was instead rooted in the strug-gle for power among Arab elites. And Israel, by 1967 approaching the twentieth anniversary of independence, was simultaneously distracted by a stagnating domestic economy and aggressive in confronting the challenges posed by a new generation of rejectionist Arab regimes.

As such, the Six-Day War occurred despite the global Cold War, not because of it. Both superpowers sought to manipulate regional tensions to enhance their influence; yet a broader regional war and the atten-dant possibility of direct superpower conflict were of interest to neither. Instead, domestic and regional political pressures drove local actors to subordinate the interests of their superpower patrons in pursuit of their own. The United States and the Soviet Union were to go along for the ride, hostages to their clients' will.

Washington was luckier in its choice of allies than was Moscow. Both superpowers failed at every turn to shape events to their interests or to impede the Arab-Israeli escalatory spiral. The superpowers, though, were not simply bystanders. They did err in omission or commission at points that facilitated the war. But Arab-Israeli interests and fears made war very difficult to prevent. The insecurities and animosities that drove the hostilities lingered and continued to define the Arab-Israeli conflict, despite peace agreements that eventually followed between Israel and Egypt and Jordan.

THE SOVIET UNION: STIRRING THE POT

By June 1967, the Soviet Union had made significant bilateral inroads in the Middle East, but its influence over regional powers was limited.

Soviet ideology did not resonate well. Its Arab nationalist clients in Syria and Egypt were inconstant friends. Soviet leaders saw the Middle East as an area of opportunity for gains against the United States but one shot through with risk and ideological compromise.

Thus, it is unsurprising that the goals of Soviet Middle East policy in the mid-1960s were specific and limited. The Soviet Union sought regional advantage at the expense of the United States, but generally at the least possible cost and risk. This tended to devolve to stoking the embers of local conflict while stopping short of combustion. The Arab-Israeli conflict presented an easy opening for Moscow to pursue this cycle by supporting Arab nationalists in Syria and Egypt against Israel. The U.S. intelligence community at the time assessed the situation in just this way: "[The Soviets]," wrote CIA analysts in a 1970 postmortem of the war, "continue to believe that the maintenance of Arab-Israeli tension at a high pitch augments Soviet influence in the area."[2]

Despite setbacks stemming from the rise of the Arab nationalist left, the United States found useful allies in Israel, the Arab monarchies, and Iran. Militarily, the U.S. Navy's Sixth Fleet dominated the eastern Mediterranean, effectively denying the maritime domain to the Soviet navy. In addition, the Central Treaty Organization (CENTO), which succeeded the Baghdad Pact following Iraq's departure in 1959, stretched across the northern tier of the Middle East and Central Asia, providing base access and staging areas for U.S. strategic bombers. On balance, the Soviets had the greater cause to see strategic threats emanating from the Middle East than did the United States.

The origins of increased Soviet involvement in the Middle East, however, lay in the reorientation of Soviet foreign policy in the wake of Stalin's death in 1953. A more pragmatic generation of leaders favored "peaceful coexistence" with the United States to reduce the risk of an apocalyptic war beginning on the north German plain.[3] With the battle lines thus fixed in Europe, geopolitical competition migrated to peripheral battlefields.

This strategic shift called for fierce political and economic competition between the superpowers, but stopped short of promoting armed conflict with the United States, whether direct or by proxy. Hence the CIA's 1966 judgment that "on balance . . . the men who took over from Khrushchev [Leonid Brezhnev and Alexei Kosygin] almost two years ago have been conspicuous in their cautious approach to both foreign and domestic problems."[4] The prevailing U.S government perspective was that, despite its aggressive designs, the Soviet Union could be a force for restraint in the Middle East and, in particular, in the Arab-Israeli conflict. According to another contemporary intelligence estimate:

> Although periods of increased tension in the Arab-Israeli dispute will occur from time to time, both sides appear to appreciate that large-scale military action involves considerable risk and no assurance of leading to a solution. In any event, the chances are good that the threat of great power intervention will prevent an attempt by either side to resolve the problem by military force.[5]

Israelis seemed to have agreed with this broad assessment but saw little ground for optimism. In their view, Soviet Middle East policy followed what then Mossad chief Meir Amit called a "Cuban model," because the strategic logic of the Cuban Missile Crisis of 1962 seemed to symbolize best the provocative impulse that Jerusalem believed animated Soviet policy. Amit maintained that the Soviet approach was "practically transmitted to the Egyptians and Syrians . . . to play at brinksmanship, to go up to a point and then retreat and gain some political benefits out of this movement."[6] Israelis described the Soviet desire for "small rather than big trouble" and "tensions without explosions."[7] The available Soviet documents do not explicitly endorse brinksmanship by proxy as the Soviet Union's mid-1960s Middle East policy, but General Secretary of the Central Committee of the Communist Party Leonid Brezhnev came close in a 1967 postmortem on the Arab defeat in the Six-Day War: "The fundamental aims," he declared, "of our party's policy in this region [include] strengthening our influence, undermining the positions of imperialism, and utmost support of the struggle of peoples for national liberation."[8]

The "Cuban model" required a degree of control over Arab nationalist regimes in Egypt and Syria. But this was not so easily established. The Soviets "did not consider Arab leaders to be dutiful 'clients' like the leaders of the Warsaw Pact countries . . . Yet, the Soviet leaders were genuinely convinced that the Arabs would never undertake serious steps without consulting them and when they did so in fact, the Soviet Union believed it would be able to rein them in."[9] It was enough for the Soviet leadership that Nasser and the Syrian Ba'athists were anti-American; any differences could be mitigated by arms transfers and artful sloganeering, such as labeling the often explicitly anticommunist regimes "non-capitalist revolutionary democrat[s]."[10]

THE UNITED STATES: IN BIG MUDDY

As the Soviets were deepening their involvement in the Middle East, the United States was increasingly bogged down in Vietnam. By 1967, American casualties and domestic ferment were peaking, and the Middle East could not compete with Southeast Asia for the attention and resources of President Lyndon Johnson's administration. Policy makers were not oblivious to Soviet maneuvering in the Middle East, but they lacked the time, energy, and focus to grapple systematically with regional geopolitical dynamics.

Johnson administration documents consistently depict the Middle East as the source of potentially dangerous distractions from the war in Vietnam. A year before war broke in June 1967, Johnson's national security advisor, Walt Rostow, warned the president, "Few other events would be as likely to tempt a pre-emptive Israeli attack and trigger a major Mid-East fracas as the threat of a Nasserist takeover in Jordan.

We cannot afford to get caught in a mess like that, especially while we are pushing ahead in Vietnam."[11] The administration, of course, would be swept up in an eerily similar scenario in the run-up to the June war.

The political fallout of Vietnam loomed large over American Middle East policy before the Six-Day War. The perceived bait-and-switch of the 1964 Gulf of Tonkin Resolution had made both Congress and the electorate chary of any further overseas involvements. At that time, the Johnson administration had justified bombing North Vietnam by insisting that Hanoi had attacked American naval vessels patrolling international waterways. The truth was that those U.S. ships had been involved in espionage and sabotage operations along the coast of North Vietnam. William Quandt, who served on the National Security Council staff, later recalled that:

> It's necessary . . . to say that Vietnam was a powerful background element in . . . American thinking in the 1967 crisis. The president was beginning to experience a strong domestic reaction to his Vietnam policy. Congress, which had supported the Gulf of Tonkin resolution, was turning against the war, and over and over again Johnson referred to Congress and what happened in Vietnam. There's even a phrase in one of the documents about "Gulf of Tonkinitis" as a kind of disease that has infected the Congress.[12]

American policy makers believed that the best course would be to keep the Arab-Israeli conflict "in the icebox."[13] This fell short of the more activist posture advocated by Middle East experts in the government. Hal Saunders, who served on the NSC staff before and during the war, advised that the United States had an interest in "building the kind of Middle East that will stop the U.S.S.R. short of eventual predominant influence à la Eastern Europe or Cuba" and concluded, somewhat optimistically, that "[the United States was] doing pretty well" in achieving this goal.[14]

Reality dictated otherwise. The U.S. relationship with Gamal Abdel Nasser, which had held a measure of promise as recently as John F. Kennedy's administration, was in disarray, while in Syria an intraparty coup had installed anti-American hardliners Salah Jadid and Hafez al-Assad.

Having lost Arab nationalists to Soviet influence, American policy makers focused on preserving the U.S. relationship with the conservative Arab monarchies and Israel. A triangular alliance, even a tacit one, was unavailable given the Arab monarchies' reluctance to be tarred with the Israeli brush via their relationship with Washington. But their choices were constrained by their fears of the Soviet Union and radical Arab states and these dictated reliance on U.S. patronage. The U.S. relationship with Israel in any case was cautious and relatively distant.

Washington's hands-off policy was possible only because the Middle East did not yet occupy a central space in American political discourse. The American Jewish community still had an ambivalent relationship with Israel and Israelis. Despite the important role played by American Jews in Truman's decision to recognize Israel in 1948, the domestic Jewish community was not galvanized by Zionist ideals. By the mid-1960s only twenty thousand American Jews had immigrated to the new state.[15] Where Israelis had expected strong identification with the Jewish state, a 1967 report on American Jews by Zionist activist Eliezer Livneh, who had been dispatched to the United States by Israeli Prime Minister Levi Eshkol, stressed that many of them were uncomfortable with Israel's dependence on the United States. He concluded that this perception "greatly decreases [Israel's] moral standing."[16] Elie Wiesel, a towering moral authority and Holocaust survivor, told the Israeli newspaper *Ha'aretz* that "the Jewishness of [American] Jewish youth can still be reached, but not through Israel."[17] Self-conscious assimilation—what in 1964 *Look* magazine termed "the vanishing American Jew"—was the order of the day.[18]

What the large community of liberal American Jews did care about was Vietnam. Rabbi Joachim Prinz, the chairman of the Conference of Presidents of Major American Jewish Organizations, deplored Israel for its "lack of social concerns, the fact that we do not hear the voice of religious Israel in terms of peace and war, social justice, integration, and similar issues."[19] He went on to warn Eshkol in a letter that "American Jews' commitment to Israel was not so profound as to influence their position on Vietnam."[20]

Johnson was seriously disconcerted by American Jewish foreign policy priorities. The president had hoped to bargain for Jewish support, or at least acquiescence, on Vietnam in return for his support for Israel. According to former Israeli president Zalman Shazar, Johnson told him "[American] Jewish support for the Vietnam involvement was his due in light of his record of support for Israel."[21] When one did not follow the other, Johnson was characteristically furious. He threatened to link continued American support of Israel with a more cooperative attitude on the part of American Jews. In a call with President Shazar, Johnson asked if

> because of critics of our Vietnam policy, we did not fulfill our commitments to the 16 million people in Vietnam, how could we be expected to fulfill our commitments to 2 million Israelis? Yet some friends of Israel in the United States had publicly criticized U.S. policy in Vietnam . . . Our failure to carry through in Vietnam would be bound to affect our ability to carry through in our commitment to other small states such as Israel.[22]

These were private ruminations. For public consumption, Johnson said that he considered himself a "Jewish non-Jew" in whom Israel had found "an even better [friend]" than Kennedy, who had at times flirted with radicals such as Nasser.[23] But they provide a small but revealing window on the way the conflict in Vietnam had shaped Johnson's approach to the Middle East before the Six-Day War.

ISRAEL: SHIMSHOYN DER NEBECHDIKKER

The U.S. preoccupation with Vietnam worried Israeli officials who foresaw a day when they would need American assistance and none would be forthcoming. Ephraim "Eppie" Evron, the second-ranking Israeli official in Washington during the Six-Day War, remembered, "We watched the West wholeheartedly support part of the world, while at the same time the Soviet Union supported the other part. [Both] the United States and Britain cold-shouldered Israel at that time, which in turn weakened her politically and militarily. We felt extremely isolated and endangered. That feeling . . . prevailed until the Six-Day War."[24]

Yet, concern about American reliability was not the only—or even the primary—source of the sense of insecurity and malaise that suffused Israeli society in the mid-1960s. In this period, American-Israeli ties were warming, but were not yet the "special relationship" into which they would evolve. Israel had seen various patrons come and go in the previous two decades—the Soviet Union and France among them—and its relationship with the United States, while important, did not dominate Israeli strategic thinking.

Israel was preoccupied by domestic as well as strategic concerns. The end of postwar Holocaust reparations had led to a contraction of the Israeli economy; economic growth was nearly flat. Simultaneously, unemployment jumped to 12.4 percent in 1966.[25] The resulting emigration from Israel heightened the sense of dislocation and torpor that contributed to these statistics and was intensified by them.

In the strategic realm, Israel feared a second Holocaust, this time at the hands of the Arabs. Cross-border raids by Palestinian guerrillas had been a constant since 1949, but their tempo increased in the mid-1960s at the urging of Syria's militant new regime. Of equal concern were Nasser's persistent, if unsuccessful, efforts to unify the Arab world militarily and ideologically against Israel. Israeli diplomat Shimon Shamir recalled that "in the perception of Israelis at that time, this pressure

constituted a real danger to the survival of the state. With today's hind-
sight this may seem a somewhat exaggerated concern, but we are talking about Israel of the 1950s and 1960s, an Israel not at all certain that
time was not working in favor of its Arab adversaries."[26] Syrian rhetoric
calling for "total war with no limits" and proclaiming a resolution "to
drench this land with our blood, to oust you aggressor and throw you
into the sea for good" raised Israeli anxiety to fever pitch.[27]

To deter aggression from neighboring countries, the Israel Defense
Forces (IDF) adopted a policy of disproportionate retaliation against
Palestinian guerrillas, while at the same time reassuring Israeli society
of the IDF's substantial military superiority over the armies of Israel's
adversaries. Government ministers, some of whom were skeptical of
the so-called reprisals, tended to concur with this strategy. This acquiescence, however, concealed the fundamental tension between the IDF
Chief of Staff Yitzhak Rabin and ministers, such as Foreign Minister
Abba Eban, who were more confident in Israel's ability to emerge from
the spring 1967 crisis intact. Tom Segev, an Israeli historian, captured
the psychology that drove the IDF leaders' approach to the Arabs as
well as to their fellow Israelis:

> For Rabin and the generals, most of whom were Israeli born,
> [the reprisal policy] was not merely a professional military issue,
> but a question of their prestige, their dignity, and their image as
> Sabra warriors facing weak-spirited politicians. They viewed these
> Eastern Europeans, some of whom were three decades older than
> they, as clinging to 'Diaspora psychology.' The belief that terror-
> ism could be overcome by defensive means might bring about the
> construction of electric fences along the borders, said Rabin, and
> 'they'll turn Israel into another ghetto.' When speaking at General
> Staff meetings, Rabin used to refer to Eshkol and his ministers as
> 'the Jews.'[28]

Prime Minister Eshkol appreciated the logic of retaliation but was skeptical of the generals' oscillating aggression and timidity. Eshkol, who still thought in Yiddish and would invoke homespun epigrams, referred to the general staff as *shimshoyn der nebechdikker*—"a pathetic Samson." Nevertheless, the climate of fear played to the hawks' advantage. When one particularly disproportionate response to a Palestinian attack escalated dramatically and counterproductively in Jordanian territory, Eshkol drily observed that the IDF was supposed "to give the mother-in-law a pinch, but instead . . . beat up the bride."[29]

EGYPT: THE VOICE OF THE ARABS

Eshkol's concern about the Arab response to Israeli retaliatory raids displayed a keen and rare appreciation for the forces that drove Arab politics before the Six-Day War. Above all, the fissure between conservative monarchies and revolutionary nationalists that Malcolm Kerr, the president of the American University of Beirut until his 1984 assassination by pro-Iranian militants, called the Arab Cold War defined the Arab political landscape. This kind of intra-Arab struggle dated back to before the 1948 Arab-Israeli war, but it came into sharp relief with Nasser's rise in Egypt and subsequent nationalist coups in Syria, Iraq, and Yemen. The resultant bidding for prestige created an escalatory spiral of bloody rhetoric and proxy conflict that pushed all the Arab parties toward war with Israel.

The irony was that in the mid-1960s, Israel per se was not the key issue for either conservative or revolutionary Arab regimes. Instead, rhetorical opposition to the Jewish state was the metric by which the two sides displayed their "Arabness," the currency for rulers fearful that anemic and ineffectual assertions of nationalist prerogative would not be sufficient to buttress their popular legitimacy and immunize them from intra-regime challenges to their rule. Rococo threats of death and destruction to Israel, regardless of intention let alone capability, were required for political survival.

But, in parallel with the protagonists in the global Cold War, neither conservative nor nationalist Arab regimes desired a shooting war with Israel. Instead, as Malcolm Kerr wrote, "when the Arabs are in a mood to cooperate, this tends to find expression in an agreement to avoid action on Palestine, but . . . when they choose to quarrel, Palestine policy really becomes a subject of dispute."[30] Israel, in effect, became the symbolic bludgeon with which the two sides battered each other's pan-Arab credentials. Arab fears of one another and their own citizens—not of Israel—drove the Arab Cold War.

Against this background, the November 1966 raid on the Jordanian village of as-Samu' sparked the escalatory cycle that led to the Six-Day War. In the wake of Jordan's thrashing by the IDF at as-Samu', Nasser and Syrian Ba'athists both sensed an opportunity to undermine King Hussein. The Syrians were the first to act, accusing Jordan of having intentionally permitted an Israeli victory as part of a plot between "the reactionary Jordanian regime and imperialist Zionism."[31] Nasser's influential state radio broadcast *Sawt al-Arab* ("Voice of the Arabs") hurled similar invective. King Hussein—already insecure about his quietly pragmatic relations with Israel—found himself castigated as a Zionist factotum.

King Hussein, the ruler of a small, weak, and divided country, unleashed a rhetorical volley of his own. At a meeting of the Joint Defense Council of the Arab League, the Jordanian delegation demanded to know "why didn't Egypt renew guerrilla attacks from its own territory? Why didn't they remove UNEF [the United Nations Emergency Force monitoring the Egypt-Israel armistice agreement] and transfer troops from Yemen to Sinai? And where was the touted Egyptian air force when the Israelis were attacking Samu'—where was Syria's commitment to Arab defense?"[32] Hussein accused Nasser of "hiding behind the skirts" of the UNEF.[33]

The Jordanian riposte exploited Nasser's own deep insecurity about his status as champion of Arab nationalism. Leading, or at least appearing to lead, the Arab charge on Palestine was central to this image; his assertion that "Palestine supersedes all differences of opinion," typified Nasser's rhetoric on the issue.[34] But the seeming Egyptian indifference to Jordanian suffering in the raids damaged that self-image.

In any case, it was the other Arab nationalist regimes—not Hussein and not the Gulf States—that most concerned Nasser. Above all, he worried about being outflanked on Palestine by the revolutionary Syrian regime. The bloody series of coups and countercoups in Damascus throughout the 1950s and 1960s had made Syrian Ba'athists exceptionally aggressive about proving their own Arab nationalist credentials, and there was no better way to do this than by topping Nasser's rhetoric. Nasser disdained what he saw as Syrian pretense, but he could not ignore it. His response was to match and exceed Syrian anti-Israeli pronouncements and, in the process, turn Israeli thoughts to preemption.

THE CRISIS

These superpower and regional contexts combined in May 1967 to create a month-long crisis that ended in the Six-Day War. Regional conditions made such a crisis inevitable, but its timing and violent catharsis originated in a unique combination of chance, miscalculation, and folly. The conduct and outcome of the Six-Day War itself was largely predictable; it was the May crisis with its military, political, and diplomatic maneuvering that, against the interests of all the players, led to war.

"In retrospect," wrote former U.S. diplomat Richard B. Parker in his book *The Politics of Miscalculation*, "it is clear that the political-military solution was supersaturated and all that was required to make it precipitate was for someone to drop in a crystal of solute."[35] Tensions had been building since the disastrous 1966 Israeli raid on as-Samu', when Israel had beaten up the bride instead of pinching the mother-in-law. In April 1967, Israeli jets shot down six Syrian MiGs in response to attacks on Israeli farmers near the Golan Heights.

Victorious Israeli pilots buzzed Damascus in a show of dominance and disdain. This only inflamed Syrian insecurity and encouraged the regime's support for the Palestinian guerrilla group Fatah's cross-border raids into Israel. On May 12, Israeli military leaders including Chief of Staff Yitzhak Rabin further escalated tensions by appearing to say to reporters that an Israeli seizure of Damascus was possible if the raids continued.[36]

Israeli threats provided the Soviets a perfect opportunity to implement their strategy of "stirring the pot." In so doing, Soviet leaders also catalyzed the chain reaction that ended in war. On May 13, the Soviets used several channels to deliver false intelligence to Cairo that Israel was massing troops on the Syrian border in preparation for a possible invasion. The exact chain of transmission remains murky, but the message found its way to the highest reaches of the Egyptian government.

The Soviets knew that the dictates of Arab nationalist solidarity would require Nasser to act in defense of his Syrian allies. In all likelihood, Soviet officials anticipated a repeat of the 1960 Rotem Crisis, in which false Soviet intelligence caused Nasser to deploy forces on the Israeli border to forestall a supposed IDF incursion into Syria.[37] In that case, the IDF had quietly mobilized its reserves to counter the Egyptian deployment but had simultaneously pursued steps to de-escalate; Nasser consolidated the propaganda gains that followed and counted the episode a victory. This served Soviet regional interests by strengthening Nasser's ties to both Moscow and Damascus, deterring any future Israeli attack with the promise of a two-front war, and embarrassing an American ally—and, by extension, the United States itself.

Soviet officials have always insisted that they believed their own false intelligence in May 1967.[38] Brezhnev, in a June 20, 1967, postmortem to the Communist Party's Central Committee, claimed "many signs led us to the conclusion that a serious international crisis was in the making, and that Israel, relying on the support of Western powers, was preparing aggression."[39] Yet, the preponderance of evidence suggests otherwise. In the years leading up to 1967, the Soviets had, on multiple occasions, knowingly issued false warnings of Israeli military activity.[40] It is also nearly certain that the Soviet military had the technical intelligence-gathering capabilities to detect the massing of "eleven to thirteen" Israeli brigades, as Moscow claimed.[41] A mid-June 1967 CIA postmortem confirmed that this was the assessment of the U.S. government: "There is no indication that Soviet intelligence was bad but that it is evident that what they passed to the Arabs was not accurate and was probably not a reliable gauge of what they must have known."[42] More suspiciously, Soviet Ambassador to Israel Dimitri Chuvakhin, when offered an opportunity by Prime Minister Levi Eshkol to inspect the Syria-Israel border, declined, remarking, "it isn't a diplomat's assignment to tour frontiers and see whether forces are being massed there."[43]

Soviet intent regarding the false intelligence is important for what it reveals about the extent of Soviet machinations in the Middle East, but Nasser alone had final authority over Egypt's response. If the Soviets had dictated events, they likely would have sought to avoid the ensuing crisis by encouraging a bout of Egyptian military posturing followed by rapid de-escalation. After the Cuban Missile Crisis, the Soviets feared proxy war as the gateway to direct superpower conflict. What is more, according to Russian analyst V. A. Zolotarev, "nobody in [Soviet] diplomatic circles contemplated the possibility of an Arab victory [against Israel]."[44]

Instead, the Arab Cold War drove Nasser's reaction; the Soviets, who failed to understand the salience of inter-Arab rivalry, could only watch as the sorcerer's apprentice took on a monstrous life of its own. The Syrians initiated this process by publicizing the Soviet report, thus ensuring that Nasser would be bound by the demands of radicalized Arab public opinion.[45] From the outset, Nasser's key calculation was not "whether the [Egyptian] army could prevail over Israel but whether [after the April 1967 Israeli humiliation of Syria] his rule could survive another failure to come to Syria's defense."[46]

Between May 14 and May 18 Nasser remilitarized the Sinai Peninsula and demanded the expulsion of the U.N. forces charged with monitoring the 1949 Israeli-Egyptian armistice agreement. Ample evidence that Nasser did not believe the Soviet intelligence makes it clear that this decision was fundamentally political. The Egyptian leadership's reaction to armed forces chief of staff Muhammad Fawzi's May 14 reconnaissance visit to the Syrian frontier was especially revealing. According to Fawzi, "I returned to Cairo on May 15 and I presented my report to General Abdel Hakim 'Amr [Nasser's deputy], which denied the presence of any Israeli concentrations along the Syrian front. I didn't note any reaction from him about the problematic situation along the Syrian border. This was the origin of my belief that the subject of Israeli concentrations . . . was not the only or even primary reason for the speed with which Egypt was undertaking its deployments."[47] What is more, American officials were clear with their Egyptian counterparts about the absence of any Israeli preparations for war. In Cairo, U.S. chargé d'affaires David Nes was unequivocal in a meeting with Egyptian foreign minister Mahmoud Riad: "Based on [information available] to us in Israel, we were not aware of any major changes in the disposition of Israeli forces or of any 'mobilization' measures."[48]

The heady response of the Egyptian people and media to the purported Israeli threat largely explains Nasser's otherwise inexplicable decision to escalate. The powerful *Sawt al-Arab* broadcasts' rhetoric took an eschatological turn: "The existence of Israel has continued too long. We welcome the Israeli aggression. We welcome the battle we have long awaited. The great hour has come. The battle has come in which we shall destroy Israel."[49] Such statements, in turn, fired popular enthusiasm for war, reinforced by a belief in Egyptian military supremacy. Senior Egyptian officers, particularly those associated with the delusional General 'Amr, also pressed Nasser to escalate.

Popular pressure had a potent impact on Nasser, but his own faith in his ability—in concert with the superpowers—to forestall an escalatory spiral was certainly as important. According to Anwar Sadat, the vice president and one of Nasser's closest confidants, "Nasser was encouraged to believe Israel might not fight, especially if the United States urged a peaceful solution."[50] Instead, Egyptian leaders envisioned the same outcome as the Soviets: "[We intended] this mobilization and deployment of troops [to be] like [the]1960 [Rotem Crisis]."[51] In that episode, both Israel and Egypt believed that their respective maneuvers had deterred the other side from escalating.

The credibility of these explanations is supported by Nasser's own assessment of Egyptian military capabilities. Despite Nasser's bellicose rhetoric intended for public consumption, he was himself a former military officer and hence privately skeptical of his own military's capabilities. Through back-channel communications, according to an NSC report, Nasser conveyed "realistic respect for U.S.-backed Israeli military capabilities and [had] been a force for moderation in Arab councils."[52] John Badeau, U.S. Ambassador to Cairo in the early 1960s, captured the prevailing view of Nasser's generally cautious approach to the Arab-Israeli conflict as: "[Nasser is] singularly unwilling to risk his regime in a decisive military decision anywhere."[53]

These official American perceptions of Nasser, however accurate they had been at one time, were detached from the powerful internal logic of the Arab Cold War, which impelled Nasser to reject all efforts at mediation and de-escalation, despite his fear of defeat in a confrontation with the IDF. After all, by introducing troops into the Sinai and expelling the UNEF detachment, Nasser had seemingly reclaimed the tattered mantle of champion of Arab nationalism. By May 18, Egyptians were exultant; Nasser could have declared victory as in 1960 and consolidated his gains. Instead, he found himself a prisoner of Arab expectations and thus of his own rhetoric. On May 19, Radio Amman, in reference to continued Egyptian consent to Israeli passage through the Strait of Tiran (Israel's strategic outlet to the Red Sea), mockingly inquired, "Will Egypt restore its batteries and guns to close its territorial waters in the Tiran Strait to the enemy? What would be Cairo's excuse if it fails to do so after the evacuation of the U.N. force from the area?"[54] Partially in response, Nasser delivered a bravura performance at Egypt's Bir Gafgafa air base in the Sinai. To an audience of fighter pilots, he crowed, "The Jews threatened war . . . We tell them, welcome [*ahlan wa sahlan*], we are ready for war."[55] Nasser undoubtedly knew how far those words were from the truth as he said them, but he simply "appeared not to be interested in salvation."[56]

Nasser's next step brought the parties closer to war. On May 22, Nasser declared the Strait of Tiran closed to all Israeli shipping. Although this marked a significant escalation, it likely appeared unavoidable to Nasser. Having replaced UNEF troops with Egyptian forces at the base guarding the strait, Nasser knew his Arab rivals would condemn him if Israeli ships were allowed to pass under Egyptian guns. According to one analysis immediately following the crisis, "any action short of the *status quo ante* 1956 [when the strait was closed to Israeli vessels] would have been painted by Nasser's enemies . . . as weakness and betrayal. The only way lay forward—a *fuite en avant*—even if necessary into war."[57]

In closing the strait, Nasser did not intend to trigger a conflict, but to Israelis it was tantamount to a declaration of war. Until that point, Israeli leaders had not been unduly alarmed by Nasser's provocations; in fact, like the Soviets, they saw them as a repeat of 1960. Even as late as May 16, after Nasser's remobilization of the Sinai, Israeli officials doubted that there was "even a 5 percent threat of escalation."[58] Seeking to mollify Nasser in the first few days of the crisis, Prime Minster Eshkol instituted a gag order on provocative statements by government officials. According to one report, he went as far as to ask the Israeli press to cooperate in avoiding mention "of [Nasser's] mobilization, of freedom of shipping, or [the nuclear reactor at] Dimona."[59]

Closure of the strait, however, crossed an Israeli redline. Where before "events had been perceived in the context of . . . the pre-crisis line of thought . . . For Israel, [it became] an existential question."[60] Opening the Strait of Tiran to Israeli vessels had been the key Israeli gain from the 1956 Suez Crisis; Israel's general staff believed that to forfeit that right would call into question the entire system of deterrence upon which their security relied. In a crisis meeting of top defense officials on May 23, Rabin articulated the IDF's logic: "My opinion . . . is that we have to respond immediately . . . The behavior of Jordan and Syria will depend on the extent of our success in the Egyptian theater. For us it is a question of survival."[61]

Regrettably, Nasser also activated latent Israeli fears of annihilation. Average Israelis, many of whom had survived the Holocaust or were the children of survivors, had no reason to doubt the sincerity of the rhetoric hurled out of Cairo. On May 26, for instance, they heard Nasser describe his decision to close the strait: "The meaning of taking this step is that we must be ready to enter into a total war with Israel . . . If Israel undertakes any act of aggression against Syria or Egypt . . . the battle will be all-encompassing and our primary goal will be the destruction of Israel."[62] Rabbis began consecrating mass graves in anticipation of devastating casualties, and a gallows humor admonished the last Israeli out of the Lod international airport to remember to "turn out the lights."

At this point, it became clear to Soviet and American policymakers that something had to be done. Neither Israel nor Egypt was capable of de-escalating, and both naturally assumed the worst of the other's intentions. War, which days earlier had seemed unthinkable, now appeared inevitable.

A swift intervention proved to be beyond the capacity of both superpowers. In keeping with their precrisis meddling, the Soviets continued their double game with Nasser, at times spurring him on and at others making halfhearted efforts at restraint. This inevitably led to a muddled and ineffective policy into which Nasser could read whatever best suited his interests and his evolving assessments of the situation, which in turn neutered Soviet leverage.

The Soviet approach was on display during a pivotal May 25–26 visit to Moscow by Egyptian defense minister Shams Badran, who had been sent by Nasser to gauge Soviet intentions. Soviet premier Alexei Kosygin proffered the cautious line advanced by Moscow since the beginning of the crisis: "We are going to back you. But you have gained your point. You have won a political victory. So it is time now to compromise, to work politically . . . Now the most important thing is to cool things down and not give Israel or the imperialist forces any cause for triggering off an armed conflict."[63] Soviet military interlocutors were simultaneously delivering the opposite message. Accompanying Badran to the airport, the hawkish Soviet defense minister Andrei Grechko told him to "stand firm. Whatever you have to face, you will find us with you. Don't let yourselves be blackmailed by the Americans or anyone else"—a statement to which Badran appeared to react with astonishment. Perhaps most revealing of Soviet dysfunction was Grechko's nonchalant response when questioned later about his brazen contradiction of Kosygin's message: "I just wanted to give him [Badran] one for the road."[64] In a classic understatement, Yevgeny Primakov, the late Soviet Arabist who eventually headed Soviet intelligence and served as foreign minister and prime minister, described Grechko's throwaway line as "not thought through . . ."

A corresponding gigue occurred between Israel and the United States, but whereas the Soviets sent Nasser contradictory signals, the Americans gave Israel little direction at all. Like the Israelis and Soviets, American officials had seen little risk of escalation until Nasser closed the Strait of Tiran. According to one diplomatic cable that went out only hours before the Egyptian move, "We have no reason to believe, in [the] present situation, that any of [the] parties to Armistice Agreements between Arab States and Israel has [any] intention of committing aggression."[65]

The White House was evidently unconvinced. Johnson had been especially harsh in a May 17 telegram to Prime Minister Eshkol:

I know that you and your people are having your patience tried to the limits by continuing incidents along your border. In this situation, I would like to emphasize in the strongest terms the need to avoid any action on your side which would add further to the violence and tension in your area. I urge the closest consultation between you and your principal friends. I am sure that you will understand that I cannot accept any responsibilities on behalf of the United States for situations which arise as the result of actions on which we are not consulted.[66]

This hands-off American position was unhelpful to those in Israel—Eshkol and Eban, in particular—who were pushing for a diplomatic resolution of the crisis. The argument that the United States would ultimately come through for Israel was deployed to downplay the risk of delayed military action, but Johnson's hectoring cable inevitably undermined what little faith there was in American commitment. Instead, the narrow American approach to the crisis seemed to confirm the melancholy Israeli belief that they could rely only on themselves. Diplomat Ephraim Evron, one of the more pro-American Israeli officials, described the extent of frustration even among Israeli doves: "Israelis understood [the] U.S. desire to stay out . . . If there was anything the U.S. government did not want, it was to appear to be in collusion—conspiracy—with Israel." What is more, private messages coming from the White House were not reassuring; according to Evron, Johnson, in a moment of anger and frustration at Israeli pressure, told him that "national suicide [i.e., an Israeli decision to attack] is not an international [i.e., American] obligation."[67]

The distrust, however, cut both ways. Just as the Soviets were dismayed to watch Nasser dictate events according to his own priorities, so too did Johnson administration officials grow frustrated at perceived Israeli attempts to manipulate American decisions. On the level of policy, some American officials believed the Israelis were deliberately feeding the United States false—or at least exaggerated—intelligence reports. Regarding a May 25 Israeli assessment that Nasser intended to attack shortly, Walt Rostow wrote to Johnson:

> We do not believe that the Israeli appreciation presented was a serious estimate of the sort they would submit to their own high officials. We think it is probably a gambit intended to influence the U.S. to do one or more of the following: (a) provide military supplies, (b) make more public commitments to Israel, (c) approve Israeli military initiatives, and (d) put more pressure on Nasser.[68]

Just as disturbing to Johnson was the sense that the Israelis were maneuvering him into a political corner. The Israeli embassy in Washington had targeted both the White House and Congress with a massive letter-writing and advocacy campaign to "create a public atmosphere that will constitute pressure on the administration in the direction of obtaining our desired goals, without it being explicitly clear that we are behind this public campaign."[69] This was particularly unwelcome given the reality on the Hill of what Secretary of State Dean Rusk and Secretary of Defense Robert McNamara referred to (as did White House staffer William Quandt, quoted earlier) as "Tonkin Gulfitis"; Johnson felt he would pay a punitive political price for even minimal overseas intervention beyond the burgeoning commitment in Southeast Asia. According to Rusk and McNamara: "The problem of 'Tonkin Gulfitis' remains serious . . . An effort to get a meaningful resolution from the Congress [on the ongoing Arab-Israeli crisis] runs the risk of becoming bogged down in acrimonious debate."[70] Thus, Johnson intended to do everything he could to prevent the Israeli tail from wagging the American dog.

These efforts, however, would prove insufficient to dispel Israeli notions of American fecklessness. The Johnson administration's last, best hope was to assemble an international naval flotilla that would navigate the Strait of Tiran and so end the Egyptian blockade. The idea never got off the ground. In fact, the British—who had initially proposed it—began retreating from the plan as soon as the Americans took it up. Translated into State Department euphemistic vernacular: "the [British] Cabinet is taking a cautious approach to the Near East Crisis and will only reluctantly assume a leading role [in any flotilla]."[71] Besides continuing to urge restraint on both sides, American mediatory proposals did not extend beyond this so-called "Red Sea Regatta."

By not articulating a clear strategy for reducing tensions, American officials ensured that the Israelis would feel compelled to act without regard for American interests. Eshkol had tried to encourage a more active American role by sending Foreign Minister Eban to meet with Johnson on May 24. The mission was twofold: both to demand greater American participation and to broach the idea that Israel might have to unilaterally strike Egyptian forces. The meeting did not go well, and Eban left only with Johnson's gnomic admonition that "Israel need not be alone unless it chooses to go alone."[72]

The IDF brass seized upon Johnson's response, and the resulting backlash—which came to be known as the "Generals' Revolt"—culminated in the decisive defeat of Israeli doves. After an initial deadlocked cabinet vote on preemptive war with Egypt, Chief of Staff Rabin lacerated Eshkol: "Inaction on our part shows powerlessness. We're making ourselves look like an empty vessel, a desperate state. We've never before been so humiliated . . . Your hesitation will cost us thousands of lives."[73] Even more perplexing for Eshkol was that IDF officers voiced these extreme views about potential Israeli casualties while maintaining high confidence in their own capability to defeat a combined Arab force. As General Uzi Narkiss illustrated in a comment to the prime minister:

I don't know what you think of the military. All of us here have been in the army for twenty years or more, and I want to tell you—it is a fantastic army. There's nothing to worry about . . . [The Arabs are] a bubble of soap, and with one pin-prick they'll burst.[74]

Eshkol was ultimately overwhelmed by public and IDF pressure. His impassioned response to Rabin's concerns about eroding IDF deterrent capability—"Will we always live by the sword?"—and his reminder that "there are no widows or orphans of prestige"[75] did little to sway a general staff obsessed by the putative costs of inaction. There was even talk—but only that—of a coup. General Ariel Sharon, then a charismatic armored division commander, sketched for Rabin a hypothetical seizure of power:

We get up and say [to Eshkol]: you listen now, your decisions are putting the state of Israel at risk, and since the situation is now critical, we're asking you to go into the next room and wait. And the Chief of Staff will go over to Kol Israel [radio station] and make an announcement [that the ministers have been] relieved.[76]

The cascade of events rendered these designs moot. On May 28, Jordan's King Hussein, fearful for his reign if perceived as having abandoned the Arab cause, flew to Cairo to pledge his allegiance to Egypt in any coming conflict with Israel. The symbolic power of Hussein's shift had an enormous impact on the course of events. The same day, Eshkol, intending to reassure the nation, delivered a disastrous performance on live radio in which he appeared befuddled and utterly inadequate to the magnitude of the decisions before him. Two days later he was sidelined; the cabinet elected to transfer the defense portfolio to Moshe Dayan— a rakish hero of Israeli victories past. By June 1, all signs pointed to war. Nasser refused to initiate an attack but could not de-escalate. The Israelis, having mobilized the IDF reserves, were financially, politically, and, above all, emotionally unwilling to sustain the status quo. The superpowers, having failed to control the crisis at the outset, were incapable of staging a deus ex machina. The tortured last-minute wrangling between the superpowers and local states reflected the desperate nature of the situation.

After Badran's May 25 visit to Moscow, the Soviets had made no further substantive attempts to restrain Nasser. Rather, they seem to have hoped the Israelis might be more pliable. In the dead of night on May 26, Soviet Ambassador to Israel Dimitri Chuvakhin had arrived unannounced at Eshkol's residence. According to one account, "Eshkol asked his wife what to do; she said, if the ambassador wants to see you in your pajamas, let him come up."[77] He did, and the ambassador delivered a conciliatory letter from Premier Kosygin stating that the Soviet Union desired peace above all and calling upon Israel to avoid conflict at all costs. Eshkol was receptive and proposed a direct meeting with Kosygin, but the contact progressed no farther. According to Chuvakhin, hawks in Moscow squelched that back channel.

Soviet moves aligned with American policy makers' own interest in avoiding war, and, ironically, there was progress toward a common superpower front to restrain their recalcitrant local clients. According to Secretary of State Rusk on May 24: "We are in touch with the U.S.S.R. Privately we find the Russians playing a generally moderate game, but publicly they have taken a harsh view of the facts and have laid responsibility at Israel's door—and by inference at ours. Syria and Cairo say publicly they have Soviet support; but our general impression is that this is somewhat less than complete."[78] Most notable was a flurry of letters exchanged between Johnson and Kosygin pledging mutual commitment to de-escalation and restraint.[79] Such proclamations, however, were intended as much for show as to resolve the crisis; by the last week of May, both powers were resigned to the fact that events had superseded whatever meager policy options had initially been available.

Acceptance of this reality led to a dramatic shift in discourse among American policy makers away from restraint and toward tacit acceptance of an Israeli strike. An eyes-only cable directly from Rusk, never one of Israel's closest friends in Washington, to ambassadors across the Middle East stated:

> You should not assume that the United States can order Israel not to fight for what it considers to be its most vital interests. We have used the utmost restraint and, thus far, have been able to hold Israel back. But the "Holy War" psychology of the Arab world is matched by an apocalyptic psychology within Israel. Israel may make a decision that it must resort to force to protect its vital interests.[80]

This policy shift resulted in what has come to be known as the "yellow light" episode.[81] In early June, Mossad director Meir Amit arrived in Washington to determine how the Johnson administration would react if Israel proceeded with a preventive attack. After conversations with McNamara and CIA personnel, Amit concluded that "we should wait a short while longer for an international armada, and then find a way to strike. [American] public opinion is in favor . . . McNamara does not object, either. The only ones opposed at this point are the people in the State Department."[82]

Some scholars have interpreted this episode as the American "unleashing" of Israel, but this misses the point of Amit's trip to Washington.[83] The reality was more complex; Israel was not America's to unleash. Although Amit's visit was couched in terms of consultation, the Mossad chief came to deliver a message, not to ask permission. Crucially, Amit prefaced his discussion with McNamara by telling him there was no need to respond to what he was about to say. He then told the secretary that, upon his return to Israel, he would recommend an attack on Egyptian forces to the cabinet. McNamara replied that he would inform Johnson of this straightaway, with no further elaboration. Thus, the American "red light" of restraint shifted to a "yellow light" of reluctant acceptance.

The American "yellow light" reflected the lack of available alternatives. Eshkol was out, the military was effectively at the wheel, and American policy up to that moment had proved ineffectual. If Johnson's counsel of restraint had fallen on deaf ears early in the crisis, there is little chance that last-minute pleas would have been any more effective.

A QUICK WAR

Just after dawn on June 5, the Six-Day War began when the Israeli air force launched an operation to eliminate Nasser's air force. Within hours, nearly every Egyptian combat plane sat smoldering on the tarmac. In effect, the war was won that morning; airpower was the linchpin of the Egyptian military, despite the large ground army assembled by Amr, and the Arab war effort depended on Nasser's ability to pin down the Israelis. Over the next five days, IDF ground forces routed exposed Egyptian troops in the Sinai, occupying the peninsula up to the Suez Canal. Simultaneously, the Israelis drove Jordanian troops, who had been committed only reluctantly at the last minute by King Hussein, from Jordanian territory west of the Jordan River (the "West Bank"), including East Jerusalem. In the north, the Syrians, who had been so instrumental in fomenting the conflict, scarcely factored in the fighting. The IDF's nearly uncontested seizure of the strategic Golan Heights at the war's end was merely an afterthought. In less than a week, the Israelis had acquired the strategic depth they had yearned for and realized an age-old dream of a Jerusalem once again entirely under Jewish control. Yet again, the Arabs were defeated on all fronts; although the 1948 war had become known among Arabs as "the disaster" (*an-nakba*), the Six-Day War was an even more comprehensive drubbing, despite its euphemistic appellation, "the setback" (*an-naksa*).

The Israeli victory appeared miraculous, and by any standard, the IDF triumph over larger and well-equipped Arab forces was an impressive feat of arms. Yet, the course of the war was not particularly surprising to any of the participants at the time. In fact, contemporaneous American intelligence assessments regarded an Israeli victory as virtually inevitable regardless of which side struck first. On May 23 the CIA had informed the White House:

> The judgment of the intelligence community is that Israeli ground forces can maintain internal security, defend successfully against simultaneous Arab attacks on all fronts, launch limited attacks simultaneously on all fronts, or hold on any three fronts while mounting successfully a major offensive on the fourth.[84]

The Soviets and even the Israelis themselves concurred with the thrust of this assessment.

The striking feature of the conflict was the extent to which the United States and the Soviet Union were hostage to their clients' perceived interests. Asserting control proved impossible in part because the Soviets had miscalculated at the outset in attempting to stir the regional pot. For their part, the Americans were too distracted by Vietnam and its domestic political reverberations. Responsibility for the war lies squarely with the local powers that fought it. When the Israelis emerged victorious, so too, by the logic of the Cold War, did the United States. But this was an unanticipated effect of the Truman administration's decision to recognize Israel nineteen years earlier.

LEGACY

The Six-Day War left a mixed legacy. The resounding Israeli victory ended the Arab Cold War. A humbled Nasser had to make peace with the oil monarchies that he had spent a decade assailing and subverting. He made his peace with the conservative monarchies whose petrodollars were needed to rehabilitate his economy. The slogans of pan-Arabism and claims of a new age heralded by the coming to power of the Free Officers rang hollow with the wreckage of the Egyptian army baking in the desert sun. Nasser was finally prepared to shed the burdens of radicalism, with all its costs and delusions.

For the United States, which had sought to diminish the power of Arab nationalists since the Suez Crisis, the war's outcome had its advantages. Such triumphs in the Middle East, however, are often ephemeral. The United States would ultimately confront Islamist radicals with their own trenchant critique of Washington's Middle Eastern allies and U.S. policy toward the region. The fury of Islamic militancy would not become obvious until the Islamic Revolution in Iran of 1979 and then attacks of 9/11. Yet, the rise of religious radicalism should not obscure the impact of the demise of Arab nationalism, which had commandeered state power in the pivotal nation of Egypt and at times provided opportunities for Soviet entry into the Middle East.

Paradoxically, the most lopsided victory in Israel's history made another war with the Arab states all but inevitable. The Arabs' humiliation was too deep and their defeat too catastrophic to contemplate peace with the triumphant Jewish state. First, the Arabs would have to salvage their honor and reclaim at least some of their lost lands. The superpowers would once more find themselves entangled in another local war, one that threatened a nuclear confrontation. The next war, however, would be the Arab coalition's last gasp. Egypt would leave the Arab wars, turn to America, and make its own peace with Israel. The Arab cause would then be spearheaded by obstreperous but peripheral radicals, such as Syria, that could not pose an existential threat to Israel.

As the external danger to Israel subsided a new internal one was born, a restive Palestinian population. The most enduring legacy of the war was Israel's sudden possession of new lands populated by millions of Palestinian Arabs. Israel had to police, patrol, feed, and pacify a populace looking for its own deliverance. The nearly half-century of occupation that ensued would shape Israel's politics and society as well as its relationship with the United States well into the twenty-first century, long after the Cold War had ended and Moscow's regional role had faded away.

CHAPTER 7

FROM THE YOM KIPPUR WAR TO THE CAMP DAVID ACCORDS

In the aftermath of the 1967 war, the Middle East remained a tinder-box. After three previous Arab-Israeli wars, the latest impasse seemed even more peculiar. Israel desired peace, but it seemed at ease with the prevailing stalemate. The Arab states demanded Israel's withdrawal to pre-1967 lines and yet they abjured formal negotiations. The U.N. Security Council had crafted Resolution 242, whose structural ambiguities made it essentially useless. The resolution called for the exchange of land for peace without specifying the sequence. The Arab states insisted on land before contemplating peace while Israel demanded a formal recognition of its statehood before considering territorial adjustments.

In the midst of this turmoil, Egypt underwent a political succession. The years since his catastrophic defeat had not been kind to Nasser. He had launched a war of attrition against Israel only to suffer massive retaliation against his army and cities. The more the conflict simmered the more the champion of nonalignment became dependent on the Soviet Union. Nasser's death in 1970 set the stage for the rise of his improbable successor, Anwar Sadat.[1] Disparaged by Cairo's political class as a transitional figure, Sadat would transform Egypt's foreign policy, if not its history. Sadat grew disenchanted with Moscow and expelled its advisors without dispensing with its aid. He initiated a back-channel conversation with Washington that acknowledged its centrality in recovering Egypt's lost lands. And he would launch a war against Israel not to destroy the Jewish state but to reclaim Egypt's honor.

In Jerusalem, as in Cairo, Sadat was underestimated. He was a weak politician leading an incapable army. Israeli defenses were thought to be impregnable and the mystique of the 1967 war hung over all cabinet deliberations. Beneath the façade of confidence, some cagey politicians such as Foreign Minister Abba Eban appreciated that Sadat was in an impossible position and might see force as a way out of his predicament. Still, even such figures took refuge in the cold logic of power and assumed that laws of deterrence would hold. In the end, the Israelis could not grasp the notion that a nation would go to war not to destroy its nemesis or even to reclaim its territory but merely to disrupt an unsatisfactory status quo.

In 1968, Americans had elected a new president who came into office critical of both his predecessor's Vietnam policy and his approach to the Middle East. Richard Nixon thought that Washington had tilted too far to Israel's side since the 1967 war. While Lyndon Johnson had been impressed by Israel's military prowess, Nixon was troubled by its territorial gains. As Eisenhower's vice president, he had learned the lessons of balancing America's affinities in that troubled region. A peacemaker, as Nixon thought of himself, had to enjoy not just the benediction of the conqueror but also the trust of the vanquished.[2]

Upon his inauguration, Nixon entrusted the responsibility for the Middle East to William Rogers and the State Department. This was unusual for a president who intended to centralize foreign policy in the White House and was suspicious of the professional bureaucracy, particularly the Foreign Service. And yet Nixon felt that with so many important issues such as Vietnam, arms control, and the opening to

China being directed from the White House, the State Department should have authority over at least one region. Moreover, Nixon was dubious that his Jewish national security advisor Henry Kissinger could be an impartial arbiter of the Arab-Israeli conflict. This was a mistake and during the crucial days of October 1973, Kissinger would assume full control of the situation, which he managed with skill. But first, the State Department had to play out its initiatives.[3]

Once Rogers arrived at his post he quickly embraced the prevailing State Department assumptions. The absence of a peace agreement was radicalizing Arab opinion to the detriment of American interests. And to achieve an accord, Israel would need to make substantial territorial concessions. The Soviet Union had to be involved, as coaxing Israel out of its land was thought to be a shared superpower concern. In this sense, the State Department was willing to concede to Moscow a leading role in Arab affairs that Nixon was determined to deny it.

The secretary soon offered his signature initiative, which became known as the Rogers Plan, in a speech on December 9, 1969. The proposal trod familiar terrain, trading land for peace. The plan additionally allowed for the demilitarization of the Sinai, safe passage of Israeli ships through the Suez Canal, and a Jerusalem whose sovereignty would be shared by Israel and Jordan. Although some of these measures seemed sensible, they rewarded Soviet allies and thus threatened to solidify relations between Arab radicals and Moscow. Nixon, always attuned to Cold War considerations, was unhappy about assigning Russia a pivotal role in Arab-Israeli peacemaking and spiked the plan. Through Leonard Garment, his counselor and liaison to the Jewish community, Nixon assured Israeli leaders that he had no confidence in the plan that his secretary of state was busy selling to the region. Both Rogers and his plan soon faded. The secretary did not appreciate how regional dynamics and Nixon's obsession with Cold War rivalries precluded a settlement along the lines that he envisioned.

Historians frequently lament that Rogers and the State Department were emasculated during the Nixon presidency. The processes of government seemed to have broken down as the secretary of state was left in the dark on key initiatives including the opening to China. Secrecy seemed to have replaced interagency consultation.[4] Nixon's treatment of his old friend is indeed deplorable. In 1952 Eisenhower had been prepared to dispense with Nixon as his vice presidential candidate after a financial scandal broke, and Rogers was instrumental in preserving his place on the ticket. Yet the more one probes Rogers's record on the Middle East—the sole area of his responsibility—the more one finds justification for his eventual exclusion from the administration's foreign policy deliberations.

As Vietnam and later Watergate came to dominate Nixon's second-term agenda, the Middle East receded farther into the background. Israeli intelligence did much to lull the United States into its own sense of complacency. The Arab grievances were ignored and Sadat was held in low regard in Washington. Kissinger assured Eban that Sadat had "no capacity for thinking moves ahead."[5] The Americans persuaded themselves that the Arab states may have been frustrated by the impasse in the peace talks but that, given the disparity of power, they would not contemplate war. The region was simply not ripe for substantial American diplomatic investment. Once the militant Arab states grew tired of their war of attrition and were prepared to abandon their Soviet patron, then the White House would consider peacemaking.

Paradoxically, the one state actor that seemed to see the gathering storm in the Middle East was the Soviet Union. Having served as the armory for Arab radicals, the Russians knew the type of weapons that Egypt and Syria were purchasing and the likely uses of such arms. Leonid Brezhnev did not want war in the Middle East. He needed the U.S. loan guarantees and agricultural products that flowed from détente, a shared policy intended to ease bilateral tensions as the Soviets sought to manage their strategic split with China and reduce the cost of the arms race, while the United States sought to reduce the prospect of proxy wars with Moscow in the Third World (as Washington was trying to end the war in Vietnam). For Brezhnev, there was simply too much at stake to risk a confrontation with America. As the undisputed leader of the Kremlin who had finally sidelined his collaborators and rivals, Brezhnev needed international stability. In the June 1973 U.S.-Soviet summit meeting, he warned Nixon that renewed Arab-Israeli war was imminent and that the two powers should together stop it. Still, even as the Soviets rang the alarm bells, they remained diplomatically inflexible. Brezhnev wanted to induce the United States toward a diplomatic settlement but the terms that he offered mirrored those of Arab rejectionists. Washington was not about to partner with Moscow and present terms to Israel that it knew Israel would never accept.[6]

One of Sadat's less endearing habits was his periodic invocation of "years of decision." The year 1971 was supposed to be the year of decision, and it came and went without a decision. The following year, 1972, seemed altogether different, as war preparations began in earnest in Egypt. The war plans were given impetus by the appointment of General Ahmad Ismail as the minister of war. Ismail's plan, called "High Minarets," was simple and limited in scope. Troops were to cross the Suez Canal and breach Israeli defense lines while remaining within range of Egypt's surface-to-air missiles. Mindful of Israel's airpower, Ismail sought to keep his troops within the envelope of these missiles. In practice, this meant that Egypt could conquer neither the Sinai desert nor the Gaza Strip beyond. A limited incursion was seen as sufficient for reclaiming the country's honor and reviving a moribund diplomatic process. A critical pillar of Egypt's plan was a Syrian offensive; a two-front war would prevent Israel from concentrating its power on a single enemy. As Sadat recruited his ally he kept his war aims to himself.

Hafez al-Assad was obsessed with the outcome of the Six-Day War and had convinced himself that Israel had succeeded through a combination of Arab disunity and poor planning. For Assad, the Arab states could triumph on the battlefield and reclaim their lands if they worked together. Not unlike Sadat, he also sought war as a pathway to a favorable settlement, but his illusions were grander and his ambitions greater. While Sadat had reconciled himself to most of Israel's post-1967 gains, Assad dreamt of pushing the Jewish state's frontiers back to where they had been before Israel launched its momentous assault.[7]

There have been plausible claims that Sadat deceived Assad during their war planning. The two had agreed on a comprehensive war that would involve an all-out Egyptian assault on Sinai while Assad conquered the Golan Heights. Once the war began, Egypt focused on crossing the canal while Assad was left to face the full force of Israel's armor. Sadat's deception aside, the tragedy of Assad, which became Syria's tragedy, was that he fell victim to his own delusions.

He came to believe that, should the two Arab states launch a successful war, Israel would negotiate not just over Sinai and the Golan but also over the Palestinian lands it had conquered in 1967. This was unrealism at its height. The Arab states may have been more prepared for war and Israel more complacent, but its power still dwarfed that of its neighbors. And the notion that Israel would lose a war and then cede even more territory to the Palestinians was, to say the least, a misreading of history and of Israel's worldview.

The Arab states would thus go to war with two incompatible plans. Egypt would be guided by "High Minarets," a limited war waged for a limited purpose. Assad signed on to a blueprint called "Granite II," which called for the conquest of both Sinai and the Golan Heights. This was a comprehensive war waged for conquest and redemption. Sadat lied to Assad, as much as Assad lied to himself.

Even with Syria on board, Sadat needed more allies. None proved more valuable than Saudi Arabia. The kingdom had barely survived Nasser and his brand of pan-Arabism and was only too happy to have a friendly leader in Cairo. King Faisal was not just a fierce anticommunist; he also detested Zionism. As Saudi Arabia came into its own as a regional power it began to remonstrate against America's pro-Israel tilt with greater confidence and vigor. In May 1973, Faisal lectured the executives of Western oil companies that the United States must "do something to change the direction that the events were taking in the Middle East today."[8] The impasse in the peace process was as distressing to the Saudis as it was to the frontline states.

In August, Sadat unexpectedly journeyed to Saudi Arabia and informed Faisal that he planned to attack Israel by October. Faisal appreciated that he could not stand aside and pledged five hundred million dollars in aid as well as an oil embargo. The monarch had one request: "We don't want to use the oil weapon in a battle which goes on for two or three days and then stops. We want to see a battle that goes for long enough time for world opinion to be mobilized."[9] This was fine with Sadat. His war to salvage Egypt's pride required a longer campaign than the previous Arab-Israeli confrontations. The oil weapon was critical to Sadat's objective of generating American pressure for a favorable armistice.

Having secured Assad's support and Faisal's collusion, Sadat had only one more ally left to notify. On October 3, Sadat summoned the Soviet ambassador to Egypt, Vladimir Vinogradov, and informed him that Egypt and Syria intended to "start military operations against Israel so as to break the present deadlock."[10] Sadat did not provide a date but the imminence of the conflict was obvious. All along, the Russians had warned Sadat against taking reckless chances, and Moscow now seemed genuinely taken aback by his latest gambit. Instead of indicating its support, Moscow withdrew its nonessential diplomatic personnel and removed its ships from Port Said. The Russians clearly lacked confidence in their allies' military capability. The Holy Land was about to have its fourth war in the four decades since Israel's founding.

WAR ERUPTS

On October 6, as Egypt and Syria began their concerted military assault, Richard Nixon was reading his daily intelligence report assuring him that the Arab states would not launch a war. The recently appointed successor to Rogers as secretary of state, Henry Kissinger, was in New York at the annual meeting of the U.N. General Assembly and was awoken with the news of the attack by his aide Joseph Sisco. The invasion was timed to coincide with Yom Kippur, the holiest day of the year for Jews. Israelis filed into their synagogues to commemorate the Day of Atonement, only to be shocked by the call-up of reserves for yet another war. As enemy forces advanced, most of Israel's national leadership was scattered throughout the capital while much of its standing army was on leave.

The Egyptian offensive was remarkable for its daring and precision. Massive shelling rocked the Israeli positions in western Sinai. The famed Bar-Lev Line along the eastern coast of the Suez Canal, behind which lay Israeli fortifications, was traversed by Egypt's air force as nearly half of its fleet flew over the defense perimeter. Egyptian commandos began crossing the canal and overrunning Israeli trenches. In the meantime, the northern frontier saw tank attacks by the Syrians, who made up for their lack of skill with courage and tenacity. The element of surprise proved devastating.

From the outset both Nixon and Kissinger saw the war as a Soviet provocation. "I think what happened is that the Russians told the Egyptians that there will not be any progress unless there is stirring in the Middle East and those maniacs have stirred a little too much," Kissinger confided to White House chief of staff Alexander Haig.[11] Nixon similarly mused, "It is hard for me to believe that the Egyptians and Syrians would have moved without the knowledge of the Soviets, if not without their direct encouragement."[12] Uppermost on the minds of the president and his secretary of state was how the crisis would affect great-power jockeying. Nixon, already mired in the Watergate scandal that would systematically devour his presidency, had little time to manage the war. Handling of the U.S. response largely devolved to Kissinger.

By insisting that the Russians had instigated the war, Nixon and Kissinger denigrated the achievements of their own détente policy. The Soviet leadership did not want a war in the Middle East for they feared that a crisis could entangle them in a confrontation with the United States, endangering arms-control talks and trade relations. The White House had defended détente from its critics by claiming that the policy forced the Soviets to restrain their rash impulses and privilege great-power cooperation above petty gains. And yet when the war broke out, the administration quickly discarded its own sober estimates and blamed Moscow.

Despite Arab gains, the administration's assessment of the Yom Kippur hostilities relied on impressions of the 1967 war and the notion that Israel would prevail quickly and decisively. Kissinger assured the Special Actions Group assembled from across the government to deal with the crisis that "within 72 to 96 hours the Arabs will be completely defeated."[13] The CIA affirmed his judgment as it underestimated the rate at which Israel was losing tanks and aircraft. The fear in the White House was not of Israeli defenses being overwhelmed, but rather of another resounding victory by the Jewish state that would complicate peace talks and the preservation of détente.

As he grappled with the war, Kissinger had a number of competing objectives. First, the war had belatedly convinced him that the status quo in the region was unacceptable. A serious effort had to be made to reconcile Israel with its Arab neighbors. For this to happen, Israel had to prevail but Arabs must not be humiliated. Another 1967-style military debacle would make it nearly impossible to resurrect the peace talks; the Arab regimes could not contemplate meeting Israel as supplicants who had been disgraced yet again. Kissinger also saw the war as an opportunity to diminish Soviet influence in the Middle East. The Arab radicals had to be made to realize that Soviet arms were inferior to those of the United States in combat and that Soviet backing was useless at the conference table. These objectives required complex calibration in a situation that would be defined as much by improvisation as by careful strategy.

Once Egypt and Syria made their initial gains, Soviet hesitation gave way to a more confrontational posture. Although still averse to more direct involvement, Moscow nonetheless exhorted Arab regimes to help the warring frontline states.

On October 10, the Soviet Union left platitudes behind and began a massive arms transfer to both Egypt and Syria. The Kremlin appreciated the danger of escalation and yet it seemed swept up by the momentum of the conflict.

Sadat had launched a war that the Soviets had advised against. Once the conflict started, the Russians were compelled to replenish his armory and support him diplomatically. Any cease-fire proposals crafted by the great powers had to consider the mandates of their allies. Although a staple of Cold War historiography is how the superpowers imposed their preferences on reluctant regional actors, in reality the great powers were often manipulated by their charges, who exploited Cold War rivalries to advance their parochial objectives. The 1973 war testified to the difficulty that both the Soviet Union and the United States had in managing their alliances in the Middle East.

During the first four days of the war the news out of Israel was dire. The Israelis had already lost five hundred tanks and more than fifty planes. Chief of Staff Moshe Dayan feared that the Egyptian forces would soon be in a position to threaten population centers. In cabinet deliberations, Prime Minister Golda Meir and her advisors contemplated placing Israel's nuclear weapons on alert. The initial anticipation in both Washington and Jerusalem that Israel would easily fend off the attackers proved unusually optimistic.[14]

As the conflict progressed, the tide of battle began to change. On the Syrian front, Israeli retaliation proved devastating. But on the Egyptian front Israel was having difficulty. The Israeli military had failed in its first offensive launched on October 9. The question for

Israeli military planners was how to sustain the momentum on the Syrian front while launching a more effective counteroffensive against Egypt. Israel was expending munitions at an alarming rate while its adversaries were being generously supplied by the Soviets. The Israelis appealed to Washington for a quick dispatch of arms. The request created its own tensions both within the alliance as well as within the administration itself.

Many sympathetic accounts of Kissinger suggest that he wanted to send arms to Israel but was hamstrung by a recalcitrant Pentagon led by Secretary of Defense James Schlesinger and an intelligence community that claimed Israel had sufficient reserves to meet the challenges of the war. Kissinger certainly did blame the Pentagon for various delays during the war when consulting with Israeli ambassador Simcha Dinitz. In reality both Nixon and Kissinger felt that in order to enhance America's leverage with Egypt in the eventual postwar period, Washington had to be circumspect in its dealings with Israel.

Unbeknownst to many in the administration, Kissinger was already in touch with the Egyptians through one of the back channels that he was so fond of. Through private communication with Egypt's national security advisor Hafiz Ismail, the two sides had been exchanging messages. In one of the early communications after the outbreak of the war, Sadat had assured the Americans that "Cairo does not intend to deepen the engagement or widen the confrontation."[15]

Kissinger reciprocated by noting that "the U.S. wishes to emphasize again that it recognizes the unacceptability to the Egyptian side of the conditions that existed prior to the outbreak of the hostilities."[16] The issue of arming the Israelis had to be considered in the context of this nascent relationship, which was critical for Kissinger's postwar schemes.

Hovering over these developments on the ground was the administration's confidence in an Israeli victory that would not affect attempts to lure Egypt away from the Soviet camp. Kissinger confided to Schlesinger that the "best result would be if Israel came out a little ahead but got bloodied in the process, and if [the] U.S. stayed clean."[17] Given that Nixon had already pledged to replace all of Israel's losses after the war, the question was how to navigate between Arab political sensitivities and Israel's immediate concerns. Kissinger proposed that Israel discretely pick up some military supplies using planes from its commercial airline El Al, suitably scrubbed of their insignia. The problem was that El Al only had six planes in its inventory, limiting its ability to carry the heavy weapons such as tanks that Israel insisted it needed.

Israeli ambassadors are never without recourse when meeting White House resistance and Dinitz was not shy about appealing to congressional opinion. Formidable members of Congress, such as Senator Henry "Scoop" Jackson, now beseeched Kissinger, asking him to heed Israel's pleas. These expressions of concern cannot be attributed solely to lobbying by Israel and its supporters. During the initial phase of war, Israel's plight did seem urgent. Given its previous miscalculations, Israeli officialdom was not about to risk not having enough to prevail. It is entirely possible that the administration was right in sensing that Israel had sufficient reserves to win the war, but Meir and the shell-shocked Dayan were not in a position to wait and see how events would unfold before asking for arms.

The Cold War that so often motivated Nixon's actions now redounded to Israel's advantage. America had to respond to the Soviet resupply efforts. The notion of credibility that frequently conditions Washington's approach to global crises required that the United States be seen as reliable an ally as the Soviet Union. Nixon had little use for disclaimers and discreet operations: "We are going to be blamed just as much for three planes as for three hundred," he insisted. For the president it was important "not to let the Russians come in there with a free hand."[18] On October 12, Nixon authorized a massive shipment of arms to Israel, transported by U.S. military aircraft.

The resupply effort came just in time. Armed with new hardware and munitions, Israel began to press ahead. In one of the largest tank battles in the Sinai, Israel destroyed 264 Egyptian tanks to only 10 of its own. Ariel Sharon, with his usual mixture of brilliance and insubordination, crossed the canal and moved toward Egypt's vaunted antiaircraft complexes. In the meantime, a counteroffensive on the northern front put Israeli troops only a few miles outside Damascus. The balance of power was tilting to Israel's favor.

From the outset of the war the White House had planned for a potential oil embargo. Task forces were established, contingencies contemplated, and even rationing mooted. The global oil market was already changing. The Organization of the Petroleum Exporting Countries, known as OPEC, had been founded in 1960 by producers seeking to wrest control over oil pricing from Western companies. In 1973 OPEC members had already begun to negotiate among themselves for a new, more lucrative pricing mechanism. As the war unfolded, the Gulf countries announced a 70 percent hike in oil prices. All this was bound to impact Europe more than the United States, which had yet to become dependent on Middle Eastern oil. Still, the administration hoped to avert an embargo that might further stress the Atlantic alliance.

At first, the situation seemed manageable as Nixon hosted in Washington the foreign ministers of leading Arab oil producers led by Saudi Arabia's Omar Saqqaf. Nixon tried to soothe the foreign ministers by assuring them that a postwar settlement would take place in the framework of U.N. Resolution 242. Given how Nixon himself had undermined Rogers's efforts and privately denigrated the resolution, the claim was disingenuous at best. Still, Nixon was not quite done. The president assured the assembled Arab dignitaries that his chosen mediator, Henry Kissinger, might be Jewish but that "a Jewish-American can be a good American and Kissinger is a good American."[19] A mortified Kissinger chimed in with the assurance that the American airlift should not be seen as anti-Arab but instead as part of the great game between the United States and the Soviet Union. Oil was strangely not even mentioned at the gathering.

Kissinger was buoyed by the meeting and assured the Special Actions Group that "we don't expect an oil cut-off now in light of the discussion with Arab foreign ministers this morning." Kissinger went on to banter with Deputy Secretary of Defense William Clements, a former Texas oilman, "Did you see the Saudi Foreign Minster come out like a good little boy and say they had very good fruitful talks with us?"[20] Kissinger's condescension would shortly appear misplaced, as he learned later that day that the Arab states were reducing oil production immediately by 5 percent and would reduce production by an additional 5 percent every subsequent month until Israel returned to pre-1967 lines and "restored" the rights of the Palestinian people. An irate King Faisal, who had long resented Washington's failure to force Israel's return of lands captured in 1967, imposed a comprehensive prohibition on oil sales on the United States. This was another intelligence failure on the part of the United States, as Sadat and Faisal had agreed on the oil embargo before the start of the war. Although Nixon and Kissinger complained about Arab blackmail in the wake of these announcements, to their credit they did not adjust their stance. Still, the potential damage to the global economy and the fortunes of allies in Europe and Japan made an early settlement of the war an imperative.

As the Israeli counteroffensive gained momentum, Soviet premier Alexei Kosygin secretly journeyed to Cairo to implore Sadat to cease hostilities. Kosygin sensed the direction of the war and appreciated that its reversal could not come about through more arms shipments. The conflict had already battered détente and threatened direct superpower confrontation. The Soviet premier found a receptive Sadat. Having reached his objective of crossing the canal and salvaging Egypt's honor, Sadat was prepared to stop the fighting before Israeli armor inflicted him another loss.

An ally that was not consulted by either Egypt or Russia was Syria. Sadat finally wrote to Assad, "My heart bleeds to tell you this but I feel that my office compels me to take this decision. I am ready to face our nation at a suitable moment and am prepared to give full accounting to it for the decision."[21] Protests from the besieged Assad failed to move Sadat. An alliance of convenience had now become too burdensome to endure. Assad would slink out of the war with his enmities intact, his army in shambles, and his land occupied by the Israelis.

Having secured Sadat's consent, Brezhnev dispatched a letter to Nixon with a detailed assessment of the war and how its continuation was bound to damage détente. The general secretary called on the president to dispatch Kissinger to Moscow—there he might work out a joint cease-fire appeal to the United Nations. Washington was in no hurry to have a cessation of hostilities when its ally was on the march. Still, it was never an American aim for Egypt to be humiliated and the prospect of a unilateral move by Moscow led Kissinger to embark on the trip.

As the war ebbed and flowed, Nixon's domestic political fortunes were rapidly deteriorating. The recordings of conversations in the Oval Office were now at the center of the Watergate scandal. The special prosecutor Archibald Cox had requested the tapes and Nixon refused to hand them over. Nixon next sought to have Cox fired, only to be rebuffed by his attorney general, Elliot Richardson, and Richardson's deputy, William Ruckelshaus. Both men resigned on October 20, 1973, in protest. As the two top Justice Department officials left, Solicitor General Robert Bork finally carried out the presidential deed. In the meantime, the Appellate Court ruled against Nixon and demanded the release of the tapes. Impeachment was in the air, with various congressional committees embarking on their own investigations. Given his own turmoil, Nixon had little mental energy or focus to spare on the escalating crisis in the Middle East.

When he left for Moscow, Kissinger's aim was to play for time as Israel's offensive inched forward. Nixon, however, undercut that strategy in a letter to Brezhnev assuring him that Kissinger had full authority to resolve all outstanding issues. "I was horrified. The letter meant that I would be deprived of any capacity to stall," recalled Kissinger.[22] The secretary of state could no longer pretend to consult with Washington as a means of gaining time. Having lost his leverage, Kissinger found a Soviet leadership most eager to settle the war.

The resolution that Kissinger negotiated in Moscow stipulated that the United States and the Soviet Union would jointly introduce the measure at the United Nations and that the negotiations would take place under its auspices. The resolution called for an immediate cease-fire and the implementation of Resolution 242. Given the fact that it established no real mechanism for the implementation of 242, the language was symbolic at best. On October 22, the U.N. Security Council passed Resolution 338 calling on all parties to cease firing and terminate all military activities. A bizarre series of events followed the vote.

In Jerusalem, Kissinger met the full force of Israeli determination. Having trapped Egypt's Third Army in the southeast sector of the Suez Canal, the Israeli commanders wanted their adversary destroyed. For her part, Meir was concerned that if the conflict ended prematurely Sadat and the Arabs would think they had won. In a private meeting, she informed Kissinger, "We would have been in a better position in a few days." Unwisely, Kissinger told her, "You won't get violent protest from Washington if something happened during the night while I'm flying." Meir retorted, "If they don't stop, we won't," to which Kissinger replied, "Even if they do."[23]

After signaling to Meir that the Israelis could press on with their operations after the cease-fire, the American delegation met the larger cabinet. Various Israeli ministers and generals came in to vent their frustrations. Dayan led the choir by proclaiming, "I don't want to stop." Kissinger reiterated his private comment to Meir, saying, "This is your domestic jurisdiction. I'll be on an airplane."[24] The Israelis had their green light.

Kissinger later claimed the sleight of hand had been necessary to get the Israelis to accept the resolution. In his memoirs, he sheepishly concedes that "I also had a sinking feeling that I might have emboldened them . . . in order to get Israeli support."[25] The fact is that Kissinger made a serious mistake in allowing Israel to violate the terms of the cease-fire. Kissinger failed to realize that the Israeli military moves were not designed to secure a modest advantage, but to disabuse Egypt of the impression that it had scored any kind of a victory. The Israeli operation was bound to involve more than mere tactical jockeying. Kissinger's claim that he had not anticipated this hardly absolves his misjudgment. The resumption of hostilities led to howls from both Moscow and Cairo. Each party appealed to the United States to pressure Israel to stop its war machine.

The green light aside, Kissinger was not indifferent to Egypt's difficulties. Preserving a measure of Sadat's self-respect was always part of his design. The cease-fire agreement was a product of American diplomacy and the secretary of state had journeyed to Jerusalem to sell the accord to a skeptical Israeli leadership. The essence of the U.S. case to the Arabs was that if they wanted concessions from Israel they had to appeal to Washington, not Moscow. For this logic to hold, the United States had to demonstrate the ability to discipline Israel. The cease-fire had to be reclaimed and Israel had to be made to stop. Moreover, Kissinger feared that the longer the war went on, the more the Kremlin might be tempted to directly intervene. This fear appeared to come true.

On October 24, Soviet ambassador to the United States and Kissinger confidant Anatoly Dobrynin informed the secretary of state that he had an urgent message from Brezhnev to Nixon. This was not the first dispatch from Brezhnev. During the past week he had made a liberal use of the hotline to vent his grievances. Once more, the general secretary outlined his complaints, which had some justification in fact, then called for joint U.S. and Soviet intervention to stem the conflict yet again. He also issued a warning: "I will say it straight that if you find it impossible to act jointly with us in this matter, we should be faced with the necessity urgently to consider the question of taking appropriate steps unilaterally."[26] At a time when the Soviet Union had eighty-five ships lingering in the Mediterranean and airborne divisions gearing up for deployment, this did not appear to be an idle threat. William Colby, the director of the CIA, informed the White House that Moscow had put together all the essential ingredients for a major unilateral intervention. A new crisis was at hand.

Nixon was not present at the critical National Security Council meeting to consider the Russian challenge. Haig insisted that the president not be disturbed. Haig claims that he did see the president beforehand, and that Nixon conveyed that this was the most serious event since the Cuban Missile Crisis and that a robust response was required. "You know what I want, Al; you handle the meeting,"[27] Nixon allegedly said to his chief of staff. Haig's account of the conversation as well as Nixon's own memoirs, which claim that he was in command of the situation, have been disputed. Whatever his actual level of participation, Nixon would have favored an aggressive course. Always a great advocate of sending signals to adversaries and of not backing down when challenged, he would have approved a tough approach.

Kissinger dominated the NSC meeting convened to discuss the situation and set the tone by informing Haig that the Soviets "find a cripple facing impeachment and why shouldn't they go in there?"[28] The secretary of state insisted "we have to go to the mat on this one."[29] A Defense Readiness Condition (DEFCON) 3 alert was issued. This was a step below full mobilization of the armed forces and was meant to convey firmness to Moscow without triggering fear of an immediate attack. The 82nd Airborne Division of the U.S. Army was put on notice, an aircraft carrier was dispatched to the Mediterranean, and a second was on its way from the Atlantic. Soviet intelligence could not have missed these maneuvers. To emphasize the point still further, a letter was dispatched to Brezhnev under Nixon's name, stressing, "We must view your suggestion of unilateral action as a matter of gravest concern involving incalculable consequences."[30]

The DEFCON alert and Nixon's stern note had their desired effect. The Politburo soon met to assess the situation and recognized that its unwise gamble had escalated the crisis. As Kosygin noted, "It is not reasonable to become engaged in a war with the United States because of Egypt and Syria."[31] On October 25, Brezhnev sent another letter to Nixon, this time omitting any talk of military intervention. The Soviet leader expressed a desire to cooperate with the United States on implementing the cease-fire. Threats and boasts were replaced by a respectful call for collaboration. The Russians had backed down.

Having averted a crisis with Moscow, Washington pressured Israel into allowing nonmilitary supplies to reach the Egyptian Third Army and accepting a cease-fire. Kissinger knew that Israel had to stop, but could not be seen to have ceased hostilities as a result of Soviet threats. The Soviets had to be rebuffed in a vivid way and only then could Israel be compelled to stop. To preserve its influence with Arabs and marginalize the Soviets, Washington had to embark on a dramatic move such as placing its forces on alert.

Paradoxically throughout the war, both superpowers remained committed to détente. Kissinger's notion that a web of mutually reinforcing relationships can prevent a regional crisis from undermining great-power cooperation seemed to have been borne out. The Soviet Union had too much at stake in terms of arms-control agreements and commercial contracts to allow a war in the Middle East to disrupt its growing ties to the United States. While both sides attempted to enhance the capabilities of their allies and undermine each other's influence, they remained mindful of the larger context of their relations.

AFTERMATH

In a break with the established pattern, the 1973 war spurred a sustained sequence of diplomatic maneuvers in its wake. The human and material cost of the war weighed heavily on Prime Minister Meir. The control that the United States exercised over Israeli choices during the crisis—a control only underscored by Washington's decision to resupply Israel and its ability to do so at a pace it determined—seemed to presage a profound change in Israel's geopolitical situation. Jerusalem would henceforth be reliant on Washington's largesse for its security.[32] The trauma of the recent war and the realization of its newfound vulnerability compelled Israel to seek peace with Egypt and thereby remove it from the Arab military equation for good.

After bruising Israel sufficiently in the war, Sadat was ready to pursue peace as a strategic choice. On October 29, Egyptian foreign minister Ismail Fahmy informed Kissinger that Egypt would "not only . . . accept Israel's existence . . . but . . . that it would not let the Palestinians stand in the way of a solution."[33] This was a striking departure for Cairo, which, in common with the other Arab rejectionist states, had used the Palestinians as a club in the rough-and-tumble inter-Arab politics of the era as well as against Israel. Having enhanced its prestige via the battlefield, Egypt could embark on an ambitious course toward a separate peace.

The end of the war also presented an opportunity for the United States to realize its long-standing ambition of reducing Soviet influence in the region. Whereas both superpowers could arm their respective clients to fight repeated wars, only the United States could deliver peace. Under the cover of the American-led "peace process," Egypt would be able to cut its ties with the Soviet Union and reorient itself toward the West, thus depriving Moscow of its main foothold in the Middle East.

On his first meetings in Cairo as secretary of state, on November 7, Kissinger had been impressed by Sadat's willingness to make concessions. He noted, "What looked like a negotiating breakthrough to outsiders was in fact the merging of Egyptian and American perceptions that had been approaching each other for many years. Each side for its own reasons sought partnership with the other—a partnership that unlocked the door to peace and advanced the interests of all peoples of the Middle East."[34] Meir similarly recognized this growing confluence of interests in Cairo and Washington. "Sadat, of course, was in a far stronger position than we were diplomatically, and the bait he held out to the United States was very tempting: its reentry into the Middle East, plus the removal of the oil embargo."[35]

Though Sadat's ultimate aim was to jettison the Soviets from Egypt, he was constrained by uncertain disengagement arrangements and the reaction of both Washington and Jerusalem. As Kissinger recognized, if Sadat moved too quickly he would lose Russian military and diplomatic support and invite a split with Syria before locking the United States and Israel into the new dispensation he was trying to create through the peace process. The Syrian link was especially important because Sadat had to have a credible threat of renewed war as leverage with both his hoped-for partners. Without Syria, the threat of renewed hostilities was unconvincing.[36] The United States thus needed to enter a peace process without knocking Egypt off its precarious course.

Having staved off the total defeat of the Arabs and outperformed the Soviets as a guarantor of last resort, Kissinger had to translate wartime accomplishments into a durable diplomatic arrangement. Failure to consolidate his initial successes, in Kissinger's view, could set back the gains of the war and jeopardize the American position. The "best outcome would be to extend the maneuvering room for our strategy; if it failed, disaster was probable. In the face of a demonstration of American impotence, Saudi Arabia and Jordan would no longer dare to support the moderate course; Syria would stiffen its intransigence; Egypt could wind up again in the Soviet camp. The Soviets would more than recover the ground they had lost."[37] Extending maneuvering room meant managing two parties to the conflict, who remained far apart on basic issues despite their intention to transform the cease-fires into a peace agreement.

Kissinger's position as a mediator was strengthened by Israel's military situation and the Arab belief that he possessed the diplomatic

acumen to settle their disputes.[38] Most important, however, was the
Arab perception, fostered by Kissinger, that only the United States
could influence Israel, which gave it a unique advantage over the Soviet
Union.[39]

The differences between the parties, as enumerated by Kissinger,
were vast and strangely like those of today. "We knew that Israel adamantly rejected a return to the 1967 borders, including relinquishment
of the Old City of Jerusalem. No Arab state, even the most moderate,
would ask for less in the context of a comprehensive peace." Given these
differences, the possibility of a swift agreement was "a mirage" and
the inevitable collapse of an effort to obtain such an agreement "would
make [the U.S.] the target for everybody's frustrations—the Israelis
would blame us for our exactions, the Arabs for our reticence, the allies
for their impotence; the Soviets would exploit the resulting turbulence
for their hegemonic aims."[40]

Kissinger crafted a "step-by-step" approach to these obstacles. Nixon
unveiled the strategy to Meir, stressing, "You each want peace at a cost
that the other is not prepared to pay. What we need to do is develop a
chain of events, to break the whole matter up and to move step-by-step
. . . Neither of you is in a position now to agree on the terms of an ultimate settlement. The problem is to keep the negotiations from getting
bogged down. Lacking agreement on final terms, the danger is that
you will agree on nothing else . . . The important thing is that communication has begun. You must not miss this opportunity."[41]

The piecemeal approach to peacemaking would only work, however,
if it were insulated from external forces that could disrupt it. For the
United States to control the negotiations and secure Cairo's new partnership with Washington, it would have to block the inevitable Soviet
intrusion into the process. What was needed, in Kissinger's assessment,
was "one symbolic act, to enable each side to pursue a separate course."
That act would take the form of an international peace conference
held in Geneva and cochaired by the Soviet Union. As Kissinger later

explained, "our strategy required first that we assemble the conference to defuse the situation and symbolize progress, but then we use its auspices to establish our central role."[42] The Geneva Conference was thus central to Kissinger's strategy of excluding the Soviets from the substance, if not the theatrics, of the diplomacy. Given the brittleness of the situation, the United States and the other participants needed the conference to provide official sanction to progress being made bilaterally, thus serving as a "safety net" if Sadat's high-wire act failed.[43] Nixon explained the seeming paradox to Meir: "We are going to talk to the Soviets. Our strategy is to try to isolate them by working with them. Otherwise the whole world will be ganged up against us and Israel."[44]

The Soviets took the bait. In Moscow, the Geneva Conference was seen as the fulfillment of the requirement in U.N. Security Council Resolution 338 for negotiations under "appropriate auspices," which would offer them a formal role in the talks. Until that happened, the Soviet Union continued to shore up its influence with Arab clients, mainly through large-scale arms transfers. Although hostilities had virtually ceased on October 25, the Soviet Union was already replacing Egypt's material losses from the war and also deploying nuclear-capable Scud ground-to-ground missiles manned by Soviet crews and two squadrons of MiG-23s. On the diplomatic front, they sought to join the United States as equals in regulating the implementation of the cease-fire resolution and establishing a joint U.S.-Soviet emergency force to monitor the parties' compliance. These somewhat dramatic steps, however, did not get them very far. The Soviets never mustered more than a handful of observers and a Polish battalion for the "emergency force," and disputes over arms repayment with Egypt further exacerbated tensions.[45]

Moscow accepted the early American lead in negotiations for two reasons that, in context, must have been compelling. The first was that Geneva would provide a setting in which Soviet diplomacy could dominate events by mobilizing local allies and galvanizing nonaligned support. The second was the conviction that the Nixon administration, beset by political troubles at home and an obstreperous regional ally, would fail in its efforts. Early acquiescence in the process would thus yield gains later. But Moscow's hand was much weaker than it perhaps realized. Having prioritized détente over Arab needs on the one hand, the Soviets had managed to hamstring their influence with all the local players. As a result, even the so-called radical Arab states—Soviet clients that could reasonably be expected to obstruct U.S. designs—actively sought American control of the postwar diplomacy and a new relationship with Washington. On November 2, Syrian deputy foreign minister Muhammad Zakariya Ismail met with Kissinger at the U.N. General Assembly; the significance of the encounter was underlined by Ismail's senior status within the Syrian government. Just a few days later, the Saudis notified Washington that Assad was looking for direct talks, which would take place in Damascus on December 15. In different ways, the war had made clear the indispensability of the United States to the Arab pursuit of a new order and, at the same time, Israel's effort to restore the old one.

Throughout the following two years, the Soviets would make clumsy and ultimately futile attempts to join a peace process that was unfolding without them. But Moscow was severely constrained: it could not disrupt the U.S.-dominated talks for fear of igniting another Middle Eastern war, which it had earlier sought to avoid, or undermining détente, which it prioritized in its foreign policy. Accordingly, as the region transitioned from war to peace, the Soviet Union would find itself with fewer cards to play.

KILOMETER 101

Before preparations for the conference in Geneva could begin the parties first had to deal with conditions on the ground. The military situation at the end of the war required an immediate effort to stabilize the precarious cease-fire. Despite the formal cessation of hostilities on

October 25, the Egyptian and Israeli armies continued to shoot at each other in the desert.[46]

The most pressing issue was the status of the Egyptian Third Army, which remained cut off and under the threat of annihilation. If the Israeli siege was not lifted soon, it could invite the Soviets back in to rescue Egypt, something that the United States was keen to avoid. As Dayan, an astute observer of the political situation, observed in his memoir:

> The crux of the problem was the situation itself—the isolation of the Third Army, with all the complications that arose therefrom. The Americans could not allow this Egyptian army to be destroyed, or left hungry, or weakened by thirst, or taken prisoner. If the Third Army could not receive supplies in any other way, the Soviet Union would send them, and such a move, they said, would be tantamount to Soviet military intervention. It would be a blow to American prestige. No matter how, the Third Army had to be saved from its plight.[47]

Sadat was similarly not eager for Moscow to use the crisis to restore its standing in the Arab world, nor did he want to risk a confrontation with the United States. This led him to take the bold step of authorizing direct military talks with the Israelis, the first in nearly twenty-five years.[48] Shortly after one a.m. on October 28, Egyptian general Muhammad Abdel Ghani el-Gamasy met his Israeli counterpart, General Aharon Yariv, at Kilometer 101 in Israeli-controlled territory to discuss the terms of the cease-fire.[49]

In addition to discussing bilateral military issues, the Gamasy-Yariv channel provided Sadat with an alternative flow of information about Israeli perceptions and intentions, one unmediated by Kissinger. The U.S. secretary of state, in fact, appeared to be unaware of some of the contents discussed in this channel. The insights afforded by the pair would enable Sadat to exercise occasional influence over Kissinger's approach to the negotiations and further encourage the exclusion of the Soviets.[50]

The main impediment to an agreement that would end the siege was Egypt's demand that Israel return to the lines it had occupied on October 22, before the encirclement of the Third Army had been completed. But Israel was not ready to give up its main bargaining chip to secure the release of its prisoners of war. Israel's insistence on an immediate exchange of prisoners meant that Sadat would have to accept the ignominy of his army being cut off under Israeli control until a later round of negotiations.

Kissinger took on the task of persuading the Egyptians that their insistence on the 22 October lines would lead nowhere. The United States, he told Fahmy on November 2, "will have a massive brawl with the Israelis on the question of the return to the October 22 positions. We have two choices: To do that, or to say, 'To hell with this. Let's tackle the bigger problem [of permanent cease-fire].' We can move on to the broader question. Only we can deliver. It is important that you repeat this to your President."[51]

Having road-tested his case for dropping the demand that Israeli forces immediately withdraw to the October 22 lines with Fahmy, Kissinger deployed it with Sadat in their November 7 meeting in Cairo. When he presented this hitherto unpalatable scenario, he was astonished to find that Sadat "did not haggle or argue. He did not dispute my analysis. He did not offer an alternative . . . It had been folly for Egypt, he averred, to seek its goals through harassing the United States. . . . He was prepared to accept the proposition that Israel needed confidence to engage itself in the peace process."[52]

Sadat acquiesced in the continued beleaguerment of the Third Army in return for its resupply via U.N.-controlled checkpoints along the Suez-Cairo road. The issue of Israel's return to the October 22 lines was thus absorbed into the larger issue of a disengagement of forces to be worked out in a future agreement. By opting for a partial agreement that deferred more complicated issues, Nixon and Kissinger had inaugurated the step-by-step approach they believed was the only path to a stable outcome.

On November 11, Israeli and Egyptian military representatives met at Kilometer 101 to sign a six-point agreement.[53] Subsequent meetings between the two sides were held to implement the last four of the six points: the exchange of prisoners, delivery of supplies to Suez City and to the Third Army, removal of impediments to movement of nonmilitary supplies to the east side of the canal, and the replacement of Israeli checkpoints on the resupply route with U.N. posts. As Kissinger had envisioned, the first two points—maintenance of the cease-fire and the question of separation of forces—would be taken up after the conference in Geneva.[54] But the direct talks had generated a momentum of their own, and the parties were eager to proceed with the disengagement process.

In fact, the talks at Kilometer 101 had progressed so well that Yariv and Gamasy, left to their own devices, might have reached a larger agreement on disengagement of forces before Geneva. During one of the breaks, Yariv and Gamasy took a short walk in the desert. As their conversation turned to friendly bantering, the Egyptian general suggested that they wrap it all up right there. There could be a Geneva conference, Gamasy offered, but the real negotiations would be between them.[55]

This was only a fantasy. When it appeared that the parties might embrace Gamasy's vision, Kissinger decided to call off the talks. His concern was that a bilaterally negotiated agreement would diminish the centrality of the United States and obviate the need for Geneva, which had been designed to facilitate that centrality. As soon as he got wind of the parties' independent actions, Kissinger interposed himself between the two sides. He pleaded with Eban, "For God's sake, stop the Yariv/el-Gamasy thing—put it on the Geneva level. Otherwise, we don't have an agenda in Geneva." He similarly admonished Fahmy,

"What are you doing? Why did you present this [disengagement plan] to the Israelis [at Kilometer 101]?"[56] Accordingly, Egypt killed the channel on November 29, thereby clearing the path to Geneva.[57]

Though it had been Kissinger's decision, curtailing the talks served all parties' interests: Egypt needed the cover of an international conference with other Arab participants before it signed a disengagement agreement, Israel wanted the United States involved to secure guarantees, and the Soviet Union craved the prospect of inclusion that Geneva presented. But ultimately the United States was the main beneficiary, as it took control of the negotiations thenceforth.

GENEVA

The termination of the cease-fire talks at Kilometer 101 had highlighted the convergence of Egyptian and Israeli interest in the U.S. role as guarantor of an agreement. Dayan, unlike Yariv, had been uncomfortable from the start with the bilateral format of the talks precisely because the United States was not at the table. And Sadat had wanted the Americans at the center of the diplomatic action as both guarantor and firewall against Soviet involvement in devising postwar arrangements.[58]

Having dealt with the immediate military predicament, Kissinger prepared for the upcoming Geneva Conference, which was critical to his effort to sideline the Soviet Union. As he later noted,

> The prospect of a peace conference was forcing us to maneuver within a seeming contradiction. We strove to assemble a multilateral conference, but our purpose was to use it as a framework for an essentially bilateral diplomacy. Soviet cooperation was necessary to convene Geneva; afterward, we would seek to reduce its role to a minimum. The peace conference could soothe Moscow's nerves as a prelude to a phase that would no doubt test our relations.[59]

Eban summed up the rationale for including the Soviets at this stage in a slightly less eloquent formulation: "I would rather have them inside my tent pissing outward, then outside my tent pissing inward."[60]

The proximate purpose of Geneva was thus to replay what the parties had begun to accomplish bilaterally. In that sense, it was a success. On December 21, the Geneva Conference convened under the auspices of the U.N. secretary general, with the United States and Soviet Union as cochairs, and with the foreign ministers of Egypt, Jordan, and Israel in attendance. Kissinger stated that the goal of the conference was peace but that the urgent need was to strengthen the cease-fire by achieving a disengagement of forces as the "essential first step" on the path of implementing U.N. Resolution 242.[61]

As cochair, the Soviets shared the glory but couldn't get traction. It would soon become clear that substantive progress toward disengagement agreements would be made outside the framework of the conference. Yet they had no other alternative than to participate in the charade. As Kissinger later framed Moscow's dilemma, "To sabotage disengagement in the Sinai therefore would have had the practical consequences of producing either a war as the Third Army sought to break out or, more likely, an explicitly separate agreement without even the cover of Geneva. Thus Moscow fell in with making disengagement the first phase of the Geneva Conference—and thus with a strategy designed to reduce its own influence."[62]

In a further blow to their prestige, the Soviets had failed to persuade their Syrian client to join the talks, which deprived Moscow of an alternative platform for influence. The Soviets' diplomatic misfortune was essential for convening the conference. Syrian nonparticipation removed a key obstacle, as Israel adamantly refused to sit with a country that, among other transgressions, refused to publish a roster of its prisoners of war.

Nonetheless, the Soviets still tried to show some initiative by referring in their set speech to Israel's "legitimate" borders, a departure from preexisting Soviet policy, and staging a private discussion with Israel about the possibility of renewing diplomatic ties cut off in 1967. The latter topic demanded discretion given the likely reaction of the Arab capitals to such a scheme. In a private meeting with Eban, Gromyko rhetorically recalled the Soviet role in the establishment of the state of Israel, allowing that the Soviet Union did not regret having done so, and declared, "Whoever acts against the existence and sovereignty of the state of Israel will find themselves in conflict with the Soviet Union."[63] The Israelis took notice of the change in Soviet posture, but were not seduced.

SINAI I

After the interlude in Geneva, Israel and Egypt resumed their work on a disengagement-of-forces agreement. Neither could afford to delay. Egypt needed to preserve the diplomatic momentum that Geneva had generated, having already concluded one separate agreement with Israel at Kilometer 101. The more time that passed, the longer Sadat would be exposed to attacks from radical Arab leaders. Moreover, a continuation of the peace process would strengthen the relationship between Washington and Cairo and give Egypt cover to make the switch from the Soviets.[64]

For its part, Israel could not maintain indefinitely the level of mobilization that its forces straddling the Suez Canal required.[65] Any agreement reached with Cairo also held the prospect of containing some political elements, which would signal a major transformation in its relationship with its main adversary and in Egypt's relationship with the United States.[66]

During the negotiations in January 1974, Israel refused to withdraw east of the Mitla and Gidi passes in the Sinai Peninsula and demanded that only a small Egyptian military presence be permitted to deploy in the territory vacated by the IDF. For its part, Egypt wanted two infantry divisions with one hundred tanks each on the east bank, not the token force that Israel was proposing. Kissinger worked to reconcile these incompatible positions through "shuttle diplomacy," which, like the step-by-step approach, emerged as the hallmark of his diplomatic style. Through his back-and-forth trips between Aswan and Jerusalem, Kissinger obtained Sadat's acceptance of Israeli forces remaining west of the passes in return for U.S. guarantees on the limitations of those forces.

As during the Kilometer 101 talks, it was Sadat who offered a critical concession to keep the process moving forward. On January 16, he agreed to scale down significantly the Egyptian presence on the east bank of the canal to eight battalions and thirty tanks.[67] That decision removed the final barrier to an agreement. As Eban later reflected, "Sadat had undertaken, reportedly against the advice of some military commanders, to withdraw masses of troops, tanks and missiles which had triumphantly crossed the Suez Canal in the first days of October. It was this decision by Sadat that led me, for the first time, to reflect that a substantive change of direction might have taken place in Egyptian policy."[68] On January 17, Nixon announced the agreement, and the chiefs of staffs of both countries signed it the following day.[69]

In what was quickly becoming a pattern, Moscow had found itself on the outside of the agreement, which had been aptly signed at Kilometer 101, not in Geneva. The Soviet Union wasted no time in voicing its objections. "All week long," Kissinger noted, "we had heard that the Soviets were bitter, especially toward Cairo, for being shut out of the diplomacy; that they believed we had paralyzed the Geneva Conference in order to promote our unilateral role."[70]

When Gromyko arrived in Washington in February, his frustration overflowed. He accused Kissinger of bad faith and of reneging on his pledge that negotiations take place under joint U.S.-Soviet auspices. For good measure, Gromyko added that the Soviet Union, if it wished, could act unilaterally. Kissinger later described this as a "bizarre" interpretation of what had actually been agreed, namely joint sponsorship of Geneva and Soviet endorsement of Arab participation in disengagement talks run largely by the United States. He dismissed the foreign minister's threat of independent action, given that it had been Moscow's own allies that had excluded the Soviet Union, and claimed it would be absurd to contemplate coercing Syria and Egypt to accept Soviet "auspices." Although Kissinger had told Nixon before Gromyko's visit that the Soviets could play the spoiler, he thought that Moscow recognized that the alternative to successful negotiations was war and that "disengagement . . . complicates the resort to arms by either side" while leaving room for "Soviet manipulation" down the road.[71]

To counter the growing perception in the Arab world and the West that Moscow was losing interest, if not influence, in the Middle East, the Kremlin dispatched Gromyko to Arab capitals and invited Arab foreign ministers to Moscow. These consultations were designed to elicit assurances that the Soviet Union would be included in all activities in connection with the Geneva negotiations. As a communiqué issued during Fahmy's visit to Moscow in January 1974 affirmed:

> It was emphasized that a very important factor in the struggle for a just settlement in the Middle East is close coordination of actions of the Soviet Union and Egypt at all stages of this struggle, including in the work of the peace conference on the Middle East, in all its working bodies that may be formed.[72]

Moscow also issued a stern warning to Egypt about the direction in which it was headed. In a visit to Cairo in March 1974, Gromyko reminded Sadat that Soviet-Egyptian cooperation had been important before and during the October War and was "of no less significance now, when the situation had qualitatively changed, and the period of political settlement of the Near East conflict, marked by the opening of the Geneva conference, has begun." He warned against "a drifting apart," and reminded Sadat that "every available good opportunity for moving forward must be taken . . . The Soviet Union can firmly and definitely state that it will work specifically in that direction. If Egypt does so too, our friendship will be no less strong than the famous Egyptian pyramids." He then went on to accuse Washington of harboring deceitful intentions. "The opponents of a just peace in the Near East would like to substitute various half-measures and so-called 'partial solutions' for a real settlement of the Near East conflict. For these ends they would like to split the Arabs and their allies and start them squabbling with each other. Our answer to this must be a further strengthening of unity, a still effective use of the mechanism of political consultations."[73]

Meanwhile, Soviet propaganda denigrated the settlement that had been reached without Moscow's participation. It belittled the disengagement-of-forces agreement by claiming, "When it gets down to real facts, it emerges that the mountain [U.S.] has labored and brought forth a mouse."[74] It also charged "the U.S. is trying to hold the key to the Middle East settlement so that it can turn this key in the direction required by imperialism and Zionism."[75] Radio Moscow asserted "it is not unlikely that both the United States and Israel are working to freeze the Middle East crisis, and to substitute a partial settlement for the comprehensive settlement on the basis of implementing the UN Security Council's well-known resolution."[76] Another Moscow broadcast warned "the point here is that imperialist circles beyond the seas regard the present circumstances as an opportunity to consolidate their neocolonialist positions and to expand them in the Arab countries."[77]

Their attack on the Sinai I accord, however, paradoxically did not preclude the Soviets from taking credit for the success of the negotiations. On February 22, 1974, a Moscow broadcast asked rhetorically:

Would an agreement on the disengagement of forces have been possible without the active efforts of the Soviet Union and the other socialist countries aimed at making the Security Council adopt a decision requiring Tel Aviv to withdraw its forces from the occupied Arab territories? And there is another fact: such an agreement could not have been reached at all without the military-political success gained by the Arab countries with the assistance of the Soviet Union.[78]

Portraying the Soviet Union as indispensable to further progress, Brezhnev would bluntly ask Fahmy at a meeting in October later that year, "You still think the Americans will help you get your territory back? I bet you that, unless the Soviet Union enters the talks, the Israelis will not withdraw another ten kilometers in your lifetime or mine. Now let's go and talk."[79] That same month Soviet military and economic assistance to Egypt, which had been precipitously slowing down since the war's end, would come to a close.[80]

Despite the Soviets' alternating whimpers and growls, the conclusion of Sinai I had consummated a new phase in Egypt's relationship with the United States. Sadat decided there would be no better day for the restoration of full diplomatic relations between their countries than during Gromyko's visit to Cairo on March 1, 1974. The flag-raising ceremony at the U.S. embassy eclipsed Gromyko's arrival in the media. "Sadat," Kissinger later reflected, "could hardly have made his new course clearer."[81]

On April 18, Sadat publicly declared the end of an era of Egypt's exclusive reliance on Soviet military aid. The same day, Fahmy reiterated his belief to Nixon that any visible Soviet role in the Middle East would undermine American influence and therefore Sadat's freedom of maneuver. As Kissinger recalled, "Egypt sought American political support, he said, and a 'red light' to the Soviets." Though Sadat's support for the United States was encouraging, Kissinger also acknowledged "we did not have the same interest in humiliating Moscow and flaunting its impotence as Egypt had in seeking to justify its switch from reliance on the Soviet Union to close cooperation with the United States."[82]

SYRIAN DISENGAGEMENT

The conclusion of Sinai I inevitably led the United States to turn its attention to Syria. Conditions on the front differed significantly from those in the Sinai. There was no beleaguered Syrian army in danger of collective heatstroke and starvation, although the Israeli army sat forbiddingly within reach of the Syrian capital. The urgency attached to an Israeli-Syrian disengagement agreement lay in the cover it would provide for the one Sadat had just signed. This had obvious implications for Kissinger's strategy, let alone Sadat's viability in an inter-Arab context. If Syria refused to reach a comparable disengagement agreement, Sadat would be discredited and the door opened to an empowered rejectionist bloc. The conditions for yet another war would not be far away.[83]

Sadat was accordingly vocal in his support for a Syrian disengagement, declaring publicly that Syria would have to tread the path taken by Egypt and that his advice for Assad was "Trust Henry." Sadat also implied that he would not participate in a second Geneva conference absent a Syrian disengagement agreement; this was a tacit warning to Moscow, whose interests lay in a continuation of the Geneva process, to keep its Syrian protégé on track. The Syrians themselves were willing to cooperate with the United States if doing so would remove Israeli forces from the suburbs of Damascus and avoid the isolation it would suffer if both Egypt and Jordan reached understandings with Jerusalem.

Israel had numerous strong incentives to cooperate. In Eban's recollection, "The list of Israeli gains was long: the saving of lives on the Golan Heights; the return of prisoners; the prospect that our economy could swing into full momentum; a chance for the Israeli Defense Forces to recuperate in equipment and strategic planning; the advantage of closer relations with the United States; the strengthening of American influence in Damascus; the corresponding weakening of Soviet prestige; and, perhaps, the first glimmer of some new horizon in Syrian-Israeli relations." The viability of Sadat and the stability of Egypt were also factors. "There was also the calculation," he added, "that our agreement with Egypt could become stable only if Sadat was taken out of the solitude which he had incurred in the Arab world by his agreement with Israel."[84]

Assad's principal demand was that Israel withdraw far behind the "purple line" (i.e., the prewar October 6 line) to match Sadat's recovery of the Sinai in January 1974. Syria, in Assad's view, would have to show at least some territorial gains on the Golan Heights. Israel, however, was only contemplating territorial withdrawal to some area beyond the purple line—that is, within newly captured territory. Ultimately, Israel did agree to cede the border city of Quneitra and give Assad a token of recaptured land, but it was an easy concession with little strategic value.

The negotiations that ensued were unlike those held on the Egyptian front, where war had brought the parties closer together in their desire for peace. The brutal fight in the north had only embittered the Syrians and Israelis and eroded interest in compromise, no less peace. There was no analogue to the Yariv-Gamasy talks at Kilometer 101; rather, the structure of the negotiations was such that each party, Syria and Israel, would negotiate only with the United States. This conferred a degree of leverage on Kissinger, but he was still not pushing on an open door.

For the United States, there was an additional source of urgency for beginning negotiations on the Syrian track. Progress on Israeli and Syrian disengagement was intimately linked to the oil embargo, now approaching its sixth month, which gave the process an added strategic and economic dimension. As Kissinger explained retrospectively in his memoir *Years of Upheaval,*

Insofar as Arab leaders thought that the United States and only the United States could achieve it, there was credibility to our position that we would not mediate unless the oil embargo was called off. The linkage was audacious, for we ourselves wanted to pursue such a negotiation so as to continue to dominate Mideast diplomacy and prevent the isolation of Sadat. But turning the oil weapon against the producers was more than a tactic. It was at the heart of our policy to rally the oil-consuming countries who were so worried about oil supplies that they were in danger of succumbing to political blackmail.

For their part, the Soviets were pushing to retain the embargo, framing the argument in predictable terms after Gromyko's visit to Cairo in March 1974. "The ban on oil exports to countries backing Israeli aggressors proved an effective weapon in the Arabs' hands . . . [it] had enabled the Arabs to overcome obstacles in the Arab-Israeli negotiations and had drawn the attention of the entire world to their demands. Most important, it put an end to the military and political humiliation they had suffered for a quarter of a century."[85]

Nixon left the embargo for Kissinger to resolve. Kissinger had earlier sent a private message to Prince Fahd, a son of the Saudi king, who had been named second deputy prime minister in October 1973 and had emerged as heir apparent, warning that the boycott was not the "act of friends" and "could lead to a confrontation." He then followed up with a stern public statement cautioning that "those countries who are engaging in economic pressures against the United States should consider whether it is appropriate to engage in such steps while peace negotiations are being prepared, and, even more, while negotiations are being conducted."[86]

Nixon also sent a letter to King Faisal underscoring Kissinger's points, but this time with the explicit threat that the United States would not pursue disengagement on the Syrian front as long as the embargo was in place. The Saudis countered that they would make known the degree to which the administration's diplomacy was geared to Nixon's domestic travails; the threat stung but was not credible. Kissinger proceeded to send Sadat and Assad "harsh messages" saying "if they believed what they professed—that we were indispensable to obtaining Israeli withdrawals—the shoe was now on the other foot: They, not we, had to find a way to end the embargo."[87]

On March 15 and 16, Kissinger met with Eban and explained his approach to isolating Syria from the radical Arabs, stressing the need for continued movement in the diplomatic arena for him to succeed. Israel would have to pull back at least to the October 6 lines and give up Quneitra but would be able to retain settlements established on the Golan Heights. Dayan was instructed to bring an Israeli proposal based on this plan when he visited the White House. With the arrival of the Israelis in Washington the negotiations officially began, which was just enough cover for the Arabs to lift the oil embargo before the month was out.[88]

After weeks of deadlock in the ensuing talks, Assad retreated from his unrealistic demands for a deep Israeli withdrawal within the Golan Heights and began to contemplate a line in the vicinity of that proposed by Israel. On May 13, Kissinger received an Israeli agreement to a Syrian civilian presence in all of Quneitra, and, later, Israel agreed to pull back to the base of the hills near the city. Assad was then persuaded to drop his insistence on Syrian control of the hills west of Quneitra, in effect permitting Israel to hold on to them, provided that Kissinger guaranteed that no Israeli heavy weapons capable of firing into Quneitra would be placed there.[89]

By the time of Kissinger's next visit to Damascus on May 23, Assad had moderated his position still further to accept a large U.N. force and a wider buffer zone of ten kilometers and limited-force zones of fifteen kilometers. On May 28, Assad gave Kissinger an oral commitment that he would not allow the Syrian side of the disengagement line to become a source of terrorist attacks against Israel. Kissinger flew to Israel and on May 29, an announcement was made that Syria and Israel had reached agreement on terms of disengagement. Two days later, Syrian and Israeli military representatives signed the necessary documents in Geneva.[90]

Soon after, the Soviets made yet another ineffectual attempt to involve themselves in the diplomacy, but were shut out by the Syrians, prompting Kissinger to make the sardonic observation that "the President of Syria, remarkably, preferred to negotiate *without* his principal ally."[91] By his own admission, Kissinger could not have excluded the Soviets had Assad decided otherwise. The perceived U.S. ability to pressure Israel had a powerfully centripetal effect on Arab leaders. It was a claim the Soviets could never make.

This was clearly awkward for Moscow. During Kissinger's Damascus shuttle, no better example of Soviet impotence appeared than a visit by Gromyko to Syria at the end of February. The Syrians had even let Kissinger know ahead of time that the Soviet foreign minister was coming and offered to cancel the visit if Kissinger thought it would disrupt the negotiations. Kissinger did not object, but let Gromyko know that he would not be able to meet with him in Damascus, where the Russians were publicly calling for Israel to withdraw from all Arab lands taken in the 1967 war. Under the circumstances, Kissinger could afford to be facetious—and wounding. When Gromyko argued that Israel had to be forced to retreat from half of the Golan Heights, as the Syrians were demanding, Kissinger suggested that Gromyko fly to Tel Aviv to try to persuade the Israelis. Gromyko sensibly flew back to Moscow instead. He was not heard from again during the negotiations.[92]

SINAI II

The second disengagement of forces agreement between Israel and Egypt did not come as easily as the first. It was achieved through a more drawn out negotiation fraught with tension and burdened by high emotion. It also precipitated a difficult period for U.S.-Israeli relations, which culminated in Washington's "reassessment" of Middle East policy. With an untested leader in Israel (Prime Minister Yitzhak Rabin, who took office in April 1974) and an unelected one in Washington (President Gerald Ford, who took office in August 1974), both needed to prove themselves to their domestic audiences. This time, Sadat was not as forthcoming with concessions, and so the United States had to make significant bilateral commitments to Israel, which had ripple effects on negotiations yet to come.

Egypt now wanted Israel to withdraw beyond the Mitla and Gidi passes and relinquish control over the Abu Rudeis and Ras Sudr oil fields in western Sinai. Israel's objective, which had been publicly acknowledged by Rabin, was to decisively split Egypt from Syria and thus diminish the prospect of another combined Arab offensive. This would require that Egypt make substantial concessions in exchange for further Israeli territorial withdrawals. The concession the Israelis had in mind would be Egypt's public renunciation of the state of belligerency between the countries in advance of an Israeli pullback from the strategic passes or the oil fields. For Sadat such a dramatic down payment for a limited Israeli withdrawal within the Sinai Peninsula held obvious political dangers. He clearly preferred to treat an incremental withdrawal as just another step in a technical process of military disengagement. He rejected the idea of nonbelligerency, believing that he could not afford to be seen in the Arab world as having withdrawn from the confrontation with Israel.[93]

Negotiations ground to a halt as Israel held firm, much to the consternation of Kissinger and Ford. During Kissinger's shuttle of March 1975, Sadat would say only that conflict with Israel would not be solved by military means; Egypt would not resort to force; it would observe the cease-fire and prevent all military and paramilitary forces from operating against Israel from Egyptian territory; hostile propaganda against Israel in Egyptian-controlled media would be reduced; and the economic boycott would be selectively eased. This was not an ungenerous position, given the preexisting state of Egyptian-Israeli relations and in the aftermath of a brutal war. Yet Israel would still not withdraw from the strategic passes for anything less than nonbelligerency, despite the lack of any legal definition of nonbelligerency, a murky concept that, as a practical matter, might well entail nothing more than Sadat had already pledged. Kissinger threw up his hands. On March 22, he departed Israel, announcing the suspension of his negotiating effort. Two days later Ford announced his "reassessment" of U.S. policy toward the Middle East, a thinly veiled warning to Israel that it would not tolerate continued intransigence.[94]

In the latter half of June, Israel's leaders finally recognized that an Egyptian commitment to nonbelligerency could not be pried out of Sadat and that their own obduracy was pointlessly straining relations with Washington. Israel agreed to withdraw to the eastern ends of the passes, while maintaining control over the high ground above the passes. Both sides agreed to a continued monitoring role for the United Nations Emergency Force II (UNEF II), a unit that had first been deployed to the Suez area following the initial cease-fire between Egypt and Israel in 1973. (Its predecessor, UNEF I, had been withdrawn at Nasser's request in 1967, a blunder that contributed to the subsequent outbreak of hostilities.) Sadat consented to continued Israeli use of an intelligence facility at Umm Khisheiba, provided he was given one facing the Israeli lines as well. At the end of August, Israel gradually began to soften its position on the precise line of withdrawal from the Gidi pass. After months of arduous negotiations and acrimonious exchanges, the second disengagement-of-forces agreement was signed in Geneva on September 4, 1975.[95]

As the negotiations proceeded, the Soviets were gamely trying to get back into the diplomatic process via the multilateral Geneva format. Soviet-Egyptian communiqués issued throughout 1974 and 1975 affirmed the need for a return to Geneva, as at the conclusion of Gromyko's visit to Cairo in February 1975:

> The U.S.S.R. and the Arab Republic of Egypt reiterated their conviction that the Geneva conference on peace in the Middle East was the most suitable forum for discussing all aspects of the settlement. The two sides call for the resumption of the Geneva conference immediately with the participation of all the parties concerned, including representatives of the PLO.[96]

The Soviets had even sent envoys on a secret mission to persuade Israeli leaders to seek a settlement at Geneva, reportedly in return for the promise of renewed diplomatic relations and a Soviet guarantee of Israel's security within the 1967 lines. At a banquet in Moscow held for Syria's foreign minister on April 23, Gromyko stated, "Israel may receive, if it wishes, the strictest guarantees with the participation in an appropriate agreement of the Soviet Union, too, [guarantees] which would ensure peaceful conditions for the existence and development of all governments in the Middle East."[97] With the United States demonstrably in Israel's corner and years of Soviet animosity preceding this forlorn offer, there could not have been much hope that Israel would leap at this opportunity. The Soviet gambit, however, did show that Moscow was capable of a modicum of creativity as the weakness of its position was becoming increasingly undeniable.

Omar Sirry, an Egyptian Foreign Ministry official at the time, recalled that "the Soviets were feeling very strongly that they were losing ground in Egypt and in the Middle East. They were beginning to feel their own weakness. They were marginal. They could not deliver the goods the way the Americans would. And they were upset about that. But Fahmy managed to continue to get arms from them."[98] Nonetheless, Moscow's waning fortunes in the Levant were at least partially offset by deft moves elsewhere, most notably in North Africa, where the Soviets signed two successive arms deals in 1974 and 1975 with Colonel Muammar al-Qaddafi of Libya. Qaddafi's anticolonial posture and disdain for Egypt had made this possible.[99]

In the weeks after Sinai II was signed, the Soviet Union continued to press the United States on reconvening Geneva. The reply from Washington on December 1, 1975, noted the Soviets' concerns, but put the onus on the conference participants, whose misgivings about Moscow's role were well known. "Only after careful preparation," the response advised, could the Geneva Conference "serve the goal of achieving progress in the settlement of the conflict." Washington was "consulting the parties to determine their views . . . on how best to prepare the agenda and procedures for a reconvened conference."[100] Of course, at this late stage, the United States had already subverted Moscow's best efforts to influence Middle East peacemaking. As Moscow's isolation deepened, U.S.-Soviet diplomacy—as this December 1975 exchange shows—had devolved to pantomime.

In light of the diplomatic breakthroughs engineered by the United States during these two years, the Soviet Union appears to have been the biggest loser of the 1973 war. The fighting that October provided the occasion, though not the underlying conditions, for American dominance of the postwar diplomacy. Seizing this opening required the extraordinary skill of the American secretary of state, but in this endeavor he already held the trump cards that Washington had been accumulating over the preceding years. The reality in which Kissinger operated was such that none of the main protagonists were especially keen to see the Soviets strengthen their presence in the Middle East.

The most successful innovation that the United States adopted was the step-by-step approach, which broke down seemingly intractable and complicated issues into manageable pieces that both sides could digest. This strategy proved essential in generating momentum toward a sustained diplomatic process that provided tangible agreements and the means by which Egypt could leave the Soviet sphere.

By 1976 Egypt was finished with interim measures and prepared to move toward a comprehensive settlement after the U.S. presidential election.[101] Yet, Ford's defeat at the polls brought a precipitous end to Kissinger's conduct of the peace process. The new president, Jimmy Carter, came into office with ideas of his own for promoting peace in the region, to which the parties now had to adapt.

CAMP DAVID ACCORDS

The outcome of the 1973 war created the conditions for one of the only enduring diplomatic achievements in the long-running U.S. effort to broker a peace between Israel and the Arabs. The peace treaty between Israel and Egypt was not inevitable, however, despite the favorable conditions engendered by the war. Kissinger had played his hand well, in part because Sadat had signaled his moves so clearly, but he did not try to break the bank. From Kissinger's perspective, the conditions at the end of the disengagement phase were still not ripe for a full-fledged peace deal between Israel and Egypt, let alone Syria.

Jimmy Carter entered office in January 1977 determined to resolve the conflict. As is the case with every new U.S. administration, Carter's rejected its predecessor's reliance on incremental arrangements in favor of a decisive push for a final peace agreement. With this goal in mind, Carter's immediate priority was to convene, with the Soviet Union, a meeting of the moribund Geneva Conference. Carter assessed a revived Geneva process as the best venue to jump-start bilateral negotiations with the blessing of both key Arab states and with the two superpowers cochairing the event. It was not, however, an easy sell. He came under fire immediately from domestic opponents of détente. They argued that reliance on a process that required inclusion of the Soviet Union would unnecessarily legitimize a Soviet role in regional security. Moreover, they claimed that the Kremlin would exploit Soviet involvement by playing the spoiler in order to buttress its dwindling importance in

Arab capitals where it once held sway. Carter conceded that the Soviets had not been particularly helpful in resolving regional conflicts; but he expressed the hope that a substantive role in Geneva would encourage constructive behavior on the part of the Soviets, who maintained that renewed war was not in their interest. In any case, he pointed out, the structure of the Geneva process called for both the United States and Soviet Union to serve as conveners. Thus, by definition, the Soviets would have to be included in any resumption of Geneva.

Within the U.S. government, there was skepticism about the utility of involving the Soviets. In June 1977, the intelligence community released an assessment entitled "The Soviet Role in the Middle East." The document concluded, "The Soviet economic, military, and political position has eroded over the past five years and shows no signs of early improvement . . . President Sadat's estrangement from the Soviets . . . was one of the most significant failures of Soviet foreign policy during the Brezhnev leadership." The analysts contended that "Soviet prestige" in the Middle East depended on their inclusion in the process but that their interests, once inside the tent, would lie in the "failure of the negotiations," which would "discredit" both the United States and its Arab allies.[102] From a policy perspective, this suggested that the United States would have to find a sweet spot for the Soviets, where they might be useful in persuading the Palestine Liberation Organization (PLO) to recognize Israel, but not have the maneuvering room to impede progress. At the State Department, the view was somewhat more sanguine. Undersecretary of State for Political Affairs Philip Habib judged that the United States could outbid the Soviets for the PLO's cooperation.

There was significant pushback from Arabs as well. They saw no advantage in conferring an imprimatur on a process involving Israel because of the tacit recognition that participation would entail. Israelis were not enthusiastic, either, fearing isolation in a multilateral setting in which only one other participant could be counted a friend. Israeli reluctance turned into more principled opposition with the May 1977 upset victory of Menachem Begin's Likud party in Israel's national elections. Begin had been a leader of the right-wing opposition to Israel's unbroken record of Labor-led governments since the establishment of the state in 1948. He subscribed to an ideology that privileged the idea of "greater Israel," that is, a modern Israel whose borders would replicate those of biblical Israel, encompassing the territory between the Jordan River and the Mediterranean. He was not, in short, disposed to negotiate with Arabs on the basis of the U.N. Security Council Resolutions 242 and 338, which elevated the idea of land for peace. The timing of Begin's accession to power could scarcely have been worse, in a narrow sense, for Carter's Geneva initiative and, more broadly, for Carter's determination to win autonomy for West Bank Palestinians and transform the Egyptian-Israeli disengagement agreements into a treaty of peace.

Sadat viewed the Geneva initiative as pointless, even obstructive. In response to a November 1977 letter from Carter pleading for Sadat's "early public endorsement" of a meeting, support Carter characterized as "vital," the Egyptian leader began to work with Israel directly. His clear objective was to short-circuit Carter's plan. Sadat succeeded by virtue of his offer to visit Israel and speak to the Knesset in Jerusalem. This was a staggering gambit—in a sense the concluding act of the war of 1973.

On November 16, 1977, the Israelis invited Sadat to Jerusalem. He accepted and, on November 20, delivered a tough speech, but his uncompromising tone was offset by the fact that it was delivered from the podium of the Knesset. A clearer signal of recognition would have been hard to imagine. The parties nevertheless were unable to pursue the opening provided by Sadat's historic visit. The truth was that the parties were still far apart, especially with respect to Sadat's demands that Israel withdraw from the West Bank and Gaza with minor border modifications. Moreover, the two leaders—Sadat and Begin—were ideologically and temperamentally incompatible. Any hope of progress reposed with U.S. diplomatic mediation, which was quickly forthcoming. Whatever Carter's drawbacks, he was flexible enough to abandon his quest for a

Geneva conference once he saw that the parties were off in a very different and possibly more promising direction. The Soviets had little leverage given the determination of both Israel and Egypt to exclude them. U.S. mediation culminated in a thirteen-day high-stakes encounter between Begin, Sadat, and Carter that began on September 5, 1978, at the presidential compound at Camp David, Maryland. Carter shuttled back and forth between Begin's and Sadat's cabins once the antagonists found each other's company intolerable. At one point, Carter even had to personally intervene with Sadat to prevent him from leaving.

Israel and Egypt had come to the meeting with objectives that only partially overlapped. Sadat wanted to solidify Egypt's relationship with the United States, gain meaningful Israeli concessions for Palestinians under occupation, and regain the Sinai Peninsula. Israel sought to drive a wedge, to the extent possible, between Washington and Cairo, avoid any concessions on the Palestinians, and extract as much from the United States as possible in exchange for the return of the Sinai to Egyptian control. As negotiations drew to a close, Sadat failed to win a halt to Israeli settlement activity in the West Bank and Gaza or autonomy for the Palestinians, but he did forge a strong relationship with the United States while regaining all Egyptian land lost in June 1967. Israel got a peace treaty with a major Arab state, a stupendous accomplishment in itself; protected its territorial ambitions in the West Bank; and won an unprecedentedly large military and economic assistance package from the United States. Both countries were soon able to reorient their military postures, more or less free from concern about war between them.

Camp David fundamentally changed the structure of Middle Eastern geopolitics for the better, by greatly reducing the risk of major war, strengthening the U.S. position in Egypt, and airbrushing the Soviet Union out of a region where its position had once been so prominent. The 1973 war had paved the way for these changes. But it was America's diplomacy that helped facilitate the cessation of the war and ultimately the accords that fostered a lasting peace between two age-old antagonists.

CHAPTER 8

IRAN REVOLTS

In 1971, Muhammad Reza Pahlavi, the shah of Iran, celebrated the two thousand five hundredth year anniversary of the Achaemenid Empire. At the event, thousands of soldiers masqueraded in traditional uniforms, with heads of state lingering in air-conditioned tents in the ancient city of Persepolis and French caterers preparing authentic Persian cuisine. The estimated cost of the spectacle ranged from one hundred million to three hundred million dollars.[1] A diffident monarch had come of age, establishing a mystical connection between his dynasty and Persia's past. This was the shah's great civilization.

The tributes kept coming as the seventies moved forward. The shah led the revolt of the petroleum-producing countries and broke the backs of the corporate oil giants, forcing dramatic price increases. Iran's gross domestic product grew by as much as 40 percent.[2] Flush with cash, the shah offered to protect the Persian Gulf on behalf of a weary America undergoing domestic retrenchment in the aftermath of the Vietnam War.[3] A vast conventional army, an air force equipped with sophisticated planes, and a blue-water navy were to transform Iran. The infusion of arms, however, obscured the fact that the Iranian military was ill-trained and incapable of absorbing all the arms at its disposal. More ominously, Iran's strategists focused on thwarting external threats and had no plans for dealing with an internal insurrection.

As oil revenues shot up, the shah exhibited all the eccentricities of an absolute ruler. In 1975, he dissolved the two prevailing official parties and replaced them with one national organ, the Rastakhiz ("Resurrection") Party.[4] Ironically, the shah's gambit contradicted the principles he had laid down in his memoir, *Mission for My Country*, published in 1962. "If I was a dictator rather than a constitutional monarch, then I might be tempted to sponsor a single dominant party such as Hitler organized or such as you find today in Communist countries," he wrote.[5] To offset the embarrassment, the shah's secret police, Sazaman-e Ettela'at va Amniyat-e Keshvar (SAVAK), had to censor the monarch's own book.

Shortly after its establishment, the Rastakhiz Party set up groups among farmers, students, industrial workers, and all sectors of the bureaucracy. The party would discipline the nation and ensure its compliance with the shah's decrees. The impact was immediate, as SAVAK's repression grew harsher. Censorship rules were stiffened, the intelligentsia cowed, civil society abused, and dissent criminalized. SAVAK was never as vicious as the Islamic Republic would later claim—and the shah's brutality never matched that of his clerical successors—but the King of Kings was isolating himself from his subjects.

The creation of the Rastakhiz Party was followed by other bizarre acts. The shah suddenly replaced the calendar that was based on the Prophet Muhammad's migration to Medina with one that started with King Cyrus's enthronement (approximately 559 B.C.). Iran went from year 1355 to year 2535. The royal court was seemingly seeking to contrive a new national identity, one that privileged royal mythologies over the country's religious foundation.

The façade of authoritarian stability soon was disturbed by new intellectual currents and a new type of activism among the youth. A radical cadre of thinkers led by the French-trained academic Ali Shariati had grown weary of Marxism and socialism and viewed Islam as an authentic ideology of dissent.[6] In their attempt to reconcile religious tradition with modernity, they reconceptualized their faith and its role in national affairs. Their Islam had a distinct political content. In their view, the Prophet Muhammad was not just a spiritual leader but also a revolutionary who challenged vested interests, a reformer who rearranged the existing socioeconomic order, a man of faith who constructed a progressive society. Such ideas helped foster the notion that religion could help mobilize a populace.

In some ways the shah was bedeviled by his own success. His educational investments had led to an increase in the number of university students at home and had dispatched thousands of Iranians to study abroad. Attuned to the sermons of Shariati and Third World intellectuals, the college campuses simmered with political tension, even producing guerrilla organizations such as Feda'iyan-e Khalq.[7] In the early 1970s, the Feda'iyan mounted spectacular attacks on government offices and police barracks. Although disarmed by the security services, they left an impression on the public. Among those impressed by the guerrillas' daring was the shah himself, who confessed in private that "the determination with which they fight is quite unbelievable. Even the women kept battling on to their very last gasp."[8] Suddenly the shah did not seem as invincible.

The monarch was not the only one to notice the guerrillas. Even as the shah was being acclaimed by Nixon as the guardian of American interests in the Gulf, the U.S. intelligence community was beginning to ring the alarm bells about the nature of the Pahlavi state. In 1972, the CIA stressed that the rise of guerrilla groups signaled that there were "soft spots, real or potential in the Iranian situation." The agency noted that the shah was being isolated and that there was a "regrettable lack of communications upward to him from his ministers."[9] As with future intelligence warnings, such analysis did not impact the White House's assessment of the monarchy.

In many ways, the armed struggle of the 1970s proved as illusory for the participants as for the royal court. Bijan Jazani, the theoretician of the Feda'iyan, had hoped that violence by a vanguard force would foment a popular uprising. Such a revolt did not result from his group's sacrifices. In the meantime, guerrilla violence by radical students convinced the shah that the challenge to his rule would come from the left and not the clerical right. The shah's background and temperament had conditioned him to fear Soviet clients. After decades of repression, the Tudeh Party was a shell of its former self and the real threats to the shah were increasingly coming from the seminaries rather than leftist enclaves.

Long accustomed to dismissing the religious classes as reactionary relics of the past, the shah did much to antagonize the clergy. The establishment of theology schools in universities, dispatch of state-sanctioned religious corps to the countryside, gender-mixing in public institutions, and general empowerment of women greatly distressed the priestly class. They complained about the relaxation of cultural strictures, denounced foreign films and modern art, and inveighed against the rampant corruption that so often accompanies sudden wealth. For the most part, the senior ayatollahs confined themselves to warning the shah's emissaries and advising him to change his ways. The royal court had willing interlocutors in the shrine city of Qum, but increasingly the voice of clerical dissent was coming from a distant figure languishing in exile.[10]

Ayatollah Ruhollah Khomeini had come to national prominence in 1964, when he led the revolt against parliamentary legislation exempting U.S. military personnel from Iranian law.[11] After his expulsion from Iran, he took up residence in the Shia sanctuaries of Iraq. During his exile he established the blueprint for an ideal government. In a series of lectures later compiled in a book titled *Islamic Government*, Khomeini called for the direct assumption of power by the clergy.[12] The notion of a single ayatollah ruling in the name of God contravened established norms of Shia political thought. However, Khomeini did not limit himself to abstract theological musings as he castigated the shah for his close association with the United States, his dictatorial rule, and for wasting Iran's oil wealth. Although physically distant from Iran, Khomeini forged ties with student groups in Europe and America and maintained close connections to Iran through his network of mid-level clerics, who disseminated his messages and reached out to opposition figures from a wide variety of backgrounds. In exile, Khomeini was free to thunder against the monarchy and take maximalist positions that his clerical contemporaries in country could not afford to adopt.

In the midst of this turmoil, the shah struggled with a disease that he tried to conceal from his most intimate associates, including his wife. In 1974, the shah was diagnosed with cancer, forcing him to consider the future of the Pahlavi dynasty without him. The shah had made himself indispensable to his government: no decision could be made without his consent and all initiatives had to originate from the palace. He sensed that his callow son Reza was not ready to manage this system of personalized rule. Perhaps a more tolerant government, with competing centers of power, would be a better foundation for his youthful successor. The shah believed the time was right for reforms; his monarchy rested on a durable foundation and his economic achievements had produced a reservoir of national goodwill. Even before the advent of the Carter administration in 1977 and its human rights advocacy, the shah considered fine-tuning his governing order.

It is hard to see how the shah envisioned political reforms. He was clearly disdainful of democracy and believed that a strong leader was necessary for ruling the benighted masses. As with most of his contemporaries, he was prone to conspiratorial thinking and looked for plots and cabals where none existed. He seemed to have appreciated that his system had to change, but possessed neither a blueprint nor a vision for directing that change. The royal court increasingly stood for nothing other than a source of patronage. Although all developing countries suffer from corruption, the scope of venality in Iran was truly staggering.

By the late 1970s, the boom turned to bust. A global recession had reduced oil purchases and caused Iran's impressive economic performance to falter. Rising inflation sharply affected food prices and housing, which was already scarce. The shah blamed the increase in prices on profiteers and dispatched gangs of students to the bazaar to control prices by fining and imprisoning merchants who overcharged. The economic challenges also led him to dismiss his long-standing prime minister, Amir Abbas Hoveyda, for the technocratic Jamshid Amouzegar. The new premier set about worsening the situation. An austerity program designed to curb government spending and tame inflation led to an increase in unemployment. The economic problems compounded the financial difficulties of the middle class and the poor, creating political tensions at a time when the system featured few safety valves.

The shah seemed to have succeeded in alienating nearly every social class. The intelligentsia was agitating for more freedom, the clergy resented loosening cultural mores, the industrial working class faced shrinking wages, the universities were in turmoil, and peasants and farmers grew frustrated by an indifferent agricultural policy. The army of civil servants that was supposed to be the backbone of the regime was angered by the monarchy's nepotism and corruption in bureaucratic management. Even worse for the shah, the surge of economic growth had created popular expectations for continued progress that could not possibly be met. A corrosive spirit of pessimism descended on the country. The Iranians seemed to be searching for a more responsive government and an end to entitlements of a privileged class that benefited from its proximity to the palace.

In January 1977, a despondent shah summoned his most trusted advisor, Minister of Court Asadollah Alam, and confessed, "We're broke. Everything seems doomed to grind to a standstill, and meanwhile many of the programs that we had planned must be postponed."[13] In his moment of distress, the shah seemed strangely alone, as his isolation had limited his circle to a very few confidants. Alam, who also had terminal cancer and in fact died in April 1978, attempted to console the monarch, assuring him that he would be remembered as Persia's greatest ruler, the one who had dragged his country into the age of modernity. It would be the tragedy of Muhammad Reza Pahlavi that as he entered the most serious crisis of his tenure he would be without Alam's wisdom and courage—two traits that the shah distinctly lacked. And as Iran came undone, America elected a new president.

THE REVOLUTION

Upon his assumption of the presidency, there was little indication that Jimmy Carter would spend the better part of his tenure focused on Iran. Arms-control diplomacy with the Soviet Union, brokering peace between Israel and its neighbors, and normalizing relations with China topped the administration's priority list. A global survey produced by the new secretary of state, Cyrus Vance, only mentioned Iran as an important relationship that needed to be preserved. For his part, Carter barely referenced Iran on the campaign trail and seemed more focused on other Cold War hot spots.

And yet, the Carter team came into office with instincts that made it an unsteady partner for a monarch experiencing an existential crisis. The president seemed genuinely offended by right-wing dictatorships and was reluctant to urge repressive measures against a populace seeking democratic rights. Too often, Carter believed, America had reflexively sided with autocrats and allowed anticommunism to blind it to progressive social movements. A Democratic Party that had gained power by critiquing Richard Nixon's and Henry Kissinger's amoral realism was bound to emphasize human rights and democratic accountability. For Carter, an assertion of America's values was compatible with preserving its interests, as he believed that Washington's allies could actually strengthen the foundations of their rule with calibrated reforms.[14]

The beginnings went well enough. The shah made a state visit to the United States shortly after Carter's inauguration and held high-level talks with the new administration. Although student protests and the use of tear gas by the Washington police had marred the White House welcoming ceremony, Carter was impressed by the shah's grasp of international affairs. A reciprocal visit by Carter to Tehran on New Year's Eve 1977 even led the president to exclaim, "Iran, because of the great leadership of the shah, is an island of stability in one of the more trouble areas of the world." The Shah later confessed, "I have never heard a foreign statesman speak of me in quite such flattering terms he used that evening."[15]

As Air Force One departed Mehrabad Airport, Carter had been swayed by the shah's image of himself as a strong leader in control of his affairs. The U.S. government had long since abandoned its assessment of the shah as an indecisive politician incapable of managing tensions. The impressions of the 1950s, with the shah eager to abdicate when confronted with a determined opposition, had evaporated after two decades of monarchical image manipulation. Even more disturbingly, no one in Washington seemed to know that the shah was suffering from a terminal disease, this despite a Tehran filled with rumors about his health and visits to the shah by prominent French doctors specializing in cancer treatment.

The notion of intelligence failure in Iran has been stressed by Carter and his senior advisors to deflect criticism from their misjudgments.[16] The claim is not without justification. Washington's perception of the shah as a strong leader inevitably affected intelligence collection. The CIA and the U.S. embassy downgraded their focus on internal politics and preoccupied themselves with the Soviet threat to Iran. This created a vicious circle: the more that domestic politics of Iran were downgraded, the less the embassy officials paid attention to opposition figures. It is at times suggested by historians that the Americans feared antagonizing the shah and thus neglected his detractors. The documentary record belies such claims. It is not so much that U.S. functionaries were being deferential to the shah; they simply did not think the oppositionists were consequential. Moreover, the notion of a clerical-led revolution was so unprecedented that it would have required unique wisdom to predict it.

Despite such limitations, there were enough warnings in early intelligence reports to have concerned a probing policy maker. In August 1977, the CIA issued its infamous analysis concluding that the shah would remain in power well into the 1980s. This assessment has been proffered by various politicians and scholars as evidence of a blind spot in American intelligence. However, the same report highlights the importance of economic growth to Iran's continued stability. "All programs are of course dependent on a constant flow of income from oil revenues; declining oil sales have recently forced a cut back in some programs and a sharp decline could affect everything else,"[17] the report stressed. This may not be the same as predicting a revolution, but it is also impossible to read this passage and come away confident in the independent strength of the Pahlavi dynasty.

In February 1976, the CIA had conducted an elaborate assessment of the Iranian elite and come away with some important insights about the clerical community. It has often been claimed that given their Cold War mind-set, the American intelligence apparatus was too narrowly focused on left-wing activists, particularly the moribund Tudeh Party. In its survey, however, the CIA stressed that "the clergy would probably not prefer the elimination of the monarchy, but would be happy to see the present Shah go. In the eyes of the religious leaders, Muhammad Reza Pahlavi has betrayed one of the essential elements of his rule, protection of Islam."[18] Had Carter read this report, he may not have been so startled when the mullahs took up the mantle of opposition to the monarchy.

For its part the State Department's own Bureau of Intelligence and Research (INR) conducted a comprehensive study in 1977 for the incoming administration. The INR report asserted, "The undercurrent of terrorist violence notwithstanding, the Shah rules Iran free from serious domestic threat. At age 57, in fine health, and protected by an elaborate security apparatus, the Shah has an excellent chance to rule for a dozen or more years." Yet, the same report stressed that "among intelligentsia, the professional middle class, and the religious conservatives, dissatisfaction is felt over the Shah's arms purchases and over the effects of a 'top-down' program of modernization on traditional values and on what many think are Iran's most pressing needs."[19] At the outset of the Carter administration, the intelligence community had too easily accepted the image of a forceful shah, but they were also reporting undercurrents of resentment and the emergence of opposition sentiments among critical sectors of society. As the crisis unfolded, intelligence reporters would become sharper and more incisive.

Throughout his life, the shah relied on the affirmation of the United States. As with most Iranians, including his Islamist successors, the shah attributed much power to the West. A modernizing monarch who distrusted the Soviets, the shah came to appreciate the importance of America as both a source of protection and a model of development. This was not so much a strategic relationship but a psychological dependency. By the 1970s, the shah trusted very few Iranians and suspected that most of his aides were unwilling to or incapable of offering him sound advice. He relied on U.S. presidents and envoys for both guidance and solace.[20] A perennially indecisive leader who held his countrymen in contempt, he required America's acknowledgment. Confusion in the White House or mixed signals from America's ambassadors was bound to increase his propensity toward indecision.[21]

To please the new administration, the shah eagerly pursued an ill-conceived and rashly implemented liberalization program. The rapid opening up of a political order that had been closed for so long invited dislocation and chaos. To reform a political system without first establishing institutions to absorb the inevitable shocks could only endanger the entire structure. Iranian opposition elements came to perceive the liberalization program as a sign of the shah's weakness and as an indication that Washington no longer supported the monarchy. That the shah's opponents rejected an opportunity to create a constitutional order for the sake of a revolution led by the most reactionary elements of the clerical community is Iran's tragedy.

The SAVAK was the first to warn the shah about the dangers of his course. The intelligence organization reported that a disgruntled coalition of members of the urban middle class, student associations, the intelligentsia, and the radical clergy were poised to challenge the monarchy. The Carter administration's human rights advocacy and the perception of American dissatisfaction with the monarchy could, the SAVAK warned, galvanize a formidable protest movement.[22] The shah was scathing in his rejection of the report. A monarch who perceived that his great accomplishments were valued by his people did not fear liberalization. Arrogance and a desire to win the White House's favor propelled the shah toward a perilous path.

The liberalization program began with the release of a number of political prisoners and commencement of dialogue with Amnesty International and other Western human rights organizations. Suddenly, the National Front, the Freedom Movement, and various lawyers' and writers' guilds resumed their activities in earnest. On October 1977, the Goethe Institute in Tehran sponsored a series of poetry readings that morphed into speeches denouncing the shah's excesses. Calls to establish a constitutional monarchy, end censorship, and reform the judiciary were freely aired. Although at this point the intelligentsia and old-school activists led the charge, they would soon be displaced by more militant forces.

Khomeini reemerged in the public sphere after the death of his son, Mustafa, in 1977.[23] In Iran of the 1970s, it appeared no one died of accidents or natural causes, and the death of Mustafa was soon attributed to SAVAK. A cagey politician, Khomeini sensed that the time had come to press his cause and assume leadership of the nascent opposition movement. "Today in Iran, an opportunity has appeared. Make the most of this opportunity," warned Khomeini in a speech.[24] His disciples, such as Morteza Motahhari, Muhammad Beheshti, Hussein Ali Montazeri, and Ali Akbar Rafsanjani, led the charge, reviving a number of dormant clerical associations. They quickly forged links with the bazaar and anchored themselves in the network of mosques. Religion and money had once again found each other. The more senior ayatollahs kept their distance from Khomeini, but the exiled cleric's followers had always been drawn from the legion of mid-level mullahs, not his skeptical peers.

As Khomeini leveled charges against the monarchy, an infuriated shah struck back. On January 7, 1978, an article entitled "Black and Red Imperialism" was dispatched by the Ministry of Information to one of Iran's largest dailies, Ettela'at, for publication.[25] The article claimed that Khomeini was an agent of the British interest and communist powers whose conduct was disapproved by the more esteemed clerics. The article went on to accuse Khomeini of being foreign born and of living a debauched lifestyle. The draft so unsettled the paper's editor that he inquired whether the court really wanted it published. Without even reading it, Prime Minister Amouzegar stressed that the shah had already approved it and thus it must be printed. This was the Iran of the 1970s: if the shah wanted something unwise and incendiary published, the press he controlled had to oblige. The monarchical system had grown so rigid that the shah's aides could not protect him from himself.

The impact of the article was electric. The seminaries in Qum were the first to erupt, with four thousand students taking to the streets. Demonstrations in other major cities followed, particularly in Tabriz, where the local authorities lost control. The army had to be called in to quell the riots. With scant training in crowd control, the army opted for violence and a number of demonstrators were killed. The protests propelled senior clerical figures such as Ayatollah Muhammad Kazem Shariatmadari and Ayatollah Muhammad Reza Golpaygani, once dubious of Khomeini's radical postulations and his theories about clerical rule, to join the chorus of condemnation of the violence. The shah was now immersed in a Shia ritual cycle of forty-day commemoration after each death. Demonstrations would cause deaths that were observed forty days later, leading to more fatalities and thus more protests. Safe in exile, Khomeini rejected compromise and called for more resistance.

As the protest movement moved along a religious cycle, the practical organization of the revolution passed from the intelligentsia to an informal structure of mosques, bazaar, and seminaries that had managed to preserve a degree of autonomy under state repression. It was perhaps inevitable that religious leaders and their lower-middle-class constituents would lead the revolution. They had a more coherent vision and a more resilient network. The secular forces with their petitions and poetry readings were destined to play a secondary role. The publication of the shah's inflammatory article ensured that one of the most dogmatic figures in Iran's modern history gained national prominence.

As turmoil engulfed Iran, Washington seemed unconcerned if not indifferent. The newly appointed U.S. ambassador to Iran, William Sullivan, had decided to take a prolonged vacation. Still, the embassy did warn the White House that "what the Qum incident and its aftermath have done is to elevate religious opposition to a more visible, significant position among those who have taken advantage of the new liberalization."[26] Carter at the time was preoccupied with settling the Arab-Israeli conflict and Secretary of State Vance was negotiating the second Strategic Arms Limitation Talks (SALT II) agreement with Moscow, so such embassy warnings went unnoticed. The president was going to defer to a monarch who had stayed in power for nearly four decades. Kermit Roosevelt, who had firsthand knowledge of the shah's personal shortcomings during times of crisis, tried to warn the administration. He was politely rebuffed.[27] The real shah remained hidden from the Washington elite.

All revolutions move in stages, with moments of deceptive silence followed by an eruption of intense activity. By the summer of 1978, the shah seemed to have stabilized the situation as he promised free parliamentary elections by the following June and dismissed the notorious head of SAVAK, General Nematollah Nasiri. The opposition seemed hesitant and the demonstrations wound down. Old-guard figures such as Mehdi Bazargan of the Freedom Movement and Karim Sanjabi of the National Front did not anticipate the collapse of the monarchy and were intrigued by the possibility of nudging the shah toward a genuine constitutional order. For the revolutionary pressures to surge ahead, something dramatic was required.

FEEDING THE CROCODILES

On August 19 a fire in Rex Cinema in the city of Abadan took the lives of 477 people. This was an act of arson, meticulously planned and carefully executed. The popular mood was to blame the shah and SAVAK. The Western press that was reduced to printing the opposition's sensationalist claims joined the chorus and faulted the regime. Later trials and testimonials would reveal that the fire had been set by Islamist militants with connections to the religious classes.

To this day no conclusive evidence has surfaced directly tying Khomeini to the Rex Cinema fire. However, the imam, as his followers now called him as a means of elevating him above other senior clerics, did establish a context that justified such acts of terror. Khomeini abhorred movies and viewed them as licentious Western exports designed to distance the Iranian youth from their traditions and sense of piety. By August 1978, approximately two dozen cinemas had already been burned by violent mobs. Moreover, Abadan was central to the monarchy's vitality; it housed the oil refineries that were the lifeblood of Iran's economy. As mayhem swept other cities, Abadan had remained quiet. A tragedy here could not just galvanize the stalled revolution but also cripple the nerve center of the government.

In the aftermath of the fire, Khomeini indulged in contradictions that seemed to be ignored by the frenzied crowds and the compliant press. The imam insisted that the Rex Cinema fire had been the shah's handiwork, designed to intimidate the populace. It showcased the cruelty of the regime and its determination to hold power by massacring innocent filmgoers. Yet, Khomeini remained implacable in his denunciations of movie theaters. A month after the Rex tragedy, he proclaimed that cinemas were being destroyed because they offended religious sensibilities.[28] Somehow the Abadan fire was the shah's doing and the rest were spontaneous acts of an aggrieved public.

By this time the shah's government was so confused that it could not refute Khomeini's cynical tales. Given the regime's unwillingness to use violence on a large scale and its seeming complicity in a horrific act of terrorism, it confronted demonstrations that now doubled in size, reaching hundreds of thousands. Abadan refinery workers walked off their plants, introducing strikes as an element of revolutionary agitation. The shah lost his narrative and then he lost his street.

In a belated act of wisdom, the shah finally removed Amouzegar from power. Amouzegar has been described as a technocrat, a manager capable of sorting out Iran's economy. He had no flair for politics and how to handle constituencies that demanded change. At a time when Iran needed a politician capable of placating, pressuring, and cajoling its merchants, mullahs, and students, Amouzegar preoccupied himself with American business schools' paradigms for economic management. Arrogant and distant, he had no capacity to stem the coming storm or even appreciate its approach.

In his place, the shah made another spectacularly bad choice, appointing an old-school, corrupt politician, Jafar Sharif-Imami, to the premiership. Sharif-Imami had been prime minister in the early

1960s, a president of the senate, and, most recently, the head of the Pahlavi Foundation. A fixture of the system, he was thought to have good relations with the clerical class and could thus ease the monarchy's troubles in the seminaries. Instead, his policy of conciliation—labeled by the U.S. embassy as "feeding the crocodiles"—was tantamount to dismantling the state's security apparatus. The prisons were now emptied, newspaper censorship was lifted, and the military was restrained to the point of emasculation. The one move that Sharif-Imami made that outdid his other misjudgments was to press for Khomeini's relocation. The imam's disciples were uneasy about his remaining in Saddam Hussein's Iraq and looked for another sanctuary, eventually settling on the suburbs of Paris with its freedom of travel and easy communication links to Iran.

September 8 began in an ominous manner with a large, angry crowd gathering in Tehran's Jaleh Square to commemorate the end of Ramadan. By now the protesters were calling for the abdication of the monarchy and the establishment of something called an Islamic Republic. Martial law had been declared, but not soon enough to alert the entire crowd. The soldiers tried to disperse the demonstrators with tear gas and warnings but their orders were ignored. As the crowd kept pushing forward, the poorly trained conscripts opened fire, killing eighty-eight demonstrators. The government's accurate figures were typically drowned out by claims that hundreds had died, some at the hands of Israeli commandos. The Western press followed suit, reporting scenes of carnage by firing squads. The famed French philosopher turned journalist Michel Foucault outdid his colleagues and claimed that four thousand protesters had been shot.

In the aftermath of what became known as Black Friday, strikes as well as demonstrations paralyzed the government. From exile, Khomeini thundered, "From now on it is time for us to close our businesses, not forever, but for the short time it will take to overthrow the ruling oppressor."[29] Central Bank officials, power-plant managers, bazaar merchants, and private-sector employees all began periodic work stoppages. In line with the regime's incompetence, the strikers continued to collect their salaries. There was essentially no penalty for going on strike.

Although it is routinely claimed that oil production came to a standstill, the industry maintained its output for some time. Prior to the onset of the strikes, Iran was producing approximately 5.8 million barrels per day. That production level was reduced to 3.4 million barrels by November 1978 and then down to 2.3 million in December.[30] It would not be until January 1979 and the tail end of the revolution that oil production was essentially shut down.[31]

Black Friday and the demonstrations that followed had an important impact on both the shah and the opposition. The realization that the public was calling for his overthrow sparked the shah's psychological paralysis. In the coming months, he would often summon Western envoys and ask them why his citizens were turning against him.[32] Long isolated from his subjects and unaware of the changing dynamics of his nation, the shah had come to believe the tributes paid to him by his sycophantic aides. The protests and marches calling for his abdication and even death shocked him, fueling his existing tendency to vacillate. It is hard to assess how his illness might have affected his judgment, but his indecisiveness at times of crisis predated his cancer diagnosis. In the end, the shah was an aloof but essentially benevolent man who was reluctant to use wide-scale force to preserve his throne.

The key turning point in any revolution is when an average citizen decides that it is both safe and advantageous for him to join the protest movement. The longer a revolution lasts, the more it is bound to grow. The regime's decision to avoid violence led the public to perceive that it could express its grievances, demonstrate its moral outrage, and gain a measure of peer acknowledgment with relative impunity. By fall of 1978, the cost-benefit analysis would lead many a fence-sitter to join the revolution—the casualties were small and the cause appeared great.

Political actors were similarly affected. At various junctures important opposition leaders had been disposed to compromise with the shah. Not all of the shah's critics were revolutionaries and most hoped for a new national compact that preserved the monarchy while placing serious restraints on its authority. Yet by autumn, most oppositionists were calling for the shah's overthrow. Once Khomeini achieved his supreme status, his uncompromising stance stifled all mediation efforts. In a ritual that was becoming all too familiar, opposition figures would journey to France, display their loyalty to Khomeini, forswear all efforts at reconciliation with the monarchy, and return home to carry forth the revolution. The price of Khomeini's benediction was adherence to his maximalist injunctions. Khomeini's obduracy and the mayhem sweeping the streets made a compromise solution more and more remote.

The shah now looked for signals from the United States and hoped that somehow Washington would take the tough decisions for him. In his memoirs, he recalls asking himself, "What were they [Westerners] thinking? What did they want—for Iran and me?" Prone toward conspiracy thinking in times of trouble, the shah asked a startled Ambassador Sullivan why the CIA was "suddenly turning against" him. "Had he done something?"[33] Sullivan could only assure the shah that the demonstrations engulfing his capital were not sponsored by the U.S. intelligence services.

As Black Friday unfolded, Carter and his senior aides were ensconced at Camp David trying to settle the Arab-Israeli account. Still, Carter managed to call the shah, expressing regret for the loss of life and affirming his support for the liberalization policies. It testifies to the extent of the shah's disillusionment with the United States that he would later claim that no such call had been made. What is clear is that Washington was too absorbed with arms-control talks with Moscow and brokering peace between Egypt and Israel to take serious notice of a collapsing pillar of its Middle East policy.

Although the shah's accusation that the CIA was plotting against his rule is outlandish, his claim that he confronted a confused U.S. policy has some justification. There was a split in Washington that never resolved throughout the revolution. Cyrus Vance, his State Department aides, and eventually William Sullivan pressed for reforms at all cost. To them, the problem was not that Iran was experiencing a revolution but that the shah had too much power. In the meantime, National Security Advisor Zbigniew Brzezinski eventually came to advocate restoring order and taking tough measures to shore up the shah. Carter never resolved this fundamental division and chose instead to split the difference. The United States would express its backing for the shah, suggest that reforms continue, and occasionally indicate that it would support the monarch should he consider alternative actions. Whenever the shah asked for clarification, the same essential formula would be repeated.

By November Iran was in flames. Demonstrations and riots were daily occurrences. Thousands of banks, shops, schools, and public buildings were either damaged or destroyed. Even Sharif-Imami, the architect of the policy of appeasement, seemed to appreciate its hazards and warned Sullivan that the "Shah was incapable of making any decisions."[34] Having failed to stem the tide of the revolution, Sharif-Imami resigned and left the shah to persist in his ambivalent strategy of liberalization during a national revolt.

At this point, an idea evolved in the royal court that the shah should concede to the verdict of the revolution. In essence, the shah should go from being the prime target of the revolution to one its leaders. Why not have a revolution without regime change? In a momentous speech on December 6, 1978, a visibly haggard shah confessed, "I, too, have heard the message of the revolution of you, the Iranian people . . . After all the sacrifices that you have made, I pledge that in the future the Iranian government will be founded in Basic Law, social justice and the people's will and know nothing of despotism, tyranny and corruption."[35] A chastised shah tried to convince his subjects to choose constitutionalism over chaos.

The conciliatory speech was a curious way to introduce a military government and its new head, General Gholam Reza Azhari. In choosing Azhari, the shah had bypassed the more determined general Gholam Ali Oveissi, the hardline military governor of Tehran, in favor of an officer who had no stomach for the job. The first act of the military government was to placate the revolutionaries by arresting prominent members of the shah's own regime, including his longest-serving prime minister, Amir Abbas Hoveyda. Sensing the mood in the palace, Khomeini assured his supporters that "their tanks, machine guns, and bayonets are all rusty, they will not withstand your iron will."[36] Once the mobs poured into the streets, they faced the same reticence from the armed forces as before. Azhari's conduct demystified the notion of a military government and removed the last vestige of monarchical authority. At every step, the shah's hesitation enabled Khomeini's success.

The ensuing chaos provoked a stream of American officials to journey to Tehran. Secretary of the Treasury Michael Blumenthal, senators Mike Mansfield and Robert Byrd, and numerous diplomats all met with the shah. Each returned with a warning: the regime had no plans for arresting the revolutionary momentum. Suddenly the façade of monarchical control was shattered and Washington began to appreciate that perhaps the shah was not in command of the situation. Carter confided to his diary that "He [the shah] is not a strong leader but very doubtful and unsure of himself."[37] The only problem was that the administration also had no plan of action and was mired in endless debates.

Although the intelligence community would later be scapegoated by Carter-era officials, at this point it offered the administration a series of incisive warnings. The CIA insisted in November 1978 that "Khomeini is determined to overthrow the Shah and is unlikely to accept a compromise. His influence now is so strong that neither other clerics nor civilian opposition leaders will take actions he opposes."[38] The INR went to the heart of the problem and stressed that "His [the shah's] reversion to the moods of depression and vacillation that he displayed in the early 1950s makes it doubtful that he can move to salvage what remains of national unity unless others intervene on his behalf."[39] In essence, the intelligence community claimed that a coalition government would not forestall the revolution. Washington would have to make the tough decisions that the shah was incapable of making. It is surprising how little impression such assessments made on senior officials.

Spurred to action by the bad news coming out of Tehran, the White House established the Iran Coordinating Committee to deal with the crisis. From its very first meeting the committee's deliberations expressed the policy chasm within the administration. For his part, Brzezinski correctly noted that Iran's military government should be pressed to take stern measures. The point that the national security advisor missed was that although the shah had an impressive apparatus of power at his disposal, he had lost the will to use it. After all, this was precisely the point of the earlier INR report. The State Department, represented in much of these discussions by Deputy Secretary of State Warren Christopher, maintained that the shah had to make further concessions to the opposition. It had become an article of faith in Foggy Bottom that the revolutionary fervor could be quenched only if the shah persisted in his liberalization policy. The impasse between the State Department and the National Security Council went unresolved.

As if the confusion in Washington were not enough, Sullivan now decided to pursue his own policy. The perennially confident ambassador dispatched a somber memorandum to the White House titled, "Thinking the Unthinkable." Seldom has a diplomatic cable been so wrong. Sullivan insisted that "it may eventuate that both the Shah and the more senior military would abdicate, leaving the armed forces under the leadership of younger officers who would be prepared to reach an accommodation with the religious leaders under Khomeini."[40] The ambassador assured his superiors that Khomeini would embrace a "Gandhi like" position and leave politics to moderate figures such as

Bazargan. Sullivan's postulations would gradually gain adherents, particularly in the State Department.[41]

Sullivan and the State Department officials who pressed for an accommodation with Khomeini missed the primacy of anti-Americanism in his revolutionary cosmology. The notion of the shah's subservience to America was a defining indictment. Any deviation from that line meant disloyalty to the cause of national emancipation. The moderates who so enchanted the U.S. embassy and the State Department were bound to have a limited tenure on Khomeini's future national stage. Their contacts with the Americans were useful to the imam as he guided his revolution to success, but in the aftermath of his triumph they would be quickly discarded.

On December 11, during the commemoration of Ashura, a Shia ritual, millions of people marched in Tehran proclaiming Khomeini as their leader and the Islamic Republic as their preferred form of government. The event was preceded by an agreement between the mullahs and the military whereby the government kept the troops out of sight and the demonstrators confined themselves to established routes. The discipline of the crowd testified to the diligence and control of its organizers and allowed them to frame the massive outpouring as a referendum on the monarchy.

By this time even the shah's ineffectual military governor was complaining about restrictions imposed on his limited authority. The army was being demoralized as soldiers were ordered to avoid bloodshed at all cost. As Tehran burned, Sullivan was summoned to the prime minister's office and found him surrounded by medical equipment, an apparent victim of a mild heart attack. Azhari implored the ambassador that "the country is lost because the Shah cannot make up his mind."[42] This was the second prime minister in a row who had advised Sullivan that the shah could not handle the situation.

Seeking a way out of his administration's impasse, Carter empowered an outside advisor to review America's policy options. George Ball, a former State Department official and a Democratic Party trouble-shooter, accepted the thankless task.[43] As a member of Lyndon Johnson's team, Ball had distinguished himself by his early and prescient opposition to the escalating Vietnam War. However, when it came to Iran he produced an altogether useless set of recommendations. Ball professed that the United States would be "inviting disaster if we were to continue to prop up the Shah as a monarch retaining any substantial powers of government."[44] Instead, Ball proposed a council of notables that would choose the government. Apparently, the shah would remain on his throne but concede most of his powers to the council as it charted Iran's future.[45] Out of his depth, Ball seemed not to realize that the shah already had tried and failed to recruit credible political figures to his government. And by this time, as the CIA assessment had suggested, anyone defying Khomeini would risk expulsion from an opposition that appeared on the verge of victory.

As Washington wandered through its confusion, the shah once again asked Sullivan for guidance. In a plaintive manner, the monarch asked the envoy whether the United States wanted him to use an iron fist. The ambassador merely replied that "You are the Shah, you must take the decision as well as the responsibility."[46] This was a different experience for the shah than in 1953, when he had faced a resolute American president and a coherent U.S. policy. Carter persistently assured the shah of his support and yet never told him what should be done to salvage the situation. "I knew he needed all the support the United States could properly give him, short of direct intervention in the internal affairs of his country," Carter recalled.[47] Given the opposition's exaggerated view of the United States, it perceived that if Washington really wanted the shah to survive it would have pressed him to use force. The fact that so little force was used during the entire revolution was seen by the shah's opponents as an indication of American indifference to his fate.

Having failed to obtain a clear U.S. preference, the shah continued his search for an opposition figure to install as premier. Shapur

Bakhtiar, a member of the National Front and a former deputy labor minister in Muhammad Mossadeq's government, finally stepped forth in January 1979 and accepted the monarch's mandate. Bakhtiar brought a measure of credibility and courage to his task. He seemed indifferent to his expulsion from the National Front and shrugged off Khomeini's denunciations. Even more dramatic was the shah's decision to leave the country under the pretext of needing rest. To anyone still willing to listen the monarch would mournfully ask why his countrymen had turned against him despite all that he had done for them. On January 16, Muhammad Reza Pahlavi and his wife left Iran, never to return.

DENOUEMENT

Although the monarchical edifice was rapidly crumbling, Bakhtiar approached his premiership with democratic energy. He outlawed press censorship, freed the remaining few political prisoners, and disbanded the SAVAK. In a nod to Iran's new identity, he prohibited the sale of oil to Israel and South Africa. Iran now left the Cold War, as Bakhtiar renounced its membership in the U.S.-led Central Treaty Organization. A member of the generation of politicians who had come of age during the Mossadeq interlude, Bakhtiar viewed himself as an heir to a liberal tradition deformed by monarchical absolutism. He was open to dialogue with Khomeini but would not prostrate himself in front of him as his secular counterparts did.

Bakhtiar's vision and moderation were bound to be devoured by the revolution. On February 1, a triumphant Khomeini returned from exile. He was welcomed by a frenzied crowd of approximately five million. He quickly established his authority by appointing Mehdi Bazargan as the head of the new interim government. Tehran was a scene of a war of nerves with Khomeini and the revolutionaries facing Bakhtiar and the military. A showdown loomed, but for now neither side was entirely sure of its strength.

For his part, Sullivan was prepared to welcome the new order. In yet another erroneous cable, he assured the White House, "Our best assessment to date is that the Shia Islamic movement commanded by Ayatollah Khomeini is far better organized and able to resist Communism than its detractors would have us believe."[48] The ambassador went on to claim, "It is possible that the process of governing might produce accommodation with the anti-clerical intellectual strains which exist in the opposition to produce something more closely approaching Westernized democratic process."[49] Sullivan's absurdities seemed to have made an impression on Vance, who claimed, "The National Front representatives seemed confident that they would be able to keep the revolution in democratic channels, but stressed that we should disassociate ourselves from Bakhtiar soon because he was going to disappear quickly."[50] It may have been the president's official policy to support Bakhtiar, but key officials were already thinking well beyond those parameters.

The need to assess the state of Iran's military led Carter to dispatch General Robert Huyser, the deputy commander of the U.S. European Command, to Tehran. Huyser was to maintain the cohesion of the military, ensure its support for Bakhtiar, and possibly prepare the ground for a coup attempt. In the wake of the shah's departure, Huyser found the senior generals demoralized and unsure of themselves. Two years into the revolution, they had done little planning for the actual takeover of the country and operation of its key industries. The revolutionaries had launched an impressive psychological campaign against both the foot soldiers and the generals, using appeals to religion and nationalism to veer them away from their commitments. Still, Huyser helped steady the generals and made sure that the armed forces held together.[51]

In February 1979, the liberals such as Bazargan and the leaders of the National Front played an indispensable role in the collapse of the monarchy. Khomeini had returned to Iran, the military seemed largely intact, and stalemate was the order of the day. The Islamists detested the old regime and the generals distrusted the new claimants of power. The liberals were in touch with the Islamists, the generals, and the U.S. embassy. They assured their interlocutors that the new government would be not vengeful, but forgiving, if not inclusive. Their pledges made it easier for the generals to acquiesce and for the embassy to believe in a tolerant republic. For Khomeini to succeed without further violence, he needed Bazargan and his ilk. It was they who helped navigate the revolution to its final triumph. It would be the last time in the history of the Islamic Republic that liberals and secularists played an important role on the national stage.

Still, the demise of the existing order needed a spark. And that came on February 9 with the insurrection of air force technicians, leading to one last gasp of conflict between the demonstrators, street guerrillas, and the military. Bakhtiar implored the generals to restore order and use the ample power at their disposal to repress the revolt. But the shah's generals declared neutrality, opting to die at the hands of Khomeini's tribunals rather than preserve the order that the shah had given up on. Theirs was a double tragedy: first, they believed in the shah, and then they believed in the revolutionaries' promise of justice and amnesty. On February 11, 1979, twenty-five hundred years of Persian monarchy came to an end.

Could the Iranian revolution have been stopped? Could the shah have been saved? These questions have been pondered by both scholars and politicians ever since Iran's momentous revolution. By the fall of 1978, the only manner in which the popular revolt could have been quelled was through a massive use of force. In the end, neither the shah nor Carter was willing to use such measures to save the Pahlavi dynasty. "A sovereign may not save his throne by shedding his countrymen's blood," insisted the shah in his memoirs.[52] Too many accounts of the revolution mimic the mullahs' claim that tens of thousands perished during the uprisings. In the aftermath of the revolution, the Islamic Republic's own Martyrs Foundation assessed that between October 1977 and February 1979, 2,781 demonstrators were killed, the majority in Tehran.[53] The fact was that the shah recoiled from violence and did not want to use indiscriminate force against his own subjects. He tried to placate the population by claiming to have heard their message of change, he tried to intimidate the protesters by deploying his armed forces, and he tried to divert the opposition by pledging a constitutional monarchy. The arrogance and megalomania that typified the shah's actions in the early 1970s had been replaced by pathetic indecisiveness as the storm gathered. The shah switched tactics so often that he only succeeded in confusing his supporters and empowering his enemies.

The irony was that the shah had at his disposal the means to forestall the revolution. The armed forces and the monarchy were indivisible and the military had long been the pillar of shah's rule. Had the shah given the order for the army to crack down, it is likely that the revolution would have been stillborn. It is important to stress that the protests in the streets gained momentum after the public realized that it would pay little price for its defiance. In a similar manner, Khomeini's stature and authority grew when his claims that the shah would react passively came to fruition. At every step of the way, Khomeini's steely determination was rewarded by monarchical retreat.

Even after the shah's departure, there was a possibility of saving the situation if the United States had assumed responsibility for guiding Iran's generals. The Iranian armed forces neither crumbled nor melted like snow. General Huyser estimated that defections from the ranks were fewer than one hundred soldiers a day, this from a force of 480,000 men. Moreover, Huyser calculated that a coup would require twenty thousand troops that he thought could be supplied from the Imperial Guards—the special detachment of the military most loyal to the shah. A week before the revolution triumphed, Huyser assured the White House that the military had the capacity to execute a coup.[54] The reports from the U.S. military attachés confirm Huyser's assessments.

The junior officers and the conscripts largely maintained their posts and would probably have executed their orders had any been issued.

The problem was all along that the generals were as tentative as the monarch himself and it was unclear on behalf of whose authority they would act. The military did not trust Bakhtiar and his contemplations of a republic. The shah's generals were tentative men of limited initiative and may have been prodded to action by monarchical edict or American injunction but not by the prime minister's pleas. In exile, the shah had cut himself off and he seemed indifferent to the plight of his own country. And in Washington, a different scene played itself out.

By the early days of February, the one person who conceivably could have stepped in and salvaged the monarchy was Jimmy Carter. However, Carter did not break the stalemate that he encountered among his advisers and he simply watched the monarchy collapse. At his core, Carter was a new type of politician suffused with idealism and distrustful of dictators such as the shah. A man who had come to power emphasizing human rights and self-determination could not bring himself to tell the shah or his generals to crack down. Throughout the revolution, Carter kept his distance from the shah, calling him only once. Once more, Brzezinski succinctly captures Carter's dilemma, stressing, "The President was clearly pulled in opposite directions by his advisors and perhaps by conflict between his reason and emotion."[55]

The imperatives of the Cold War and the need to maintain stability in the Middle East had traditionally pressed the United States to resist radical actors. Washington usually feared that unreliable leaders such as Gamal Abdel Nasser and Muhammad Mossadeq would endanger America's interests and might even pave the way for Soviet inroads. Many influential voices in the Carter administration managed to convince themselves that the shah would be displaced not by rash revolutionaries led by Khomeini but by moderate politicians inclined to deal with the United States. They believed that even though Iran might no longer serve as the linchpin of America's containment network in the

Middle East, it would remain a nation ruled by pragmatic politicians inclined to respect international norms. As such, there was no need for the White House to implore the Iranian generals to shed blood, for Iran would remain a constructive actor at ease with the U.S. domination of the Middle East. Indeed, instead of relying on an unsavory right-wing despot like the shah, Washington would have a chance to deal with politicians with a measure of popular legitimacy. Such sentiments appealed to Carter, who seemed implicitly to share the hope that Khomeini and his clerical disciples leading the revolution in the name of Islamic militancy and anti-Americanism would fade from the scene while the moderate members of the revolutionary coalition would succeed. To say the least, this was a gross misreading of Iran's revolt.

In the end, 1979 unfolded differently than 1953 had. At every step of the way, the shah had the capability to quell the revolution. Through judicious reforms in the early 1970s, or a more forceful response once the revolution broke out, the monarchy had many cards at its disposal. Even after the shah's departure, the military may have been able to execute a coup. In Washington, Carter confronted a confused bureaucracy and ultimately chose not to make the tough decisions. Somehow, it was hoped that reasonable Iranians would reclaim the revolution from the firebrands. In a paradoxical way, the success of Iran's improbable revolution relied heavily on an Iranian monarch and an American president.

CATASTROPHE

The 1979 Iranian revolution constituted one of the most dramatic setbacks for the United States. It proved that American interests can be imperiled not just by the Soviet Union and its proxies or by Arab neutralists but by militant actors beholden to neither superpower. Iran's revolutionaries were not agents of the Soviet Union and had no qualms about prosecuting leftists and communists. Under the banner of "Neither East nor West" they seemed to abhor both superpowers, although given the contentious history of U.S.-Iran relations they had a particular animus for the United States. Still, as the dominant power in the Middle East, the newly rising Islamic Republic was more damaging to Washington. Moscow seemed to relish the advent of a stridently anti-American state, even if that state had no need for its communist ideology.

As its first act on the international scene, the Islamic Republic breached the sanctuary of a diplomatic compound in November 1979 and held U.S. embassy officials hostage for 444 days. In its second major act, in 1983, it engineered the bombing of U.S. Marine barracks in Lebanon, killing 241 U.S. service personnel. The theocratic state would go on to become the benefactor of an array of radical forces such as Hezbollah and Hamas. It would seek to subvert the Gulf sheikdoms and emerge as an implacable foe of Israel. It would pursue weapons of mass destruction and go on to construct an elaborate nuclear infrastructure. The Islamic Republic would also be a participant in the longest war in the history of the Middle East.

CHAPTER 9

THE IRAN-IRAQ WAR

The Iran-Iraq war, one of the longest conflicts in the history of the modern Middle East, defined the politics of the Persian Gulf for decades to come. A revolutionary Iran emerged from the fight with its enmities intact but its revolution exhausted. Iraq left the conflict empowered but embittered toward its Arab allies, who had invested in Iraq's war but refused to aid its reconstruction. A fragile armistice brought the war to the end without removing the underlying causes of the conflict.

For the United States, the showdown offered an opportunity to regain confidence and find firmer footing in the region after the Carter administration's mishandling of the Iranian revolution. The war remained confined to the two Gulf giants and did not embroil the entire Middle East. Iran was not permitted to win the war, and the Soviet Union did not gain greater influence in the region. Oil continued to fuel the global economy and Iran's revolutionary threat to the sheikdoms subsided. Saddam appeared menacing but contained.

IRAQ GOES TO WAR

Iran's revolution, with its assault on the prevailing order, portended conflict. War frequently follows revolutions, as newly empowered militants look abroad for redemption of their cause. Revolutionaries, who believe that their claims are universally applicable, and blur the distinction between domestic and foreign affairs, are inherently unpredictable. International relations offer a means of affirming the vitality of the larger mission as opposed to realizing national interests. Iran's theocratic revolt not only shared these impulses, but, given its religious characteristics, cast all issues in a distinct binary: the forces of piety battling a profane order. For Ayatollah Khomeini, the success of his revolution at home mandated its wider regional observance.

The onset of the revolution did not immediately change the uneasy truce between Tehran and Baghdad, which had been in place since the 1975 Algiers Accord had settled the two countries' dispute over the Shatt al-Arab waterway. The Ba'athist regime in Iraq even welcomed the demise of the shah, whose great power pretensions and close ties to the United States had led to frequent clashes with Iraq. The moderate and judicious Bazargan government, with its neutralist foreign policy and a determination to improve relations with Iran's neighbors, did not overtly concern the masters of Iraq. Indeed, Bazargan was even invited to Baghdad in July 1979 with an eye toward improving relations.

Soon, however, a disturbing pattern emerged with Iran mixing aggressive propaganda, subversion, and terrorism to advance its cause in other nations. As always, Khomeini and his clerical cohort would begin by denying the legitimacy of the existing ruling class and castigating the Gulf sheikdoms for their close ties to the United States. Terrorism and violence were not far behind, as such measures were a necessary response to what the clerics deemed to be iniquitous regimes. Whether it was plotting a coup in Bahrain, planning bombings in Kuwait, or instigating riots during the annual hajj (pilgrimages) to the holy city of Mecca in Saudi Arabia, Iran quickly estranged its neighbors. In a retrospective gaze, Ayatollah Hussein Ali Montazeri, Khomeini's heir apparent who was himself eventually ousted from power, noted Iran's complicity in its fate, stressing, "Our harsh slogans against them and talk of exporting the revolution provoked them to act against us and these slogans became the basis for provoking Iraq and causing eight years of war."[1] To be sure, the Gulf states had vulnerabilities. Many of them harbored sizeable Shia populations that had historically been kept out of the spoils of power. The blatant discrimination of the Sunni rulers had confined the Shias to second-class status, deprived of political standing or an important share in the national economy. By providing sanctuary to opposition forces and misusing its diplomatic missions for political agitation, Tehran made itself a source of animosity.

Perhaps nowhere was Iran's message of Shia empowerment received with greater acclaim than in Iraq. A defiant and resolute Ayatollah Muhammad Baqir Sadr shattered the conventions of political passivity and openly embraced Iran's revolution and its clerical patron. In a 1979 fatwa, Sadr declared his "total support for the Imam," and even suggested that it was dishonorable for Muslims to join the Ba'ath Party.[2] These were not the idle claims of an errant cleric, as Sadr's stature, his close connections to the leading Shia political party, al- Da'wa, and his street power made him an important opponent of the state. Sadr's frequent arrests by Saddam's police not only led to his further radicalization, but sparked riots in the shrine cities of Karbala and Najaf. In the meantime, a number of Iraqi Shia parties united under the banner of Islamic Liberation Movement, dedicating themselves to armed struggle against the Ba'athist rule.[3]

In April 1980, these trends culminated in a failed assassination attempt against Tariq Aziz, the deputy prime minister, by Shia forces during a speech at the University of Baghdad. Saddam's reaction featured all the brutality and excess that characterized his tenure. Spooked by the example of the Iranian revolution, in which a rebellious cleric had led a national revolt through the force of his personality and religious pedigree, Saddam executed Sadr. The ayatollah's death was followed by random arrests, summary executions, and expulsion of countless Shias to Iran. Saddam seemed to have genuinely feared the spread of Khomeini's Islamist revolt and blamed his Shia problems on Iranian manipulation.[4]

The rise of dogmatic clerics in Iran made the conflict between the two powers ideological as well as practical. The religiosity of Khomeini's revolution and his unique appeal to the hard-pressed Shia masses threatened to undermine a secular regime that was governing a restive majority. For Khomeini, the Arab socialist republics were as anathema as the monarchical states that he had always disparaged. On the strategic front, Khomeini's assertion of predominance over the Persian Gulf unnerved an Iraqi state that had its own hegemonic aspirations. Moreover, as a leading pan-Arab state, Iraq saw an opportunity to rebuff a Persian nation that had grown comparatively weaker after the ravages of the revolution.[5]

However, Iran's provocations cannot alone account for the war, as opportunism and greed also pressed Saddam toward conflict.[6] Iraq's changing regional position reinforced Saddam's ambition to emerge as the leading actor in the Middle East. By 1979, the Iraqi regime was at its most stable, as it had largely silenced a Kurdish insurgency that had begun in the early 1970s, and as its oil wealth stood second only to that of Saudi Arabia. Within the Middle East, Egypt's expulsion from the councils of Arab states because of its peace treaty with Israel made Iraq the focal point of Arab order. The size of its army, its rising oil revenues, and its geopolitical centrality further enhanced its predominance. Saddam seems to have thought that his move against Iran was a necessary step toward consolidating his regional position. "We have to stick their noses in mud so we can impose our will over them. This cannot take place except militarily," Saddam advised his aides.[7]

The opportunity to tame Khomeini and emerge as the Arab hegemon also coincided with internal convulsions in Iran that seemingly made that task much easier. Saddam must have noticed how the Islamic Republic was dismantling its armed forces, musing at one point, "In other words, do they have the mind to fight us while they are in this bad military condition?"[8]

The mullahs' statecraft was at its most confused immediately prior to the start of hostilities. On the one hand, Iran was providing sanctuary to Saddam's opponents and engaging in similarly inflammatory acts throughout the Gulf region. Yet, the revolutionaries' distrust of the military and their perception that the armed forces were an instrument of monarchical repression simultaneously led them to downgrade the shah's impressive force. Iran was canceling military purchase orders, reducing the size of its armed forces by a third, and delaying conscription calls. The revolutionaries who had come to power rebelling against the prevailing order disdained conventional military preparations in favor of people's militias. The Revolutionary Guards recruited from among the regime's young loyalists would be the bulwark of Iran's defenses. In the Islamic Republic's initial frenzied days, Iranian mullahs perceived themselves to be vanguards of a new epoch immune from the constraints of politics and history. Iran indulged in rhetorical assaults and mischievous practices while at the same time making itself vulnerable to retribution.

Far from seeking to entrap Iran in a war with its neighbor, the Carter administration used its good offices to warn the theocracy. Washington appreciated that the provisional government was a moderate regime under political stress. Given the anti-American frenzy of the time, the United States had to be circumspect and deal gingerly with Bazargan. But the essence of U.S. policy aimed to improve bilateral relations. U.S. embassy personnel were in touch with their Iranian counterparts and were attempting to deal with issues such as the remaining commercial contracts and outstanding arms sales. Although the Islamic Republic likes to pretend otherwise, many of its leading clerical politicians were also in contact with American diplomats.

As part of its routine exchanges, U.S. officials began sharing intelligence assessments with the provisional government. The main conduit appears to have been the deputy prime minister—and later ambassador to Sweden—Abbas Amir Entezam, who would go on to be the Islamic Republic's longest-serving political prisoner. Once Entezam became Iran's envoy to Sweden in 1979, many of these meetings were held in Stockholm. Among the issues discussed during these sessions were the Soviet Union's priorities, the developments in the Middle East, and particularly Iraq's intentions.

In October 1979, George Cave of the CIA led a delegation to Tehran to meet with Foreign Minister Ibrahim Yazdi and Entezam. The U.S. officials outlined Iraqi military preparations that seemed to suggest plans for an invasion. The Iraqi military exercises, the prepositioning of supplies, and the dispatch of large units to the border areas appeared ominous. In the meantime, Iraq had also set up an organization called the Arab Liberation Front that was to instigate uprisings among Iran's ethnic Arabs once the invasion began. Three weeks after the briefing, on November 4 Iranian militants took over the U.S. embassy and instigated a 444-day crisis, holding fifty-two Americans hostage. The provisional government soon collapsed and the nascent U.S.-Iranian intelligence cooperation came to an end.[9] In this sense, the hostage crisis not only damaged Iran's international reputation but also endangered its national interests.

By the summer of 1980, Iraq had begun to establish the antecedents for an invasion of Iran. Saddam's rhetoric went through a subtle transformation, directly indicting the theocratic regime for Iraq's internal disturbances. In a pointed measure, Saddam called on the Iranian masses to overthrow the "mummy Khomeini," stressing his hope that the "Iranian people would find someone else other than this rotten Khomeini."[10] In an even more belligerent tone, Saddam virtually promised war, claiming, "It is not a bad thing to avoid a clash with Iran, unless a clash is patriotic and national duty."[11]

As border skirmishes between the two states intensified, Saddam simply renounced the 1975 treaty that had provided a peaceful means for operating the Shatt al-Arab waterway. In his impetuous style, he claimed that "since the rulers of Iran have violated this agreement from the beginning of their reign as [did] the Shah before them, I announce before you that we consider the March 1975 agreement abrogated."[12] Finally, on September 22, 1980, the Iraqi dictator took the predictable yet catastrophic decision to invade Iran, provoking one of the most devastating wars in the annals of modern Middle East history.

As with any other war, the Iran-Iraq war has generated its share of conspiracies. At times, it is suggested that an aggrieved Carter administration gave the Iraqi dictator a green light to invade. Yet as we have seen, prior to the takeover of the U.S. embassy American intelligence was steadily warning Tehran of Baghdad's designs. Washington's first reaction to the invasion was to try to restore the status quo and preserve Iran's sovereignty. Zbigniew Brzezinski stressed, "We should actively seek new contacts with Iran to explore the possibility of helping it just enough to put sufficient pressure on Iraq to pull back from most, if not all, its current acquisitions. Only by attempting to do this can we make the needed effort to safeguard Iran from Soviet penetration and internal disintegration."[13] Carter conceded in a public address that "We oppose any effort to dismember Iran."[14] In the end, the theocracy was too enchanted with its anti-American animosities to respond to Carter's sympathetic outreach.

The United States did not want to see a war in the Persian Gulf. Washington neither offered Iraq a green light nor looked with favor on Saddam's invasion. Iraq, after all, was an ally of the Soviet Union and had signed a friendship treaty with Moscow in 1972. Baghdad had purchased Russian arms, spearheaded the opposition to the Camp David Accords, and sought to mobilize the radical Arab states against Israel.

In light of the ongoing hostage crisis, there was enmity toward Iran, but the historical records suggest that this animosity never led Carter to conspire with Saddam.

THE WAR CONTINUES

As the war went on, it became the domain of the newly inaugurated Reagan administration, which took office on January 20, 1981. During the campaign, Ronald Reagan had criticized Carter's handling of the Iranian revolution, insisting that the United States had "undercut the shah" and that it was a "blot on our record that we let him [the shah] down." Reagan was determined to buttress America's alliances in the Middle East and push back on a revolutionary theocracy that seemed determined to upend the regional order. It was imperative for the new administration that oil continue to flow from the Gulf, the war not expand, and the sheikdoms not be intimidated by the Islamic Republic into complying with its mandates. In due course, this meant tilting toward Iraq.

Iraq's invasion initially scored impressive gains, as the Iranian city of Khurramshahr fell and the important industrial cities of Abadan and Ahvaz were besieged and isolated in a matter of weeks. Saddam flamboyantly proclaimed his desire to fight "until every inch of usurped land was restored to Arab control," an unsubtle claim on the oil-rich Khuzistan province.[15] Saddam's ambitions soon outstripped his military acumen. His forces encountered logistical difficulties resulting from poor planning and unexpectedly stiff Iranian resistance. Even at the early stages of the conflict, Saddam's misjudgments were manifest. The Iraqi dictator's anticipation that his battlefield successes would lead to a mass uprising grossly misunderstood the mood of the Iranian people. Moreover, the notion that a revolutionary regime claiming to be in command of a new epoch would quickly cede vast portions of its territory and resettle itself in a truncated terrain as Saddam had anticipated was a profound misperception.

In January 1981, Iran began its counterattack, quickly scoring notable gains. The siege of Abadan along the Persian Gulf ended in the spring, and Iran moved to expel the remaining Iraqi forces from its territory. Despite battlefield success, however, Iran's military establishment was plagued by tensions: the task of coordinating between the Revolutionary Guards, the regular armed forces, and the Basij militias was not always easy. The differing command structure and lack of coordination made the military tasks much more difficult. Sayyad Ali Shirazi, the commander of the ground forces, who had established a good relationship with the clerical leadership, noted these challenges:

> In these circumstances we did not have just one or two problems. It was not just a shortage of supplies, but the leadership of the forces. During such sensitive times, this was difficult as on the one hand were elements with a revolutionary spirit and on the other those whose long years during the reign of decadence gave them a different culture. This was very difficult.[16]

The ostensible Iranian strategy was to have the Basij and the Revolutionary Guard units conduct human-wave assaults that would overwhelm the ill-prepared Iraqi defenses. Once an opening was achieved, the regular military contingents would finish the attack. Such unrelenting offensive operations did prove successful, as they conserved munitions while achieving victories.

The war was not without its share of mediation and diplomacy seeking to resolve the conflict. The foreign ministers of the Islamic Conference launched their own fact-finding tours, while Yasir Arafat, chairman of the Palestine Liberation Organization, made unsuccessful visits to both Tehran and Baghdad. Rafsanjani, the speaker of the Iranian parliament and one of Khomeini's closest aides, rebuffed all these efforts by simply asserting, "As we are sure of victory and do not want to reward aggression, we refuse to negotiate."[17] The U.N. Security

Council also issued a call for the termination of the war and the restoration of the borders. In 1981, the United Nations went beyond mere declarations and assumed an activist posture, with the appointment of the former Swedish prime minister, Olof Palme, as its emissary. However, Palme's mission was frustrated by both parties. Iran insisted on designating Iraq as an aggressor and on the removal of all ground troops from its territory before any discussion could begin. Baghdad balked at any withdrawal of its forces and claimed that such a move could only be considered as part of negotiations. Both sides appeared willing to continue the war, and engaged in laborious discussions over technicalities in the hope of impeding an actual settlement. The war would be decided on the battlefields.

The conflict placed the Gulf emirates in a precarious position, as they distrusted both Iran's Islamist aspirations and Iraq's pan-Arabist pretensions. The pull of Arabism and disdain for an Iranian regime that was openly calling for their overthrow seemingly made supporting Saddam an easy choice. Yet, inter-Arab relations were never simple, as the radical republics had long contested the legitimacy of the monarchical states. As the war dragged on and Iran grew determined to export its revolution, the sheikdoms chose the Iraqi strongman. They augmented Iraq's military capabilities and birthed an unprecedented anti-Iranian alliance in the form of the Gulf Cooperation Council (GCC). The decision to stand with Saddam would be a fateful one for the Gulf states.[18]

By June 1982, Iran had essentially evicted Iraq from its territory, and was focused on whether it should cross into Iraq. Given the economic costs and the human toll that it extracted, the decision to attack Iraq remains one of the most contentious in Iran's modern history. In today's Islamic Republic one rarely finds a politician who does not claim that he had qualms about the invasion and even opposed it. In a grotesque act of historical revisionism, it is even suggested at times that Khomeini himself was against the move and wanted to end the war.[19] The theocratic state's attempt to whitewash its history does not change the fact that besides Bazargan and his party, Freedom Movement, and various commanders of the regular military, there was a consensus within the regime to continue the conflict. As Rafsanjani would concede nearly two decades after the end of the war, "During that time in Iran no one was prepared to accept a cease-fire. At that time we convened a meeting regarding the direction of the war, and the Imam commanded that no one should speak of a cease-fire and that the war must achieve its goals."[20] A combination of ideological convictions, the misperception that the war would be quick, and the fear that Saddam would not remain contained pressed Iran toward the disastrous decision to prolong the conflict.

Not unlike Saddam, the theocratic regime indulged in its own misperceptions, exaggerating the opportunities available to it, while diminishing the costs of a military surge into Iraq. To begin with, Tehran suspected that its military victories might in fact provoke Saddam's overthrow. In March 1982, when Iran was assuming the initiative in the war, the commander of the Revolutionary Guards, Mohsen Reza'i, claimed that given recent battlefield victories there was a "smell of a military coup in Iraq in the air and we have to prepare ourselves for that."[21] Rafsanjani recalled a conversation with Montazeri, at that time when the latter had implored him to quickly dispatch forces into Iraq given the imminence of a coup. "Mr. Montazeri spent half the night calling me, asking me what are our forces waiting for? Why are we not entering Iraq? Iraq is in chaos and we can go to Baghdad and finish this whole thing. There are some waiting to implement a coup as soon as we enter Iraq."[22] Should Iran's armies cross into Iraq, the clerical rulers assured themselves of Iraqi peoples' support. As Montazeri noted elsewhere, "We are certain that the Muslim nation of Iraq will assist us."[23]

To the extent that Iran had a plan for post-Saddam Iraq, it was that once the liberated Iraqis had a chance to choose their own government, they would opt for an Islamic one. Khomeini went even farther when he stated that the Iraqis would select not only a government that realized their "Islamic hope," but one that would establish intimate ties with Iran.[24] Given the clerics' belief that all the inhabitants of the Middle East desired an Islamic government, they had no doubt that a free choice for Iraqis would yield an Islamic polity. Somehow, Tehran convinced itself that the incursion into Iraq would quickly achieve the desired results without either a prolonged war or a cumbersome occupation, and that the Iraqi people would welcome the invading armies as liberators.

As the fortunes of the war appeared to be changing, the panicked Gulf states undertook another diplomatic gambit to entice Iran to lay down arms. The Saudis now stepped forward proffering their good offices for mediation of the conflict and a seventy-billion-dollar reconstruction package to Iran. Saddam, eager to put the war behind him, accepted this potential cessation of the hostilities only to be rebuffed by the triumphant and vengeful mullahs. Indeed, as Iran scored battlefield successes, its attitudes toward the Gulf emirates hardened. Khomeini, in his expanded declaration of war aims, not only called for close ties with a "liberated Iraq," but hinted at the outright control of the Gulf. "If Iran and Iraq can merge and be amalgamated, all the diminutive nations of the region will join them," exclaimed the imam.[25] The cleric's rhetoric solidified the Gulf states' support for Saddam and brought along an international community that did not want to cede this crucial area to a radical theocracy.

On July 13, the die was finally cast. It was Iran's turn to miscalculate, as it transformed itself from a victim to an aggressor. Operation Ramadan witnessed the mobilization of approximately one hundred thousand Iranian troops whose initial target was Basra. The crossing into Iraq quickly petered out, as Iran did not have sufficient tactical dexterity, adequate air cover, or sophisticated arms to carry out a concerted attack. The character of the war now came into focus, with limited territorial gains acquired at huge cost. The war most closely resembled the carnage of World War I with trenches, fixed movement of forces, and, in due time, ample use of chemical weapons.

A WAR OF ATTRITION

Once Iranian troops crossed the border into Iraq in 1982, the tactics of the two antagonists changed in important ways. During the initial phase of the war, Iraq had been the belligerent, launching wide-scale offensive operations. Once Iran became the aggressor, Iraq largely retreated into a defensive formation, rebuffing persistent Iranian attacks in the hope that Tehran would grow weary of war. As the conflict dragged on, both sides would modify their strategies, experiment with new weapons, and cultivate opposition forces. In the end, however, all the strategic tinkering failed to reset the essential parameters of the conflict. The Iran-Iraq war had become a classic stalemate.

In the White House none of this was obvious. Iran appeared to be winning, its Islamist revolution sweeping the Middle East. Washington had legitimate concerns regarding Iran and its destructive impact on the Arab world. The clerical regime routinely used the annual religious pilgrimages to Mecca to stage protests against the House of Saud, and the regime had tried to assassinate Kuwaiti leaders and plotted coups in Bahrain. The U.S. intelligence community warned that these regimes could soon be replaced by "ones more compatible with Tehran."[26] The preservation of America's alliance system in the Middle East pushed Washington toward Baghdad.

The Reagan administration's tilt toward Iraq was neither intermittent nor tentative. To facilitate official contacts and commerce, Iraq was taken off the terrorism list in 1982. The administration claimed (without much evidence) that Iraq had reduced its support for terrorism. This new strategy was not without its justifications, as Secretary of State George Shultz stressed:

Our support for Iraq increased in rough proportions to Iran's military success. The United States could not stand idle and watch the Khomeini revolution sweep forward. In this situation, a tilt toward Iraq was warranted to prevent Iranian dominance of the Persian Gulf and the countries around it.[27]

To be sure, it was the concern with Iran rather than devotion to Saddam that was conditioning America's policy. The Iraqi strongman was seen as an indispensable barrier to Iranian expansionism, and thus his violations of international law were reluctantly tolerated. The imperative of repelling Khomeini's revolution spurred Washington's embrace of the Iraqi dictator.

The United States now began providing Iraq with aid in the form of Commodity Credit Corporation guarantees for the purchase of agricultural products. This assistance amounted to $652 million dollars by 1987. The agricultural credits allowed Iraq to divert funds it would otherwise spend on foodstuffs to military appropriations. By the late 1980s, the annual trade between the two countries reached $3.7 billion dollars and entailed sale of trucks, transport vehicles, and helicopters.[28] Even more significant was the decision by the United States to begin a "limited intelligence sharing program with Iraq."[29] This "limited" program provided Saddam information on Iran's battlefield positions and critical data for bombing targets.

The United States may have refrained from directly selling arms to Iraq, but it did much to facilitate Iraq's weapons trade with other nations. The administration sought to "encourage other countries to arm and finance Iraq's war effort."[30] The French proved particularly eager, as they soon accounted for 40 percent of all Iraqi arms sales. Washington also made direct appeals to South Korea and Italy and promised Egypt that if it sold its surplus Soviet military equipment to Iraq, America would replenish its stocks. These moves buttressed Iraq's military effort and fortified its spirit of resistance.

Iran's entry into Iraqi territory had also altered the Soviet Union's calculus. Khomeini's revolt had been greeted with enthusiasm by the Kremlin. As with many secular ideologues uneasy about religion, the Soviet communists perceived that the Islamist phase of the revolution was a passing one. Soon their long-cherished client, the Tudeh Party, would assume greater influence if not outright control. These hopes were dashed when Khomeini's revolution unfolded in an explicitly anticommunist manner. His slogan "Neither East nor West" meant severing ties with Washington and no subordination to Moscow. While the Soviet Union benefited tactically from Iran's anti-Americanism and its attacks on Israel, Khomeini would go on to castigate communism as an alien and inauthentic ideology while Iran condemned Soviet occupation of Afghanistan, which had begun in 1979.

The complexity and contradictions of Soviet policy fully manifested when the war broke out. Moscow sought to preserve its ties with Iraq while seeking warm relations with Iran. This proved an uneasy balancing act, as the Soviets placated Iran by suspending direct arms deliveries to Iraq while permitting the Eastern bloc countries to continue such sales. In the end, Iran remained unimpressed by Soviet gestures, while Iraq grew estranged from its erstwhile ally.

Less well known is the Soviet Union's own tilt toward Iraq in 1982. Once Iran's forces entered Iraq, Moscow was confronted with stark choices. Russia did not relish the idea of the collapse of the Ba'athist regime and a forward march of Khomeini's fundamentalism. In the meantime, the mullahs had turned on the Tudeh Party, closing its offices, shuttering its newspapers, and purging its cadre from government. This was followed by a more sustained campaign of repression, with public recantations and executions. Now all pretense of neutrality was set aside as Moscow began direct arms sales to Iraq and condemned Iranian offensives. The Kremlin still hoped that the conflict could be resolved diplomatically, but it had no choice but to side with Saddam.

As part of its pattern of escalating the war, Iraq began attack-

ing Iran's oil facilities. The purchase of French Super Étendard aircraft in 1983 allowed Iraq's air force a greater range and brought
Iran's main oil installations on Kharg Island, in the Gulf, within its
striking capability. Baghdad's gambit did have an economic impact,
but it failed to diminish the clerical regime's determination. The
Islamic Republic's retaliation ended up interfering with Gulf commerce. With Iraq's oil exported largely overland, there were few
Iraqi vessels that Iran could target. Consequently, Tehran chose to
retaliate against the Gulf emirates that were financially sustaining
Saddam's war machine by attacking their shipping fleets. Despite
later recriminations, it was Iraq that had initially disturbed the Gulf
and made oil shipping a target of military reprisal. Iran had a limited interest in extending the war to the Gulf waters, since its main
focus was on ground operations. As Rafsanjani noted, "Saddam's
policy is to bring the Persian Gulf states into the war, but we don't
want to destabilize the region."[31] It was Iraq that wanted to internationalize the war and perceived that by threatening the critical
waterways it could induce the great powers to impose a settlement
on Iran. As with many facets of the conflict, Iraq had expanded the
hostilities—in this case, the "tanker war"—but the clerical regime
in Iran took the blame.

Iran would be the subject of further Arab machinations, as the
Middle East largely coalesced around Saddam. Oil policy eventually
became another area of tension between Iran and its neighbors. After
its battlefield successes in the mid-1980s, Iran had to contend with a
Saudi-led Gulf community that increased oil output to depress the
prices and damage Iran's financial prospects. Tehran denounced the
"oil conspiracy," with Khomeini warning that the "price of the war
is no less important to us than the price of oil."[32] Rafsanjani similarly
complained about plots by "enemies to reduce the price of oil." The
Saudi ploy eventually succeeded, as by 1986 the oil prices had plum-
meted to nearly ten dollars per barrel. Despite the economic pressure

exerted on Iran, the Islamic Republic absorbed the costs and persisted with its policies.[33]

The problem with Iran's regional diplomacy was that it simply could not sustain a coherent approach toward the Gulf sheikdoms. At times, Tehran would try to decouple Iraq from the emirates, dispatching various foreign ministry delegations with offers of better ties. In 1984, when the Saudis shot down an Iranian military aircraft, Tehran's reaction was muted if not conciliatory. Yet, the longer the Gulf states supported Saddam, the more difficult it was for the clerics to maintain a policy of reconciliation. In the end, Iran's determination to prosecute the war, its frequent denunciation of these states' legitimacy, and its support for local opposition groups obscured its hesitant and modest efforts to reach out. The fact that the Gulf states remained a steady source of support for Saddam had much to do with Iran's self-defeating and contradictory practices.

Among the most egregious developments of the war was Iraq's use of chemical weapons against Iranian combatants. As early as 1983, Iraq began deploying chemical agents as an integral part of its war strategy. The purpose of the gas was not just to blunt Iran's human-wave assaults, but also to terrorize the enemy and sap its morale.[34] Although initially the use of such weapons failed to achieve these objectives, in due time, they offered Iraq a great advantage in the war. Once more, Saddam's brutal behavior was largely ignored. The international community's focus was on the Persian menace, not the Iraqi dictator's gross violations of the laws of war.

Baghdad's proclamations on its use of chemical weapons were usually couched in ambiguity, stressing the need to employ "all measures" to defend the country. However, at times, such gauzy denials would give way to open acknowledgment, if not outright boasting. Major General Maher Abdel Rashid captured the essence of Iraq's position by claiming, "The invaders should know that for every harmful insect there is an insecticide capable of destroying it whatever their numbers and that Iraq possess this annihilation insecticide."[35] The theme of using pesticide to exterminate the "swarms of mosquitoes" became a frequent reference of the Iraqi leadership.[36] At times even such subtleties would fall away. In a heated exchange with Les Aspin, the chairman of the House of Representatives' Armed Services Committee, Tariq Aziz exclaimed, "Yes of course we use chemical weapons. These are savages and we need to defend ourselves. We would use nuclear weapons if we had them."[37] Not since World War I had a nation relied so heavily on chemical agents to achieve its strategic objectives.

Despite Iraq's continued employment of gas, there is no indication of comparable Iranian use. Neither the many United Nations investigations at the time, the testimonials of Iraqi officers, nor documents captured since the American invasion of Iraq in 2003 suggest that Iran used such weapons. It appears that Iran did begin research into chemical munitions, but never developed sufficient capacity for battlefield use.[38]

The U.S. position of tilting toward Iraq did not change with the well-documented revelations of chemical weapons use by Iraq. The United States did view Iraq's use of such munitions as distressing and was concerned about the behavior of its ally of convenience. The State Department led by George Shultz did condemn the use of chemical weapons by Iraq as violating international conventions, but the essence of cooperation remained intact. Richard Murphy, Assistant Secretary of State for Near East Affairs, insisted on this position by stressing that "The U.S.-Iraqi relationship is important to our long-term political and economic objectives in the Gulf and beyond . . . We believe that economic sanctions will be useless and counterproductive in terms of our ability to influence the Iraqis."[39]

The desire to buttress Iraq's war efforts was all too evident when Donald Rumsfeld, then a presidential emissary, journeyed to Iraq in 1983. On his trips to Baghdad, Rumsfeld was to inform the Iraqis that "[the United States'] chemical weapons condemnation was made strictly out of our strong opposition to the use of lethal and incapacitating chemical weapons, wherever it occurs." However, Rumsfeld was also to stress that "[American] interests in 1) Preventing an Iranian victory and 2) Continuing to improve bilateral relations with Iraq, at a pace of Iraqi choosing, remain undiminished."[40]

Iraq's use of gas confronted its American ally with a difficult choice. The United States had genuine qualms about Saddam's violations of the laws of war. Yet, its principal objective remained containment of Iran's revolution and preventing the Islamic Republic from winning the war. In his memoirs, Shultz insists that he was shocked when he heard that his condemnation of Iraq's chemical weapon attacks had provoked the intelligence community to stress, "We have demolished a budding relationship [with Iraq] by taking a tough position in opposition to chemical weapons."[41] The relationship, of course, was not demolished, as America protested the use of chemical weapons but did not adjust its fundamental policy.

The ebb and flow of the stalemated conflict eventually was challenged by one of Iran's most enterprising and successful operations. In February 1986, Iran launched an operation that involved two attacks, one aimed at Basra that was largely diversionary and the other at Faw Peninsula nearly forty miles south of Basra. The real aim of the operation was to capture Faw, which would cut off Iraq from the Persian Gulf and its essential communication links with Kuwait. The occupation of Faw would allow Iran an opportunity to move against Basra with the real hope of capturing an important city. The Iranian operation—particularly the tactical skill it displayed under poor weather conditions—surprised the Iraqis.[42] However, after an initial promising surge, Iran was not capable of sustaining its attack. Iraq's heavy use of chemical weapons, as well as disarray within Iran's command structure, did much to undermine the operation. The perennial conflict between the Revolutionary Guards with their amateurish war planning and the regular military with its deliberate tactics led to yet another purge of the army officers. Iran followed up its operation with a series of inconclusive attacks. The war returned to a deadlock.

As Iran entered its sixth year of the war, internal divisions over the course of the conflict began to more clearly manifest. Although it is still difficult to decipher the internal deliberations of the theocratic regime, it appears that an important faction of the government began to sense that the war was endangering the Islamic Republic. Speaker of the parliament Rafsanjani and President Ali Khamenei were among those who were advising caution and even probing for a diplomatic solution. Saddam's international support and his capacity to wage chemical warfare were ruefully noted by Rafsanjani, who warned, "They will do all they can to rescue Saddam and will not cease efforts to prevent our victory. We also have to think about defense against those dangerous weapons."[43]

Yet, these moderates were confronted by a Revolutionary Guard leadership and important clerical firebrands who still insisted that the cause of the revolution had to be redeemed in the deserts of Iraq. Ironically, these divisions within the regime initially led to a more aggressive prosecution of the war. From 1982 to 1987, Iran had largely limited itself to a strategy of attrition with periodic offensives designed to exhaust its adversary. As the population's patience with the war diminished, the Revolutionary Guards called for a mass mobilization to achieve the final victory. As Reza'i noted in 1986, "The war today should be completely transformed into a people's war, in accordance with a scheme in which all industrial schools will begin manufacturing military hardware."[44] It was hoped that a massive offensive could defeat Saddam's armies before the Iranian populace completely gave up on the war.

Whatever the internal debates, Khomeini still supported the radicals. Even after all the devastation, he was not prepared to abandon the conflict or his quest to export the revolution through the force of arms. Khomeini seemingly accepted the Revolutionary Guard leaderships' arguments that through more forceful effort Saddam would fall. Echoing those sentiments, Khomeini warned the regional states, "Those who inhabit the Gulf should not devote themselves to Saddam, for he will soon be gone."[45] The supreme leader's decision prolonged the war and led to one of its most hazardous periods.

INTERNATIONALIZATION OF THE WAR

The final years of the war were difficult ones for an Islamic Republic that had made the demise of Saddam's regime the centerpiece of its strategy. Iran had managed to sustain the war despite isolation, economic difficulties and popular disenchantment. However, as the stalemate lengthened and tensions in the Persian Gulf threatened to draw in the great powers, the theocracy had to revisit its most fundamental national decision. Given Iran's intense factionalism and ideological divides, it was difficult for Tehran to act quickly or decisively.

The United States also underwent its own set of reconsiderations during this period. The Reagan administration had made much of its attempts to isolate Iran and in 1983 had even launched Operation Staunch to prevent arms sales to the theocratic regime. As part of the operation, American envoys crisscrossed the world pressuring countries not to sell arms to Iran. Yet U.S. strategy was complicated by the developments in Lebanon. By the mid-1980s, Iran's Hezbollah client was busy taking Americans hostage. The predicament of those hostages eventually led Reagan to sell arms to Iran as a means of retrieving them. This did not just violate his policy but endangered his presidency. The administration that had made so much of its arms embargo against Iran was suddenly caught selling military hardware to the mullahs.

The origins of the Iran-Contra affair lay in the intelligence community's concern that Iran's isolation might serve Soviet purposes. The CIA perceived that Khomeini was on the verge of death and America needed to influence the theocracy's impending succession crisis. Failure to do so would leave the field open to Moscow. Such conceptions were eagerly affirmed by the Israelis, who were already selling arms to Iran given their identification of Iraq as the more immediate threat to their state. The Israelis harbored no illusion about Iran's pragmatic tendencies but merely sought to buttress its war effort against Saddam. America soon became entangled in Israel's enterprise with its share of duplicitous arms dealers, cunning Iranians, and Israeli realpolitik.

In the summer of 1985, the U.S. national security advisor, Robert McFarlane, landed in Tehran with a cake and a Bible signed by Reagan as a gesture of goodwill, hoping to meet the moderates he had come to empower. McFarlane was relegated to seeing second-tier officials, including a young Hassan Rouhani. In the meantime, a shipment of sophisticated American weapons including the antitank TOW (Tube-launched, Optically-tracked, Wireless-guided) missiles arrived in Tehran. A few of the American hostages in Lebanon were released, but this led to more being captured given that they were proving a valuable commodity of exchange for the mullahs. The eventual exposure of the plot by a Lebanese newspaper led to an outcry in Washington with congressional investigations and even legal proceedings. In the region, the scandal caused a considerable erosion of America's credibility. Reagan now had to fend off Democratic lawmakers while reassuring Arab allies who were disturbed by his double-dealing.

In the midst of America's political drama, Iran was inexplicably moving toward an expanded conflict on the high seas. Iran's relations with Kuwait had never been harmonious, as the Islamic Republic had previously plotted the ouster of the tiny emirate's leadership. Not only was Kuwait a generous benefactor of Iraq, but its geographic proximity to Iran and its weak military capabilities made its oil commerce a tempting target. However, Kuwait now effectively manipulated Cold War rivalries, insisting that unless the United States protected its oil vessels it would turn to the Soviet Union. The fear of Moscow reaching into the Gulf and the need to demonstrate resolve to Arab allies in light of Iran-Contra pressed the Reagan administration toward the reflagging of Kuwaiti ships.[46] As Reagan confessed, "If we don't do the job, the Soviets will. And that will jeopardize our national security as well as our allies."[47] The theme of credibility was stressed more directly by Assistant Secretary Murphy when he acknowledged, "Frankly, in the light of the Iran-Contra revelations, we had found that the leaders of the Gulf states were questioning the coherence and seriousness of U.S. policy in the Gulf along with our reliability and staying power."[48] At any rate, Washington's decision to reflag brought it into direct confrontation with the Islamic Republic.

The Gulf waters were now the scene of simmering conflict between the United States and Iran. Tehran responded to the U.S. reflagging of Kuwaiti vessels by launching speed-boat attacks and mining the Gulf. The United States Navy soon responded by sinking a number of Iranian ships and oil platforms. The more Iran attempted to interfere with Gulf commerce, the more it came into direct confrontation with the United States. The Reagan administration did not want to expand the conflict and was reluctant to use the massive naval firepower at its disposal, but it was gradually drawn into a more intense confrontation with Iran.

The U.S. convoys and naval deployments provoked still more heated debate within the theocracy. For the more moderate elements, the prospect of provoking the American armada was not a promising development. Rafsanjani took the lead in emphasizing to the Gulf States and the United States that "We do not want anything from you except that you stay neutral."[49] However, for the regime's firebrands the prospect of clashing with the "Great Satan" offered another means of proving Iran's revolutionary mettle. Mohsen Rafiqdust, the head of the Revolutionary Guard's ministry, flamboyantly proclaimed, "We are ready to go to war against America to resist any threat against the Islamic Republic's interests."[50] Reza'i, the disastrous commander of the Revolutionary Guards whose countless miscalculations inflicted serious damage on his country, boasted, "Americans should be assured that so long as they are in the Persian Gulf they are at war with us."[51] This was another self-defeating move; while Iran's position was weakening it invited additional belligerents into the conflict.

The setbacks in the Gulf were mirrored by Iran's difficulties on the ground. Since 1982, Iraq had been largely reacting to Iran's offensives in the hope of exhausting its enemy. By spring of 1988, Iraq finally moved beyond its static defenses and recaptured the Faw Peninsula, handing Iran a demoralizing defeat. Faw had become a symbol of Iranian success, a single tangible conquest after years of inconclusive fighting. The rapid collapse of Iran's fortifications concerned a military leadership accustomed to believing that Iraqis lacked the courage and daring to resume offensive operations. Suddenly, Iraq not only evicted Iran from its territory, but for the first time since 1982 it reentered Iranian lands.

Baghdad's more effective prosecution of the war did not stop at the border, as it intensified its attacks on Iran's urban areas with its missiles and aircraft.[52] The so-called "war of cities" meant that Iraq was effectively targeting Iran's population centers. The importance of the "war of cities" was not so much the damage that it inflicted, as only about two thousand Iranians lost their lives in the missile attacks. The significance of the assaults was their psychological impact, as they provoked a panic among urban dwellers leading to mass exodus from cities such as Tehran. The Iranian regime had lost control of events, as it could neither offer assurances to a frightened public nor meaningfully retaliate against Iraq's latest act of aggression.

By 1988, Iran was exhausted from having waged eight years of war without any measurable international support. Iraqi counterattacks, American assaults in the Gulf, and the "war of cities" undermined the arguments for continuing the war. The difficulties of the war were compounded by a smaller than expected pool of volunteer soldiers, which undercut Iran's strategy of utilizing manpower to overcome technological superiority. The inability of Iran to muster sufficient volunteers forced a more rigorous conscription effort that further estranged the population. Even then, the draft calls failed to generate enough troops, as Iran simply could not provide forces to relaunch its typical human-wave-led offensives.

Throughout the war, there had been ample feelers and peace proposals from a variety of actors and institutions. Given its depiction of the war as a conflict between Islam and disbelief, Iran abjured all such entreaties. However, the United States in 1987 had sought to pressure Iran by drafting U.N. Security Council Resolution 598, which outlined an eight-stage plan for terminating hostilities. The resolution stressed that whichever power rejected the proposal would be subject to mandatory sanctions. Baghdad's acceptance of the resolution placed Iran in a bind. Should the Islamic Republic dismiss the offer, it would confront more debilitating sanctions. In a gesture of uncharacteristic restraint, Iran did not summarily reject the scheme but raised questions and asked for various clarifications. It would be wrong, however, to suggest that Tehran's more tempered approach was motivated strictly by a desire to avoid sanctions. The regime seemed divided about how to proceed.

It is hard to determine at which exact point Iran decided to accept Resolution 598. The accidental shooting down of an Iranian airliner in July 1988 by a U.S. naval vessel appears to have convinced Khomeini that it was time to end the war. The destruction of the aircraft seemingly persuaded Khomeini and the leading members of the state that a sinister American conspiracy was afoot. Iran had long feared the internationalization of the conflict, but now it sensed that given Saddam's inability to conquer Iran, the United States had decided to finish the job itself. Rafsanjani warned, "It is obvious that the Global Arrogance has decided to prevent our victory."[53] An influential newspaper stressed the conspiracy theme, noting, "This was in no way an accident, and in our view, it is a notification."[54] Coming on the heels of the ongoing clashes with the United States in the Persian Gulf, the airliner incident was viewed as the beginning of a new and more robust American military campaign against Iran.

The other factor that facilitated the end of the war was Iraq's persistent use of chemical weapons. The indiscriminate use of chemical agents against the Kurdish population in the city of Halabja in 1988 caused considerable consternation in Tehran. There was widespread fear within the ruling elite that similar measures could be used against Iran's urban centers. Rafsanjani later recalled, "Iraqis constantly used chemical weapons, and an example of that was Halabja where people fell like autumn leaves. We thought that it would be a huge event if similar crimes took place against our cities such as Tabriz and Kermanshah."[55] The Iraqi chemical weapons attacks that had successfully blunted various Iranian offensives proved instrumental in the decision to conclude the conflict.

Despite overwhelming pressures on the state, resistance to ending the war persisted in Iran. In his final appeal for the continuation of the war, Reza'i listed his requirements for achieving victory. In a letter to Khomeini, he acknowledged that the war would probably last another five years and its prosecution would require "350 infantry brigades, 2,500 tanks, 300 fighter planes and 300 helicopters as well as an ability to make substantial number of laser and atomic weapons."[56] Despite such a daunting list, the commander of the Revolutionary Guards recommended that the war continue. Prime Minister Mir-Hussein Musavi, who oversaw the management of the economy, further tipped the scales against the Guards by claiming that the country could not meet their demands.[57] Musavi seems to have been the pivotal figure in ending the war, as he reportedly warned that the "government does not have the capacity for an appropriation of a single dollar."[58] In his own private response to his disciples, the supreme leader finally acquiesced to the termination of hostilities. Khomeini noted that given that the "commanders who are specialists openly confess that the Islamic military will not be victorious for some time, and in light of the recent defeats and the enemy's extensive use of chemical weapons and our lack of equipment to neutralize them, I give my consent to a cease-fire."[59]

It was only after Khomeini's decision that the Revolutionary Guards reluctantly accepted the armistice.

The imam now had to confront his countrymen with his momentous decision. A humbled Khomeini proclaimed,

> Today, this decision was more deadly than drinking hemlock. I submitted myself to God's will and drank this drink to His satisfaction. To me, it would have been more bearable to accept death and martyrdom. Today's decision is based only on the interests of the Islamic Republic.[60]

Khomeini's statement was followed by more elaborate explanations by the clerical leaders, particularly Rafsanjani and Khamenei. In its latest narrative, the Islamic Republic stressed that prolonging the war would only distract Iran from the more important goal of spreading its divine message. This was an ironic confession, given the state's previous insistence that the war would define the success of the revolution. In the end, the conflict that was to transform the Middle East threatened the very survival of the Islamic Republic, forcing it to sue for peace.[61]

AN UNCERTAIN LEGACY

Since the outset of the Cold War, the United States had committed itself to sustaining its alliance system in the Middle East. This eventually meant preserving the conservative order and the monarchies that underpinned it. The need to resist radical actors and revolutionary changes became a cornerstone of U.S. policy. It was often feared that political upheaval would pave the way for Soviet entry and thus endanger core U.S. interests. The Iran-Iraq war was an unusual episode because both superpowers were concerned about the scale of Iran's ambitions. For Washington the war signified that the threat of radicalism need not emanate just from the Soviet Union and that it was possible for the United States to suffer setbacks not engineered by Moscow.

Upon assuming office, the Reagan administration's principal concern was to prevent an Iranian victory. The clerical regime was still enchanted by its revolutionary mission and sought to undermine the established regional authorities. The militant republic openly proclaimed its desire for displacement of Saddam and the overthrow of his Gulf monarchical accomplices. These were not empty threats—Iran often acted upon its impetuous claims. Once Saddam presented himself as the guardian of the Gulf and offered his state as a barrier to Iranian power, America tilted toward him. The tilt seemed to help, as Washington's provision of intelligence, financial credits, and lobbying for arms on behalf of Iraq helped Saddam rebuff Iranian assaults. The theocracy finally exhausted itself and sued for peace without achieving any of its objectives. It is hard to argue with the practical success of U.S. policy, as Iran's revolution was confined within its borders and its leaders came to appreciate the need for a more tempered approach to statecraft.

During the 1980s, America also managed to hold its alliances together. Iran's revolt initially unsettled the Gulf rulers, as they feared the contagion of its revolution and the appeal of its Islamist message. The United States commitment to the Gulf also manifested itself in diplomatic outreach and military sales to the sheikdoms. Eventually that commitment saw America's armada shield Kuwait's commerce and destroy much of Iran's navy. The alliance system that America had nurtured for so long held its own during one of the most stressful periods of its existence.

The Islamic Republic did much to generate an international consensus against itself. Iran's refusal to end the war, its continued revolutionary exhortations, and its meddling in the Levant caused the Europeans and even the Russians to suspect its motives. Saddam's aggression seemed pale compared to Khomeini's revisionism. The Iraqi strongman might have been a ruthless dictator, but Khomeini threatened to unleash an Islamist revolution that would subvert the regional order. Iran's improvised war strategy led it to obtain arms from a diverse array of sources, but it could not enlist the Soviet Union on its side the way Arab radicals had done during earlier wars. The Islamist coloration of its revolution proved disturbing to a Russia that had to manage its own substantial Muslim population. The Cold War demarcations did not rescue the mullahs in the way that they had salvaged Nasser's wreckage.

America has always done better at wars than at planning for their aftermath. The end of the Iran-Iraq war presented the White House with unresolved challenges and unsettled tensions. Iraq's strongman had endured and wanted his reward. Iranian revolutionaries had survived and were still nursing their grievances. The Gulf rulers seemed unresponsive to the pleas of Iraq for aid and indifferent to changes in Iran. The stability of the Gulf seemed more illusory than real. And that illusion was shattered come August 1990.

CHAPTER 10

THE GULF WAR

The American people usually elect presidents whose principal preoccupation has been domestic affairs. Most of the governors and senators who become president have to learn the intricacies of international relations on the job. This was not the case with George H. W. Bush, who arrived at the White House in 1989 with an impressive résumé and a well-defined worldview. The new president had already served as the ambassador to the United Nations, an envoy to China, the head of the CIA, and as vice president for both terms under Ronald Reagan.

Bush assumed the office of the presidency at a time of unprecedented change. The collapse of the Soviet Union, the unification of Germany, and the need to establish the parameters of the post–Cold War international order would define his presidency. Although he would leave office after only one term, his deft handling of myriad crises has rescued his reputation. His combined caution and integrity, his prudence and daring, made him an ideal president for tumultuous times.

Bush's internationalism emphasized stability and order. Although not prone to the rhetorical flourishes of his predecessor, he focused on achieving practical results at a limited cost. As president, Bush relied much on personal diplomacy and developing relations with other world leaders. This allowed him to call on his counterparts during times of crisis and mobilize the international community behind various U.S. initiatives. The administration's realist bent did not exclude the promotion of democracy, but it did place assertion of such values in the context of ensuring stability.[1]

Upon his inauguration, no one could have imagined that Bush would spend much of his presidency dealing with Iraq. The notion that Saddam Hussein would invade Kuwait and annex a sovereign state was considered outlandish even for such an impetuous leader. Once Saddam unexpectedly launched his attack, the administration managed to craft an international consensus and assembled a formidable coalition against him. The notion of resisting aggression was a key principle of Bush's new world order and did much to condition his response to Saddam's dangerous foray. But America does not always end its wars well, and the Gulf War proved no different. Iraq, still ruled by Saddam, survived the war and continued to menace the region.

PRELUDE TO INVASION

As we have seen, the end of the Iran-Iraq war had not resolved the fundamental security challenges of the countries in the Persian Gulf. The eight-year war had left the region heavily armed, while essential disputes went largely unresolved. The international community may have been reliant on the region's oil, but its attention was diverted to Europe. The Middle East for once took a backseat to the exhilarating events that culminated in the end of the Cold War.

The Bush administration was determined to maintain its predecessor's policy of reaching out to Iraq. Saddam had been a useful ally during the war and had managed to check Iranian expansionism. Although the Bush team had no illusions about Saddam, it hoped that exhaustion, and the need for economic rehabilitation, would cause Iraq to relinquish its legacy of radicalism. An Iraq focused on its internal reconstruction and acting as a reasonable member of the Arab community could still serve as a bulwark against Iran.

The best means of tethering Iraq to such a regional order was thought to be trade. During the Bush administration's first year in office, the guiding thesis of U.S. policy was that incentives offered the most suitable means of tempering Saddam's ambitions and perhaps obtaining his cooperation on regional issues. As Bush's secretary of state, James Baker, recalled, "We wanted to explore the proposition that closer political and economic ties with Iraq might persuade it at the very least to be less of a stumbling block."[2] Agricultural credits were the preferred commodity of influence as Iraq's needs were outpacing its resources. However, the administration was open to other commercial ventures. This was American pragmatism at its most obvious; economics was thought to transcend ideology and history as conditioning national motives.

Iraq policy was in many ways an offshoot of the administration's overall Middle East strategy. As often in the past, the resolution of the Arab-Israeli conflict topped Washington's priority list. The Palestine Liberation Organization's tentative recognition of Israel in 1988 had generated enthusiasm about resolving one of the region's debilitating conflicts. Saddam was seen as potentially a constructive actor on that front. The fact that he had formed the Arab Cooperation Council along with Egypt and Jordan indicated his alignment with moderate Arab states. The perennial rivalry between the two Ba'athist states of Iraq and Syria was also viewed as advantageous. Saddam could be counted on to buttress his Lebanese proxies at the expense of the militant Hafez Assad. As the United States sought to strengthen the forces of moderation and press ahead with its peace process, Iraq was seen as an important pillar of that diplomacy.

The White House's penchant for dealing with Iraq was not always shared by Congress. The end of the Iran-Iraq war led to criticisms from lawmakers regarding Iraq's human rights abuses and use of chemical weapons, particularly against Kurdish civilians. To fend off a congressional push for sanctions, the administration doubled down on its policy of changing Iraq's behavior through incentives. On October 2, 1989, Bush signed National Security Directive 26 that stated, "The United States Government should propose economic and political incentives for Iraq to moderate its behavior and to increase our influence with Iraq."[3] Along these lines, the Commodity Credit Cooperation pledged one billion dollars in agricultural credits to Baghdad.

The policy of accommodation was now in full swing. The promised assistance was being delivered and Iraq's sensitivities were seemingly being assuaged. In February 1990, Baghdad decried a Voice of America editorial that denounced Saddam's tyrannical rule. The State Department cabled to U.S. Ambassador April Glaspie to stress to her Iraqi counterparts that "It is [in] no way U.S. Government policy to suggest that the Government of Iraq is illegitimate and that the people of Iraq should or will revolt against the Government of Iraq."[4] The note of contrition was sent after Saddam's agents were thought to be planning attacks on Iraqi dissidents on American soil.

This back and forth did not seem to matter much to Saddam as he confronted an impossible situation. Shattered by war, Iraq's economy was now burdened by nearly one hundred billion dollars in debt. After years of suffering and hardship, the population began to agitate for economic stability and a measure of freedom. Returning war veterans, always a dangerous constituency for a dictatorship, were expressing their own grievances with the state of affairs. The collapse of Soviet satraps in Eastern Europe and the advent of people power had unhinged despots worldwide. Saddam reacted with further repression, with purges of the military, and by embarking on an aggressive foreign policy.

As he had done during the war with Iran, Saddam presented himself as the leader of the Arab world, a modern-day Nasser who had a right to impose his preferences on the Middle East. Suddenly he began to inveigh against Israel, warning, "We will make fire eat up half of Israel."[5] For a leader who had already used chemical weapons on a massive scale these chilling threats did not seem like idle rhetoric. The plight of the Palestinians, a tempting target for Arab opportunists, became Saddam's cause. He was not interested in America's peace plans but exhorted the Palestinians to rise up and liberate all Arab lands. The PLO opened offices in Baghdad while the notorious Palestinian terrorist Abu Nidal found sanctuary in Iraq.

Washington may have wanted to placate Saddam, but his ambition to be the leading Arab ruler led him in a different direction. Always distrustful of the United States and continuously pointing to the Iran-Contra affair as an indication of American perfidy, Saddam viewed the U.S. presence in the Gulf as a barrier to his ambitions. He called for the eviction of U.S. forces from the region and stressed that the Middle East could not claim its true independence so long as an American armada lurked in the Gulf. Visiting U.S. officials were often subjected to harangues by Saddam about how their government was plotting against his rule and wanted to remove him from power. Persistent American assurances may not have dented his well-honed sense of conspiracy, but they did make him question U.S. resolve.

Even more ominously, Saddam turned his gaze to the Arab sheikhdoms. Having long complained about their ingratitude as his country shielded them from Khomeini's Islamist rage, Saddam now charged that the Gulf monarchies were conspiring with the United States to keep oil prices down, thus making it impossible for him to revive his economy. In the February 1990 meeting of the Arab Cooperation Council, Saddam pulled aside King Hussein of Jordan and President Hosni Mubarak of Egypt and asked them to convey a message to the Gulf rulers: Iraq needed not only debt relief but also an additional thirty billion dollars in aid. To make himself clear, Saddam stressed that "if they do not give the money to me, I will know how to get it."[6] His attempt at extortion failed to move the Gulf rulers.

As his country's economy deteriorated, Saddam demanded an

increase in oil prices. As was his wont by now, he called for all states to adhere to their OPEC quotas while exempting himself from such impositions. Kuwait and the United Arab Emirates were two states that routinely exceeded their allotted share, provoking Saddam's ire. In a speech, he warned that "the continued violation of oil quotas by some Arab states amounts to a declaration of war on Iraq."[7] As oil prices continued to plummet, Iraq's economic woes worsened. Unwilling to cut his military budget and scale back state expenditures for fear of a popular backlash, Saddam was reduced to issuing more threats against his erstwhile allies.

By the spring of 1990, Saddam had begun to zero in on Kuwait and made a series of demands of the sheikhdom. As with most colonial demarcations, the boundary between the two states was disputed. In 1961, Iraq had even amassed troops on Kuwait's border, only to be deterred by a timely British intervention.[8] Saddam now resurrected those territorial claims and again stressed his refusal to pay his war debts. He contested the Rumalia oil field that straddled the two countries, demanding a greater share of its output. And then there were the two islands of Warbah and Bubiyan that Iraq wanted from Kuwait in order to enhance its access to the Persian Gulf. The Kuwaitis were in no mood to concede.

By this time, Washington was beginning to recognize that its attempt to lure Saddam into cooperation by providing him with aid was not working. The American posture stiffened as agricultural credits were suspended and Glaspie informed the Iraqis that they were "on a collision course with the U.S. if it [Iraq] continued to engage in actions that threaten the stability of the Gulf."[9] The U.S. warnings, however, did not have the optimal effect as they were usually coupled with gestures of goodwill. To be fair, even if the administration had spoken with a consistent voice it may not have had an impact on Saddam. The scope of his grievances and ambitions seemed to outstrip a diplomatic settlement.

Among the unhelpful maneuvers at this point was the dispatch of a high-level congressional delegation to Baghdad to assuage Saddam. Senator Robert Dole, the senior member of the bipartisan group, informed Saddam that "only twelve hours earlier President Bush assured me that he wanted better relations and that the United States government wanted better relations with Iraq."[10] Senator Alan Simpson took note of critical American press commentaries that had agitated the Iraqis and advised Saddam that the problem was that the U.S. press was "haughty and arrogant."[11] Given his unsophisticated understanding of American politics, Saddam may have convinced himself that the United States would not object to his contemplated act of hostility.

Although they would be victims of Saddam's aggression, the Kuwaitis must bear a measure of blame for what transpired. The United States was prepared to demonstrate its commitment to Gulf security by forging closer military collaboration with the sheikdoms. Such an occasion arose when the United Arab Emirates accepted an offer of joint military exercises with the United States. Kuwait, supported by Saudi Arabia, declined to participate in the exercises and insisted that such displays might further inflame Saddam's suspicions. The Kuwaiti conduct at this point was a curious mixture of being both mindful and dismissive of Saddam's threats. On the one hand, they did respond to Iraq's intimidation by filing protest petitions with the Arab League and the United Nations. And yet, they kept the United States at arm's length. It is difficult to assess whether a different Kuwaiti posture would have caused Saddam to reconsider his invasion. But, the princely state's conduct certainly did not improve its position.

The news of joint military exercises between the United States and the United Arab Emirates finally led Saddam to summon Glaspie. This was to be the ambassador's first and only encounter with the Iraqi president. A surprised Glaspie did not have time to consult with Washington and went into the meeting with outdated talking points. A brutish Saddam went through his list of grievances, denigrated American power, and boasted of Iraq's military strength. "Yours is a society which cannot accept ten thousand dead in one battle," claimed Saddam.[12] He was not beyond threatening terrorism: "we cannot come all the way to you in the United States but individual Arabs may reach you."[13] Glaspie stressed that the United States took no position on Iraq's border dispute with Kuwait but insisted that the issue be resolved peacefully.

Glaspie finally got to the point and asked Saddam about his intentions given Iraq's military buildup along Kuwait's border. Saddam, who interrupted the meeting to take a call from Hosni Mubarak about a forthcoming summit to settle the dispute, confided to the ambassador that "When we meet and when we see that there is hope, nothing will happen." Then he added, "but if we are unable to find a solution then it will be natural that Iraq will not accept death, even though wisdom is above everything."[14]

Glaspie followed her meeting with a cable to Washington injudiciously titled "Saddam's Message of Peace." The ambassador asserted that Saddam was sincere in his claim that he wanted a peaceful settlement of the quarrel with Kuwait. The American military exercises in conjunction with the United Arab Emirates were largely unnecessary and she recommended that the United States "ease off our public criticism of Iraq until we see how the negotiations develop."[15]

Much has been made of Glaspie's assurance to Saddam that the United States took no position on the border dispute between Iraq and Kuwait. Although the ambassador's tone during the encounter was unwisely obsequious, in this case she was expressing standard American policy. The United States would not take a position on how the border dispute was settled but it was opposed to its revision by force of arms. The State Department's own guidance to its regional ambassadors noted that the "U.S. takes no position on the substance of bilateral issues concerning Iraq . . . We remain committed to ensuring the free flow of oil from the Gulf states and to support the sovereignty and integrity of the Gulf states."[16] In his own letter to Saddam after his meeting with Glaspie, Bush noted that "my administration continues to desire better relations with Iraq," while also stressing that "we believe that differences are best resolved by peaceful means and not by threats involving military force or conflict."[17] Washington's perception, reinforced by its Arab allies, was that Saddam was merely trying to intimidate the Kuwaitis and that an excessively confrontational policy would push him into a corner that he could not escape without lashing out.

Evidence that has come out of Iraq since the collapse of the Ba'athist regime reveals how Saddam misinterpreted his meeting with Glaspie. A former Iraqi official noted that after the meeting Saddam was "relieved that America was not going to get involved."[18] While in captivity in 2004, Saddam himself recalled the conversation as affirming his decision to invade. Saddam seems to have thought that the CIA was omniscient. The United States must have known that he was planning to invade Kuwait. If Washington objected, then its representative would have said so. To a leader who often interpreted evidence selectively, the meeting seemed to have affirmed his instincts.

A retrospective assessment of the full record of Saddam's discussion with Glaspie leads to the conclusion that the Iraqi strongman was using the occasion to deter the United States. Saddam issued numerous threats and boasted that the American people were averse to casualties. As with many Third World leaders of his generation he was enchanted by the Vietnam War and felt that the United States lacked the resolution to confront recalcitrant adversaries. He kept insisting that Iraq was not afraid of America and would defend its rights irrespective of the costs. The transcript of the conversation may not shed much light on Iraq's intentions toward Kuwait, but they do constitute an unmistakable warning to the United States not to underestimate Iraq's determination. Saddam seemed to have already made the decision to invade and the purpose of the meeting was to scare Washington from taking any forceful reaction.

The ongoing rancor between Kuwait and Iraq finally led the Arab

League to empower Mubarak as a mediator. In a critical July 24 meeting, Saddam made false assurances to Mubarak that would go on to haunt him. "As long as discussions last between Iraq and Kuwait, I won't use force. I won't intervene with force before I have exhausted all the possibility for negotiations," assured Saddam.[19] The Iraqi president went on to insist that the buildup of his forces on Kuwait's periphery was a routine troop movement.

As the pressure on Kuwait mounted, Saudi Arabia joined the chorus urging its ally to moderate its stance. At a meeting of the oil ministers, Kuwait agreed to reduce production although not to the extent that Iraq deemed sufficient. Still, Iraq and Kuwait did agree to meet on August 1 in Saudi Arabia to work out their remaining differences. The message coming out of Arab capitals was that Saddam was bluffing. The forthcoming summit would finally put an end to the crisis. Even the Kuwaitis went so far as to describe the crisis as fading summer clouds.

Kuwait approached the critical summit with the same air of complacency that had characterized its previous encounters with Iraq. Kuwait's leader, Jaber al-Ahmad al-Jaber al-Sabah, still thought that conceding to Saddam would only whet his appetite and thus it was better to rebuff the Iraqi strongman. This reasoning was even more astounding in light of a report from Kuwait's military attaché in Baghdad that Iraq's elite Republican Guard was gearing up for an invasion.[20] Neither Saudi advice for moderation, nor Iraq's military buildup on its border, dissuaded Kuwait from its policy of defiance. The summit predictably failed when the Iraqi delegation stormed out of the meeting.

By this time, U.S. intelligence was reporting that Iraq had committed too many troops to an offensive formation for this to be a bluff. As diplomacy faltered, the CIA grew more certain that an invasion was afoot. The warnings of the intelligence services had to be balanced by the assurances of key regional allies. Bush was a president who believed in personal contact with his counterparts and relied on them for information and advice. What the president heard from King Hussein and President Mubarak was that Saddam was pretending and that his military moves were part of an elaborate ruse. Moreover, even if military action came it would likely be confined to the disputed oil field. The history of the Arab world is filled with deceit and intrigue, but there was no precedent for a country to invade and annex another one. The CIA's warnings were thus going against the stream of Arab advice and history.

Archival records obtained after the 2003 overthrow of Saddam shed light on some of Iraq's key decisions in 1990. It appears that the Iraqi leadership considered the changing international situation to be a propitious time for its invasion. There were simply too many competing priorities for the United States to preoccupy itself with tiny Kuwait. As one of Saddam's advisors confided to him, "I believe the present circumstances in the world today have given us the opportunity of a lifetime and this opportunity [will] not happen again in fifty years."[21] All the international community cared about was the region's energy supplies—and Saddam was happy to sell Kuwait's oil to all customers.

On August 2, Iraqi forces invaded Kuwait.

Could the United States have deterred Saddam with a more robust policy during the spring of 1990? The fact remains that a more confrontational policy would not have had the support of the regional allies or of an American public awaiting its post–Cold War peace dividend. The pull of continuity is always compelling and the notion that incentives could sway an adversary remains a hallmark of U.S. diplomacy. As we have seen, the policy of accommodating Saddam did shift during the summer of 1990, but not in a decisive enough manner to impress the Iraqi leader bent on invasion.

Yet on August 2, no one could have guessed that America would assemble a vast international coalition, deploy half a million troops in the desert, and forcefully reclaim Kuwait.

DESERT SHIELD

Saddam's invasion initially caught American officials flat-footed. After being notified of the attack, Bush later confessed, "I had no idea what our options were."[22] The first meeting of the National Security Council (NSC) went badly. There was neither a consensus on objectives nor a strategy about how to move forward. Bush compounded the problem by stating to the assembled White House press corps that he did not contemplate intervention. The meeting degenerated into a squabble between those who wanted a robust response and others who were still trying to figure out what redlines to draw and where.

Brent Scowcroft, the president's national security advisor, was distressed at the meandering nature of the conversation and the willingness of some present to accept Saddam's conquest. "I was frankly appalled at the undertone of the discussion, which suggested resignation to the invasion and even adaptation to a fait accompli," Scowcroft later recalled.[23] Dick Cheney, who was secretary of defense at the time, similarly recalled that "when the Gulf crisis first started, there were two camps. There were those of us who believed this really was a major strategic threat to the U.S. We could not afford to let Saddam dominate the Gulf. The other school thought it was more a matter of Kuwait, who cares about Kuwait?"[24] The administration had to come up with a coherent and unified response to the crisis.

Bush was scheduled to travel to Aspen, Colorado, to give a major address at the annual Aspen Institute Conference on the foreign policy challenges of the post–Cold War era. Scowcroft used the time on the plane to convince the president that the emerging international system should not allow dictators to swallow up weak nations. America had to compel Saddam to disgorge his ill-gotten gain. Bush was already thinking along the same lines and seemed poised to commit U.S. forces to repel Saddam's aggression if diplomatic and economic pressures did not settle the issue.

When Bush landed in Aspen he met a determined British prime minister Margaret Thatcher, who insisted on a firm response. Much would be made later about how Thatcher had bucked up a wavering Bush. In reality, she only affirmed his instincts, as by now Bush was determined to restore Kuwait's sovereignty.

By the time of the second NSC session, the mood of indecision and despair had all but disappeared. With Bush's permission, Scowcroft took command of the meeting and stressed that the "stakes for the United States are such that to accommodate Iraq should not be a policy option."[25] There was a fear that the tempestuous Iraqi dictator might not stop at Kuwait and might actually invade Saudi Arabia. Even if he curtailed his operations at Kuwait, he would still be in command of more than 20 percent of the world's known oil supplies, allowing him to manipulate prices to the detriment of the global economy.

The one persistent voice of skepticism in the inner circle was the chairman of Joint Chiefs of Staff, Army general Colin Powell. A veteran of the Vietnam War, Powell was leery of embarking on military campaigns without firm and sustained public support. Shortly after Iraq invaded Kuwait, Powell claimed that "I don't see the senior leadership taking us into armed conflict for the events of the last twenty-four hours."[26] From the beginning, Powell insisted that deterring Saddam from invading Saudi Arabia would be much easier than dislodging him from Kuwait. As the situation progressed, he would remain cautious, reluctant to go to war, and eager to end the conflict as soon as possible.

A few days after the invasion, the administration made the momentous decision that there would be no compromise with Saddam nor face-saving off-ramps for the Iraqi dictator. The president would have to convince a skeptical Congress, a lukewarm public, and an unwieldy alliance system to support a tough line. The remarkable aspect of the Gulf War was that the administration managed to stitch together a truly global effort on America's terms. In time, both the Congress and the United Nations would endorse Bush's strategy and the generals who were uneasy about going to war would perform their task with precision and skill.[27]

Given its determination to affirm legal norms, the administration resolved to work through the United Nations. If Saddam's conduct was unlawful, America would do the opposite and observe all legal niceties. The support of the United Nations would also ease the way for other nations to impose sanctions on Iraq and eventually contribute troops to the effort. A series of U.N. resolutions would legitimize America's action and underpin its coalition. On August 6, after condemning Iraq, the U.N. Security Council passed Resolution 661, essentially prohibiting all trade with Baghdad. Soon, the two pipelines carrying Iraq's oil through Saudi Arabia and Turkey were shut down. Iraq had to revert to a war economy with rations, accelerated agricultural production, and looting of Kuwait to stay afloat. For a state that relied on income from oil sales, such belated measures of self-sufficiency could not overcome the international embargos.

As it contemplated its course of action, the White House decided that the first step was to contain Saddam and prevent any further military incursions by Iraq. Saudi Arabia proved the prized actor, both as a frontline state that needed protection and as a leading Arab power that could rally regional support. The Saudis were anxious and angry with Saddam, but it remained uncertain whether they would accept a sizeable U.S. troop presence on their territory. The politically risky move of hosting Western forces near Islam's holy shrines weighed heavily on the Saudis. Indeed, many in Washington feared that instead of leading the Arab charge against Baghdad, Riyadh might be tempted to reach some kind of accommodation with Saddam.

The Bush team's entreaties to the House of Saud soon ran up against doubts about American credibility. Two episodes colored the Saudis' perception of U.S. promises. In 1979, the Carter administration had sought to reassure the Saudi kingdom after the fall of the shah in Iran by dispatching a squadron of F-16 fighter jets to the Gulf. However, not wishing to antagonize the Iranian revolutionaries, the administration had revealed that the aircraft were unarmed. Next was the Reagan administration's quick retreat from Lebanon in 1983 after Hezbollah attacked a U.S. Marine barracks. Paradoxically, much like Saddam, the Saudis doubted the credibility of U.S. pledges and its staying power once it encountered hardship.

The White House started with Prince Bandar bin Sultan, the wily longtime Saudi ambassador to Washington who maintained close ties to King Fahd. Scowcroft took the lead in convincing Bandar that this time America was serious. A further round of presentations of military plans at the Pentagon seemed to clinch the case.[28] Despite this, Bush decided to dispatch Cheney and Powell to Riyadh to make a direct appeal to the king. The powerful presentation by the high-level American delegation made an impression on Fahd. The mounting Iraqi forces in Kuwait and the prepositioning of artillery and Scud missiles implied that Saddam was gathering at least the capability to invade Saudi Arabia. The fate of Kuwait and the fact that Saddam had all along misled Fahd about his intentions convinced the monarch that delay would not serve his interests. The kingdom authorized the deployment of U.S. forces on its territory. Operation Desert Shield was under way.

A similar set of calculations propelled Egypt to join the coalition. During Iraq's war with Iran, Egypt had been at the forefront of efforts to assist Saddam. The Iraqi leader reciprocated by helping to rehabilitate Cairo after its peace treaty with Israel led to its eviction from the councils of Arab states. Saddam's false promises on the eve of the invasion of Kuwait had humiliated Hosni Mubarak. As the Egyptian leader informed Cheney and Powell during their visit to Cairo, "I don't care anything about Kuwaitis. They are a bunch of shysters and they deserve everything they got. They won't help us and now they are asking for our help. I don't care about Kuwaitis but Saddam lied to me."[29]

Once Fahd and Mubarak were on board the remainder of the Arab coalition began to come together. On August 7, the Gulf Cooperation

Council issued a resolution denouncing Iraq's invasion. Shortly afterward, the Arab League offered its own condemnation. Despite a number of U.N. resolutions that had already passed, the affirmation of the Arab League must have unsettled Saddam. All along he had assumed that the fractious Arab world would not coalesce behind the United States. In the end, he could count only on the support of the PLO and King Hussein of Jordan, both of whom acted disreputably throughout the crisis. Saddam had miscalculated that fear of popular backlash would deter the Saudis from inviting American troops, and that the remaining Arab states would side with him as opposed to the disliked Kuwaitis.

Hafez al-Assad of Syria seemed a natural choice to join the alliance as his animosities and ambitions made him a foe of Saddam. The two leaders of the contending Ba'ath parties had long accused each other of ideological heresy and competed for influence in the Levant. Assad appreciated that his Soviet patron was increasingly a spent force. He needed new allies. Suddenly, Saddam's reckless invasion offered Assad a chance to cut his rival down to size while earning American and Saudi gratitude. In the end, Syria's contribution of 14,500 troops may have been modest but as a symbol its participation was all too important.

As the threat gathered, Saddam remained confident that a casualty-averse America would not engage his forces. He assured his aides that "all they can do is to bring their airplanes and start bombing: boom, boom, boom. Give me one instance when an airplane has settled any situation."[30] When Yemeni leader Ali Abdullah Saleh visited Baghdad, the Iraqi strongman claimed that "we considered that America and Israel may attack us without ground forces. . . . they may attack us with airplanes and missiles."[31] Still enchanted by the notion that the aftershocks of the Vietnam War precluded an American ground invasion, Saddam seemed assured that his grip on Kuwait would hold.

While the United States was mobilizing the Arab countries, Saddam decided to play the Israel card and appeal directly to the Arab masses. He now suggested that he would withdraw from Kuwait if Israel left the occupied territories. Even this offer was tentative and had to "take into consideration the historic rights of Iraq to its territory and the choice of the Kuwaiti people."[32] Saddam was not quite finished, as he also demanded that all allied forces withdraw from Saudi Arabia and all the sanctions against Iraq be lifted. These terms were summarily rejected by Washington.

Yet another of Saddam's misjudgments was that the Soviet Union would reprise its traditional role and restrain U.S. action. Soviet leader Mikhail Gorbachev, however, had a greater stake in cooperating with Washington than in preserving Saddam's gains. The fact that Baghdad had not consulted with Moscow before the invasion, as was required by the Soviet-Iraq Friendship Treaty, relieved Gorbachev of any lingering attachment to Saddam. Russia would not join the military alliance led by the United States and would eventually offer its own proposals for settling the conflict (to Washington's great annoyance), but the Soviet Union did support the various U.N. Security Council resolutions. Gorbachev also joined Bush in condemning Iraq's act and demanding the restoration of Kuwait's sovereignty.

Whatever its previous mishaps may have been, by the fall of 1990 the Bush administration had discharged a remarkable diplomatic tour de force. Both superpowers were in agreement. America's mandates were endorsed by the United Nations. The U.S. military realized a logistical miracle by deploying two hundred fifty thousand troops and two million tons of military hardware in the Saudi desert. Sanctions were imposed on Iraq. The United States did not waver, nor adjust its terms, but marshaled the entire international community into accepting its maximalist demands. On top of all that, Washington collected fifty-four billion dollars in allied contributions for the war effort. Then began a period of wait-and-see.

"I never had any faith in sanctions, and I don't believe the president did either," recalled Scowcroft.[33] After the midterm congressional elections in November, the administration moved toward war. Bush and his advisors feared that public support for the war was tenuous at best and likely to erode over time. The international coalition was similarly fragile. It was at this point that the White House secured U.N. Security Council Resolution 678, which called on Iraq to withdraw from Kuwait by January 15, 1991, or face military attack. Soon after, Bush authorized the dispatch of an additional two hundred thousand troops to Saudi Arabia.

In a concerted public effort, the administration began to question the notion that sanctions could evict Saddam from Kuwait. Cheney testified to Congress that "we do not have an indefinite period of time to wait for sanctions to produce the desired result."[34] Baker similarly stressed that "we have to face the fact that four months into the conflict none of our efforts have yet produced any sign of change in Saddam Hussein."[35] Finally, William Webster, the director of the CIA, assessed that "there is no assurance or guarantee that economic hardship will compel Saddam Hussein to change his policy."[36] The decision for war had been looming in the background for some time and by now appeared preordained. Few officials believed that sanctions alone would cause Saddam to retreat.

Saddam welcomed the passage of Resolution 678. The Iraqi dictator perceived that the escalation of the crisis would lead to more creative diplomacy that had the potential to resolve the issue on terms acceptable to Iraq. As Saddam confessed to his aides, "When the world gets frenzied, everything becomes possible."[37] To some extent Saddam's delusions were buttressed by a stream of mediators making their way to Baghdad offering all kinds of plans. The more dangerous the situation became, Saddam reasoned, the more imaginative the search for a diplomatic solution would become.

As war seemed imminent, foreign policy luminaries stepped forth with their forebodings. Zbigniew Brzezinski warned in congressional testimony that the casualty figures could exceed twenty thousand

and the economic consequences of the conflict would be devastating. A string of retired generals similarly claimed that the cost of liberating Kuwait was going to be unacceptably high. Historian Arthur Schlesinger invoked the 1960s and asked senators to "take a few quiet moments to revisit the Vietnam monument."[38] Robert McNamara, who spent a lifetime offering penance for his Vietnam folly, stepped forth with his own cautionary tales. History was to repeat itself and those present at the time of America's misadventure in Southeast Asia were determined to be heard.

Many purveyors of the Vietnam analogy failed to acknowledge how technological innovations had changed the U.S. military, particularly the air force. Old generals may have been right that airpower does not win wars, but its potency and precision could certainly weaken an enemy. Unlike Ho Chi Minh, Saddam did not have a superpower patron or a hospitable terrain that he could use to his advantage. The Soviet Union was not about to restrain the United States and the desert did not offer the sanctuary of the jungle. The Gulf War was to be a very different conflict from the wars that had gone before and would go after it.

Given the divisions in his country, Bush sought to prove to his critics that he was willing to go to the last mile to avoid war. The idea of a high-level meeting between Iraqi and American officials had been mooted for some time. After wrangling about dates and places, Bush agreed to a meeting between Baker and Tariq Aziz. The president was concerned that Saddam was not getting a correct assessment of the situation from his sycophantic and frightened aides. A clear warning in the form of a letter conveyed through Aziz, who was Saddam's confidant, may yet get the Iraqi strongman to back down. Scowcroft opposed the meeting and feared that Baker's penchant for diplomacy might lead to a protracted dialogue that would undermine the cohesion of the alliance. Still, Bush went ahead.

Saddam seemed ecstatic at the prospect of the meeting. All along he had believed that the United States did not have the resolve for war and that its concerns about casualties would override its distaste for his conduct. Perhaps the offer of talks was a way for America to avoid a war that it did not want. Saddam might not be able to keep all his spoils but a compromise solution might yet allow him to retain some of his gains. It appears that Saddam approached the talks anticipating a U.S. offer that fell well short of the U.N. Security Council resolutions.

On January 9, 1991, Baker finally met Aziz in Geneva. The meeting began inauspiciously, with Aziz refusing to take Bush's letter to Saddam. The foreign minister insisted that the threatening and insulting tone of the missive was not in keeping with normal diplomatic practice. The letter remained on the table, unclaimed by both parties. Baker made clear to Aziz that Iraq had to accept all U.N. resolutions and there would be no compromise. The secretary of state also emphasized that any Iraqi use of chemical weapons would lead to an all-out American retaliation. Aziz was hardly in a position to make sweeping concessions; thus ended the only direct encounter between the two sides before the onset of hostilities.

The next issue for the administration to grapple with was whether to seek congressional authorization. Many high-ranking officials including Cheney stressed that the president already had sufficient constitutional authority and that the possibility of a failed vote would be devastating for the White House and the assembled coalition. Again Bush overrode the advice of his more hawkish aides and appreciated that congressional consent was necessary for national unity. The fact that both houses of Congress had already signaled that they would soon commence a debate on the use of force further expedited the president's decision.

After a robust and contentious debate the House of Representatives voted 250 to 183 and the Senate 52 to 47 to support the war. A factor favoring the administration was Saddam's obduracy and his refusal to make concessions. Subsequent to the war, Bush and many of his advisors have suggested that the president would have waged war even if he had lost the vote in one or both houses of Congress. It is impossible to refute this claim, but it would be a contentious task to take the country to war after failing to secure congressional support. On January 17, the United States went to war with a divided country and a divided legislature.

DESERT STORM

The military campaign labeled Desert Storm was led by the burly and blunt-speaking General Norman Schwarzkopf Jr.[39] The war plan that Schwarzkopf designed was as simple as it was decisive. Allied airpower would first pound Iraq's military and economic infrastructure. At the conclusion of the air war, the army would launch an amphibious assault on Kuwait. In the meantime, U.S. marines and army units would be deployed in the desert separating Iraq and Saudi Arabia and trap Iraq's forces in Kuwait. It was hoped that the combined effect of all these measures would smash Iraq's army.[40]

From the outset, the United States resolved that Saddam should be defeated in a manner that did not upend the balance of power in the Gulf. Scowcroft stressed that the United States' goal should be "to reduce Saddam's military might so that he would no longer pose a threat to the region. Yet to do so in such a way that Iraq was secure from external threat and the balance of power with Iran [was] preserved."[41] This meant that the United States had to wage war against Iraq but not necessarily overthrow the Ba'athist regime.

As the six-week-long air war proceeded, Saddam reacted with measures of his own. Iraq launched Scud missiles at Israel. All along, Saddam had hoped to transform his war into a general Arab-Israeli conflict. By shooting missiles into Israel, he sought to present himself as the champion of the Palestinian cause and fracture the international alliance. The practical impact of the attacks may have been limited, but they did cause fear in Israeli cities. Given Iraq's chemical weapons, the Israeli government began equipping its citizens with gas masks. The question that the White House had to address was how to prevent Israel from retaliating and thus potentially causing the Arab states to leave the coalition.

The administration's message of restraint was not well received by Israel's hawkish prime minister, Yitzhak Shamir. The core of the Israeli defense doctrine has always been that it will respond decisively to all acts of aggression. Shamir was hardly the one to abandon this deterrent policy. Washington went into high gear, including dispatching Deputy Secretary of State Lawrence Eagleburger to Jerusalem for consultations. Eagleburger made a compelling case that nothing Israel was contemplating could match the destructive power of the allied bombing campaign. If Israel truly wanted Saddam's military destroyed, it had to sit on its hands. The dispatch of Patriot missile batteries that proved an effective barrier against the Scuds helped convince Israel to defer military action.

The one military tool at his disposal that Saddam did not use against Israel or the United States was his vast chemical weapons arsenal. Baker's warnings to Aziz on this issue seem to have been persuasive. From the postwar archives of Iraq we see that Saddam and his inner circle were concerned that the use of chemical weapons could trigger a nuclear response. As Izzat al-Douri, Saddam's vice president, noted in a private meeting, "It is dangerous for us to reveal our intentions to use chemical weapons. . . . this would give them [the United States] an excuse for nuclear attack."[42] Saddam seemed to have appreciated that if he crossed that line, the Americans were likely to march to Baghdad and topple his regime. At least in this narrow case, deterrence worked.

For much of this period, Gorbachev had complied with U.S. requests and had supported various American initiatives at the United Nations. As the prospect of a ground war loomed, important voices in the Kremlin grew uneasy about the defeat of their longtime client. Gorbachev warned Bush that "our new U.S.-Soviet cooperation, the spirit of our common values, means it is important to do the right thing." And the right thing was to "stop in this phase."[43] For the Soviet leader, the air war had taught Saddam a lesson and now it was time to provide him with a dignified path out of his predicament.

Gorbachev now summoned Aziz to Moscow and assured him that if Saddam withdrew now his regime would be spared and the sanctions lifted. Saddam instructed Aziz to "agree with him [Gorbachev] on the issue of withdrawal . . . taking into consideration that we have a large military force."[44] As far as Palestine was concerned, Aziz was to inform Gorbachev that "Saddam Hussein tells you that the Palestine issue has now become your [Gorbachev's] responsibility . . . Saddam has done his part."[45] Aziz offered to withdraw two thirds of Iraqi forces if sanctions were lifted. Once Iraq completed its withdrawal in about three weeks, then the U.N. resolutions would be formally abrogated. There were some vague references to Palestine but Iraq no longer insisted that its withdrawal be contingent on Israel leaving the occupied territories. Bush rejected this offer and insisted on complete withdrawal in a week, the release of all prisoners, and the dismantling of explosives that Iraqi troops had installed on wells in the Kuwaiti oil fields. In the absence of such stipulations, the coalition would soon begin its ground assault.[46]

On February 15, Iraq went a step farther and formally accepted Resolution 660, which called for withdrawal of all Iraqi forces from Kuwait. A mood of despair descended on the White House, as Bush conceded, "If Saddam withdrew with most of his armed forces intact, we hadn't really won."[47] The administration had settled on the notion that degrading Iraq's army was necessary to prevent future aggression by Saddam. And there were certainly reasons to doubt Saddam's sincerity. After all, at the time when Iraq was accepting the resolutions it was also busy setting Kuwait's oil fields ablaze. Still, it must be noted that the essential objectives articulated by the United Nations were seemingly met before the advent of the ground war. Bush rejected the final

Iraqi offer and gave Saddam a twenty-four-hour deadline to withdraw. Iraq's failure to comply with the ultimatum triggered the final phase of Operation Desert Storm.

Once the ground war began, Saddam had no real strategy other than salvaging as much of his army as he could. As Iraqi troops scrambled in the midst of surrender and retreat, they became an easy mark for the advancing coalition. The retreating Iraqi conscripts were subject to relentless attacks, triggering concerns in Washington about the scope of the carnage. A few days into the conflict, the mission of liberating Kuwait had been achieved, and to press ahead with the decimation of a largely disarmed force would only rankle the sensitivity of the allies, particularly the Arab members of the coalition. On February 28, Bush announced a cease-fire.

The allied victory had been decisive and stunning. In fewer than one hundred hours, they had captured nearly 74,000 square miles of land and were in possession of 15 percent of Iraq's territory. The Iraqi military was devastated; only a few of its divisions remained operational. The United States military suffered 148 deaths, testifying to the skill of its armed forces and the precision of its weaponry. This was not just the quickest war in history, but also one of the most lopsided.

The decision to stop the war short of toppling Saddam has generated its own share of controversy. Bush administration officials have justified their call by stressing the constraints of coalition warfare. A move beyond the liberation of Kuwait was bound to undermine the international alliance. The United Nations had not authorized a surge toward Baghdad and the Arab states would not have participated in such an endeavor. Even more importantly, Bush had promised multiple heads of state that his goals were limited to the eviction of Iraq from Kuwait. As a person of integrity, he was reluctant to go back on his word. Still, behind this decision lurks a more complex debate between two schools of thought.

For the administration's critics, the root cause of the conflict was the nature of the Iraqi regime and Saddam's personal system of rule. So long as Saddam remained in power, he could be counted on to behave aggressively. An administration steeped in realism, on the other hand, saw the conflict in terms of Iraq's capabilities. As a subsequent NSC study stressed, "Regardless of Saddam Hussein's motivations, the Iraqi invasion of Kuwait was possible because of a collapse of the regional balance of power."[48] The key was to ensure that Iraq's military power was degraded and its offensive potential regulated. In this line of thinking, Saddam was an opportunist who could be restrained if the cost of aggression was made clear to him. In essence, there was no need for regime change if a proper deterrence structure was in place.

Despite rhetorical exaggerations during the war and unwise comparisons of Saddam to Hitler by Bush, the administration viewed Saddam as unexceptional. The National Intelligence Estimate suggested, "Saddam Hussein is a product of an Iraqi political culture, not an aberration . . . changing the nature of Iraqi politics is a long-term process and not likely to be achieved by the fall of Saddam Hussein."[49] The United States had dealt with Saddam during his war with Iran only to find that he was less pragmatic and less predictable than it had anticipated. Still, the spectacular military defeat that he had suffered in Kuwait was bound to adjust his calculus and deflate his ambitions. Put simply, Saddam could be compelled to stay in his box.

And then there was the military brass that Bush would have had to contend with had he chosen to prolong the war. The American officer corps led by Colin Powell was haunted by Vietnam and wanted a quick exit after victory. Sorting out the messy politics of Iraq was not part of that compressed timeline. A civilian leadership leery of Vietnam comparisons was quick to yield to the generals. If Lyndon Johnson had micromanaged his war, then George Bush was going to leave it in the hands of his cautious officers. The military performed its task magnificently, precisely because its objectives were so limited. Given the power and precision of its weapons, the United States could evict

Iraq from Kuwait, but those same armaments could not fashion a new Iraqi society.

An element of magical thinking pervaded the administration's rationalizations for ending the war. The continuation of Saddam in power was clearly undesirable and yet the situation would somehow take care of itself. Bush confessed in his diary that "it seems to me that the more suffering the people of Iraq go through, the more likely that somebody will stand up and do that which should have been done a long time ago, take the guy out of there—either kick him out of the country or do something where he is no longer running things.[50] Cheney confidently predicted, "Saddam will be gone in six months."[51] Theses perceptions defy a basic premise of history: things do not happen simply because they should. Saddam's intricate security system and his ability to manipulate Iraq's sectarian divisions allowed him to retain power much longer than the Bush team anticipated.

The administration's postwar planning suffered from similar intellectual missteps. Washington assumed that after the war, Iraqi society would somehow settle back into previous routines, hopefully without Saddam at the helm. Among the scenarios that the administration had not anticipated was a popular uprising in the Kurdish north and the Shia south. "The truth is they were the last thing we wanted and needed," recalled Deputy National Security Advisor Robert Gates.[52] Even more unforeseen was how some Iraqi military units would reconstitute themselves and try to crush the rebellions. The administration that had all along been reluctant to intervene in Iraq was pulled in two different directions. The desire to stay out was eventually overwhelmed by the moral imperative of ending the slaughter.

The Shia rebellion in the south was put down by Saddam almost as quickly as it started. In the north, the conflict lingered. As Saddam unleashed his assault, nearly two million Kurds fled to the mountains and refugees began to spill into Turkey. The humanitarian crisis marred the news of America's decisive victory, compelling the administration to act. The Kurds—victims of so many of Saddam's previous war crimes—seemed destined to suffer another atrocity. The gravity of the situation led to Operation Provide Comfort, which offered safe havens for the displaced population. The United States would now be committed to patrolling from the air a zone of Iraq that gradually evolved into an autonomous Kurdish entity.

In a sense, the Gulf War was destined for an untidy end. The administration had built a vast coalition, secured U.N. resolutions, and assured the public of its limited goals. Regime change in Iraq was seemingly beyond the writ of law and the patience of the American people. The administration could have changed course and followed Truman's model of attempting to move beyond repelling North Korea's attack and unify the Korean peninsula. But that seemed more costly than wise. Washington assured itself that Saddam could not possibly survive such a catastrophic defeat. No one anticipated what would happen if he did.

The paradox of the Gulf War is how quickly its claims were reversed. After all the fretting the Bush administration did about the balance of power, the United States eventually was the one to step in and preserve the security of the Gulf. And that meant a substantial commitment of American forces to the region. The United States flew air missions over Iraq, protected civilian sanctuaries, and stationed a formidable armada in the Gulf waters. This was hardly what Bush had in mind before the start of hostilities. His Democratic successor, Bill Clinton, would reverse another pillar of the Gulf War by making regime change in Iraq official U.S. policy. The means of changing that regime would be economic sanctions that provoked a humanitarian crisis without actually getting rid of Saddam. In the aftermath of 9/11, George W. Bush would finally invade Iraq, triggering a conflict whose ramifications unfold to this day.

A WAR WITHOUT AN END

The Gulf War was the final conflict of the Cold War. The Soviet Union accepted Saddam's eviction from Kuwait and the destruction of his armed forces. Its diplomatic maneuverings notwithstanding, Moscow was not prepared to sacrifice America's goodwill for the sake of rescuing an impetuous client. The Gulf War, as with Iran's revolution, reveals that at times during the Cold War, America's interests were jeopardized not just by Russia but by radical actors nurturing their own schemes. Saddam did not invade Kuwait to pave the way for Soviet advances but to realize his ambition of becoming a great Arab leader.

One of the most dramatic lessons of the Gulf War is the difficulty of assessing the intentions of an opaque regime. At times, critics have suggested that the Bush administration could have prevented the invasion of Kuwait if it had clearly expressed redlines. It is not so much that the Bush team failed to devise a clear deterrence strategy, but that no administration could be expected to craft one. A precise deterrence posture required a perfect estimation of Saddam's objectives. The Washington establishment and indeed all the Arab rulers were convinced that in 1990 Saddam was bluffing and that his war of nerves was designed to extract concessions from Kuwait. All the saber-rattling and the troop deployments were merely Saddam's version of coercive diplomacy.

Still, once the war started, Bush's great advantage was an adversary whose aggression was obvious and whose offers of compromise came too late. Saddam's miscalculations were staggering. He assumed that by invading Kuwait he could solve his economic problems and turn himself into an Arab hero. He dismissed the possibility of a robust U.S. reaction by taking refuge in the stale Vietnam syndrome. Failing to see how the geopolitical landscape had changed, he assumed that the

Soviet Union would restrain American power. Most importantly, he failed to see how the United States could not leave him in charge of the Persian Gulf.

The intriguing aspect of the Gulf War is how soon its legacy evaporated. All the lofty talk of a new world order quickly faded. The international system reverted to timeworn chaos and rivalry. The United Nations has had a better track record in the post–Cold War era as evidenced by its numerous sanctions resolutions imposed on Iran, but it is still too divided to serve as a platform for sustained international cooperation. The newly arrived Russian Federation would prove more antagonistic than Gorbachev's Soviet Union, and China would find its own voice as an emerging power. Thus, the Gulf War may have benefited from a steady United Nations but did not presage great power harmony. The United States would remain a superpower, but one that has difficulty building a global consensus behind its preferences.

Nor did the war fundamentally adjust Saddam's perspective. The Iraqi archives reveal that Saddam actually thought that he had won. He had survived an onslaught by an impressive international coalition led by a superpower. If the United States could have deposed him, it would have. Saddam assured his inner circle that "the strongest scientific, technological and military powers and the highest financial and economic potential existing in the region and the world without any exception . . . all got together against us and they did not succeed despite what happened. They did not dare to attack Baghdad."[53] The Iraqi despot lived in a zero-sum universe; in it rivals and adversaries were eliminated, not given another chance. The United States had not surged ahead, he reasoned, because it feared Iraq and its forces.

The Gulf War continues to be debated by historians and policy makers, often with reference to its more contentious successor. However, to assess the war properly, one must do so on its own terms. The Gulf War achieved its primary and essential objective: the liberation of Kuwait.

And it did so at a modest cost to the United States. A central and defining principle of international law was redeemed and an aggressor was suitably punished. America's alliances were not battered nor were its politics polarized as a result of the conflict. And that may be the Gulf War's most important lesson and its most crucial legacy.

CONCLUSION

In the nuclear age, war between the superpowers may have been unthinkable but competition was all too common. The Cold War compelled the United States to defy its own isolationist past and seek permanent alliances beyond its borders. Given the resources and geographical position of the Middle East, all U.S. presidents recognized that the region played an important role in America's struggle against Russia. And it was in the Middle East that America discharged its containment obligations with minimal cost.

America's successes in the region started early. In 1946, the Soviet Union's attempt to extend its sphere of influence into northern Iran was repelled. In 1953, Iran was the scene of another Cold War flashpoint when its well-meaning but reckless prime minister was ousted. In 1958, the imperiled conservative order proved resurgent. America's Israeli ally succeeded in its wars in such a lopsided manner that Arab states were left to question the value of Soviet arms and support. The most devastating conflict in the history of the modern Middle East, the Iran-Iraq war, remained largely confined to the two antagonists and did not destabilize the entire region. And the first Gulf War proved the apex of American power in the Middle East.

America's successes during the Cold War did not stem from the limits of its ambitions. The United States sought to preserve access to the region's oil, ensure the safety of Israel, and thwart Soviet inroads into the Middle East. These were not modest objectives, but they were practical. The Gulf states had their own interest in making certain that their oil reached the global markets. Conservatives had ample incentives to battle the tides of radicalism and preserve their regimes. The Israelis had an existential stake in their military superiority and went to great lengths in disabusing the Arab states of the notion that they could smother the Zionist enterprise.

Throughout the Cold War, America succeeded best when it was buttressing an already resilient ally. Iran's Prime Minister Ahmad Qavam was already inclined to resist Soviet encroachment in 1946, and that determination was much strengthened by Truman's backing. Without Washington's stance, Qavam may have acquiesced to Stalin's land grab. In 1953, the United States helped steady the shah and his generals as they took the initiative to oust Muhammad Mossadeq. In 1958, the conservative order was on the brink of collapse after the decapitation of the Iraqi dynasty. It was America's aid and military deployments that fortified the monarchies of Jordan and Saudi Arabia. The conservatives won the Arab Cold War with no small measure of U.S. support. In all its wars, Israel understood that it had the support of the United States—a support that proved indispensable in 1973 when Arab states appeared to threaten the survival of the Jewish state. And in the Gulf War, the Bush administration put together a formidable alliance that not only evicted Saddam Hussein from Kuwait but also reclaimed sovereignty as an indispensable principle of international law.

The United States' record in the Middle East was not one of uninterrupted success; it did suffer some staggering setbacks. America usually faltered when its presidents made the wrong assumptions and its allies displayed poor judgment. Eisenhower initially assumed that Colonel Gamal Abdel Nasser and his nationalist allies would spearhead America's Cold War priorities in the Middle East. Eisenhower was correct in noting the arrival of Arab nationalism but he discounted its neutralist tendencies and its refusal to choose sides in the Cold War struggle. His administration spent much of its first term in office investing in Nasser and devising elaborate Arab-Israeli peace proposals that had no chance of being accepted by either party. As his first term expired, Eisenhower was bedeviled by Nasser as well as by U.S. allies' rash invasion of Egypt. The British, French, and Israeli attack on the Suez Canal in 1956 inflamed regional tensions and polarized an already divided Middle East. Nasser survived but the British presence in the Arab East did not.

Still, if the Soviet Union viewed these events as a pathway toward the projection of its own power, it proved wrong. Eisenhower's deft response to the Suez Crisis and its aftermath indicated a rare propensity among U.S. presidents: a willingness to discard existing assumptions and forge new policies. The United States did much to reverse the invasion of Egypt by its allies, as such outdated imperial ventures had no role in an international system roiling with colonial awakenings. The Eisenhower Doctrine, announced shortly after the Suez War, was a more subtle means of undermining the influence of Arab radicals. By the time Eisenhower left office, the conservatives had reclaimed the initiative and the radicals were divided and bickering among themselves.

Nowhere was America's misapprehension of an adversary greater than the Carter administration's assessment of Ayatollah Ruhollah Khomeini and Iran's revolution. In 1979, Jimmy Carter's ambivalence only compounded the shah's indecision and psychological paralysis. In the later stages of the uprising, the Carter administration convinced itself that the monarchy was going to be replaced by the moderate elements of the revolutionary coalition and that Khomeini and his clerical disciples would yield to secular forces. There are no inevitabilities in history and there is no reason to believe that Iran's revolution was destined to succeed. The shah was primarily responsible for the fate of his monarchy, but the Carter administration must bear its own measure of blame for the collapse of an essential pillar of American power in the Middle East. While Eisenhower helped to salvage the Arab conservative monarchies in 1958, Carter helplessly looked on as the Pahlavi dynasty crumbled.

It has been the central claim of many academics and diplomats that America suffered in the Arab world because of its alliance with Israel. The historical record belies such casual claims. The conservative monarchies never contemplated severing relations with America because of its ties to the Jewish state and even found occasions of common cause with Israel. After all, it was Israeli armor that finally put an end to Nasserism in the Six-Day War in 1967, causing the radicals to come to terms with the monarchs. And it was Egypt's costly defeats in the Arab-Israeli wars that finally led Anwar Sadat to decouple his nation from the Arab rejectionist camp. Sadat understood that to leave the Arab morass he had to switch sides in the Cold War and embrace Washington. The United States managed to sustain its alliance with Israel without causing permanent harm to its relations with Arab states.

A more serious question is whether the United States invested too much diplomatic capital in solving the Arab-Israeli dispute. Should the resolution of one of the most enduring conflicts in the history of the Middle East have been an American priority? The answer during the Cold War era is yes. The reality is that wars between Israel and the Arab states did threaten to destabilize the region and provided openings for the Soviet Union. In 1973, the Yom Kippur War did summon the possibility of nuclear confrontation, but leaders on both sides quickly walked it back. The fact that the United States was involved in peacemaking offered both parties a platform to express their grievances and cover for retreat from the brink. And eventually the cumulative efforts of successive administrations did produce the Camp David Accords, still one of the more durable agreements in the Middle East. The story of American diplomatic efforts to cajole recalcitrant Israeli leaders while propitiating aggrieved Arab rulers provides the backdrop of the Cold War era.

As significant as the resolution of the Arab-Israeli conflict was during the Cold War, its importance has now diminished. The Soviet Union has disappeared and the possibility of a general Arab-Israeli war is nonexistent. The conflict between Israelis and Palestinians neither conditions the politics of the Middle East nor constitutes a barrier to American power. This is not to suggest that the United States should not mediate the differences between Israel and its Palestinian neighbor. The emotionally charged issue of Palestinian displacement still tugs at Arab consciousness and both Israelis and Palestinians would be better off with a Jewish state coexisting with a Palestinian one next door. However, the time when this issue should have defined America's priorities in the Middle East has passed.

Looking over the entire span of the Cold War, the intriguing question remains: Did the United States win the Cold War in the Middle East or did the Soviet Union lose it? America's policy makers were not always the wisest nor were its strategists always the most thoughtful. Yet, the United States prevailed because the Soviet Union faced even more insurmountable barriers to its political objectives. The fusion of communism and nationalism that defined politics in East Asian states such as China and Vietnam never took hold in the Middle East. Communism, with its prescribed stages of history, materialism, and atheism, may have inspired a segment of the intellectual class, but it never became a creed for the masses. Islam and its holistic worldview was too powerful to be displaced by an alternative ideology with similar aspirations.

Thus, the Kremlin never developed reliable allies. Nasser and the Ba'athist army officers who came to power in Syria and Iraq may have appreciated Soviet support, but they were ill suited to become instruments of Russian power. Egypt was one of the largest recipients of Soviet aid in the Middle East, but that did not stop Nasser from sporadically reaching out to the United States when his interests dictated.

Nor did his successor, Anwar Sadat, have any compunction about expelling Soviet advisors. The problem for Moscow was that Arab radicals did not believe in its ideology and were often mere opportunists who tactically switched sides. The Soviet Union offered Arabs neither a model worthy of emulation nor resources to enable their economics and militaries.

It appears that throughout the Cold War, the Middle East was more of a priority for the United States than for Russia. Despite its globalist reach, the core Soviet concerns remained Eastern Europe and Asia. Of course, the Russians also were inclined to mischief and saw in the rise of postcolonial nationalism an opportunity to poke the West. Russia would aid Arab militants, fan the flames of revolutions in Latin America, and support African liberation movements. But it would also retreat in the Middle East in a manner that was unthinkable in Eastern Europe. Stalin's withdrawal from Iran would never have been replicated, let alone considered, in the case of Poland. Brezhnev accepted the expulsion of his advisors from Egypt, while such a move in East Germany would have been inconceivable to him. This focus on Europe and Asia only changed during the reign of Gorbachev, when the Cold War receded and the Soviet Union retreated from its client states en masse.

In documents from across the U.S. administrations spanning the Cold War, nearly every strategic review insists that the Middle East was one of the most important priorities for the United States. This was as true for Truman as it was for Reagan. The consistent theme that binds all Cold War administrations together was their shared perception that they had to succeed in the Middle East. The region's petroleum wealth meant more to America than to an oil-producing Russia, and its pivotal location was more critical to a distant United States than to a land-power like the Soviet Union. This mismatch in priorities partly explains why the Americans often came ahead in their competition for influence with the Russians. Simply put, it meant more to us than to them.

Finally we must question whether the inexpensive U.S. successes in preserving stability geared to American interests yielded an instability that lately has come to define the Middle East. The administrations that have come to power since the Cold War ended have chosen priorities that did not always enhance the region's stability. The Clinton administration's inordinate focus on Israeli-Palestinian peacemaking came at a time when the conflict was no longer a touchstone in Arab politics. In the meantime, the Gulf simmered with unresolved tensions and terrorism festered in the background. The Clinton administration mistakenly believed that the resolution of the Israeli-Palestinian conflict would somehow transform the region's politics.

In the aftermath of the 9/11 tragedies, the George W. Bush administration also sought to refashion the Arab order. The administration came to define the Arab world's authoritarian stability as a problem, which it then proceeded to solve by destroying the Iraqi state. The unusual logic at play here was that the demise of Saddam's regime would transform the Middle East. In this sense, the administration discounted how difficult it would be to reconstitute a functioning Iraqi state, much less transform the stubborn politics of the Arab world. America's prolonged occupation of Iraq, with all its hazards and costs, tempered Washington's ambitions and produced a president who was wary of engaging in the region's many crises. Barack Obama's administration arrived in power in 2008 determined not to be preoccupied with the complexities of the Arab world. The Obama presidency stood aside from all its predecessors by intimating that the traditional American emphasis on the Middle East was misplaced. The future lay in Asia, and the administration contemplated its pivot away from the Middle East. The drone wars would handle the vexing problem of terrorism without inordinate American involvement. Washington appeared confused in 2011 as the Arab uprisings brought about a tidal wave of revolutions and civil wars. In the Levant, a humanitarian catastrophe unfolded with the Syrian civil war; and farther east, Iraq once more tottered on the brink of collapse and Iran menaced the region. The one place where the Obama team did intervene militarily was in Libya, spreading a malaise of state incapacity, followed by anarchy, to a large swath of North Africa. It would be the tragedy of the Obama administration that its neglect of the Middle East came at a precise time when the region came undone.

Still, whatever miscalculations America may have made, the principal cause of the region's disorders are its leaders and the choices and decisions that they have made. They cannot be absolved of responsibility or forgiven because their region played a central role in the great powers' competition. Once the Cold War ended, Arab leaders could have focused on the rehabilitation of their nations, instituting economic reforms and creating inclusive governments. The Arab ruling class knew that it was presiding over a region marred by vast corruption, demographic disaster, environmental degradation, infrastructural decay, and so on. Instead of reforming their societies, they chose to nurture their conflicts, engage in a costly arms buildup, and ignore the pleas of their citizens for better governance. No external actor, even one as powerful as the United States, can compel a ruling elite to alter its ways and adapt to new circumstances. The Arab potentates' lust for power too often blinded them to the undercurrent of tension that marks their social order. Even the cataclysmic Arab uprisings have not detracted much of this leadership from its previous patterns of poor governance. America's Cold War policies cannot be blamed for the lack of vision that has characterized Arab order well into the twenty-first century.

ACKNOWLEDGMENTS

RAY TAKEYH wishes to acknowledge Richard Haass and James Lindsay for the generosity and assistance for a project that took longer than anticipated. The Council on Foreign Relations (CFR) continues to provide me with the most remarkable place to work. The library staff at the Council did much to facilitate the research for this book and responded to my many arcane requests with alacrity and aplomb. The CFR is an independent, nonpartisan membership organization, think tank, and publisher. The Council takes no institutional positions on policy issues and has no affiliation with the U.S. government. All views expressed in this book are the sole responsibility of the authors.

STEVEN SIMON wishes to acknowledge James Fromson and Max Peck for their superb research and analysis. He also wishes to thank his coauthor for single-handedly demonstrating how wrong Truman was when he proffered his oft-quoted advice on how to get a friend in Washington.

We both wish to thank our esteemed editor, Brendan Curry, and all the staff at Norton. Brendan was an ideal editor for us in terms of his uncanny eye and his comradeship throughout our long journey together. Our agent, Andrew Wiley, was also an indispensable source of support and guidance.

NOTES

CHAPTER 1: THE IRAN CRISIS OF 1946 AND THE COLD WAR'S FIRST CONFLICT

1. Norman Stone, *The Atlantic and Its Enemies: A History of the Cold War* (New York: Basic Books, 2010), 1–18; Tony Judt, *Postwar: A History of Europe Since 1945* (New York: Penguin, 2005), 13–41.

2. Melvyn Leffler, *A Preponderance of Power: National Security, the Truman Administration and the Cold War* (Stanford: Stanford University Press, 1992), 101.

3. Bruce Kuniholm, *The Origins of the Cold War in the Near East: Great Power Conflict and Diplomacy in Iran, Turkey, and Greece* (Princeton: Princeton University Press, 1980), 310.

4. Ibid.

5. Anne Applebaum, *The Iron Curtain: The Crushing of Eastern Europe, 1944–1956* (New York: Doubleday, 2012), 19.

6. John Lewis Gaddis, *George F. Kennan: An American Life* (New York: Penguin, 2011), 218; Walter Hixon, *George F. Kennan: Cold War Iconoclast* (New York: Columbia University Press, 1989), 25–45; Andres Stephanson, *Kennan and the Art of Foreign Policy* (Cambridge, Mass: Harvard University Press, 1989), 4–53.

7. Gaddis, *George F. Kennan: An American Life*, 220.

8. Ibid.

9. George F. Kennan, "The Sources of Soviet Conduct," *Foreign Affairs* 25, no. 4 (July 1947); also George F. Kennan, *Memoirs, 1925–1950* (Boston: Little, Brown, 1972), 583–98; Barton Bernstein and Allen Matusow, eds., *The Truman Administration: A Documentary History* (New York: Joanna Cotler Books, 1966), 198–212; Nicholas Thompson, *The Hawk and the Dove: Paul Nitze, George Kennan, and the History of the Cold War* (New York: Henry Holt, 2009), 57–64.

10. Eduard Mark, "The War Scare of 1946 and Its Consequences," *Diplomatic History* 21, no. 3 (Summer 1997).

11. Dean Acheson, *Present at the Creation: My Years in the State Department* (New York: W. W. Norton, 1986), 86.

12. Charles Bohlen, *Witness to History, 1929–1969* (New York: W. W. Norton, 1973), 26–29.

13. Memorandum of Conversation by Patterson, August 21, 1947 (RG 59) 741.83/8-2147, National Archives and Records (hereafter NARA).

14. Ibid.

15. Fraser Harbutt, *The Iron Curtain: Churchill, America, and the Origins of the Cold War* (Oxford: Oxford University Press, 1986), 186.

16. William Manchester and Paul Reid, *The Last Lion: Winston Spencer Churchill: Defender of the Realm, 1940–1965* (New York: Little, Brown, 2012), 957–63.

17. Randall Woods and Howard Jones, *Dawning of the Cold War: The United States' Quest for Order* (Oxford: Oxford University Press, 1991), 98–133; Robert Dallek, *The Lost Peace: Leadership in a Time of Horror and Hope, 1945–1953* (New York: HarperCollins, 2010), 211–41.

18. John Lewis Gaddis, *Strategies of Containment: A Critical Appraisal of American National Security Policy during the Cold War* (Oxford: Oxford University Press, 2005), 89–127.

19. John DeNovo, *American Interests and Policies in the Middle East: 1900–1939* (Minneapolis: University of Minnesota Press, 1963), 96–97.

20. Galia Golan, *Soviet Politics in the Middle East: From World War Two to Gorbachev* (Cambridge: Cambridge University Press, 1990), 4–44.

21. Louise Fawcett, *Iran and the Cold War: The Azerbaijan Crisis of 1946* (Cambridge: Cambridge University Press, 1992), 88.

22. Vladislav Zubok, *A Failed Empire: The Soviet Union in the Cold War from Stalin to Gorbachev* (Chapel Hill: University of North Carolina Press, 2007), 41.

23. Kuniholm, *The Origins of the Cold War in the Near East*, 164–67.

24. Rouhollah Ramazani, *Iran's Foreign Policy, 1941–1973: A Study of Foreign Policy in Modernizing Nations* (Charlottesville: University of Virginia Press, 1975), 92.

25. Gary Hess, "The Iranian Crisis of 1945–1946 and Cold War," *Political Science Quarterly* 89, no. 1 (March 1974); Fraser Harbutt, *Yalta 1945: Europe and America at the Crossroads* (Cambridge: Cambridge University Press, 2010), 202–3.

26. *Foreign Relations of the United States* (hereafter *FRUS*): *Conferences at Malta and Yalta, 1945* (Washington, DC: Government Printing Office, 1975), 439–500.

27. Ibid.

28. *FRUS*, 1944, vol. V: *The Near East, South Asia and Africa* (Washington, DC: 1965), 105.

29. Zubok, *A Failed Empire*, 42.

30. *FRUS*, 1945, vol. VIII: *The Near East and Africa* (Washington, DC, 1969), 510–17.

31. Barry Rubin, *Paved with Good Intentions: The American Experience and Iran* (Oxford: Oxford University Press, 1980), 31.

32. *FRUS*, 1944, vol. IV, 345–55.

33. Kuniholm, *The Origins of the Cold War in the Near East*, 277–78.

34. *FRUS*, 1946, vol. VII: *The Near East and Africa* (Washington, DC, 1969), 344.

35. For the shah's own account of the crisis, see Mohammad Reza Pahlavi, *Answer to History* (New York: Stein and Day, 1980), 63–77. For important accounts of the shah during this period, see Abbas Milani, *The Shah* (New York: Palgrave Macmillan, 2011), 111–41; Gholam Reza Afkhami, *The Life and Times of the Shah* (Berkeley: University of California Press, 2009), 86–110.

36. Fawcett, *Iran and the Cold War*, 60.

37. Kuniholm, *The Origins of the Cold War in the Near East*, 313–14.

38. *FRUS*, 1946, vol. VII, 293.

39. Richard Pfau, "Containment in Iran, 1945: The Shift to an Active Policy," *Diplomatic History* (Fall 1977), 364.

40. Ibid., 365.

41. Wilson Miscamble, *From Roosevelt to Truman: Potsdam, Hiroshima, and the Cold War* (Cambridge: Cambridge University Press, 2007), 34–124, 307–33; Arnold Offner, *Another Such Victory: President Truman and the Cold War 1945–1953* (Stanford: Stanford University Press, 2002), 47–185.

42. *FRUS*, 1946, vol. VII, 733.

43. Harry S. Truman, *Memoirs of Harry S. Truman: 1946–52: Years of Trial and Hope* (New York: Doubleday, 1956), 95.

44. Ervand Abrahamian, *The Coup: 1953, the CIA, and the Roots of Modern U.S.-Iranian Relations* (New York: The New Press, 2012), 43.

45. Fawcett, *Iran and the Cold War*, 68.

46. Simon Davis, "A Projected New Trusteeship? American Internationalism, British Imperialism, and the Reconstruction of Iran, 1938–1947," *Diplomacy and Statecraft* 17, no. 1 (2006).

47. Ramazani, *Iran's Foreign Policy, 1941–1973*, 126.

48. *FRUS*, 1946, vol. VII, 357.

49. Harbutt, *The Iron Curtain*, 61.

50. Zubok, *A Failed Empire*, 45.

51. Ibid., 49.

CHAPTER 2: THE PALESTINE QUESTION

1. Peter L. Hahn, *Caught in the Middle East: U.S. Policy Toward the Arab-Israeli Conflict, 1945–1961* (Chapel Hill: University of North Carolina Press, 2004), 15.

2. Hahn, *Caught in the Middle East*, 36.

3. Yaacov Ro'i, *Soviet Decision Making in Practice: The USSR and Israel, 1947–1954* (New Brunswick, NJ: Transaction Publishers, 1980), 48.

4. Cabinet Meeting. 47/6. Minute 3. Confidential Annex, January 15, 1947, Public Record Office. See also Bruce J. Evensen, *Truman, Palestine, and the Press: Shaping Conventional Wisdom at the Beginning of the Cold War* (New York: Greenwood Press, 1992), 121.

5. William Roger Louis, *Ends of British Imperialism: The Scramble for Empire, Suez, and Decolonization* (London: I.B. Tauris, 2006), 443.

6. *Foreign Relations of the United States* (hereafter *FRUS*), 1944, vol. V: *The Near East, South Asia, and Africa, the Far East* (Washington, DC: Government Printing Office, 1965), 590–91; Hahn, *Caught in the Middle East*, 18.

7. Harrison Report, Harry S. Truman Office File (HSTOF), Part III, Reel 33, Roosevelt Study Centre (RSC), Middleburgh, The Netherlands.

8. Hahn, *Caught in the Middle East*, 33.

9. Ibid., see Gallup poll cited.

10. "President's Statement on Palestine," *New York Times*, October 5, 1946.

11. See Michael J. Cohen, "Truman and Palestine, 1945–1948: Revisionism, Politics and Diplomacy," *Modern Judaism* 2, no. 1 (February 1982): 8n30.

12. Hahn, *Caught in the Middle East*, 35.

13. Michael Ottolenghi, "Harry Truman's Recognition of Israel," *The Historical Journal* 47, no. 4 (December 2004): 967.

14. *FRUS*, 1945, vol. VIII: *The Near East and Africa* (Washington, DC: Government Printing Office, 1969), 742–43.

15. Memorandum from the Joint Chiefs of Staff for the State-War-Navy Coordinating Committee, 21 June 1946, HSTOF, Part III, Reel 34, RSC.

16. Evensen, *Truman, Palestine, and the Press*, 132.

17. *FRUS*, 1947, vol. V: *The Near East and Africa* (Washington: Government Printing Office, 1971), 1147; and Ottolenghi, "Harry Truman's Recognition of Israel," 973.

18. "The Problem of Palestine," JCS 1684/5, October 10, 1947, Records of the Joint Chiefs of Staff, National Archives. See also Ottolenghi, "Harry Truman's Recognition of Israel," 973.

19. *FRUS*, 1947, vol. V, 1166–70. Hahn, *Caught in the Middle East*, 42.

20. Hahn, *Caught in the Middle East*, 29.

21. Ottolenghi, "Harry Truman's Recognition of Israel," 968.

22. *FRUS*, 1947, vol. V, 1147. See also Ottolenghi, "Harry Truman's Recognition of Israel," 973.

23. Central Intelligence Agency: Office of Reports and Estimates, "The Current Situation in Palestine," October 20, 1947, C.I.A. FOIA Archives, http://primarysources.brillonline.com/browse/us-intelligence-on-the-middle-east/

central-intelligence-agency-intelligence-estimate-the-current-situation-in-pal estine-october-20-1947-secret-cia;umeoumeob01090.

24. "Impact of Loss of Arab Oil Production on World Petroleum Situation," July 8, 1948, 800.6363/7-848, RG 59 NA, cited in Daniel Yergin, *The Prize: The Epic Quest for Oil, Money and Power* (New York: Simon and Schuster, 1991): 408.

25. Yergin, *The Prize*, 408.

26. Ro'i, *Soviet Decision Making in Practice*, 25.

27. "The Palestine Question: Speech by Andrei Gromyko at General Assembly, First Special Session, 14 May 1947, *General Assembly, 1st Special Session, 77th Plenary Meeting*, vol. 1, 127–35; Yaacov Ro'i, *From Encroachment to Involvement: A Documentary Study of Soviet Policy in the Middle East, 1945–1973* (New York: Halsted Press, 1974): 37–40.

28. *FRUS*, 1947, vol. V, 1095.

29. Ro'i, *Soviet Decision Making in Practice*, 77.

30. Ibid.

31. Ibid., 72. The State Department had missed this crucial cue, although it was right that the Soviets were attempting to "play both ends against the middle." See *FRUS*, 1947, vol. V, 1089.

32. *FRUS*, 1947, vol. V, 1166–70.

33. E. Epstein to Sumner Welles, May 29, 1947, CZA, S25/483, see Ro'i, *Soviet Decision Making in Practice*, 73.

34. *General Assembly, 2nd Session, Ad Hoc Committee on the Palestine Question*, pp. 69–71, 13 October 1947, see Ro'i, *From Encroachment*, 50.

35. *Pravda*, September 30, 1946, see Ro'i, *Soviet Decision Making in Practice*, 40n95.

36. "73. M. A. Maksimov and S. Nemchinov to A. Ia. Vyshinskii (Moscow), AVP RF, F.07, OP. 12A, P.42, D.6, LL. 130–3, "The Palestine Question" (Moscow, 5 March 1947)," in *Documents on Israeli-Soviet Relations, 1941–1953*, eds. Eytan Bentsur and Boris Leonidovich Kolokolov (Portland, OR: Frank Cass Publishers, 2000), 166.

37. *Jewish Telegraphic Agency*, June 9, 1946, see Ro'i, *Soviet Decision Making in Practice*, 43n103.

38. Ro'i, *Soviet Decision Making in Practice*, 96–97.

39. Ibid., 17.

40. *FRUS*, 1945, vol. V: *Europe* (Washington, DC: Government Printing Office, 1945), 712.

41. *New York Times*, March 7, 1947, cited in Ro'i, *Soviet Decision Making in Practice*, 50.

42. Ro'i, *Soviet Decision Making in Practice*, 51.

43. June 12, 1946, CZA, S25/286, see Ro'i, *Soviet Decision Making in Practice*, 45.

44. "90. E. Epstein to the Jewish Agency Executive, CZA, S25/9299, 31 July 1947,

'Conversation with Mr. Mikhail S. Vavilov, First Secretary of the Soviet Embassy in Washington,'" in *Documents on Israeli-Soviet Relations*, 217–18.

45. "118. Demioshkin to Gromyko, 13 April 1948, 'The Situation in Palestine After the UN Resolution on the Partition of the Country,'" in *Documents on Israeli-Soviet Relations*, 273.

46. Ro'i, *Soviet Decision Making in Practice*, 74.

47. Ibid., 43.

48. *Public Papers of the Presidents of the United States: Harry S. Truman, 1948* (Washington, DC: Government Printing Office, 1964), 101. See also Ottolenghi, "Harry Truman's Recognition of Israel," 980.

49. Eben A. Ayers, "Diary Entry of February 17, 1948," Ayers Papers, box 16, folder 4, Harry S. Truman Library (hereafter HSTL); Harry S. Truman, *Memoirs of Harry S. Truman: 1946–52: Years of Trial and Hope*, (Garden City, NY: Doubleday, 1956), 159; *FRUS*, 1948, vol. V, 632–33; Bruce J. Evensen, "The Limits of Presidential Leadership: Truman at War with Zionists, the Press, Public Opinion and His Own State Department over Palestine," *Presidential Studies Quarterly* 23, no. 2 (Spring 1993): 269–87 (276).

50. *FRUS*, 1948, vol. V, 573.

51. Arthur Krock, Truman interview, April 8, 1948, box 1, Mudd Manuscript Library; Evensen, "Limits," 276.

52. Frank Brecher, *American Diplomacy and the Israeli War of Independence* (New York: McFarland Publishing, 2013), 46.

53. Menahem Kaufman, *An Ambiguous Partnership: Non-Zionists and Zionists in America, 1939–1948* (Jerusalem: Magnes Press, 1991), 7.

54. Oral History Interview: Loy Henderson, Harry S. Truman Library, 126; *FRUS*, 1947, vol. V, 1173–80; Bruce J. Evensen, "Truman, Palestine and the Cold War," *Middle Eastern Studies* 28, no. 1 (January 1992): 120–56 (129).

55. *FRUS*, 1947, vol. V, 1263–64.

56. Ibid.

57. Ibid., 655–6.

58. *FRUS*, 1948, vol V, 695.

59. Ibid., 667, 674.

60. Ibid., 1180–84; 1240–47; 1270.

61. Cohen, "Truman and Palestine," 14.

62. Evensen, "Truman, Palestine and the Cold War," 122.

63. "Memorandum by Kennan to secretary of state, 20 Jan. 1948," *FRUS*, 1948, vol. V, 546–54. See also Ottolenghi, "Harry Truman's Recognition of Israel," 980.

64. "President Truman to secretary of state, 22 Feb. 1948," *FRUS*, 1948, vol. V, 645. See also Ottolenghi, "Harry Truman's Recognition of Israel," 980.

65. *FRUS*, 1948, V, 730.

66. Brecher, *American Diplomacy and the Israeli War of Independence*, 18.

67. Ibid., 6.
68. *FRUS*, 1948, vol. V, 750.
69. Ibid., 759.
70. Ibid., 987.
71. Melvyn P. Leffler, *A Preponderance of Power: National Security, the Truman Administration, and the Cold War* (Stanford: Stanford University Press: 1992), 240–1.
72. Kaufman, *Ambiguous Partnership*, 8.
73. *New York Times*, 5 May 1948, in Papers of Clark Clifford, Subject File 1945–54, Palestine, Press Clippings, HSTL. See also Ottolenghi, "Harry Truman's Recognition of Israel," 982.
74. *New York Times*, 6 May 1948, in Papers of Clark Clifford, Subject File 1945–54, Palestine, Press Clippings, HSTL. See also Ottolenghi, "Harry Truman's Recognition of Israel," 982.
75. Eleanor Roosevelt to Truman, 11 May 1948, Papers of Harry S. Truman, PSF, Personal File, Roosevelt Eleanor, Folder 2, HSTL. See also Ottolenghi, "Harry Truman's Recognition of Israel," 982.
76. See *FRUS*, 1948, vol. V, 972–77, and *FRUS*, 1948, vol. 5, 1005–7, for doubts about Israel.
77. Evan M. Wilson, *Decision on Palestine: How the U.S. Came to Recognize Israel* (Stanford: Hoover Institution Press, 1979), 137; Cohen, "Truman and Palestine," 17.
78. Leffler, *Preponderance of Power*, 242.
79. "Bakulin to Zorin, 5 June 1948, AVP RF, F.089, OP.1, P.1, D.L, L.3," *Documents on Soviet-Israeli Relations*, 291.
80. "*Security Council, 3rd Year, No. 128,* 2 December 1948, p. 23," see Ro'i, *From Encroachment*, 64–66.

CHAPTER 3: AMERICA, IRAN, AND THE COUP

1. William Roger Louis, *The British Empire in the Middle East: Arab Nationalism, the United States and Postwar Imperialism, 1945–1951* (Oxford: Oxford University Press, 1984), 632–91; John Darwin, *Britain and Decolonisation: The Retreat from Empire in the Postwar World* (London: Palgrave Macmillan, 1988), 51–103.
2. H. W. Brands, "The Cairo-Tehran Connection in Anglo-American Rivalry in the Middle East, 1951–1953," *International History Review* 11, no. 3 (August 1989).
3. Daniel Yergin, *The Prize: The Epic Quest for Oil, Money, and Power* (New York: Simon and Schuster, 1991), 458.
4. Francis J. Gavin, "Politics, Power, and U.S. Policy in Iran, 1950–1953," *Journal of Cold War Studies* 1, no. 1 (Winter 1999), 11.

5. Ervand Abrahamian, *The Coup: 1953, the CIA and the Roots of Modern U.S.-Iranian Relations* (New York: The New Press, 2013), 61.

6. Farhad Diba, *Mossadegh: A Political Biography* (London: Croom Helm, 1986); James A. Bill, *The Eagle and the Lion: The Tragedy of American-Iranian Relations* (New Haven, CT: Yale University Press, 1989), 53–57.

7. Homa Katouzian, *Musaddiq and the Struggle for Power in Iran* (London: I.B. Tauris, 1999), 78–113; see also Katouzian, "Problems of Democracy and the Public Sphere in Modern Iran," *Comparative Studies in South Asia, Africa, and the Middle East* 18, no. 2 (1988): 31–37.

8. Ervand Abrahamian, *Iran Between Two Revolutions* (Princeton, NJ: Princeton University Press, 1982), 250–52; Richard W. Cottam, *Nationalism in Iran* (Pittsburgh: University of Pittsburgh Press, 1979), 264–68; T. Cuyler Young Jr., "The Social Support of Current Iranian Policy," *Middle East Journal* 6, no. 2 (Spring 1952): 125–43.

9. Shahrough Akhavi, "The Role of the Clergy in Iranian Politics, 1949–1954," in *Musaddiq, Iranian Nationalism and Oil*, eds. James A. Bill and William Roger Louis (Austin: University of Texas Press, 1988), 91–118; see also Akhavi, *Religion and Politics in Contemporary Iran: Clergy-State Relations in the Pahlavi Period* (Albany: State University of New York Press, 1980), 60–72.

10. British Embassy, Foreign Office (hereafter FO), 371/1952/105.

11. *Foreign Relations of the United States* (hereafter *FRUS*), 1952–1954, vol. X: Iran, 14.

12. Mark Gasiorowski, *U.S. Foreign Policy and the Shah: Building a Client State in Iran* (Ithaca: Cornell University Press, 1991), 57–85; Melvyn Leffler, *A Preponderance of Power: National Security, the Truman Administration, and the Cold War* (Stanford: Stanford University Press, 1992), 446–95.

13. Thomas Walton, "Economic Development and Revolutionary Uupheavals in Iran," *Cambridge Journal of Economics* 4, no. 3 (September 1980): 288–9.

14. Irvine H. Anderson, "The American Oil Industry and the Fifty-Fifty Agreement of 1950," in *Musaddiq, Iranian Nationalism and Oil*, eds. James A. Bill and William Roger Louis (Austin: University of Texas Press, 1988).

15. Bill and Louis, eds., *Musaddiq, Iranian Nationalism and Oil*, 17.

16. Mary Ann Heiss, *Empire and Nationhood: The United States, Great Britain, and Iranian Oil, 1950–1954* (New York: Columbia University Press, 1997), 53.

17. *FRUS*, 10.

18. Dean Acheson, *Present at the Creation: My Years in the State Department* (New York: W. W. Norton, 1969), 503.

19. *Time*, January 7, 1952.

20. *New York Times Magazine,* September 28, 1952.

21. Bill and Louis, eds., *Musaddiq, Iranian Nationalism and Oil*, 180.

22. Heiss, *Empire and Nationhood,* 87.
23. Richard Stobaugh, "The Evolution of Iranian Oil Policy," in *Iran Under the Pahlavis,* ed. George Lenczowski (Stanford: Hoover Institution Press, 1978), 212.
24. Kamran M. Dadkhah, "Iran's Economic Policy during the Mosaddeq Era," *Journal of Iranian Research and Analysis* 16, no. 2 (November 2000); Homa Katouzian, "Oil Boycott and the Political Economy: Musaddiq and the Strategy of Non-Oil Economics," in *Musaddiq, Iranian Nationalism and Oil,* eds. James A. Bill and William Roger Louis (Austin: University of Texas Press, 1988), 203–28.
25. *FRUS,* 70.
26. *FRUS,* 74.
27. *FRUS,* 60–61.
28. Acheson, *Present at the Creation,* 506.
29. Gholam Reza Afkhami, *The Life and Times of the Shah* (Berkeley: University of California Press, 2009), 127.
30. Rudy Abramson, *Spanning the Century: The Life of W. Averell Harriman, 1891–1986* (New York: W. Morrow, 1992), 466–85.
31. *FRUS,* 94.
32. *FRUS,* 98.
33. Abrahamian, *The Coup,* 127.
34. Anthony Eden, *Full Circle: The Memoirs of Anthony Eden* (London: Cassell, 1960), 213.
35. For an impressive collection of essays on Churchill, see *Churchill: A Major New Assessment of His Life in Peace and War,* eds. Robert Blake and William Roger Louis (Oxford: Oxford University Press, 1993).
36. Vernon A. Walters, *Silent Missions* (Garden City, NY: Doubleday, 1978), 262.
37. *FRUS,* 274.
38. Fakhreddin Azimi, *Iran: The Crisis of Democracy: From the Exile of Reza Shah to the Fall of Musaddiq* (London: I.B. Tauris, 2009), 257–93; see also Azimi, *The Quest for Democracy in Iran: A Century of Struggle Against Authoritarian Rule* (Cambridge, MA: Harvard University Press, 2008), 19–157.
39. Sepehr Zabih, *The Mossadegh Era: Roots of the Iranian Revolution* (Chicago: Lake View Press, 1982), 56–88.
40. Acheson, *Present at the Creation,* 685.
41. Robert R. Bowie and Richard H. Immerman, *Waging Peace: How Eisenhower Shaped an Enduring Cold War Strategy* (Oxford: Oxford University Press, 1988); Fred I. Greenstein, *The Hidden Hand Presidency: Eisenhower as Leader* (New York: Basic Books, 1982); also Greenstein, "Eisenhower as an Activist President: A New Look at New Evidence," *Political Science Quarterly* 94, no. 4 (Win-

ter 1979–1980); Richard H. Immerman, "Eisenhower or Dulles: Who Made the Decisions?" *Political Psychology* 1, no. 2 (Autumn 1979); Douglas Kinnard, *President Eisenhower and Strategy Management: A Study in Defense Politics* (Lexington: University Press of Kentucky, 1989).

42. The historiography of Eisenhower's presidency had gone through many changes. The initial views of Eisenhower were overwhelmingly negative, stressing that the president's subordinates essentially conducted national affairs; see Townsend Hoopes, *The Devil and John Foster Dulles* (Boston: Little, Brown, 1973). The important studies that introduced Eisenhower revisionism are Evan Thomas, *Ike's Bluff: President Eisenhower's Secret Battle to Save the World* (New York: Little, Brown, 2012); Jean Edward Smith, *Eisenhower in War and Peace* (New York: Random House, 2012); Herbert S. Parmet, *Eisenhower and the American Crusades* (New York: Macmillan, 1972); Peter Lyon, *Eisenhower: Portrait of a Hero* (Boston: Little, Brown, 1974); Stephen E. Ambrose, *Eisenhower: Soldier and President* (New York: Simon and Schuster, 1990); John Lewis Gaddis, *Strategies of Containment: A Critical Appraisal of Postwar American National Security Policy* (Oxford: Oxford University Press, 1983); Richard H. Immerman, "The Confessions of an Eisenhower Revisionist: An Agonizing Reappraisal," *Diplomatic History* 14, no. 3 (July 1990); George H. Quester, "Was Eisenhower a Genius?" *International Security* 4, no. 2 (Fall 1979).

43. The John Foster Dulles that is emerging in the most recent revisionist studies is different from the traditional view of him as a dogmatic Cold Warrior with a rigid ideological view. In recent studies, the secretary is seen as inclined to pursue a more flexible strategy. Among more important works of Dulles revisionism are Richard H. Immerman, ed., *John Foster Dulles and the Diplomacy of the Cold War* (Princeton, NJ: Princeton University Press, 1990); John Lewis Gaddis, "The Unexpected John Foster Dulles: Nuclear Weapons, Communism, and the Russians," in John Lewis Gaddis, *The United States and the End of the Cold War: Implications, Reconsiderations, Provocations* (Oxford: Oxford University Press, 1992); Ronald W. Preussen, "Beyond the Cold War—Again: 1955 and 1990s," *Political Science Quarterly* 108, no. 1 (Spring 1993).

44. William Blum, *The CIA: A Forgotten History* (London: Zed Books, 1986); John Prados, *Presidents' Secret Wars: CIA and Pentagon Covert Operations Since World War II* (New York: W. Morrow, 1986); 229–348; Gregory F. Treverton, *Covert Action: The Limits of Intervention in the Postwar World* (New York: Basic Books, 1987), 44–84.

45. Gavin, "Politics, Power, and U.S. Policy in Iran, 1950-1953," 82.

46. Afkhami, *Life and Times of the Shah*, 150.

47. Ibid.

48. *FRUS*, 323.

49. *FRUS*, 351.

50. Royal Institute of International Affairs, *Documents on International Affairs,* 1953 (London: Oxford University Press, 1954), 349–51.

51. Dwight D. Eisenhower, *Mandate for Change, 1953–1956: The White House Years* (New York: Little, Brown, 1963), 162.

52. Mark Gasiorowski and Malcolm Byrne, eds., *Mohammad Mosaddeq and the 1953 Coup in Iran* (Syracuse, NY: Syracuse University Press, 2004), 76.

53. Donald N. Wilber, "Clandestine Service History: Overthrow of Premier Mossadeq of Iran, November 1952–August 1953," *New York Times*, April 16, 2000), 7.

54. Barry M. Rubin, *Paved with Good Intentions: The American Experience and Iran* (Oxford: Oxford University Press, 1980), 80.

55. H. W. Brands, *Inside the Cold War: Loy Henderson and the Rise of the American Empire, 1918–1961* (Oxford: Oxford University Press, 1991), 235.

56. Wilber, *Clandestine Service History*, 11.

57. Mervyn Roberts, "Analysis of Radio Propaganda in the 1953 Iran Coup," *Iranian Studies* 45, no. 6 (November 2012).

58. Mark J. Gasiorowski, "The 1953 Coup d'État in Iran," *International Journal of Middle East Studies* 19, no. 3 (August 1987), 284.

59. Wilber, *Clandestine Service History*, 34–35.

60. Darioush Bayandor, *Iran and the CIA: The Fall of Mosaddeq Revisited* (New York: Palgrave Macmillan, 2010), 92.

61. Abrahamian, *The Coup*, 184.

62. Wilber, *Clandestine Service History,* 64.

63. Ibid.

64. *FRUS*, 749.

65. Fakhreddin Azimi, "The Overthrow of the Government of Mosaddeq Reconsidered," *Iranian Studies* 45, no. 6 (September 2012), 701; Maziar Behrooz, "Tudeh Factionalism and the 1953 Coup in Iran," *International Journal of Middle East Studies* 33, no. 3 (August 2001).

66. *FRUS*, 754.

67. Ardeshir Zahedi, *Khaterat'e Ardeshir Zahedi*, vol. 1 (Maryland: Ibex Publishers, 2006), 190.

68. *FRUS*, 753.

69. Mohammad Mossadegh, *Musaddiq's Memoirs*, trans. S. H. Amin and Homa Katouzian (London: JEBHE, National Movement of Iran, 1988), 359.

70. *FRUS*, 710.

71. For a flawed account of the crisis, see Kermit Roosevelt, *Countercoup: The Struggle for the Control of Iran* (New York: McGraw-Hill, 1979).

72. Wilber, *Clandestine Service History*, 62.

73. Ray Takeyh, "Coupdunnit: What Really Happened in Iran," *Foreign Affairs* 93, no. 5 (September/October 2014), 166.

CHAPTER 4: THE SUEZ WAR

1 For the nature of the American foreign policy establishment and its overall common outlook, see G. Hudson, "The Establishment," *Foreign Policy* (Spring 1973); Leslie Gelb, Anthony Lake, and Mike Destler, *Our Own Worst Enemy* (New York: Simon and Schuster, 1984); David Clinton, "Interests, Values and the American Consensus on Foreign Policy," in *Political Traditions and Contemporary Problems*, ed. Kenneth Thompson (Washington, DC: University Press of America, 1982), 4–10.

2. Background study prepared for Eisenhower's meeting with Congressional Leaders, January 5, 1954. Ann Whitman File: DDE Diary (Box 3), Dwight D. Eisenhower Library (hereafter DDEL).

3. Dwight Eisenhower, *Mandate for Change: Memoirs, 1953–1956* (New York: Doubleday, 1963), 35; Iwan Morgan, *Eisenhower versus the Big Spenders: The Eisenhower Administration, the Democrats and the Budget, 1953–1960* (New York: St. Martin's, 1990); John Sloan, *Eisenhower and the Management of Prosperity* (Lawrence: University Press of Kansas, 1991); Robert Griffith, "Dwight D. Eisenhower and the Corporate Commonwealth," *American Historical Review* 87, no. 1 (February 1982).

4. *Foreign Relations of the United States* (hereafter *FRUS*), 1952–1954, vol. II: *National Security Affairs* (Washington, DC: Government Printing Office, 1984), 397.

5. NSC 161/1, October 30, 1953, Office of Special Advisor for National Security Affairs (hereafter OSNSA): NSC Policy Papers (Box 5), DDEL.

6. Note by Executive Secretary to National Security Council with Respect to Near and Middle East, July 15, 1953, OSNSA: NSC Policy Papers (Box 5), DDEL.

7. Ibid.

8. R. Hrair Dekmejian, *Egypt under Nasir: A Study in Political Dynamics* (New York: University of London Press, 1971), 97–108; Nadav Safran, *Egypt in Search of Political Community* (Cambridge, MA: Harvard University Press, 1961); Joseph Lorenz, *Egypt and the Arabs: Foreign Policy and the Search for National Identity* (Boulder, CO: Cambridge University Press, 1990), 21–36; Leonard Binder, *The Ideological Revolution in the Middle East* (South Bend, IN: University of Notre Dame Press, 1964), 75–116; Anwar Chejne, "Egyptian Attitude toward Pan-Arabism," *Middle East Journal* (Summer 1957).

9. Report by the State Department, April 2, 1953, Ann Whitman File: Dulles-Herter Series (Box 1), DDEL.

10. *FRUS*, 1952–1954, vol. 9, 339.

11. Gamal Abdel Nasser, *The Philosophy of the Revolution* (Washington, DC: Public Affairs Press, 1955), 49.

12. Jean Lacouture, *Nasser: A Political Biography* (New York: Knopf , 1973), 188.
13. Evelyn Shuckburgh, *Descent to Suez: Diaries, 1951–1956* (New York: W. W. Norton, 1987), 76.
14. Ibid.
15. Memorandum by Eden, Egypt, The Alternatives, February 10, 1953, CAB 129/56 C(53). Public Record Office. United Kingdom.
16. Progress Report on NSC 155/1, July 23 1954, S/S NSC Lot File 53 D31. National Archives and Records (hereafter NARA).
17. Robert Stephens, *Nasser: A Political Biography* (London: Penguin Press, 1971), 262; E. Be'eri, *Army Officers in Arab Politics and Society* (New York: Frederick A. Praeger, 1970), 375–85; Joseph Lorenz, *Egypt and Arabs: Foreign Policy and the Search for National Identity* (Boulder, CO: Westview Press, 1990), 26–27; Sylvia Haim, *Arab Nationalism: An Anthology* (Berkeley: University of California Press, 1974), 49–55; Nissim Rejwan, *Nasserist Ideology: Its Exponents and Critics* (New Brunswick, NJ: Transaction Publishers, 1974), 50-54; Albert Hourani, *A Vision of History* (London: The Center for Lebanese Studies, 1962), 132; Uriel Dann, *King Hussein and the Challenge of Arab Radicalism, 1955–1957* (Oxford: Oxford University Press, 1991), 22–23.
18. Jean Lacouture, *Egypt in Transition* (New York: Criterion, 1958), 137.
19. Jean Lacouture, *Nasser: A Political Biography*, 184.
20. NEA Report, January 17, 1955, NEA Files: Lot File 58 D332. NARA.
21. Foreign Office Report, February 3, 1955, FO 371/115488. PRO.
22. Glubb to Eden, November 28, 1955. FO 371/115526. PRO; Dann, *King Hussein and the Challenge of Arab Radicalism* (Oxford: Oxford University Press, 1991), 26.
23. Uriel Dann, "The Foreign Office, the Baghdad Pact and Jordan," *Asian and African Studies* 21/3 (Fall 1987), 251.
24. Harold Macmillan, *Tides of Fortune, 1945–1955* (New York: Harper Collins, 1969), 256.
25. Ibid.
26. Patrick Seale, *The Struggle for Syria: A Study of Postwar Arab Politics, 1945–1958* (London: Oxford University Press, 1965), 195.
27. Eisenhower Diary Entry, January 10, 1956, Ann Whitman File: DDE Diary (Box 9), DDEL.
28. The 206th NSC Meeting, October 6, 1955, Ann Whitman File: NSC Series (Box 7), DDEL.
29. Dulles to Caffery, September 8, 1954 (RG 59) 780.5/9-854. NARA.
30. Joint Anglo-American Planning on Alpha, January 26, 1955, NEA Files: Lot 59 D518. NARA.
31. Eisenhower Diary Entry, January 10, 1956, Ann Whitman File: DDE Diary (Box 9), DDEL.

32. Keith Kyle, *Suez* (London: Weidenfeld and Nicolson, 1991), 91–2.
33. *FRUS*, 1955–1957, vol. XV: *Arab-Israeli Conflict, January 1 to July 26, 1956*, 123.
34. Ibid., 297.
35. Ibid.
36. *FRUS*, 309.
37. Ibid., 306.
38. Memorandum of Conversation between Eisenhower, Dulles and Anderson, March 7, 1956, JFD Papers: White House Memorandum Series (Box 4), DDEL.
39. *FRUS*, 306.
40. Memorandum for the President, March 28, 1956, JFD Papers: White House Memorandum Series (Box 5), DDEL.
41. Anthony Nutting, *No End of a Lesson: The Story of Suez* (New York: Constable, 1967), 34–35.
42. Makins to Dulles, March 29, 1956, Ann Whitman File: International Series (Box 9), DDEL.
43. Memorandum for the President, March 28, 1956, JFD Papers: Subject Series (Box 10), DDEL.
44. Eisenhower Diary Entry, March 28, 1956, Ann Whitman File: DDE Series (Box 10), DDEL.
45. Douglas Little, "Cold War and Covert Action: The United States and Syria, 1945–1958," *Middle East Journal* (Winter 1990), 66.
46. Memorandum for the President, March 28, 1956, JFD Papers: Subject Series (Box 5), DDEL.
47. Possible Course of Action in the Near East, March 14, 1956, OMEGA Lot File 59 D518, NARA.
48. Byroade to Dulles, May 25, 1956, OMEGA Lot File 59 D518, NARA.
49. Townsend Hoopes, *The Devil and John Foster Dulles* (Boston: Little, Brown, 1973), 330–44; Donald Neff, *Warriors at Suez: Eisenhower Takes America into the Middle East* (New York: Linden Press/Simon and Schuster, 1981), 8–103.
50. Memorandum of Conversation between Dulles and Hussein, July 19, 1956 (RG 59) 874.2614/7-1956, NARA.
51. Mohamed H. Heikal, *Cutting the Lion's Tail: Suez Through Egyptian Eyes* (New York: Arbor House, 1987), 70.
52. *FRUS*, 1955–1957, vol. XVI: *Suez Crisis, July 26–December 31 1956*, 167.
53. Ibid., 173.
54. Memorandum of Conversation between Eisenhower and Dulles, July 31 1956, Ann Whitman File: DDE Diary Series (Box 16), DDEL.
55. Evelyn Shuckburgh, *Descent to Suez*, 360–61.
56. Dillon to Dulles, July 27, 1956 (RG 59) 974.7301/17-2956, NARA.
57. Robert Murphy, *Diplomat Among Warriors* (Garden City, NY: Doubleday, 1964), 308.

58. Murphy to Dulles, July 29, 1956, (RG 59) 730.1/7-2956.

59. Diane Kunz, *The Economic Diplomacy of the Suez Crisis* (Chapel Hill: University of North Carolina Press, 1991), 81.

60. Roger Owen and William Roger Louis, eds., *Suez 1956* (Oxford: Oxford University Press, 1989), 198.

61. *FRUS*, 1955–1957, vol. 16, 407.

62. Kyle, *Suez,* 264.

63. *FRUS*, 790.

64. Memorandum for the Record, October 5, 1956, Ann Whitman File: DDE Series (Box 5), DDEL.

65. Israeli Statement, October 29, 1956, 684A.56/10-2956, NARA.

66. Aldrich to Dulles, 29 October 1956 (RG 59) 684A.56/10-2956, NARA.

67. Eden's Ultimatum to Egypt, House of Commons, *Parliamentary Debates,* 5th Series, vol. 1558, Columns 1273–75; D.C. Watt, ed., Documents on Suez (London 1957), 85.

68. Memorandum of Conversation between Dulles and Coulson, October 30, 1956 (RG 59) 684A.86/10-3056, NARA.

69. Dwight D. Eisenhower, *Waging Peace, 1956–1961* (Garden City, NY: Doubleday, 1965), 70.

70. *FRUS*, vol. XVI, 796.

71. Memorandum of Conversation with the President, November 5, 1956, Ann Whitman File: Staff Papers (Box 19), DDEL.

72. Progress Report on U.S. Objectives with Respect to the Near and Middle East, November 21, 1956, NSC Staff Papers: OCB Series (Box 78), DDEL.

73. Memorandum of Conversation between Dulles and Eisenhower, December 20, 1956, Ann Whitman File: DDE Diary Series (Box 20), DDEL.

74. Memorandum for the President, December 17, 1956, Ann Whitman File: Dulles-Herter Series (Box 7), DDEL.

75. Ibid.

76. Meeting with Congressional Leadership, December 31, 1956, Ann Whitman File: Legislative Meeting Series (Box 20), DDEL.

77. Eisenhower, *Waging Peace*, 178.

78. Ibid.

79. "Statement by the Honorable John Foster Dulles before a Joint Session of the Foreign Relations and Armed Services Committee of the Senate, January 14, 1957," Dulles-Herter Series (Box 8), DDEL.

CHAPTER 5: 1958: THE YEAR OF THE REVOLUTIONS

1. For critiques of Eisenhower's handling of the Third World, see Douglas Little, *American Orientalism: The United States and the Middle East Since 1945* (Cha-

pel Hill: University of North Carolina Press, 2002), 117–37; Robert McMahon, "Eisenhower and Third World Nationalism: A Critique of the Revisionists," *Political Science Quarterly* 101, no. 3 (Spring 1986).

2. David Lesch, *Syria and the United States: Eisenhower's Cold War in the Middle East* (Boulder, CO: Westview Press, 1992), 80–120.

3. Andrew Rathmell, *Secret War in the Middle East: The Covert Struggle for Syria, 1949–1961* (London: I.B. Tauris, 1995), 125–45.

4. John Foster Dulles Papers (Telephone Series: Box 12). Dwight D. Eisenhower Library (hereafter DDEL).

5. Bonnie Saunders, *The United States and Arab Nationalism: The Syrian Case, 1953–1960* (Westport, CT: Praeger, 1996), 63.

6. John Foster Dulles Papers (Correspondence Series: Box 1), DDEL.

7. Dwight D. Eisenhower, *Waging Peace, 1956–1961* (Garden City, NY: Doubleday, 1965), 199.

8. Ibid., 198.

9. Patrick Seale, *The Struggle for Syria, 1945–1958* (Oxford: Oxford University Press, 1965), 307–27.

10. Adeed I. Dawisha, *Egypt in the Arab World: The Elements of Foreign Policy* (New York: Macmillan, 1976), 21–33; Tawfiq Hasou, *The Struggle for the Arab World: Egypt's Nasser and the Arab League* (London and Boston: Routledge and Kegan Paul, 1985), 89–136.

11. Malcolm H. Kerr, *The Arab Cold War: A Study of Ideology in Politics* (Oxford: Oxford University Press, 1965), 2–30.

12. Salim Yaqub, *Containing Arab Nationalism: The Eisenhower Doctrine and the Middle East* (Chapel Hill: University of North Carolina Press, 2004), 197; Lesch, *Syria and the United States,* 127–38.

13. Sarah Yizraeli, *Politics and Society in Saudi Arabia: The Crucial Years of Development: 1960–1982* (London: C. Hurst, 2013), 19–31.

14. Nadav Safran, *Saudi Arabia: The Ceaseless Quest for Security* (Ithaca, NY: Cornell University Press, 1985), 73–110; Naif bin Hethlain, *Saudi Arabia and the U.S. Since 1962* (London: Saqi Books, 2010), 31–117.

15. John Foster Dulles Papers (Telephone Series: Box 12), DDEL.

16. Briefing Paper, Eisenhower Papers (White House Central File—Confidential Series, Box 9), DDEL.

17. *Foreign Relations of the United States* (hereafter *FRUS*), 1958–1960, vol. XII: *Near East Region: Iraq, Iran, Arabian Peninsula* (Washington, DC: Government Printing Office, 1993), 40.

18. Nigel John Ashton, *Eisenhower, Macmillan and the Problem of Nasser: Anglo-American Relations and Arab Nationalism, 1955–1959* (London: Macmillan, 1996), 160.

19. Charles Tripp, *A History of Iraq* (Cambridge: Cambridge University Press,

2000), 148–55; Adeed I. Dawisha, *Iraq: A Political History from Independence to Occupation* (Princeton, NJ: Princeton University Press, 2009), 171–209.

20. Hanna Batatu, *The Old Social Classes and the Revolutionary Movement of Iraq: A Study of Iraq's Old Landed and Commercial Classes and of Its Communists, Baathists, and Free Officers* (Princeton, NJ: Princeton University Press, 1978), 795.

21. Mohamed Heikal, *The Cairo Documents: The Private Papers of Nasser* (London: Doubleday, 1972), 126.

22. Uriel Dann, *Iraq Under Qasim: A Political History, 1958–1963* (New York: Praeger, 1969), 19–77.

23. Fawaz Gerges, *The Superpowers and the Middle East: Regional and International Politics, 1955–1957* (Boulder, CO: Westview Press, 1994), 117.

24. Aleksandr Fursenko and Timothy Naftali, *Khrushchev's Cold War: The Inside Story of an American Adversary* (New York: W. W. Norton, 2006), 163.

25. Robert Fernea and William Roger Louis, eds., *The Iraqi Revolution of 1958: The Old Social Classes Revisited* (London: I.B. Tauris, 1991), 106–18.

26. White House Office of Staff Secretary (International Series: Box 11), DDEL.

27. *FRUS*, vol. XII, 163.

28. White House Office of Staff Secretary (International Series: Box 11), DDEL.

29. Nigel Ashton, "A Great New Venture? Anglo-American Cooperation in the Middle East and the Response to the Iraqi Revolution July 1958," *Diplomacy and Statecraft* (March 1993).

30. Uriel Dann, *King Hussein and the Challenge of Arab Radicalism: Jordan, 1955–1967* (Oxford: Oxford University Press, 1989), 86–99; Douglas Little, "A Puppet in Search of a Puppeteer? The United States, King Hussein, and Jordan, 1953–1970," *International History Review* 17, no. 3 (August 1995); Kamal Salibi, *The Modern History of Jordan* (London: I.B. Tauris, 1998), 197–222.

31. Roby C. Barrett, *The Greater Middle East and the Cold War: U.S. Foreign Policy under Eisenhower and Kennedy* (London: I.B. Tauris, 2007), 69.

32. *FRUS*, vol. XII, 98.

33. Alexander George and Richard Smoke, *Deterrence in American Foreign Policy: Theory and Practice* (New York: Columbia University Press, 1974), 309–63; Zachary Karabell, *Architects of Intervention: The United States, the Third World and the Cold War, 1946–1962* (Baton Rouge: Louisiana State University Press, 1999), 136–73; H. W. Brands, *Into the Labyrinth: The United States and the Middle East: 1953–1993* (New York: McGraw-Hill, 1994), 69–80.

34. David Lesch, *The Middle East and the United States: A Historical and Political Reassessment* (Boulder, CO: Westview Press, 1999), 100–128.

35. Douglas Little, "His Finest Hour? Eisenhower, Lebanon, and the 1958 Middle East Crisis," *Diplomatic History* (Winter 1996), 45.

36. Ritchie Ovendale, "Great Britain and the Anglo-American Invasion of Jordan and Lebanon," *International History Review* (May 1994).

37. William Roger Louis and Roger Owen, eds., *A Revolutionary Year: The Middle East in 1958* (London: I.B. Tauris, 2002), 94.

38. Galia Golan, *Soviet Policies in the Middle East: From World War II to Gorbachev* (Cambridge: Cambridge University Press, 1990), 44–58.

39. Barrett, *The Greater Middle East and the Cold War*, 113.

40. White House Staff Secretary (International Series, Box 8), DDEL.

41. Barrett, *The Greater Middle East and the Cold War*, 114.

42. Ibid., 120.

43. Andrew Rathmell, "Brotherly Enemies: The Rise and Fall of the Syrian-Egyptian Intelligence Axis, 1954–1967," *Intelligence and National Security* (Winter 1998).

44. Fernea and Louis, eds., *The Iraqi Revolution of 1958* (London: I.B. Tauris, 1991), 95–106.

45. *Life,* July 2, 1959.

46. Ashton, *Eisenhower, Macmillan and the Problem of Nasser* (London: Macmillan, 1996), 198.

47. *FRUS*, 149; Burton Kaufman, *The Arab Middle East and the United States: Inter-Arab rivalry and Superpower Diplomacy* (New York: Twayne, 1996), 17–31.

48. *FRUS*, 132.

49. Ibid., 198.

50. Abraham Ben-Zvi, *Eisenhower, Kennedy and the Origins of the American-Israeli Alliance* (New York: Columbia University Press, 1998), 59–97; Douglas Little, "The Making of a Special Relationship: The United States and Israel, 1957–68," *International Journal of Middle East Studies* 25, no. 4 (1993).

CHAPTER 6: THE SIX-DAY WAR

1 Malcolm H. Kerr, *The Arab Cold War: Gamal Abd al-Nasir and His Rivals, 1958–1970* (Oxford: Oxford University Press, 1971).

2. "Intelligence Report: Soviet Policy and the 1967 Arab-Israeli War" (Directorate of Intelligence: Central Intelligence Agency, March 16, 1970).

3. Galia Golan, "The Cold War and the Soviet Attitude," in *The Cold War in the Middle East: Regional Conflict and the Superpowers 1967–73*, ed. Nigel Ashton (London: Routledge, 2007), 59–60.

4. *Foreign Relations of the United States* (hereafter *FRUS*), 1964–1968, vol. XIX: *Arab-Israeli Crisis and War, 1967* (Washington, DC: Government Printing Office, 2004), 132.

5. *FRUS*, 1964–1968, vol. XVIII: *Arab-Israeli Dispute, 1964–1967* (Washington, DC: Government Printing Office, 2000), 404.

6. Amit testimony in Richard Parker, *The Six-Day War: A Retrospective* (Gainesville: University Press of Florida, 1996), 49.

7. Abba Eban and Shlomo Argov quoted in Michael B. Oren, *Six Days of War: June 1967 and the Making of the Modern Middle East* (New York: Ballantine Books, 2003), 43.

8. "On Soviet Policy Following the Israeli Aggression in the Middle East, 20 June 1967" (Cold War International History Project), http://digitalarchive.wilson center.org/document/112654.

9. Yaavov Ro'i and Boris Morozov, eds., *The Soviet Union and the June 1967 Six Day War.* Cold War International History Project Series. (Washington, D.C.: Woodrow Wilson Center Press, 2008), 16, 53.

10. Oren, *Six Days of War*, 28.

11. *FRUS*, vol. XVIII, 300.

12. Quandt testimony in Parker, *The Six-Day War,* 204.

13. For examples of the desire to keep U.S. policy "in the icebox" see *FRUS*, vol. XVIII, 4, 87, 200, 234, 381, and 399.

14. *FRUS*, 1964–1968, vol. XX: *Arab-Israeli Dispute, 1967–1968* (Washington, DC: Government Printing Office, 2001), 14.

15. Tom Segev, *1967: Israel, the War, and the Year that Transformed the Middle East* (New York: Metropolitan Books, 2007), 106.

16. Eliezer Livneh cited in Segev, *1967*, 106–7.

17. Ibid.

18. Samuel C. Heilman, *Portrait of American Jews: The Last Half of the 20th Century*, Samuel and Althea Stroum Lectures in Jewish Studies (Seattle: University of Washington Press, 1995), 58.

19. "American Jewish Congress Head Says He Regards Viet Nam as a 'Jewish Issue'" (Jewish Telegraphic Agency, April 7, 1967), http://www.jta.org/1967/04/07/archive/a -jj-congress-head-says-he-regards-viet-nam-as-a-jewish-issue#ixzz2qfxQl374.

20. Segev, *1967*, 124.

21. Shazar quoted in Judith Klinghoffer, *Vietnam, Jews, and the Middle East: Unintended Consequences* (New York: St. Martin's, 1999), 57.

22. *FRUS*, vol. XVIII, 314.

23. Harry McPherson quoted in Segev, *1967*, 122; and Johnson quoted in Oren, *Six Days of War*, 26.

24. Evron testimony in Parker, *The Six-Day War*, 127.

25. PRO FCO 17/577: "Israel—Defense: Report of Defense Attaché, Nov. 16, 1966," cited in Oren, *Six Days of War*, 27.

26. Shamir testimony in Parker, *The Six-Day War*, 24.

27. Evron testimony, ibid., 127.

28. Segev, *1967*, 155.

29. Ofra Lev-Eshkol, *Humorous Eshkol*, 150, quoted in Segev, 153.

30. Malcolm H. Kerr, *The Arab Cold War: Gamal Abd Al-Nasir and His Rivals, 1958-1970* (Oxford: Oxford University Press, 1971), 114.

31. Oren, *Six Days of War*, 35.

32. Ibid., 36.

33. Asher Susser, *On Both Banks of the Jordan: A Political Biography of Wasfi Al-Tall* (Portland, OR: Frank Cass, 1994), 55.

34. Quoted in Avraham Sela, *The Decline of the Arab-Israeli Conflict: Middle East Politics and the Quest for Regional Order* (Albany: State University of New York Press, 1998), 59.

35. Richard Parker, *The Politics of Miscalculation in the Middle East* (Bloomington: Indiana University Press, 1993), 5.

36. Oren, *Six Days of War*, 52.

37. Ro'i and Morozov, *The Soviet Union and the June 1967 Six Day War*, 5.

38. Some scholars continue to believe this narrative. See, for instance, Parker, *The Politics of Miscalculation*, 27.

39. See Brezhnev report, Appendix 7, CPSU Central Committee, 20 June 1967, RGANI, f.2, op.3, d.20, 5–76 in Ro'i and Morozov, *The Soviet Union*, 308.

40. See Moshe Gat, *Britain and the Conflict in the Middle East, 1964–1967: The Coming of the Six-Day War* (Westport, CT: Praeger, 2003), 150.

41. Abba Eban, *Abba Eban: An Autobiography* (New York: Random House, 1977), 330.

42. *FRUS*, 1964–1968, vol. XIX: *Arab-Israeli Crisis and War, 1967* (Washington, DC: Government Printing Office, 2004), 298.

43. Quoted in Isabella Ginor and Gideon Remez, *Foxbats over Dimona: The Soviets' Nuclear Gamble in the Six-Day War* (New Haven, CT: Yale University Press, 2008), 99.

44. Zolotarev cited in Ro'i and Morozov, *The Soviet Union*, 9.

45. See Syrian Foreign Ministry report of May 13, *ibid*. 6.

46. Oren, *Six Days of War*, 57.

47. Author's translation, Muhammad Fawzi, *Harb al-Thalath Sanawat* (Beirut: Dar al-Moustaqbal al-Arabi, 1984), 71–72.

48. *FRUS*, vol. XIX, 5.

49. Quoted in Hasia R. Diner, *The Jews of the United States, 1654 to 2000* (Berkeley: University of California Press, 2006), 322.

50. Anwar Sadat, *In Search of Identity: An Autobiography* (New York: Harper and Row, 1978), quoted in "Dangerous Illusions," in *The 1967 Arab-Israeli War*, eds. William Roger Louis and Avi Shlaim (Cambridge: Cambridge University Press, 2012), 66.

51. Fawzi quoted in BBC documentary, "Fifty Years War," quoted ibid.

52. Background Paper: UAR General Information, 22–26 February 1966 in LBJ Files, 1963–1969, reel 8 of 8, quoted in Fawaz A. Gerges, *The Superpowers and the Middle East: Regional and International Politics, 1955–1967* (Boulder, CO: Westview Press, 1994), 213.

53. Cairo to Department of State, Subject: US-UAR Relations, 11 April 1964, in LBJ Files, 1963–1969, quoted ibid., 213.

54. BBC, Summary of World Broadcasts. Part 4: The Middle East and Africa 1967.

55. Author's translation, "The Address by President Gamal Abdel Nasser during His Visit to the Advanced Command Unit of the Air Force (Arabic)," May 22, 1967, http://nasser.bibalex.org/Speeches/browser.aspx?SID=1215&lang=en.

56. Parker, *The Politics of Miscalculation*, 73.

57. Michael Howard and Robert Hunter, Adelphi Paper, October 1967, "Israel and the Arab World: The Crisis of 1967" in *The Evolution of Strategic Thought: Classic Adelphi Papers*, ed. The International Institute for Strategic Studies (London: Routledge, 2008).

58. Ami Gluska, *The Israeli Military and the Origins of the 1967 War: Government, Armed Forces and Defence Policy 1963–1967* (London: Routledge, 2007) 125.

59. Eshkol quoted ibid., 134.

60. Ibid., 130.

61. Rabin quoted in Louis and Shlaim, eds., *The 1967 Arab-Israeli War*, 28–29.

62. Author's translation.

63. Kosygin quoted in Malcolm H. Kerr, et al., *Quest for Understanding: Arabic and Islamic Studies in Memory of Malcolm H. Kerr* (Beirut: American University of Beirut, 1991), 123; Muhammad Hasanayn Haykal, *The Sphinx and the Commissar: The Rise and Fall of Soviet Influence in the Middle East* (New York: Harper and Row, 1978), 178–79.

64. Haykal, *The Sphinx and the Commissar*, 178–80.

65. *FRUS*, vol. XIX, 35.

66. Ibid., 8.

67. Evron testimony in Parker, *The Six-Day War*, 133, 135.

68. *FRUS*, vol. XIX, 61.

69. Bitan to Israeli Embassy in Washington, 21 May 1967, ISA, A-3/7920, cited in Segev, *1967*, 254.

70. *FRUS*, vol. XIX, 103.

71. Ibid., 68.

72. Johnson quoted in Robert David Johnson, "Lyndon Johnson and Israel: The Secret Presidential Recordings," Research Paper, no. 3 (Tel Aviv: S. Daniel Abraham Center for International and Regional Studies, Tel Aviv University, 2008), 43.

73. Rabin quoted in Segev, *1967*, 293.

74. Narkiss quoted ibid., 295.

75. Eshkol quoted in Patrick Tyler, *A World of Trouble: The White House and the Middle East: From the Cold War to the War on Terror* (New York: Farrar, Straus and Giroux, 2009), 107; and Segev, *1967*, 290.

76. Sharon quoted in Ami Gluska, *Eshkol, Give the Order!*, 369, cited in Segev, *1967*, 308.

77. Segev, *1967*, 267.

78. *FRUS*, vol. XIX, 54.

79. See *FRUS*, 38, 41, and 84.

80. *FRUS*, 141.

81. William B. Quandt, "Lyndon Johnson and the June 1967 War: What Color Was the Light?" *Middle East Journal* 46, no. 2 (April 1, 1992): 198–228.

82. Amit to Mossad, June 2, 1967, estate of Yaacov Herzog, cited in Segev, 326.

83. See Louis and Shlaim (eds.), *The 1967 Arab-Israeli War*, 38.

84. *FRUS*, 44.

CHAPTER 7: FROM THE YOM KIPPUR WAR TO THE CAMP DAVID ACCORDS

1. Anwar Sadat, *In Search of Identity: An Autobiography* (New York: Harper and Row, 1978).

2. William Quandt, *Decade of Decision: American Policy Towards the Arab-Israeli Conflict, 1967–1976* (Berkeley: University of California Press, 1977); Salim Yaqub, "The Weight of Conquest: Henry Kissinger and the Arab-Israeli Conflict," in *Nixon in the World: American Foreign Relations 1969–1977*, eds. Fredrik Logevall and Andrew Preston (New York: Oxford University Press, 2008), 227–48.

3. Robert Schulzinger, *Henry Kissinger: Doctor of Diplomacy* (New York: Columbia University Press, 1989), 142–63; Robert Dallek, *Nixon and Kissinger: Partners in Power* (New York: HarperCollins Publishers, 2007).

4. For a critical account of Kissinger's handling of the crisis, see William Bundy, *A Tangled Web: The Making of Foreign Policy in the Nixon Presidency* (New York: Hill and Wang, 1998), 428–73.

5. Asaf Siniver, "U.S. Foreign Policy and the Kissinger Stratagem," in *The October 1973 War: Politics, Diplomacy, Legacy*, ed. Asaf Siniver (London: C. Hurst, 2012), 89.

6. For important accounts of Soviet policy toward the 1973 war, see Victor Israelyan, *Inside the Kremlin During the October War* (University Park: Pennsylvania State University Press, 1995); Yevgeny Primakov, *Russia and the Arabs* (New York: Basic Books, 2009); Alvin Rubinstein, *Red Star on the Nile: The Soviet-Egyptian Influence Relationship Since June War* (Princeton, NJ: Princeton University Press, 1977), 248–82.

7. Patrick Seale, *Assad of Syria: The Struggle for the Middle East* (London: I.B. Tauris, 1988), 202–26.

8. Daniel Yergin, *The Prize: The Epic Quest for Oil, Money and Power* (New York: Simon and Schuster, 1991), 595.

9. Ibid., 597.

10. Raymond Garthoff, *Détente and Confrontation: American-Soviet Relations from Nixon to Reagan* (Washington, DC: Brookings Institution, 1994), 411.

11. Alistair Horne, *Kissinger: 1973, the Crucial Year* (New York: Simon and Schuster, 2009), 232.

12. Richard Nixon, *The Memoirs of Richard Nixon* (New York: Grosset &Dunlap, 1978), 921.

13. Patrick Tyler, *A World of Trouble: The White House and the Middle East: From the Cold War to the War on Terror* (New York: Farrar, Straus and Giroux, 2009), 130.

14. Golda Meir, *My Life* (New York: G. P. Putnam's Sons, 1975), 380–461; Moshe Dayan, *The Story of My Life* (New York: William Morrow, 1975).

15. Yornam Meital, "The October War and Egypt's Multiple Crossings," in Siniver, ed., *The October 1973 War*, 57.

16. *Foreign Relations of the United States* (hereafter *FRUS*), 1969–1976, vol. XXV: *Arab-Israeli Crisis and War, 1973* (Washington, DC: Government Printing Office, 2011), 542.

17. Walter Isaacson, *Kissinger: A Biography* (London: Faber and Faber, 1992), 514.

18. *FRUS*, 498.

19. Yergin, *The Prize*, 607.

20. *FRUS*, 577.

21. Mohamed Heikal, *The Road to Ramadan* (New York: Quadrangle/New York Times Book Co., 1975), 239.

22. Henry Kissinger, *Years of Upheaval* (Boston: Little, Brown, 1982), 547.

23. *FRUS*, 658.

24. Jussi Hanhimaki, *The Flawed Architect: Henry Kissinger and American Foreign Policy* (Oxford: Oxford University Press, 2004), 314.

25. Kissinger, *Years of Upheaval*, 569.

26. *FRUS*, 735.

27. Garthoff, *Détente and Confrontation*, 426.

28. Tyler, *A World of Trouble*, 165.

29. Ibid., 736.

30. *FRUS*, 748.

31. Joel Migdal, *Shifting Sands: The United States and the Middle East* (New York: Columbia University Press, 2014), 95.

32. Kissinger, *Years of Upheaval*, 620.

33. Ibid., 618.

34. Ibid., 646.

35. Meir, *My Life,* 439.

36. Kissinger, *Years of Upheaval,* 747–48, 768.

37. Ibid., 768.

38. Memcon between Kissinger, Meir, and Party, 3 November 1973, 10:45 p.m.–1:10 a.m., Source: RG 59, Records of Henry Kissinger, 1973–1977. Box 3. Nixon Presidential Library (hereafter NPL).

39. Kissinger, *Years of Upheaval,* 623–24.

40. Ibid., 615.

41. Memcon between Meir, Nixon, and Kissinger, 1 November 1973, 12:10 p.m., Source: RG 59, Records of Henry Kissinger, 1973–1977. Box 2. NODIS Action Memos, 1973–1976. NPL.

42. Kissinger, *Years of Upheaval,* 752.

43. Ibid., 645–46.

44. Memcon between Meir, Nixon, and Kissinger, 1 November 1973, 12:10 p.m. Source: RG 59, Records of Henry Kissinger, 1973–1977. Box 2. NODIS Action Memos, 1973–1976. NPL.

45. Yaacov Ro'i, *From Encroachment to Involvement: A Documentary Study of Soviet Policy in the Middle East, 1945–1973* (New York: Halsted Press, 1974), 583.

46. Memcon between Kissinger, Meir, Dinitz, and General Yariv. 1 November 1973, 8:10 a.m.–10:25 a.m. Source: RG 59, Records of Henry Kissinger, 1973–1977. Box 2. NODIS Action Memos, 1973–1976. NPL.

47. Moshe Dayan, *Moshe Dayan: Story of My Life* (New York: William Morrow, 1975), p. 544.

48. Ibid., 547.

49. Kenneth W. Stein, *Heroic Diplomacy: Sadat, Kissinger, Carter, Begin, and the Quest for Arab-Israeli Peace* (New York: Routledge, 1999), 102–3.

50. Stein, *Heroic Diplomacy,* 108.

51. Memcon between Fahmi and Kissinger, 2 November 1973, 8:19 p.m. Source: RG 59, Records of Henry Kissinger. Box 1. Misc Docs, Tabs, 1973–77. NPL.

52. Kissinger, *Years of Upheaval,* 640.

53. William B. Quandt, *Peace Process: American Diplomacy and the Arab-Israeli Conflict Since 1967,* 3rd edition (Brookings Institution Press and the University of California Press, 2005), 137.

54. Kissinger, *Years of Upheaval,* 751.

55. Matti Golan, *The Secret Conversations of Henry Kissinger: Step-by-Step Diplomacy in the Middle East* (New York: Quadrangle, 1976) 102.

56. Stein, *Heroic Peace,* 111–12.

57. Dayan, *The Story of My Life,* 120–21.

58. Stein, *Heroic Diplomacy,* 113.

59. Kissinger, *Years of Upheaval,* 755.

60. Stein, *Heroic Diplomacy*, 120.

61. Quandt, *Peace Process*, 140–41.

62. Kissinger, *Years of Upheaval*, 749.

63. Dayan, *The Story of My Life*, 138.

64. Kissinger, *Years of Upheaval*, 811.

65. Kissinger, *Years of Upheaval*, 815; Golan, *The Secret Conversations of Henry Kissinger*, 146–47.

66. Dayan, *The Story of My Life,* 569–70.

67. Quandt, *Peace Process,* 142–43.

68. Abba Eban, *Abba Eban: An Autobiography* (New York: Random House, 1977), 561.

69. Quandt, *Peace Process,* 142–43.

70. Kissinger, *Years of Upheaval*, 843.

71. Ibid., 940–42.

72. Radio Moscow, January 24, 1974; Foy D. Kohler, Leon Goure, and Mose L. Harvey, *The Soviet Union and the October 1973 Middle East War: The Implications for Détente* (Center for Advanced International Studies, 1974), 118.

73. FBIS/USSR, March 5, 1974, F3. Rubinstein, *Red Star on the Nile*, 294.

74. T. Kolesnichenko, "The International Week," *Pravda*, March 14, 1974, in Kohler, *The Soviet Union and the October 1973 War*, 108.

75. Kohler, *The Soviet Union and the October 1973 War*, 113.

76. Ibid., 114.

77. Ibid., 113.

78. Ibid., 108.

79. Quoted by Henry Tanner, *International Herald Tribune*, November 23–24, 1974.

80. Stein, *Heroic Diplomacy*, 173.

81. Kissinger, *Years of Upheaval*, 969.

82. Ibid., 1036.

83. Quandt, *Peace Process*, 148.

84. Eban, *Abba Eban: An Autobiography*, 573–74.

85. From *Novosti* quoted by Alvin Rubinstein from *Le Matin-an-Nahar Arab Report,* 5, 10 (March 11, 1974), in Rubinstein, *Red Star on the Nile*, 296.

86. Kissinger, *Years of Upheaval*, 879–80.

87. Ibid., 893.

88. Quandt, *Peace Process,* 147.

89. Ibid., 150–51.

90. Ibid., 151.

91. Kissinger, *Years of Upheaval*, 1033–34.

92. Golan, *The Soviet Union and the 1973 October* War, 195–96.

93. Quandt, *Peace Process*, 160.

94. Ibid., 162–66.

95. Ibid., 168–69.

96. BBC/ME/4824/E/1-2 (February 7, 1975).

97. *Pravda*, April 24, 1975, cited in Rubinstein, *Red Star on the Nile*, 312.

98. Stein, *Heroic Diplomacy*, 173.

99. Rubinstein, *Red Star on the Nile*, 303.

100. U.S. State Department, text of U.S. reply to a Soviet proposal on reconvening the Middle East peace conference, December 1, 1975, Washington, DC, *US Policy in the Middle East: November 1974–February 1976, Selected Documents*, no. 4 (Washington, DC: Bureau of Public Affairs, 1976).

101. Stein, *Heroic Diplomacy*, 183.

102. William Steding, *Presidential Faith and Foreign Policy: Jimmy Carter the Disciple and Ronald Reagan the Alchemist* (New York: Palgrave, 2014), 74.

CHAPTER 8: IRAN REVOLTS

1. Michael Axworthy, *Revolutionary Iran: A History of the Islamic Republic* (Oxford: Oxford University Press, 2013), 77.

2. Said Amir Arjomand, *The Turban for the Crown: The Islamic Revolution in Iran* (Oxford: Oxford University Press, 1988), 110.

3. Roham Alvandi, "Nixon, Kissinger and the Shah: The Origins of Iranian Primacy in the Persian Gulf," *Diplomatic History* 36, no. 2 (2012), 337–72.

4. Shaul Bakhash, *Reign of the Ayatollahs: Iran and the Islamic Revolution* (New York: Basic Books, 1984), 10–14.

5. Mohammed Reza Pahlavi, *Mission for My Country* (New York: McGraw Hill, 1962), 172–74.

6. Ali Rahnema, *An Islamic Utopian: A Political Biography of Ali Shariati* (London: I.B. Tauris, 1998); Mansoor Moaddel: *Class, Politics and Ideology in the Iranian Revolution* (New York: Columbia University Press, 1993), 130–54.

7. James Bill, *The Eagle and the Lion: The Tragedy of American-Iranian Relations* (New Haven, CT: Yale University Press, 1990), 190–93.

8. Asadollah Alam, *The Shah and I: Confidential Diary of Iran's Royal Court* (London: I.B. Tauris, 2009), 463.

9. Andrew Scott Cooper, *Oil Kings: How the U.S., Iran, and Saudi Arabia Changed the Balance of Power in the Middle East* (New York: Simon and Schuster, 2011), 60.

10. Roy Mottahedeh, *The Mantle of the Prophet: Religion and Politics in Iran* (New York: Simon and Schuster, 1985); Shahrough Akhavi, *Religion and Politics in Contemporary Iran: Clergy-State Relations in the Pahlavi Period* (Albany: State University of New York Press, 1980), 91–117.

11. For the 1963 crisis, see Ervand Abrahamian, *Iran Between Two Revolutions* (Princeton, NJ: Princeton University Press, 1982), 473–75; Hamid Algar, "The Oppositionist Role of the Ulama in Twentieth Century Iran," in *Scholars, Saints and Sufis: Muslim Religious Institutions in the Middle East Since 1500*, ed. Nikki Keddie (Berkeley: University of California Press, 1972), 231–55.

12. Ruhollah Khomeini, *Islamic Government* (Tehran, 1980). See also *Islam and Revolution: The Writings and Declarations of Imam Khomeini*, trans. Hamid Algar (Berkeley, CA: Mizan Press, 1981).

13. Asadollah Alam, *The Shah and I: The Confidential Diary of Iran's Royal Court, 1968–1977* (London: I.B. Tauris, 2008), 535–36.

14. Gaddis Smith, *Morality, Reason and Power: American Diplomacy in the Carter Years* (New York: Hill and Wang, 1987), 180–208; Scott Kaufman, *Plans Unraveled: The Foreign Policy of the Carter Administration* (De Kalb: Northern Illinois University Press), 28–56; Betty Glad, *An Outsider in the White House: Jimmy Carter, His Advisors, and the Making of American Foreign Policy* (Ithaca, NY: Cornell University Press, 2009), 167–76.

15. Mohammed Reza Pahlavi, *Answer to History* (New York: Stein and Day, 1980), 152.

16. For the best assessment of the U.S. intelligence community during the Iranian Revolution, see Robert Jervis, *Why Intelligence Fails: Lessons from the Iranian Revolution and the Iraq War* (Ithaca, NY: Cornell University Press, 2010), 1–123.

17. "Iran in the 1980s," August 1977, Central Intelligence Agency. Digital National Security Archive (Iran Revolution Collection).

18. "Elites and the Distribution of Power in Iran," February 1976. Central Intelligence Agency (Research Study). Digital National Security Archive (Iran Revolution Collection).

19. "The Future of Iran: Implications for the United States," January 28, 1977. U.S. State Department: Bureau of Intelligence and Research. Digital National Security Archive (Iran Revolution Collection).

20. R. K. Ramazani, "Who Lost America? The Case of Iran," *Middle East Journal* (Winter 1982), 13–15.

21. For the best account of the shah's psychological makeup, see Marvin Zonis, *Majestic Failure: The Fall of the Shah* (Chicago: University of Chicago Press, 1991).

22. Abbas Milani, *The Shah* (New York: Palgrave, 2011), 375–77.

23. For important studies on Khomeini, see Baqer Moin, *Khomeini: The Life of the Ayatollah* (New York: St. Martin's, 1999); Hamid Dabashi, *Theology of Discontent: The Ideological Foundations of the Islamic Revolution in Iran* (New York: New York University Press, 1993), 409–85.

24. Charles Kurzman, *The Unthinkable Revolution* (Cambridge, MA: Harvard University Press, 2004), 22.

25. *Ettela'at* (Tehran), January 7, 1978.

26. "Religion and Politics: Qom and its Aftermath," Cable from U.S. Embassy (Tehran) to Department of State, January 2, 1978. Digital National Security Archive (Iran Revolution Collection).

27. Barry Rubin, *Paved with Good Intentions: The American Experience and Iran* (Oxford: Oxford University Press, 1981), 205.

28. James Buchan, *Days of God: The Revolution in Iran and its Consequences* (London: John Murray, 2012), 214.

29. Kurzman, *The Unthinkable Revolution*, 78.

30. *Worldwide Crude Oil and Gas Production*, Volume 77, February 26, 1979, 166.

31. *Worldwide Crude Oil and Gas Production*, Volume 77, March 26, 1979, 204.

32. Anthony Parsons, *The Pride and the Fall: Iran, 1974–1979* (London: Jonathan Cape, 1984), 60–131.

33. William Sullivan, *Mission to Iran* (New York: W. W. Norton, 1981), 157.

34. Gary Sick, *All Fall Down: America's Tragic Encounter with Iran* (New York: Random House), 95.

35. Buchan, *Days of God*, 241.

36. Gholam Reza Afkhami, *The Life and Times of the Shah* (Berkeley: University of California Press, 2009), 486.

37. Jimmy Carter, *White House Diary* (New York: Farrar, Straus and Giroux, 2010), 258.

38. "The Politics of Ayatollah Ruhollah Khomeini," November 20, 1978. Central Intelligence Agency. Digital National Security Archive (Iran Revolution Collection).

39. "The Gathering Crisis in Iran," November 2, 1978. Bureau of Intelligence and Research (Briefing Memorandum). Digital National Security Archive (Iran Revolution Collection).

40. "Thinking the Unthinkable," November 9, 1978, Cable from U.S. Embassy (Tehran) to the Department of State, Digital National Security Archives (Iran Revolution Collection).

41. Sullivan, *Mission to Iran*, 200–214; Sick, *All Fall Down*, 81–102.

42. Afkhami, *The Life and Times of the Shah*, 488.

43. James Bill, *George Ball: Behind the Scenes in U.S. Foreign Policy* (New Haven, CT: Yale University Press, 1997).

44. George Ball, "Issues and Implications of the Iran Crisis," December 12, 1979. Digital National Security Archives (Iran Revolution Collection).

45. Sick, *All Fall Down*, 109.

46. Sick, *All Fall Down*, 125.

47. Jimmy Carter, *Keeping Faith: Memoirs of a President* (New York: Bantam Books, 1982), 447.

48. "Iran: Understanding the Shia Islamic Movement," February 2, 1979. U.S.

Embassy (Tehran) to the Department of State. Digital National Security Archives (Iran Revolution Collection).

49. Ibid.

50. Cyrus Vance, *Hard Choices: Critical Years in America's Foreign Policy* (New York: Simon and Schuster, 1983), 79.

51. Robert Huyser, *Mission to Tehran* (New York: Harper and Row, 1986), 138–286.

52. Pahlavi, *Answer to History*, 167.

53. Ervand Abrahamian, *A History of Modern Iran* (Cambridge: Cambridge University Press, 2008), 161.

54. Robert Huyser, *Mission to Tehran*, 138–286; Zbigniew Brzezinski, *Power and Principle: Memoir of the National Security Adviser 1977–1981* (New York: Farrar, Straus and Giroux, 1983), 385.

55. Ibid., 355.

CHAPTER 9: THE IRAN-IRAQ WAR

1. Ali Husayn Muntaziri, *Matn-i Kamil-i khatirati-i Ayatollah Husayn Ali Muntaziri* (Spanga, Sweden: 2001), 244.

2. Amazia Baram, "The Impact of Khomeini's Revolution on the Radical Shi'i Movement of Iraq," in *The Iranian Revolution and the Muslim World*, ed. David Menashri (Boulder, CO: Westview Press, 1990), 142.

3. F. Gregory Gause III, "Iraq's Decisions to Go to War, 1980, and 1990," *Middle East Journal* (Winter 2002), 65.

4. Shahram Chubin and Charles Tripp, *Iran and Iraq at War* (Boulder, CO: Westview Press, 1988), 53–68; Gause, "Iraq's Decisions to Go to War, 1980, 1990," 63–69; Eric Davis, *Memories of State: Politics, History and Collective Identity in Modern Iraq* (Berkeley: University of California Press, 2005), 176–200.

5. Efraim Karsh, "Geopolitical Determinism: The Origins of the Iran-Iraq War," *Middle East Journal* 44, no. 2 (Spring 1990), 265–67; Mohssen Massarrat, "The Ideological Context of the Iran-Iraq War: Pan-Islamism versus Pan-Arabism," in *Iran and the Arab World*, eds. Hooshang Amirahmadi and Nader Entessar (New York: St. Martin's, 1993).

6. For important accounts of Saddam, see Marion Farouk-Sluglett and Peter Sluglett, *Iraq Since 1958: From Revolution to Dictatorship* (London: I.B. Tauris, 1990), 255–69; Phebe Marr, *The Modern History of Iraq* (Boulder, CO: Westview Press, 1985); Charles Tripp, *A History of Iraq* (Cambridge: Cambridge University Press, 2000), 193–275; Kannan Makiya, *Republic of Fear: The Politics of Modern Iraq* (Berkeley: University of California Press, 1989).

7. Kevin Woods, David Palkki, and Mark Stout, eds., *The Saddam Tapes: The*

Inner Workings of a Tyrant's Regime, 1978–2001 (Cambridge: Cambridge University Press, 2011), 137.

8. Ibid., 135.

9. Mark Gasiorowski, "U.S. Intelligence Assistance to Iran, May–October 1979," *Middle East Journal* 66, no. 4 (Autumn 2012), 623–25.

10. Marr, *Modern History of Iraq*, 67.

11. Ibid.

12. R. K. Ramazani, *Revolutionary Iran: Challenge and Response in the Middle East* (Baltimore: Johns Hopkins University Press, 1986), 61.

13. Christian Emery, *U.S. Foreign Policy and Iranian Revolution: The Cold War Dynamics of Engagement and Strategic Alliance* (New York: Palgrave Macmillan, 2013), 187.

14. Ibid.

15. Ralph King, *The United Nations and the Iran-Iraq War* (New York: Ford Foundation, 1987), 15–17.

16. Sayyad Ali Shirazi, *Khatirat-i salha-yi nabard: Khatirat-i shahid' Ali Sayyad Shirazi/ intikhab va sadah-nivisi-i Mohsen Mumini* (Tehran, 2009), 209.

17. Majid Khadduri, *The Gulf War: The Origins and Implications of the Iran-Iraq War* (Oxford: Oxford University Press, 1988), 95.

18. John Parott, "The Response of Saudi Arabia to the Iran-Iraq War," *Journal of South Asian and Middle Eastern Studies*, no. 2 (Winter 1986); James Bill, "The Arab World and the Challenge of Iran," *Journal of Arab Affairs* (October 1982); Itamar Rabinovich, "The Impact on the Arab World," and Barry Rubin, "The Gulf States and the Iran-Iraq War," in *The Iran-Iraq War: Impact and Implications*, ed. Efraim Karsh (New York: St. Martin's, 1989); Saideh Lotfian, "Taking Sides: Regional Powers and War," in *Iranian Perspectives on the Iran-Iraq War*, ed. Farhang Rajaee (Gainesville: University Press of Florida, 1997).

19. The principal propagator of this view was Ahmad Khomeini, who years after the war suggested that his father was prepared to end the war in 1982.

20. www.Aftabnews.com, July 7, 2008.

21. Ali Akbar Rafsanjani, *Karnamah va khatirat-i 1361*, 234. (Tehran, 2001)

22. www.tabank.ir September 15, 2008.

23. *Kayhan* (Tehran), June 23, 1982.

24. Ruhollah Khomeini, *Dar justuju-yi rah az kalam-i Imam: Daftar 2, jang va jihad* (Tehran, 1984), 142.

25. Chubin and Tripp, *Iran and Iraq at War*, 164.

26. James Blight, et al., eds., *Becoming Enemies: U.S.-Iran Relations and the Iran-Iraq War, 1979–1988* (New York: Rowan and Littlefield, 2012), 311.

27. George Shultz, *Turmoil and Triumph: My Years as Secretary of State* (New York: Scribner's, 1993), 237.

28. Bruce Jentleson, *With Friends Like These: Reagan, Bush, and Saddam, 1982–1990* (New York: W. W. Norton, 1994), 46.

29. Lawrence Freedman, *A Choice of Enemies: America Confronts the Middle East* (New York: Public Affairs, 2008), 165.

30. Jentleson, *With Friends Like These*, 45.

31. *Kayhan* (Tehran), April 2, 1985.

32. Chubin and Tripp, *Iran and Iraq at War*, 173.

33. R. K. Ramazani, "The Iran-Iraq War and the Persian Gulf Crisis," *Current History* 87, no. 526 (1988), 61–64; Anthony Cordesman, "Lessons of the Iran-Iraq War: The First Round," *Armed Forces Journal International* 119, no. 8 (1982), 32–46.

34. Joost R. Hitlermann, *A Poisonous Affair: America, Iraq, and the Gassing of Halabja* (Cambridge: Cambridge University Press, 2007), 30–32.

35. Ibid., 37.

36. Ramazani, *Revolutionary Iran*, 70–86.

37. Hitlermann, *A Poisonous Affair*, 75.

38. Joost Hitlermann, "Outsiders as Enablers: Consequences and Lessons from International Silence on Iraq's Use of Chemical Weapons during the Iran-Iraq War," in *Iran, Iraq and the Legacies of War*, eds. Lawrence Potter and Gary Sick (New York: Palgrave, 2004), 151–67.

39. Zachary Karabell, "Backfire: U.S. Policy Toward Iraq: 1988–2 August 1990," *Middle East Journal* 49, no. 1 (Winter 1995), 30–31.

40. Hitlermann, *A Poisonous Affair*, 52.

41. Shultz, *Turmoil and Triumph*, 239.

42. Efraim Karsh, "From Ideological Zeal to Geopolitical Realism: The Islamic Republic and the Gulf," in Efraim Karsh, ed., *The Iran-Iraq War 1980–1988*, 33; Saskia Geiling, *Religion and War in Revolutionary Iran* (London: I.B. Tauris, 1999), 28; Ramazani, *Revolutionary Iran*, 233.

43. Rafsanjani, *Karnamah va khatirat-i 1361*, 317.

44. Islamic Republic News Agency (hereafter IRNA), May 31, 1986.

45. IRNA, November 10, 1986.

46. Eric Hooglund, "Reagan's Iran: Factions behind US Policy in the Gulf." Middle East Research and Information project (MERIP). *Middle East Report* (March–April 1988) 31; Gary Sick, "Trial by Error: Reflections on the Iran-Iraq War," *Middle East Journal* (Spring 1989), 240.

47. *New York Times*, July 22, 1987. See also Shahram Chubin, "The Last Phase of the Iran-Iraq War: From Stalemate to Ceasefire," *Third World Quarterly* (April 1989); Nader Entessar, "Superpowers and Persian Gulf Security," *Third World Quarterly* (October 1988); Thomas McNaugher, "U.S. Policy and the Gulf War: A Question of Means," and Maxwell More Johnson, "The Role of U.S. Military Force in the Gulf War," in *The Persian Gulf War: Lessons for*

Strategy, Law and Diplomacy, ed. Christopher Joyner (New York: Greenwood Press, 1990).

48. Freedman, *A Choice of Enemies: America Confronts the Middle East*, 197.
49. Chubin and Tripp, *Iran and Iraq at War*, 177.
50. *Kayhan* (Tehran), July 9, 1987.
51. *Tehran Times*, October 15, 1987.
52. S. Taheri Shemirani, "The War of Cities," in Farhang Rajaee, ed., *The Iran-Iraq War: The Politics of Aggression*, 32–41.
53. *Kayhan* (Tehran), July 19, 1988.
54. *Jumhuri-i Islami* (Tehran), July 19, 1988.
55. www.Aftabnews.com, July 17, 2008.
56. Iranian Labor News Agency, September 29, 2006.
57. In his recollection of the encounter between Khomeini and Rezai, Nateq-Nuri recounts the following: When asked what he needed for victory after eight years of war, the commander of the Guards answered 300 airplanes, 3,000 tanks and seven more years were necessary. Also, the size of the army must be doubled while the size of the guards had to increase by fivefold. The imam asked Prime Minister Mussavi what the possibility was of providing that budget. The answer was negative. Still, the commander of the Guards expressed his readiness to continue the war. The imam declared that these were mere slogans. For the sake of protecting Islam and the revolution, they would have to drink the poison chalice. Ali Akbar Natiq-Nuri, *Khatirat-i Hujjat al-Islam va al-Muslimin Ali Akbar Natiq Nuri,* vol. 2 (Tehran, 2005), 68.
58. Rajanews.com, March 10, 2008.
59. Iranian Labor News Agency, September 29, 2006.
60. Kenneth Pollack, *The Persian Puzzle: The Conflict between Iran and America* (New York: Random House, 2004), 232.
61. *Ettela'at* (Tehran), September 7, 1988.

CHAPTER 10: THE GULF WAR

1. Jeffrey Engle, "A Better World . . . but Don't Get Carried Away: The Foreign Policy of George H.W. Bush Twenty Years on," *Diplomatic History* (January 2010); Ryan Barilleaux and Mark Rozell, *Power and Prudence: The Presidency of George H.W. Bush* (College Station: Texas A&M University Press, 2004); Ryan Barilleaux and Mary Stuckey, eds., *Leadership and the Bush Presidency: Prudence or Drift in an Era of Change?* (Westport, CT: Praeger, 1992).
2. Peter Hahn, *Missions Accomplished? The United States and Iraq since World War I* (Oxford: Oxford University Press, 2012), 90.
3. http://fas.org/irp/offdocs/nsd/nsd26.pdf.

4. Bruce Jentleson, *With Friends Like These: Reagan, Bush, and Saddam, 1982–1990*, (New York: W. W. Norton, 1994), 146.
5. Foreign Broadcast Information Service. FBIS-NES-90-064, Daily Report, April 3, 1990, 32–36.
6. Lawrence Freedman and Efraim Karsh, *The Gulf Conflict: 1990–1991: Diplomacy and War in the New World Order* (Princeton, NJ: Princeton University Press, 1993), 45.
7. Ibid., 46.
8. Adeed I. Dawisha, *Iraq: A Political History from Independence to Occupation* (Princeton, NJ: Princeton University Press, 2009), 171–209; Charles Tripp, *A History of Iraq* (Cambridge: Cambridge University Press, 2000), 148–85.
9. Steven Hurst, *The Foreign Policy of the Bush Administration: In Search of a New World Order* (London: Cassell, 1999), 89.
10. Zachary Karabell, "Backfire: U.S. Policy Toward Iraq: 1988–2 August 1990," *Middle East Journal* 49, no. 1 (Winter 1995), 47.
11. Ibid.
12. "Meeting between President Saddam Hussein and the American Ambassador to Iraq," July 25, 1990. U.S. Department of State. The Digital National Security Archives (Iraq Collection).
13. Ibid.
14. Patrick Tyler, *A World of Trouble: The White House and the Middle East: From the Cold War to the War on Terror* (New York: Farrar, Straus and Giroux, 2009), 363.
15. *Washington Post*, July 12, 1991.
16. James Baker III with Thomas DeFrank, *The Politics of Diplomacy: Revolution, War and Peace, 1989–1992* (New York: G.P. Putman's Sons), 271.
17. Hurst, *The Foreign Policy of the Bush Administration*, 91; Richard Haass, *War of Necessity, War of Choice: Memoir of Two Iraq Wars* (New York: Simon and Schuster, 2009), 58.
18. Charles Duelfer and Stephen Benedict Dyson, "Chronic Misperception and International Conflict: The U.S.-Iraq Experience," *International Security* (Summer 2011), 88.
19. Freedman and Karsh, *The Gulf Conflict*, 50.
20. Ibid., 56.
21. Jeffrey Engel, "The Gulf War and the End of the Cold War and Beyond," in *Into the Desert: Reflections on the Gulf War*, ed. Jeffrey Engel (Oxford: Oxford University Press, 2013), 26.
22. Stephen Sestanovich, *Maximalist: America in the World from Truman to Obama* (New York: Alfred Knopf, 2014), 250.
23. George Bush and Brent Scowcroft, *A World Transformed* (New York: Alfred Knopf, 1998), 317.

24. Interview with Richard B. Cheney: George H. W. Bush Oral History Project (Miller Center, University of Virginia, 2011), 55.

25. Bob Woodward, *The Commanders* (New York: Simon and Schuster, 1991), 220–21.

26. Peter Rodman, *Presidential Command: Power, Leadership, and the Making of Foreign Policy from Richard Nixon to George W. Bush* (New York: Alfred Knopf, 2009), 197.

27. Colin Powell with Joseph Persico, *My American Journey* (New York: 1995), 401–529; Karen DeYoung, *Soldier: The Life of Colin Powell* (New York: Knopf, 2006).

28. Haass, *War of Necessity, War of Choice*, 67.

29. Interview with Robert Gates: George H. W. Bush Oral History Project (Miller Center, University of Virginia, 2000), 51.

30. Kevin Woods, David Palkki, and Mark Strout, eds., *The Saddam Tapes: The Inner Workings of a Tyrant's Regime, 1978–2001* (Cambridge: Cambridge University Press, 2011), 176.

31. Ibid.

32. Freedman and Karsh, *The Gulf Conflict*, 101.

33. Hurst, *The Foreign Policy of the Bush Administration*, 91.

34. Ibid., 114.

35. Ibid.

36. Ibid.

37. Kevin Woods, *The Mother of All Battles: Saddam Hussein's Strategic Plan for the Persian Gulf War* (Annapolis, MD: Naval Institute Press, 2008), 113.

38. Peter Beinart, *The Icarus Syndrome: A History of American Hubris* (New York: HarperCollins, 2010), 258.

39. Norman Schwarzkopf, *Doesn't Take a Hero: The Autobiography of General H. Norman Schwarzkopf* (New York: Bantam Books, 1993); Michael Gordon and Bernard Trainor, *The Generals' War: The Inside Story of the Conflict in the Gulf* (New York: Little, Brown, 1995).

40. Lawrence Freedman, *A Choice of Enemies: America Confronts the Middle East* (New York: Public Affairs, 2008), 234–54.

41. Interview with Brent Scowcroft: George H. W. Bush Oral History Project (Miller Center, University of Virginia, 1999), 432–33.

42. Amatzia Baram, "Deterrence Lessons from Iraq," *Foreign Affairs* 91, no. 4 (July/August 2012), 85.

43. Engle, "The Gulf War and the End of the Cold War and Beyond," 47.

44. Woods, *The Mother of All Battles*, 251.

45. Ibid.

46. Mikhail Gorbachev, *Memoirs* (New York: Doubleday, 1995), 559–65.

47. Bush and Scowcroft, *A World Restored*, 473.

48. Gideon Rose, *How Wars End: Why We Always Fight the Last Battle* (New York: Simon and Schuster, 2010), 216.

49. Ibid., 218.

50. Ibid., 222.

51. Ibid.

52. Gates, George H. W. Bush Oral History Project, 60.

53. Kevin Woods, David Palkki, and Mark Strout, eds., *The Saddam Tapes*, 214.

INDEX